T0277679

IN
DEEP

The Collected Surf Writings

In Deep: The Collected Surf Writings is published under Catharsis, a sectionalized division under Di Angelo Publications, Inc.

Catharsis is an imprint of Di Angelo Publications.
Copyright 2023.
All rights reserved.
Printed in the United States of America.

Di Angelo Publications
4265 San Felipe #1100
Houston, Texas 77027

Library of Congress
In Deep: The Collected Surf Writings
ISBN: 978-1-955690-45-4
Paperback

Words: Matt George
Cover Photo: Bernie Baker - Pictured: Matt George (Standing) and brother Sam, Nusa Lembongan, Indonesia, 1984.
Back Cover Photo: Everton Luis
Interior Photos: Matt George, unless otherwise noted
Cover Design: Thai Little
Interior Design: Kimberly James
Editors: Cody Wootton, Ashley Crantas, Willy Rowberry

Downloadable via Kindle, NOOK, iBooks, and Google Play.

For educational, business, and bulk orders, contact sales@diangelopublications.com.

1. Sports & Recreation --- Water Sports --- Surfing
2. Travel --- Special Interest --- Sports
3. Sports & Recreation --- Essays

IN

DEEP

The Collected Surf Writings

MATT GEORGE

FOREWORD BY KELLY SLATER

CONTENTS

FOREWORD

KELLY SLATER

I was a junior at Cocoa Beach High School in 1989, the year Matt George came to write the piece on me for *SURFER* magazine ["The Seduction of Kelly Slater"]. I was flattered that they wanted to do such a big article, but also kind of intimidated. I'd been interviewed by some newspapers and a couple other magazines, but those were nothing like having a writer from the biggest surf magazine in the world come do a prominent feature on me. As a seventeen-year-old, I was stoked enough if somebody videoed me at the beach. I knew I needed to have my game face on, really wanting to impress Matt with my surfing abilities, so I was surprised when, soon after he arrived at my house, it became clear that his story wasn't going to be about my surfing, but all about me.

Matt analyzed every aspect of my life, writing not just about me, but my family, my friends, where I surfed, how I ate, and what I thought. It wasn't like any interview I'd ever done. My first impression of Matt was just how eccentric he was. He spoke almost as if in a poem, speaking haikus off the top of his head, and I'd never met anyone like that. I think it was a little daunting for me because he obviously thought so deeply about surfing.

Not only was Matt's story my first major profile in a surfing magazine, but it was probably the most memorable, becoming controversial long before there was such a thing as "going viral." The opening line, "He sleeps like an angel," was the thing I remember most because it became such a big deal. It definitely became a talking point—perhaps because homophobia was more rampant in those days, especially in high school—and the part of the story that everyone brought up to to me all the time.

One thing that struck me about Matt is that he would romanticize the smallest thing, finding some deep, eloquent, layered story in even the simplest of experiences. Like in his article "The Blood, The Booze, and the Barking Dogs of Herbie Fletcher's Annual Cabo Contest." I was at that surf contest in San Jose Del Cabo at the tip of Baja, and none of us had much money, so we were cramming as many of us as we could in a hotel room. Everyone (except for me, because I was the straight kid) was getting blind drunk, puking in the pool. I even remember having to pull a dead local man out of the water after he had drowned. But somehow, Matt found a way to tell this romantic story about the beauty and the purity of whatever was happening, however down and dirty it seemed at the time.

I can look back on that story now and appreciate the writing, admiring the way that Matt captured that moment in time. In a generation or two, these types of stories may no longer exist. When I was coming up, a large part of keeping the surfing culture alive was left up to the magazines. In recent years, we've lost the two major surf magazines—*SURFER* and *SURFING*—and what we've been left with is technology. With websites, we're now being spoon-fed everything; we don't have to work as hard or know as much about surfing. You used to have to go live it to learn it. There was more intuitive knowledge required. Now we have emojis and single word descriptions on social media. If you cut out all of today's technology and had to go out and learn it on your own like we did, it would take you decades. Instead, it's all boiled down to algorithms on your smartphone. When we lose our critical thinking and our connection to nature, we lose our humanity. Writers like Matt George, who observe and soak in every detail, are the ultimate critical thinkers, and we were lucky to have them, and him, around.

Matt has also been a constant figure in my life—at arm's length often, but a constant nonetheless. A few years ago, I ran into Matt after he and his wife had parted ways, and he was so sad, his emotions so raw. Matt and his wife have reconnected since then, but at the time, I really felt bad for him. There's something like a safety net when you have people in your life for so many decades, and times like those reminded me of how important it is to have these people in your life.

I have a lot of Matt George stories, but here's one of my favorites. Years ago, I was told about this surf contest in Ventura, California. Matt, who was covering the event, was standing there, arms crossed and watching the surf. It was cold out. A bunch of kids from the surf class were playing around, and one of them comes up behind Matt and pantsed him, pulling his sweatpants down around his ankles. And Matt doesn't even flinch—just stands there like nothing has happened. So there he is, basically naked, and all the kids are pointing and laughing.

But after about thirty seconds, they start begging him to pull his pants up. Matt does nothing. Nothing, that is, until he quietly demands that the kid who pulled his pants down come pull them back up, which the kid did. I thought it was the funniest thing, but it speaks to Matt's character, sensitive but steadfast in his resolve—and that shows in his writing.

Matt's book, *In Deep,* captures an important time in surfing's written history—a time when you didn't know people by looking at their Instagram; when you learned who they were by traveling with them, riding with them, and experiencing life with them. This is what Matt George did, and continues to do, and I hope his stories are as important to today's young surfers as they were to me.

PREFACE

AUTHOR, MENTAWAI ISLANDS
PHOTO: MICK CURLEY

The book you hold in your hands is not a memoir. Not another tedious tale of youth lost to surfing, nor a tiresome recounting of a penniless, drug-addled sojourn on the global Dharma Bum trail in the guise of self-discovery. No, those memoirs shortchange professional surfing life. This is a book of people who spend their lives surfing not as a pastime, but as an aim. People who have committed their entire professional, financial, personal, and philosophical lives to surfing. And, fair enough, spent it in pursuit of a connection with the power of the cosmos itself.

This will not be a book that attempts to convince you of the allure of riding Ocean waves, nor one that tries to describe the act itself. But it will take you inside the lives of those who call surfing life itself. Many before me have expounded on the empyrean connection of surfing, but straight up, the surfing life is more a series of lightning strikes. When done properly, surfing is an injection of mindblow jacked straight into your aorta, leaving the surfer as addicted as any Times Square smacky.

And it's funny how surfing keeps these secrets. Not even the drama of film can truly describe it, no matter how many times the "mainstream media" has thrown itself at the sport, including my 1998 Columbia TriStar feature film release, *In God's Hands*, which the powers of Hollywood eviscerated. The reason why is simple: surfing doesn't work as a spectator experience. A spectator must stand too far away from the action. Watching from dry *terra firma*, the spectator cannot hear it or feel it. A spectator of surfing is sensory deprived, like watching a title fight from the nosebleeds. And then there is the lack of rules in surfing, the undefined playing field, the randomness of the waves, the hissing chaos, the endless waiting for the right wave, and, most of all, that distance from the waves' merciless reality. For the spectator, surfing is literally *out there*. Watching from land, surfing will always look like a stunt, not a sport.

I feel I am allowed to say all this because I am not a writer who surfs—I am a surfer who writes. I have not just been an observer, some cub reporter, some acolyte or dilettante; I have been a professional surfer for my entire life. I have been immersed in surfing's evolution from its penniless throes of the '60s to its 22-billion-dollar industry of today. And the characters in this book are my peers, not my subjects. And the places in this book are our world.

By way of explanation, I offer this: I was taught to surf in Waikiki at eight years old while my Navy dad was stationed at Pearl. I was paid to surf and compete professionally from 1979 to 1984. I was then taken on by SURFER Magazine as their Senior Contributing Editor. My beat was the global scene. I traveled, lived, ate, and breathed surfing, shoulder to shoulder with my fellow believers. Over the decades, I strove to articulate ideas about surfing, not just information. Daring readers to imagine, not simply ingest. Expressing, in every case, the belief that in the act of surfing and living a surfing life, lay something noble, something lodged deep in one's soul. And it was this deep relationship with the Ocean that drove me to live my life as a series of feats both in and out of the water. Yet never straying far enough from the sea to lose my connection with it. I always returned from my more outlandish adventures, at the cost of great professional and financial sacrilege, to recapture that meaning I felt while riding inside a wave. I have been a writer, a photographer, a Hollywood screenwriter, a remote region aid relief worker, a teacher, a magazine editor, and an emergency medical technician. I have performed jet ski rescues in the Ninth Ward of New Orleans in the wake of Hurricane Katrina. I have built emergency shelters and helicopter pads by hand in remote Kashmir in the wake of Pakistan's 2006 earthquake. I have evacuated villagers off the slopes of Indonesia's great Mt. Merapi eruption. I have sailed boats full of aid to the most remote islands off Aceh in the wake of the 2004 Indian Ocean tsunami. I held the first tsunami evacuation test in Indonesian history in a city of one million people. I have taught Journalism at Sea off West Sumatra, and I run Indonesia's first surfing magazine.

I am confident that this book is a view of surfers and the world of surfing that you just won't get anywhere else. In these stories, I hope you will see a sincere love fueled by a profound sport populated by characters living remarkable lives. And it is my hope that these tales will stand the test of time and serve as a kind of portal into a sport that is as arresting as it is mystifying. Not only adding a new perspective to surfing's unfolding mythology, but providing readers new to this world with a deeper understanding of the enthralling sport that has given me, and my fellow devotees, a life of meaning.

—Matt George
Kuta, Bali
January 10, 2023

For Maryanne

AUTHOR, SUMBAWA
PHOTO: ERIC LEE

"You have navigated with raging soul
Far from the paternal home
Passing beyond the seas' double rocks
And now you inhabit a foreign land"
—From Euripides, *Medea*

RED WATER

BETHANY HAMILTON AND THE TEETH OF THE TIGER
SURFER MAGAZINE, USA, 2003

The maiming horror of a shark attack. Every single surfer on earth has shuddered at the thought. And thanks to Steven Spielberg, most civilians as well. But this youthful survivor surprised us all. Bethany Hamilton, all grown up now, a surfing champion, a global inspiration, a mother of three, proved that youthful dreams can be changed, but never crushed.

—Mg.

October 31, 2003 — Hāʻena, Kauai

She had been leading a daredevil life for weeks now. And in the end, she had no idea the trouble she was getting herself into. Swimming beneath the moon, swimming beneath the sun, but swimming. Always swimming. And starving. Patrolling the reefs for opportunity, for blood, for flesh. Swinging her massive, blunted head with the regularity of a metronome, propelling her fourteen feet of mass through the depths with effortless power. With her ragged dorsal fin breaking the surface, she had been bumping into surfers for weeks now. Testing them, feeling their fear, waiting for her time. They seemed such easy prey. Slow, awkward, lounging on the surface like something dying. And now, one of them was in her path; it was time. Another was here, apart from the rest. Alone and weak. And this one looked so small and frail. She approached her prey from the side, taking her time, timing the strokes of the thin, pale arm that dipped off the surfboard in a rhythm of bubbles. With one last savage kick of her great tail, she opened her jaws in a ragged yawn, and taking the thin, pale arm in her throat, she clamped down with over sixteen tons of sawing pressure. And as her teeth met, she effortlessly plucked it from the human body and swallowed it whole.

The bite was so clean and painless that Bethany Hamilton, just thirteen, noticed that the sea had turned red before she realized that her arm was gone at the shoulder. A strange serenity came over her, a warmth, as her body began to scream its outrage. Spurting gouts of rich, burgundy blood, Bethany struggled over to her best friend, Alana Blanchard, also thirteen, and could only manage the words, "I think a shark just attacked me." Alana told Bethany to "not even joke about that." Then Alana's eyes saw something that her mind couldn't grasp.

The bleeding stump where her best friend's left arm used to be. Alana's stomach revolted and purged twice before she could call for her father and her brother, who were paddling for a nearby wave.

Imagine the dilemma of Holt Blanchard, 45, who was now a quarter mile offshore with his son, his daughter, and a profusely bleeding and gravely injured thirteen-year-old Bethany Hamilton. And somewhere below his feet was a large, dangerous shark. With Bethany's arm gone at the shoulder, a tourniquet was out of the question. To stem the blood, Holt could only manage a compress with the t-shirt he was wearing. Holt now had an impossible decision to make. Should he send his children on ahead, across the deep lagoon, to keep them away from a bleeding Bethany? And if so, how could he protect them? Should he keep them close, where at least he imagined he could put himself between them and the shark should it return for Bethany? For one brief moment, he even thought of somehow opening his own wrists and slipping into the sea to await his fate while the other three made for shore. With no time to deliberate, he made his decision on instinct. Keep the family close; face the danger together. He instructed his daughter to keep the pressure on the blood-soaked t-shirt and to keep talking to a fading Bethany. Then he and his son rigged their surfboard leashes and began dragging Bethany and Alana to shore on a raft made of their surfboards.

Cheri Hamilton, mother of Bethany, who had yet to see her daughter, was driving so fast behind the ambulance that some cops pulled her over. It wasn't until the ambulance driver radioed back that the cops let Cheri go. As she mashed the accelerator to the floor of the salt-rusted family station wagon, a call came in on her cell phone. It was Holt Blanchard. Cheri asked him how badly Bethany was hurt. The conversation went like this:

> Holt: You mean you don't know?
> Cheri: Know what?
> Holt: Cheri . . . her arm is gone.
> Cheri: (Long Pause) Gone where?

Tom Hamilton, Bethany's father, was just about to be put under for a knee operation on the only operating table that the small local hospital owned. A shaken nurse poked her head in the room and informed the team that a terrible emergency was coming in and that they needed the table right away. Tom limped into the corridor in his hospital gown as the operating theater made ready for an emergency surgery. Tom blanched when a brusque orderly asked him what his blood type was. Learning that there had been a shark attack on a young girl at Makua Beach, Tom's heart squeezed. He knew he had only a fifty-fifty chance, since Bethany and Alana were the only thirteen-year-old girls on the island with the guts enough to surf the reef at Makua Beach. Tom stood in the corridor in his hospital gown as the victim was being wheeled into the hospital. He held his breath; he would know in a second. Alana had dark brown hair. Bethany's was blonde. As the gurney turned the corner, all the air in Tom's chest disappeared. The hair was blonde.

It has been widely known that the tiger shark's characteristic serrated tooth shape and grotesquely powerful jaws have evolved for specialized feeding on large sea turtles. Sea turtles whose shells cannot be split by a grown man with an axe. Called the hyena of the sea, the tiger shark strikes with a sawing motion of its bottom jaw against the bone razor blades of its top jaw. It is known as the deadliest bite of any shark. Bethany's arm was removed so cleanly, with such precision and efficiency, that the operating doctor, upon first seeing the wound, was confused. He wanted to know who the son of a bitch was that had amputated without his permission.

The next day, after word had spread through the islands, legendary big wave surfer Laird Hamilton, no relation to Bethany, called his father, Billy, another legendary surfer, and told him if he didn't go out and "kill this fucking shark," he was going to do it himself. Fourteen days later, much to the outrage of the indigenous Hawaiian population, Billy Hamilton and Ralph Young hauled to the beach a fourteen-foot female tiger shark with a ragged dorsal fin. It took a gutted five-foot gray shark as bait and a barbed hook the size of dinner plate to do it. Butchering the beast offshore, away from prying eyes, they found no evidence of Bethany's arm or her pink watch or her charm bracelet or the eighteen-inch semi-circle of her surfboard that the shark had taken all at once. Experts claimed that the shark would have long before regurgitated the irritating fiberglass and probably the arm with it. However, removing the jaws from the carcass and matching them to Bethany's board, the Hawaiian Fish and Game forensic team revealed that it was a perfect fit. Aside from the jaws, the only other part of the shark that was saved was a section of its dusky, striped skin. This skin was presented to Boy Akana, a local Kahuna, or Polynesian priest, who would stretch the skin over ceremonial drums to call on the ancient spirits to calm the seas. Twenty-four hours later, Hawaiian Governor Linda Lingle was said to decree that the matter was now closed and that the tourist industry should get back to normal.

Seven days after the catch of the great fish, Bethany Hamilton pays a visit to Ralph Young's fishing compound with her father, Tom. Bethany, at her own request, is there to visit the jaws that took her arm. Bethany crouches in the middle of the lawn, where the jaws come up to her shoulder. They are still bloody and have shards of feeding tissue hanging from their teeth. For long moments, the men stand around uncomfortably as Bethany curiously pokes at the razor-sharp teeth one by one. Then she looks up and asks her father if she can have one of the teeth for a necklace she would like to make. An amulet to protect her in the future. The men are so stunned that nobody speaks. Upon leaving the compound with her father, Bethany is overheard saying, "I hope I don't have dreams."

On the drive home, it rains. With a sleeping Bethany next to him in the car, with the windshield wipers beating time, Tom Hamilton begins to hum a tune. He has not thought of this tune for a long, long time. Not since he was in the US Navy as a young gunner's mate. His lips move slightly as he recalls the words of the Navy Hymn:

> "Eternal Father, strong to save,
> Whose arm does bind the restless wave,
> Who biddest the mighty Ocean deep,
> Its own appointed limits keep,
> O hear us when we cry to thee,
> For those in peril on the sea."

Driving on through the rain, these are the only words Tom Hamilton can remember.

He reaches out to gently take his daughter's hand.

But it is not there.

OLD SMOKE

NORTH OF THE BRIDGE
SURFER MAGAZINE, USA, 1997

He was smoking a joint in a remote Northern California Pub when I ran into him. He wasn't long for this world. —Mg.

He is a surfer. He is forty-one years old. He has worn a beard for the last twenty of those years. Along with a threadbare Pendleton shirt under a light blue down vest with a flap of duct tape covering its torn right pocket. In his mud-spattered white Ford F-150 pickup truck, at all times, he carries a beat-up surfboard, seven feet, two inches long, a thick, tattered wetsuit, a hoe, a shovel, three five-gallon restaurant buckets, two fifty-pound sacks of manure, and a loaded revolver.

On this day, he arrives at the Point Arena Pier a little earlier than usual: around 3:00 p.m. He parks his truck and walks out onto the pier to check the surf. He does this every day, every single day, even though lately, he has been wondering why. He sees that the surf is up again. He guesses that means he'll have to go surfing. Because he guesses that is what he has lived for. He looks out onto the breaking waves off the point. He sees that a former friend of his is in the lineup. This reminds him of his own work that has caused the falling out between he and most his friends. The work that made his wife take the kid and split. The work that he's begun to despise. He looks around once. Unbuckles his belt. He unzips the hidden pouch on the back of his belt and pulls out a thumb-sized marijuana joint. A resiny bit of his latest harvest. The good shit. The stuff that next week's big sale is about. He looks around out of habit. But no one would give a damn down on the pier. He sparks it and draws deeply, burning a good half inch. He feels the smoke soar into his lungs and work up into his forehead. The polecat scent sweeps up behind his bloodshot eyes, and the universe slows on its axis for the millionth time in his life.

A big set of waves hiss through the lineup. Some teenager in a bright orange wetsuit drops into one of them and starts hacking around on its face, slashing his tiny surfboard this way and that. The future.

Shit, what do these disco kids know about surfing? Fuck, man, all they do is go out and get in the way of real surfers. Wiggling around like a bunch of retards. These fuckin' pussies don't even smoke anymore. What the hell do they know, the little shits. He has said this to himself a thousand times. It's a thought that he's tired of. It's old and useless.

"SHIT!" This time out loud. Then he tries, for the first time in a long time, to think of something that makes him happy. That's what his ex wanted him to do all the goddamned time. And that fucked up marriage counselor too. Think nice all the goddamn time. It was hard enough in front of the both of them. But now? Alone? He tries again. Nothing. Only all the crap he has been putting up with. *Fuckin' cops and their fuckin' heat-seeking helicopters. Fuckin' busts. The fuckin' payoffs. Those fuckin' cocaine assholes movin' in. The fuckin' rip-offs between friends. Those fuckin' deer that have been eating all my best homegrown, and those fuckin' dogs of mine that won't do a fuckin' thing about it. And all those fuckin' big business yuppie college boys that are taking over the business, showing up in suits, for chrissakes, tryin' to organize us outlaw farmers into some kind of half-assed union, but only so that they can broker bales of the good shit down to the buggering San Francisco queers in the Castro. And the fuckin' wife that doesn't want to raise a kid around the whole green scene and just up and splits with our boy. The fuckin' paranoia of it all. The fuckin' surfing.* There. That was a new one. The surfing. The whole reason he got into this lifestyle in the first place. Twenty years ago, it was all so righteous. Him and all his friends dropping out of Berkeley Poli Sci, scamming a cinch life, making it too easy. Plenty bud, plenty surf, plenty bud, plenty surf. But now, now he was bored with it. Stupid with it. He stunk of it.

He takes another drag. Blows it out his nose like a horse in a frost. He wonders why it is so painful to think back these days. He blames it on the surfing. Like old smoke, the high of surfing had just worn off, leaving a sour cottonmouth. He feels old. Bitter. He admits it to himself again just to be sure that his desire to surf was about gone. And here he had gone and based his whole life on it. Dedicating his whole life to surfing and being an asshole local and yelling at people in the surf to go home and clenching his fists and throwing punches at strangers' faces and growing his goddamn weed so that he could just keep doing it over and over, day after day. Oh sure, he'd laughed along the way. Not enough though. He'd loved a woman, had a kid, had some good friends, ridden some good waves—plenty of those. But that was all gone now. *Fuck, I haven't even talked to my old man for ten years, him and his fuckin' Air Force medals, and I did all this for what? The smoke? The waves? Was this what I was supposed to end up with?*

He isn't even looking at the surf at this point. He is looking down off the pier into a sea that is undulating and sighing through the barnacled pilings. The seaweed sweeping around like a witch's hair in a storm. To him, even the water seemed colder these days. He shakes his head and does a good, long job of wiping his face with his right hand. He takes a last drag on his smoke and flicks the remaining half into the water. *Fuck, there's plenty more where that came from.*

He turns and walks back to his truck. He pulls his moldering wetsuit out of the bed and begins to turn it inside out. He strips naked and lifts himself up into the passenger side of the cab to pull his wetsuit on. Then he stops. Just sits there. His fingers let go of the wetsuit and the thing slides down into the wheel well around his ankles. He is motionless for a full five minutes. He reaches under the driver's seat, finds the holster. He pulls out the revolver, weighs it in his hand. He flicks the safety on and off a few times. The gun feels heavier to him than it ever has. He flicks the safety off. Firing position. He puts his finger inside the trigger guard. Wraps his finger around the trigger. Feels it. The power of it. The noise of it. He twists his wrist and stares straight down the barrel with his finger still on the trigger. It is not fear he feels—it's something else. A disconnection with everything. Every single thing that has ever come before. He stares down the barrel. A seagull calls over at the pier, and he turns his head and watches it swoop and then hover over a garbage can and complain. He looks back down the barrel of the revolver for another minute. Then he takes his finger off the trigger and lets his hand and the gun fall into his naked lap. The gun feels like its been on ice. Another minute. Just looking at it. Then he flips the safety on with his thumb, leans over, and fits the gun back into its holster. He sits up, eases himself back into the seat. He wonders what it would feel like. The blast. A spray of stars? Or do the lights just go out? With the sound of the sea and the smell of the smoke on him, he is as lonely as he has ever been. He stares out the dirty windshield at nothing.

ONCE THERE WAS
A WAR

THE SOLDIERS, THE SACRED CRAFT, AND THE SURF
PHOTOGRAPHER WHO FOUND HIS HEART ON THE
FORGOTTEN ISLAND OF MOROTAI

PHOTO: JASON CHILDS

SURFER MAGAZINE, USA, 2015

Growing up in a military family, I have always been fascinated by military history. But never did I expect to be surfing on a beach so instrumental in the ending of World War II. Nor one so lost in time. —Mg.

The Descendants

It is a world not easy to find. And even harder to find a reason why. But in a lost and battered hut, on a lost and battered island, by the light of a lost and battered hurricane lantern, the old, old man told his story to us. His name was Cecil Carel and he was either 98, 101, or 104 years old. He wasn't sure. Neither were the other men of the village who sat with us near midnight in Cecil Carel's fishing hut. We listened to his voice, now shaved down by the ages to no more than a sigh. His eyes, rheumy and a pale lime, seemed to look more inward than out, as if he had seen enough in his long life and now just listened to his own stories like remembered songs. He spoke of a magical and brutal time in his village when, as a boy, perched far above in his beloved coconut trees, he used to wave hello to the Japanese soldiers on their way to work. He spoke of how they would wave back and how the smallest of them would step over and catch the coconuts he would drop down to them. The soldiers were always thirsty. They would drink deeply and then, wiping their faces on their forearms, would dig the flesh out of the coconuts with their bayonets. They were always hungry. And growing smaller in numbers by the day. The jungle was eating them alive.

The Japanese soldiers would leave Cecil Carel small gifts from time to time at the base of the trees he climbed for them. The biggest prize being the broken bayonet that he used to harvest the coconuts for his village. Tired and gaunt after months of jungle war, the Japanese soldiers had stopped bothering the young women of his village on their daily patrols along the crescent-shaped beach that was his home. At first, they averaged three young women a day, the girls swelling with children not long after. Spring would bring the harvest of the girls' screams. Through pantomime with the Japanese soldiers, Cecil Carel spoke of how he made friends with the Japanese despite this. And how the small number of them were waiting for the thousands of American soldiers to make land and butcher them. As Cecil Carel spoke, the lantern hissed low and the moon spun toward the horizon. Beneath a sky so jammed with stars it seemed you could pick up a rock and hit them. The same night sky that had looked down on the slaughter that visited this place during World War II. The Battle of Morotai, where five hundred Japanese soldiers harassed MacArthur's landing forces for over a year. Cecil Carel didn't remember much of the fighting. That took place mostly to the southwest. But he did remember two old friends. One was a Japanese soldier named Teruo Nakamura, the last Japanese soldier to surrender after World War II. Nakamura, fiercely patriotic and refusing to believe that Japan had surrendered, had hidden and waited for word of a Japanese victory in the jungle behind this very beach for twenty-nine years. Until his extraordinary surrender in 1974. It took a signed letter from the Japanese Emperor to talk him into it. Cecil Carel, the only man on earth that Nakamura trusted, was tasked with bringing him the document and walking Nakamura out of the jungle. Upon telling this story, Cecil Carel smiled softly and said he could still remember the word *juken,* Japanese for bayonet.

And the one other soldier that Cecil Carel would never forget was a "giant negro" named Sam. An American Marine, actually. He'd stuck around, too. Gone AWOL after MacArthur's butchery. Sam had asked Cecil why any man in his right mind would go home to a country that hated him when he could stay here on this beach and marry a beautiful village woman? And Cecil agreed with Sam and invited him to stay. Which is exactly what Sam did. And Cecil Carel spoke of how "Big Sam" had died happy of old age on this very beach. One of the men sitting in the hut with us, tall, well built, and deep coffee of skin, was Sam's grandson. Cecil Carel said that he had always had vivid memories of Sam. Because in 1945, after all the noise and the raping and the fighting and the bloodletting and the bombs and the guns, after all that, Sam had taught Cecil Carel how to surf.

The Sacred Hearts

It is a world not easy to find. And even harder to find a reason why. Days of equatorial ground travel, stifling nights under mosquito nets, and flights on vintage Inter-Island aircraft that make room for surfboards by chucking their jungle survival kits out onto the tarmac. Then it's a long rental van drive based more on belief than anything else. With suicide drivers flying around jaw-clenching corners, doing battle with the big dirt movers that are chewing up the island to plant all the palm oil in the world. And there is the last challenge of maneuvering your car onto an old listing bamboo raft that has to be swum by hand across a black lagoon, water licking at the hubcaps. And aside from the lapping surf inside the lagoons, there is only one kind of surf on this corner of the Pacific. The untamed. With fringing reefs just offshore that face the fury of a deep indigo Ocean slamming relentlessly onto their jagged shallows. Sure, there are whispers of secret surf spots when the planets align. And there is even a rumored resort going up with a manageable break in its front yard. But mostly, this will cater to the European kite surfing crowd and anyone else with a thirst for isolation and wildly swinging winds and seas. And god help anyone in December when the big swells arrive from the North Pacific. Or the Philippine typhoon waves that hold the same raw power as General Douglas MacArthur's pounding battleships. Morotai is no place for the weekend surfer.

But there is a place where, within all this violent nature, there lies a peaceful crescent-shaped bay ringed with white sand and peopled with the child descendants of the many creeds that have foisted themselves upon their blood. The plunderers who found the Moluccas, whether for spice or war. A village peopled with children who bear the names Fernando, Sato, George, Zhang, Nando, Eka, Yunus, and Elizabeth the Albino. Dutch, English, Portuguese, Japanese, American, Chinese, African, Filipino, and all their mixes and religions and beliefs and languages look out of the eyes of these children. Children who surf her gentle beach break on wooden boards carved out of the jungle by their own hands. The same way a Black Marine named Sam taught Cecil Carel. The boards being the last vestige of Big Sam, who, having been through Pearl Harbor on his way to the South Pacific war theater, had probably picked up surfing during R&R in the waters off Waikiki.

The surfing that Sam brought here remains indelible. Even the fishermen maneuver their prahu fishing boats through the shore break standing up, both hands on the up-ended tiller, using their body language to surf their boats to shore. Surfing also serves as evening theater here. When the children take to the sea and the village elders gather to watch and mend fishing nets and gossip gaily and feed their pigs the evening slop in the sand. A tribal gathering, as the children, naked and shiny skinned, cavort in complete surfing innocence on wooden boards of their own design with a style and grace reminiscent of the ancient Polynesians. Small wooden board held out in front of the prone body, no paddling, legs kicking, the board to be pulled quickly underfoot as the wave crests beneath them. Leaping to their feet in this moment, late drops are a way of life. Length of ride means more than anything, and when they come unstuck, and they do, these child surfers make the most of it. Like the way kids jump out of the swing on the playground. Back-flips are a favorite. Expert swimmers, they look like tiny middleweight boxers, whip lean and muscled beyond their years. And their boards are a fascination. Reflecting the universal design of the Polynesian paipo board that can be found from Sao Tomé to Peru and in the countless indigenous surfing cultures that exist on our planet. Rough-hewn, blunt-nosed, parallel upturned rails. Surfboards, or their *Papan Salancar*, are surfed in the morning, left heavy and waterlogged in the scorching sun to dry during the day, and then surfed again as the sun sets and the cooking fires begin. Surfboards that are swollen with the sea twice a day, just like the children who ride them. Surfboards that, during the day, as they dry out, serve as cutting boards for the fish, or as swing set seats, tables, cafe signs, and infant beds. Surfboards hewn by machete and axe and stone and adze. Surfboards that bear the bark of leviathan trees or the painted names of foundered boats that have been battered to pieces on the outer reefs, their planking providing a boon of opportunity as they wash up on the shore. And all this up against a cup of island life where makeshift churches and mosques and Hindu temples and animistic fire pits pepper the village. Where children dream the dreams of all surfers to the beat of a windy shore break in a forgotten bay hard against a great riotous jungle that goes about its business as it has for a million years. A world where the days are not human property, but where they are owned by the imagination of children.

The Photographer

I watch a shirtless renowned Australian photographer, stamping his feet on the sand with joy. The children surrounding him have their wooden boards under their arms, and they are calling out his name and dancing with glee. It's easy to see that photographer Jason Childs has found a reason to be here. An expat in Indonesia of untold years, with a spot firmly earned in the pantheon of surfing's greatest photographers, Jason has been driven here by an ethereal desire that has surprised even him. Having once swum from an early expedition boat to these shores, curious at what he thought were fisherman in the shore break, Jason found the child surfers of Morotai, and with them, an absolution. An answer to a fury that had been gnawing at him for too long. After witnessing the continuing freefall of a beautiful, innocent empire on his adopted home of Bali, a place ravaged by a decades-long torrent of misguided tourism and salacious development, Jason was tired and angry. As are most pioneers who witness the moral and physical decay of an enchanted place due to progress. Pioneers who yearn for days past, who shake their fists against the slow tide of tourism, greed, land grabbing, and carpetbaggers and their evils. But Jason, often moody and short-fused on the subject, soldiered on. Dedicating himself to the raising of his two boys and of the meaning of being a good father and a good husband. Searching for answers, wishing they were easier to find. Hoping that they would manifest in some way. It was simple. He wanted the dream of his early days in Bali returned. And all the motivating passions that came with it.

I was lucky enough to witness him finding it. Finding it in the joy of the surfing children of Morotai. I sit on the beach in the shade of a hau tree with Karen and Alfi, eight-year-old fraternal twins and the only girl surfers on Morotai. Together, we watch Jason as he dances with delight with the little surfers on the beach as they all make their way back into the village after the mid-day surf session. A knot of brown kids swirling around Jason's much taller and, by comparison, ivory-white form. His camera held like a victory spear overhead, snapping away as the child surfing tribe carries him up the beach on their joy alone. These were his children now, these were his redemption from his thoughts and worries, these were embodiments of the search for such innocence within himself that led him to the sea in the first place. When it all meant something untrammeled.

I thought back on how my old friend Jason Childs, whom I have been on many campaigns with throughout the years, both dangerous and joyous, looked very different when he asked me to come along on this journey. To return to a place where he saw things right. And how he felt a gravitational pull to document it all before it ever went away. I saw his story of a lifetime in his eyes. I had never seen that in him before and I gladly came with him for that. And now I sat on the beach under a hau tree with two little surfing twins, watching as Jason Childs waltzed down the beach amid the child surfing tribe of Morotai. Dancing with the children until he became so far away that it was hard to tell who was who. Dancing until, in the heat waves coming off the white sand beach, Jason Childs became one of them.

Little nine-year-olds Karen and Alfi look on as well. And in the quiet hush of the tropical shade, they point at Jason and look at me and say in tandem, "*Bapak.*"

Father.

The Sacred Craft

His wooden surfboard is taking shape. It stands as high as his head and now lies propped between the two roots of the fallen tree it was carved from. It has an off-set, semi-pointed nose, a perfectly square tail, three knotholes, and is still a home for a small colony of fire ants. It is seventeen and a half inches wide, two and a half thick, weighs twelve pounds dry and twenty-one pounds wet.

His grandfather's axe hangs in his hand at his side. He can feel the power of the axe, its magic, how it makes things. Things like this surfboard before him. He runs his hands along the deck of his surfboard. He likes a concave deck. He twists the axe, chipping at a few imperfections. He lays down on the board. Gauging the contours of the deck in relation to his body. The raw smell of the wood is exciting to him. He stands, swings the axe again and again, at once smoothing the concave deck and shaping it. Chips of wood fall onto the jungle floor.

The sound of the axe echoes into the trees. The sounds stop. He spits on the axe, sharpens it on a square of hard stone that he has brought with him for this purpose. He gets back to work. An hour passes. He flips the board over. Sights it from the tail. Starts drawing the edge of the axe blade back toward himself. Great shavings of wood, the length of his forearm, peel back under his strength. The smell of the fresh wood his whole world now. He skins and thins the board toward the tail, trying an idea he has for a convex contour. Sweat droplets fall from his chin.

He stops. The cicadas suddenly break into a leaf-shaking song. A bird of paradise calls to its mate. White shafts of sunlight streak through the jungle canopy. An army of black ants, their path a moving black stripe as wide as a small creek, march off to work not far from his feet. He looks up into the sunlight. He can hear the surf. A happy sound. He looks at the position of the sun and knows the surf is only going to get better. The wind, too. He is alone with his surfboard and he is happy. He sights the board from the nose. Draws his axe. Forms another idea into the wood. He wants more speed out of this one, better paddling, more comfort. No more splinters. He has had enough of those in his chest and belly and penis and knees to last a lifetime. He stands the board up. Runs his callused palms down each rail. He has the muscles and working hands of a man three times his age, the hard work of the village in each of his fingers.

He props the board up against the tree and sits down, his back up against another tree. Out of the pocket of his sandy shorts, he pulls a mountain apple. Its taste is bitter but the juice quenches his thirst. He cocks his head and looks at the lines of his surfboard. He might take a bit off the left rail. He knows it will be one more day of work until he is finished. He looks up again. The jungle canopy is feeling the offshore wind now. A dancer's wind. Swirling through the forest branches like it used to through the hair of his mother. He forms his arms and scoops up a good pile of dead leaves, tosses a small serpent aside, flicks a large hairy spider away. He then curls up on the small mound, in the warmth of the dead leaves, closes his eyes, and sleeps.

It is the 15th of May, 2015.

He is 9 years old.

THE SEDUCTION OF
KELLY SLATER

SURFER MAGAZINE, USA, 1989

Afraid of reprisals, this story was originally edited by SURFER *Magazine so that it read that I was not sleeping next to a seventeen-year-old Kelly Slater, but watching him sleep from the doorway of his room. The Slater family at this time was half broke; a little stucco tract house in Florida, mattresses on the floor. Kelly's Dad had split. I was told by his blue-collar single mother that I would be sharing a mattress on the floor with Kelly. I never understood what the big deal was back at* SURFER *Magazine. I grew up with three other brothers in one room and we shared beds. The following is how it really came down. —Mg.*

He sleeps like an angel. Curled up on his side, dark eyebrows slightly raised, hugging his pillow to his chin. His startling moss green eyes retired for the day. An extraordinary young man in saintly repose. A face at peace with a world that is treating him so kindly. Or, so it would seem. Lying next to him in bed, I listen to the sounds of the night. Kelly's measured breathing, the hissing of the nearby Atlantic Ocean, its gummy breeze sifting through the palms and strangely, the low snorting of two manatees rolling by in the lagoon system that laces itself through the backyards of Cocoa Beach, Florida. I glance at the alarm clock. It is 3:02 a.m. on a January school night. Kelly and I had been up slumber-party talking and the conversation had just drifted off. He was gone in seconds. Now and then, the night wind would lift the tattered sheet that was nailed up over his open window and spirit its way around his room. In one corner were a few taped and split packing boxes, overflowing with surf trophies. In another was a single battered chest of drawers. Across the room was a closet with its sliding door off its grooves, and hanging inside was what looked like a salesman's ultimate sample rack of every surf apparel manufacturer in the business. Wetsuits, t-shirts, sweats, trunks, shorts, sandals, the works. Most with their hang tags still dangling. These labels would spin slowly, an odd-looking mobile.

On the cool tile floor, Kelly and I were lying on a frayed mattress under a quilted blanket the movers left behind. The look and feel of this household had been a surprise to me from the start. Considering Kelly Slater's "golden child" public image, already seasoned by years of teen beat marketing, I'd expected something a bit more silver spoon. But there were no pretenses here. This was salt-of-the-earth stuff. From the moment I walked in the house—a white stucco tract unit at the end of a small cul-de-sac—I'd been treated like family. And since I had been raised in a crowded house with three brothers, I barely batted an eye when his mother, Judy, told me I would be bunking on the deck with Kelly. There was no couch in the place. Judy was an EMT, volunteer firefighter, bartender, and currently looking for a fourth job to make ends meet. I was told stepfather Walker—just Walker—was a boat engine mechanic somewhere in town. He wasn't around during my visit. I wasn't sure if this was intentional. Older brother Sean and younger brother Stephen were around, though. They were in the next room on their mattress. The family had been nomadic for three years now. Ever since Judy's divorce from the children's natural father, Stephen Slater, the bait shop owner. Rumors of his hard drinking swirled around town, but the family in this house kept the truth of those cards close to their chest. It was also understood that father Stephen had plenty of Syrian blood in his veins to add to Judy's Irish. Hence Kelly's olive skin and green eyes.

Judy and her boys had been keeping a lot of things in cardboard boxes lately. They'd been renting this house for the last six months, but now it, too, was up for sale, and rumor had it that the realtor lady had found a buyer. There are a lot of rumors in Cocoa Beach. A place long abandoned since LBJ's ego move that stole the space industry away from this boomtown and off to Houston. The Slater family would be moving again soon. No one was quite sure when. I looked at the clock: 3:05 a.m. The sheet over the window moved again. Beyond it was what Kelly had referred to earlier as "the whole world out there." Funny how he'd put it that way. As if it were a separate entity, lying in wait. A kaleidoscope of expectations.

"I pledge allegiance to the flag of the United States of America and to the republic for which it stands . . ." I was in trouble, struggling to remember

the words, a little off cadence. After all, it had been about twenty years since I'd recited it. And to make matters worse, my voice, which was about ten times as deep as anyone else in the room, was throwing the whole class off. A little girl, in what looked like her mother's glasses, was already rolling her eyes at me.

"*Oh brother,*" she hissed. We finished up and I squeezed into a one-piece classroom desk. One forgets how miserable the things were. I was spending the day with Kelly Slater at the Cocoa Beach High School, currently in his social studies class. A day-in-the-life exercise with the world's most famous amateur surfer. An imperious Miss Burns stood in front of the chalkboard, wielding an eraser like a scepter.

"Now, class, yesterday we left off talking about what life would be like in the Soviet Union. Does anyone have any ideas on what, oh, say, Kelly's life would be like in the USSR?" The question seemed odd, but swept up in the moment with a surge of high school failures in my heart, my hand almost shot up. Someone beat me to it. A real cut-up.

"I think he'd freeze to death without a wetsuit." That really busted us up. Took a while for us all to settle down. Miss Burns continued.

"I think we can do better than that, Chummer. Now, how about a show of hands?" She scanned the room of other goofy-named boys and future single moms like a master, waiting just long enough for a few kids to start wiggling their fingers before making her choice.

"Okay, Scooter?"

"Well, I don't think he would enjoy surfing as much because. . . because . . . because he would be winning for the State. And that's not as fun as winning for yourself, I don't think." Kelly wasn't even listening at this point. He'd slipped his algebra homework over his social studies assignment and was going over the figures. Apparently, Kelly is a math prodigy. Might have even gone in that direction if not for the beach.

"Psst . . . hey, Kelly," I meant to whisper, but my voice, Jesus. "Does this kind of thing go on all the time with you?"

"*Shhhhhhh! Gawd, don't be so rude!*" Busted. It was Glasses again. Since I'd goofed up the pledge, she'd been lying in wait for another shot at me. A few heads turned my way and Glasses was frowning. Kelly was no help. The class discussion continued, with each example of imagined

Soviet life revolving around Kelly. I looked over at him again. Christ, I thought, he must be awfully used to people talking about him to be this unaffected. I mean, these were his classmates, having a rap about his theoretical life in Russia. Wasn't he at all curious about what they were saying? My answer came about three minutes later, when Kelly finished his algebra and glanced up to see how things in class were progressing. I whispered my question again. He whispered back, "I don't really mind people talking around me as long as they leave me out of it." A moment, and then a smile, "It doesn't matter anyway; there's no surf in Russia."

"Shhhhhh! Gawd! Come. On!"

It was Glasses again. She had me dead to rights. Even Miss Burns was glaring at me. I looked over at Kelly. He was sitting bolt upright, hands folded on top of his desk, playing the perfect student.

I sat on a boardwalk bench, drinking a bottle of cold Dr. Pepper and looking out at the Atlantic Ocean of Cocoa Beach's Space Coast. Behind me was a torn-up town, both literally and philosophically. Having hosted the great space race industry of the '50s and '60s, Cocoa Beach was ghostly now that Cape Canaveral was just an alternative launch site for Houston. But it still bore the remembrance in the names of its streets. Lunar Way. Trinity Base Lane. Apollo Street. Not letting any of the old folks forget JFK and Jackie and Armstrong and just what the hell happened to all of them. If everything went right, I thought, they might even name a street after Kelly someday. Cocoa Beach is big on naming streets after things that blast out beyond the stratosphere of small-town life. Kelly, a space industry all his own, would be pulling out soon too, and the whole town knew it.

In front of me, a tepid two-foot wind swell crawled in through a phalanx of bobbing surfers. Now and again, a set of dribblers would move through and trigger a flurry of action, leaving the wreckage of twenty desperate, unmade maneuvers in its wake. From takeoff to the sand, they had about five seconds to make something happen. The beach and parking lot scene was pumping more energy into the day than the waves. Ghetto blasters, all those single moms and their kids with dollar store sand pails, surly high schoolers in trucker hats and their throbbing paycheck-to-paycheck muscle cars. And the merciless Florida sun baking them all like bricks in a kiln. How humans could take heat like this on a daily basis was actually studied here when NASA was around. They ended up loosely comparing it to life on Mars.

I watched for Kelly. Everybody did. He was out there in the lineup, waiting for his wave. The one everyone knew would come. The moment he paddled out, a small group of his high school peers moved from the parking lot up to the boardwalk. Their leader sent the skinny kid across the strand for some Mountain Dew and pizza-by-the-slice. They were all settling in for the show. "There he goes, there goes Slater," one of them whispered like he'd spotted a six-point buck. And Kelly was easy enough to spot. He had the newest wetsuit, a fluorescent orange number. The crew watched as Kelly ripped the wave toward shore, his style as centered over gravity as Focault's pendulum. Strangely reminiscent of 1977 World Champion Shaun Tomson. Kelly's surfing just so damn mature and smart. Of course, this could have a lot to do with the fact that he'd already been surfing for eleven of his seventeen years. Shoulder to shoulder in the lineup with famed locals like Jeff Klugel, Rich Rudolph, Todd Holland, Charlie Kuhn, brother Sean, and his biggest influence, Matt Kechele. Kelly made all the right choices on the little wave. When to trim and flow, when to turn, when to jam. There was a connection at work that separated him from the rest of the boys.

I'd asked him about it earlier, and he'd replied, "I guess the difference is I use my body weight to its full potential. I don't know if other guys even think about that stuff."

He ended his wave with a long floater that took him onto the sand. "That was boss, man. That was really hot," someone said. The assembly agreed. Except for their leader. He just squinted, for a few seconds, at Kelly paddling back out, threw his Mountain Dew into the sand, and went to get his board. The skinny kid came back and handed out the pop and the slices. He had an extra slice. I said sure. He sat on the bench next to me and we ate the pizza and drank the pop and watched some more.

"Quite an audience Kelly's got here," I said.

"Umm, yeah," the skinny kid said with a cheek full of pizza. "Kelly always has an audience."

That stopped me. I'd heard those same words spoken of another surfer years ago. Those exact words. Of course, pointing out the similarities between World Champion Tom Curren and Kelly Slater is nothing new, but I wondered if most people understood the depth of those similarities. The same humble, troubled family backgrounds. The same unaffected, distant attitude toward early fame. The fact that both, despite their many laurels, were still what people would call "good kids." At seventeen years, Kelly is courteous and playful. Not the brat someone would expect, given his striking talent. Same with Tom Curren. Everyone loved Tommy, even kids his own age. Now everyone loved Kelly, as he wore the predictions of future world greatness like a halo, just like Tom Curren did at his age.

Yes, very similar, except for one thing. I watched Kelly take off on his next wave and thought good and hard about it. Kelly's surfing is on the same level positionally as Tom Curren's was at seventeen. But despite Kelly holding more amateur titles than anyone else in history, six ESA titles and four US titles, despite his overall technique, Kelly just isn't the same. His surfing is not as *magical* as Tom's was, not as spontaneous or instinctive. Nor, probably, will it ever be. Kelly's style is more of a hybrid emulation, honed from years of observing those who had gone before and studying what worked. Because of this, Kelly may indeed be the best in the sport someday. But his surfing will never be as otherworldly as Tom's. No, Kelly was a perfect technician, ergonomic, an explosive Nureyev to Curren's delicate Baryshnikov. Yet I doubted anyone would ever be able to actually emulate Kelly. He was like a time traveler, always years ahead of the rest. He surfed each wave as a hole-in-one. A perfect ice-skating routine with a genius for turning a misstep into a functional maneuver. And Kelly never, ever gave up on any maneuver either; there was no quit in him. Every wave a recital. A shot across the bow of any naysayer who doubted his future.

As Kelly paddled out again, I could see in the eyes of his peers that to them, Kelly Slater was the luckiest person in the world. It made me wonder if Kelly believed this too. If he knew he'd already begun to reap the benefits of thirteen boom years of professional surfing's growth. I thought about the surf clothing bull market. The million-dollar pro tour. The million-dollar athlete contracts. Here was an industry that had finally realized a top surfer's worth and was now willing to pay for it. And this industry was ready to cut Kelly the biggest checks yet. In fact, the gold rush had already begun. Kelly has also been the chief recipient of a new amateur system that allows endorsements, slush funds, world travel, and plenty of commercial exposure. Unlike most amateur hopefuls, he'd been given the opportunity to tentatively touch the world of surfing's lucrative gold reserves. And all before graduating from high school.

Later on, when Kelly had come in and plopped himself down on the bench, board on his lap, I asked him about it. If he felt lucky. If he understood the magnitude of it all. "I think I understand," he said, "but I try not to think about it much. I'm just another high school kid. I'm like my friends. I'm just like them." He nodded at the crew. I glanced over at the other kids and wondered if Kelly actually believed that, too. Kelly looked down at his board, water dripping off his nose. "But I don't know," he said quietly, just to me, as he picked at the wax on the deck of his board. "Sometimes . . . sometimes it feels like the whole world out there is watching."

"May I please speak to Kelly Slater?" It was a young female voice. Sounded long distance. Judy had me doing dishes, getting the kids off to school, mowing the lawn, and answering the phone by now. You earn your keep in this single mom's house, however tenuous the rent.

"Uh . . . yeah. Sure. Hold on," I said. I called Kelly out of his brother's room, where they were cracking up to a Steve Martin stand-up comedy CD. Kelly came out laughing and picked up the receiver.

"Hello?"

Long silence.

"Uh . . . yeah, thanks. Yeah. Hey, I gotta go, my girlfriend is on the other line. Yeah. Sure. Bye." Kelly doesn't have a girlfriend.

He looked at me and said, "Jeez! I'm getting more and more of those." Then he walked back to the Steve Martin CD. Situation handled. I asked him about it later. The girls, how they react to him. The attention he's starting to get. "Well, I guess it's pretty different. It's not so bad. But I'm concentrating on other things right now." He thought for a moment. "I guess girls are okay. I had a girlfriend, but that whole thing can be the biggest problem in the world, you know? I've seen that with my family."

Yes, I thought. So he has. From what I'd seen, Cocoa Beach was swimming in late alimony checks. Since I'd arrived, I hadn't met one kid whose parents who were still together. Not a single one. I remembered watching Kelly and the boys playing basketball during PE earlier that day when the coach and I had fallen into a conversation about the divorce problem. At a break in the conversation, one of the boys on the sideline, who I hadn't realized had been listening in, piped up with, "Yeah, I know . . . I wish all our parents were back together again."

"Well . . . I think using the word 'agent' is inappropriate in this case." I was talking on the phone to Brian Taylor, talent agent with the William Morris Agency in Los Angeles. "Kelly's still an amateur, of course, so we're walking a thin line here. The arrangement we're working out with the . . . interested party . . . is one that will allow a guaranteed stability . . . a longevity and mutual growth." Oh Jesus, here we go. Put in the tape, hit play. Still, hearing those words, I knew it was going to be Ocean Pacific Sportswear. No question. But open season had been declared on Kelly Slater. The phone had been ringing off the hook all week. Billabong, Quiksilver, Gotcha, Rip Curl, all the major surf companies were interested. So Kelly had taken on an agent. Or, as Brian Taylor put it, "an executive adviser." Taylor added, "We're not rushing Kelly by any means . . . we just have some big plans for him to consider. Right now, we're working on his travel allowance. Then, once he turns pro, a set contract situation. Further down the line, we think Kelly's going to be the first surfer to cross over to the general public through TV and, eventually, movie possibilities. He's good-looking, smart, American, and such a nice, nice kid . . . the sky's the limit." Once again, I was hearing the exact same words I'd heard about Tom Curren. A whole future laid out in steps. I considered the likelihood of this master plan actually happening. I had to admit, Kelly's chances were better than Tom's. Kelly is accessible, doesn't smoke bales of weed, and unlike Tom, isn't socially hamstrung to the point of being half recluse. Who knows, I thought, maybe this time around, the creation of a great American surf hero would go as planned.

Staring at the ceiling from under the movers' blanket, I took a deep breath and slowly let it out, remembering what all these other people were saying about Kelly Slater. I thought back to that evening, one of the only times Kelly had spoken of himself in any depth. He's a fairly private kid, has to be, now that the whole world is watching. But tonight, as he stared at the ceiling, lying next to me on the mattress and talking things out, he'd found his voice on the subject. His answers were simple, but a few stood out.

"Money? Well, I don't know. I've never had a job. I was going to bus tables once, but then I didn't."

Right. But what about the surfing money, the career money?

"Oh, that," he said. "Well, I guess that's what everyone wants . . . it would be nice. But I just look at it like I'm gonna have a job I really love once I get out of high school." What would he do if he found himself with a lot of money someday? "I don't know. I already get my boards for free. Build a wave pool for me and my friends, maybe? Ha! I'd help out here at home, too, I guess. I'd like to do that. I mean, it's not like we're starving or nothin', but I guess it could be easier. I think that's really gonna help when I turn pro, you know? 'Cause if you haven't got a lot . . . well, it's like being in the desert, real thirsty, then finding a jug of water . . . except it's being guarded by Mike Tyson. Well, if you're thirsty enough, Tyson wouldn't even matter. You're still gonna take a shot at it."

As we spoke into the night, the impression I got from Kelly Slater was damned refreshing. This kid was no product. No programmed contest machine with a myopic commercial view on surfing. I sensed a deep core love for what he's involved in. It seemed to transcend teenage stoke. When he spoke of riding waves, he didn't highlight the moves, but rather how he felt while doing them. He'd even said the best surfing could get was when he was out in perfect, empty surf with his brother Sean. The feeling of it. And perhaps that's the true connection he shares with surfers like Tom Curren. A silent communication with the Ocean. An understanding. A psychic blessing that separates surfing's true prodigies from the merely talented. "I love surfing in the rain," he'd said last. "It's like surfing inside your own dream." And with that, seventeen-year-old Kelly Slater's eyes closed, and his breath became even and steady, and he drifted off.

I looked over at Kelly and wondered just what "the whole world out there" had in store for him. Plenty of money and fame, sure. The two most bewitching seductions mortal life can offer. Powerful, sensual, and for the gifted, always dangerous. Fatal in most cases. Jimi, Janis, Morrison. Still, quite literally and only a high school diploma away, hell and waters high were all out there waiting for Kelly. Just beyond that open window. Whirling around him like a maelstrom as he lay here in the calm eye of the storm on a mattress on the floor of a rented house in Cocoa Beach, Florida. But they hadn't got a hold of him just yet. No, all the madness of fame and fortune could wait for Kelly Slater just a little while longer. Because right here, right now, he sleeps like an angel.

KEALA KENNELLY'S SYMPHONIES FOR THE DEVIL

SURFER MAGAZINE, USA, 2001

I wrote this in angry opposition to the misogyny that exists in surfing. And in my fury to get my point across, it is to my regret that I inadvertently outed Keala before she had a chance to discuss her sexuality with her family. I hope she has forgiven me. Because I love her and the physical and emotional courage that she represents. She became the female Big Wave champion of the world. —Mg.

Her name is Keala Kennelly and she has a story that most male surfers do not want to hear. Because she is a woman in the professional surfing world. Because she is supposed to behave. She is supposed to defer. And yet she sees and feels and loves exactly the same things you misogynist surfer assholes do. Probably more. She has to. Because you guys have made it so damn hard for her to love anything. Mostly herself. Think about that next time you're looking down your noses at Keala Kennelly. Yeah, I know she doesn't look like some piece doing a pole dance and I know that confuses your strip club sensitivities, but I can tell you this much: she knows what it's like to push herself over a roaring offshore ledge in scary Sumatran surf and win the contest there.

She's ridden deep at Pipeline, which is more than 99% of you will ever do. She's surfed the seven seas, which is more than 99% of you will ever do. She's wiped out horribly, been scalped by a Tahitian reef, won championships, and she has drowned and been resuscitated a long way from home. She's risked her life, bet it all, and surfed desperately for the money that no one else was ever going to give her. She earns her stay here on earth. The hard way. All alone. With absolutely no help from you. That's why she knows what it's like to be a winner against impossible odds. Don't you dare run Keala Kennelly down for trying to be a winner. Because that's what she's been doing here on earth. Trying to win. Trying to be something. Trying to rise up in a man's world that doesn't even want her there. To rise up and stand up and love and laugh and surf through life a winner, a champion. And for god's sake, gentlemen, who could possibly hate someone, anyone, for wanting that?

The Phaze Club, Honolulu, Pearl Harbor Day, 2001

It was like being inside a smoker's lung. And there is no hornier crowd on earth than the one inside a rave club in Honolulu on a Friday at midnight. It's the desperation of the place. The rock fever. The gotta fuck. The sweat that runs in rivulets down the necks of over two hundred bodies through two hundred different colognes and perfumes to spatter onto the dance floor with every shake of the head. A snake-pit of wet, writhing figures, hands held high, trancing, jumping, screaming to chest-heaving beats that pound and climax and release and pound and climax and release and pound and climax and release. *Doof! Doof! Doof! Doof!* The sound. Good Christ almighty, the racket. As if god had lost his temper between your temples. Proof that sound waves break. Then there's the smoke. The great draughts of hissing white dragon's breath, like a massive hit off some mammoth spliff. Into this collapsed lung it comes, obscuring, choking, urging, transforming, suspending gravity, suspending life. Then come the lights, the piercing, blinding laser lights that search for life forms in pinpoint beams of bio-luminescent pink and red and blue and yellow and green. Like being in an aquarium of air. Sweeping, shooting, darting, spraying over, under, and through the bacchanal, alternately dilating and snapping shut four hundred pupils already shot from the hypoxic effects of too much smoke, weed, ecstasy, estrogen, and pints of testosterone.

So why is Keala Kennelly smiling? Because she's responsible for it all. Squeezed into the DJ booth, risen throne-like above the dance floor, I watch closely as she and a guy called DS95 battle it out on the turntables. With her left hand, Keala clamps her headphones to her left ear, while her right hand delicately plays over the spinning vinyl disks before her, a lover's touch in the middle of a riot. She bobs maniacally to the pounding, crushing beats, reaching into her Pandora's box of LP's and releasing their demons into the turgid throng. Keala, then DS95 in turn, grooved in and, reacting to each other's trip, lay it down and out. In this space in time, in the center of her "blessed symbiotic energy" that Keala calls "The Vortex," she is the happiest she has ever been. A conductor to an electronic symphony that at her touch, can lead to the multitude grasping for the heavens or pave their way to straight to hell.

There's a guy, just some guy, eyes closed, bobbing half to death next to me. He's going on after Keala and DS95. God knows what he has swallowed. There's another guy crammed in behind him. Zonked. He'll be going on after-hours. And that's when it hits me. Here, in this DJ booth, Keala is once again surrounded by men, again doing something extraordinary in a male-dominated arena. Not just playing in the boy's league, but actually hitting their balls out of the park.

Taking the hard-earned lessons she has endured in the surf and applying them, chin-up, to a second world she is fascinated with. A second world dominated by male performers. An entirely different world of waves. Here, in these clubs, the waves are not of the Ocean, but of sound.

I yell into the ear of the guy standing next to me; I call him by name.

"Hey, Level Em . . . What do the guy DJs think of female DJs?"

"As long as they step up to the plate!"

If it was only that easy in surfing, I thought.

"So!" I bellowed. "Is Keala stepping up to the plate?"

"DJKK?" he yelled back. "Are you kidding me? Look at the people!"

So that's what they called them. That biomass on the dance floor. *The people.* I looked at them all right. I looked at the people connecting to something. And, for better or worse, connecting together. Connected by sound and light. Electricity at its rawest. The stuff that runs in every one of us. That runs every particle of matter in the universe. The ultimate unifier that keeps books and rocks and waves from dissolving into mounds of molecules and molecules from dissolving into atoms and atoms from dissolving into quarks and neutrinos. Pure fucking electricity. Exposed here like a toppled high-voltage tower.

With a final flourish, Keala throws her hands above her head and lets the music ride. All at once, appearing out of the smoke of the dance floor is Keala's older brother. A sylph in a tight striped t-shirt and capped sleeves and perfectly combed, gold-tipped hair, he is a beautiful young man. His name is Quest. His sexuality lithe, hungry, and ambiguous. Brother and sister embrace deeply. Keala's shift at the turntables is over, another pummeling success. Quest has tears of pride in his eyes as he yanks Keala toward the dance floor. With a scream of healed exorcism, Keala rips off her headphones and relinquishes her throne at the turntable to DJ Level M. *Doof! Doof! Doof! Doof!* The beat relentless. Keala surrenders to her brother and is dragged into the heathen swamp on the floor. At the last instant, she turns back to me just as a laser beam of eerie red flashes across her face. Just time for a wink at me before she vanishes into a six-foot ball of rolling smoke.

Doof! Doof! Doof! Doof!

The breath of god.

The Relation of Incidents

Her name is Keala Kennelly and you're goddamned right she loves to DJ. It's a fantasy world of sights and sounds and it's a long walk away from the misogynistic world of surfing. At the turntables, she's in the vortex, making it happen on the cutting edge of an entire movement of sound. A deep groundswell that, if you have the guts to ride it, feels like taking over the world. A whole tribe on a whole new Gondwana that is filled with creative minds and global thinking and unbound laughter and limos and pink champagne on ice. New York, Ibiza, Miami. The excitement is hers, and she belongs to the transcendence of it all.

So why does it envelope her so? That's easy.

First of all, Keala grew up in a spaceship. Or at least that's what she thought it was. One of those geodesic dome homes that her hippie mom got her hands on somehow. A mom who used to embarrass the hell out of Keala by sitting way up on top of the fucking thing, cross-legged and meditating at all hours. Keala got teased a lot for that. And being a blonde white chick growing up on Kauai is no yellow brick road. Especially since Keala had to raise herself as a boy just to survive the rough and tumble world of being Caucasian in a Polynesian culture. Thank god for champion surfers Andy and Bruce Irons. Like brothers to her, they were her only peers when it came to her passion of riding waves. So she dressed like them and talked like them and tried her level best to surf like them. She's actually defeated them both in surf contests. Not many people can say that. So, yeah, as she put it, she had very few "girl people" in her life. Early on, her mom flew the coop. A hurricane was all it took. Hurricane Iniki. A Norfolk pine karate-chopped their crazy house. It was pretty much all they had. Dad had said they were going to have to start over. So Keala's mom, the free spirit she called herself, split. Keala came home from school one day and there was a "Dear John" letter for her on the bed. Keala doesn't remember much about that letter from her mother, except that it was short.

She remembers that.

So she toughed it out. Keala, Dad, and brothers Gavin and Quest (her mom's idea). She wore men's surf trunks and Andy and Bruce's cast-off t-shirts, and she remained a tomboy. It was separate and safer than trying to assimilate into the mocking, taunting nightmares and sexual confusions and mean-hearted politics of high school society. She also stayed on the honor roll at school, enduring as best she could the hell that was Kapaa High School on the east side of Kauai. Physically, it was battle ground of white against brown. And with her cornflower hair and princess fair skin and wide, strong shoulders, she was a big target as a minority white. Her first fistfight was with a local Hawaiian boy. That opened the floodgates for the local beefy Polynesian "Titta" girls. And then came that defining moment with the big Samoan gal. They damn near ripped each other's heads off during that one. A miraculous draw. So impressive that the fights trailed off after that. And having more breathing room to maintain her 3.5 GPA meant she could surf as much as she liked. So she did. Aside from Bruce and Andy, who were kind to her, the other boys hated her. They used to call her a retard. They even made fun of the way she walked. Those shoulders, those strong legs. Her lean, angular body. Keala genuinely believed something was wrong with her.

And that's why Sergio happened.

Keala was out of high school at sixteen as a GED escapee. She had a falling-out with her dad about it. Not long after, she threw in with a guy named Sergio. Just Sergio. He ended up being a psycho. Keala moved from Kauai to Long Beach, California, to be with him. She didn't know anything. He was the only guy who ever showed any interest in her at all. She figured that's what love was. The guy turned out to be such a scary gangster that Keala's dad disowned her. Took two and half years for Keala to come up for air. She left Sergio under the cover of night and moved home again. Kauai never seemed so beautiful. She started surfing again. And started looking at the twilight sky, wishing on the first star that someday she would win a world title. And not long after, she met Roxanne.

December 08, 2001 — Kaimuki, Oahu, Hawaii

I come to at dawn. My mouth watering. The rich, buttery scent of toast reaching my nose.

I sit up in bed. Remembering, despite yesterday's fourth rave with her in as many nights, that I was staying in Keala's guest room of her sixteenth-floor, two-bedroom apartment overlooking Oahu's South Shore. I step over to the louvered glass window. Crank it open. Yep, it's still there. That indefinable romantic scent of Hawaii mixed with the spume of the mighty Pacific. Which I could see winter cobalt in the distance, beyond that clusterfuck of hotel buildings that used to be Waikiki. It's quiet back here on the hill in Kaimuki. Just the lonely, fluting wind. Too high to hear the mourning doves or the scratching palms below. But high enough to see the pink castle of Tripler Military Hospital, where Keala was born and named. Keala tells me there was a double rainbow in the valley above the hospital that day. The day that she was named after them. Kealalee Kennelly, the "Sweet Path."

I can hear her in the kitchen working dishes and glasses and skillets and pots and pans. A blender whirs to life. Before me, I can see giant barges out on the horizon, silently plowing clouds of white at their clumsy bows, plying their inter-island trade out in the Molokai channel. I can hear the balmy December tradewinds clatter the wooden blinds in the living room from time to time.

Mele Kalikimaka. Christmas season in paradise.

I remember Keala telling me the day before that she lived in this high-rise back from the beach because she was stuck between two worlds. A city mouse and a country mouse at once, Keala elected to move from the "beautiful but career crushing" isolation of Kauai to Waikiki, the big city by Hawaiian standards. She also avoided the microscopic lifestyle of the North Shore of Oahu to live here, close to the city and the nightlife that she is such an important part of.

"The North Shore?" Keala had said. "People living so close they know the color of each other's shit." As gentle as she can be, she could still give you a reminder of the boy's locker room world she grew up in. I stood there, breathing in that fresh air off the sea through the louvered blinds, taking stock of all that had happened to me and Keala in our days together. I would be leaving today. Headed home to the mainland.

When I'd arrived at the airport days ago, Keala was there to pick me up in her funky little Toyota four-door. She had on jeans and a sexy sparkly top and a turned-down sailor's hat. She looked powerful and beautiful and shapely and comfortable all at once. She hopped out of the car, slung a flower lei around my neck, and hugged me and kissed me on the cheek. The world smelling like Plumeria flowers. Then we looked into each other's eyes and smiled and held on with both hands. Looking at each other. Only somewhat familiar with each other before, right then and there, it felt like a moment of understanding. Of mutual appreciation. That both of us were there because of each other. That she had earned a major profile in SURFER Magazine and that SURFER had sent me to do it. It felt like the start of an adventure for us both. It felt like a kind of love.

I remembered first walking into her high-rise apartment building. A tall, round building, cored like an apple, open to the sky. From the sixteenth floor, when you looked down the inside of the thing, an optical illusion occurred. Concentric circular lines seem to spiral down into the center of the earth. We leaned over the railing together. Keala dropped a mourning dove's feather she had found in the parking lot. We watched it flit and float and tumble into the darkness below. It took a full minute to splash down. When it alighted, Keala looked at me.

"I call this the vortex, too," she said. "You can look at it forever. It's one of the big reasons I moved in here. Reminds me of the vortex in the music." I remembered we were driving out to Makaha on the west side because she had a stunt work gig on some Hollywood movie. She told me the movie money was cool, but that she preferred the social glamour of music. "When you're spinning, you only get one take, and even then, you're responsible for every heartbeat in the house."

When our talk turned to surfing, she told me she was miffed that she wasn't invited to the annual Pipeline Masters surf contest, the most prestigious contest of the sport. I mentioned that if any woman were to be invited, it would have to be the current world champion, Layne Beachley.

"Layne?" Keala said. "No way. She's scared of places like that. That's why I won at Teahupoo in Tahiti." I had to remind her that I was there when Layne was dropping into the heaviest waves of the OP Pro 2000 contest in Sumatra.

"Yeah, well," said Keala, "So did I, a year later, and at least I won the damn thing."

That evening, at her request, I found myself sitting on the counter of Keala's bathroom sink while watching her get ready for another round as headline DJ in town. Looking in the mirror, she wanted me to check her makeup at every turn, the sparkly eye shadow, the pink lipstick. It was new to her, this makeup thing. And she seemed to trust my opinion on women's makeup. There was that growing-up-with-guys thing again. Here I was, watching Keala Kennelly in her bra and panties as she got ready for the night. She seems completely comfortable with her body around guys. "I'm a surfer," she said. "I've been getting dressed in parking lots all my life".

Then she grabbed a *SURFER* Magazine and sat up on the counter next to me and showed me the underwear photo, the one that caused all the trouble at the 2001 Surfer Poll Awards. I knew it well. Everybody did. Keala was at the event with what she called her "Pussy Posse." The champagne and the laughter and the attitude were flowing that night. That's how she and her crew all ended up at the official portrait station, hiking up their skirts to expose their panties. Printed in bold on the front of their panties was the saying, "BE YOURSELF." Then Keala did it again onstage in front of the whole world when she accepted her award for best female surfer of the year.

"What the fuck was the big deal?" Keala said. "You know how many guys I've seen grab their nuts in public to make a point?" The fallout from the incident was incendiary. The very next day, both Bruce and Andy scolded her for it. She felt bad enough, but it got much worse when surf Legend Laird Hamilton called and told her to "knock that kinda shit off." Laird Hamilton. The big wave Thor of the surfing world. Bruce and Andy I could understand, but Laird Hamilton?

"Oh, Laird's my godfather," Keala replied. "Didn't you know?" *Gulp.* All I knew is that I couldn't think of many guys who could handle that kind of pressure. How on earth did the great Laird become her godfather?

"Kauai," was all Keala said.

There are a lot of photos on Keala's walls. Up above the dining room table and above the DJ station turntables and the boxes of LPs and above the rack of ten surfboards by the front door. Mostly these photos were framed pages torn out of surf magazines with images of Keala surfing. A whole mess of them. I was staggered at how many.

"I like 'em," she whispered to herself as she touched them. We took our time looking at them one by one. "They remind me that I really am somebody and that I am strong and that I'm not retarded," she said. "Besides, no one else is gonna put them up on a wall."

A life-size nude portrait of Madonna dominated her hallway, and beside that, a Medieval Times Dinner &Tournament poster wrapped with a beauty contestant ribbon that read: QUEEN OF LOVE AND BEAUTY. When I asked about the ribbon, Keala's reply brought tears to my eyes. Touching the ribbon like a living thing, she explained it was from one of those nutty places where you dress up in the costumes of King Arthur's Camelot and dine ringside as brave knights in "real suits of armor on real horses!" Joust and fight with mighty claymore swords to win the hand of the fair maidens in the crowd. Thrilled enough by the "real live horses," Keala almost passed out when the champion of the games rode over to her. "I couldn't believe it! The White Knight actually took my hand. MY HAND! In front of everybody! And he said, 'My Lady.'

I mean, *fuck, dude*, was he talking to me? I even got to wear a crown!" Her story made me want to go find anyone who had ever insulted her and knock their front teeth out.

The next morning, at the window of the guest room I slept in, I breathed in deep, glorious Hawaiian trade wind oxygen. I could hear Keala moving around in the kitchen and something sizzling in a frying pan. Nice thick bacon by the smell of it. I rubbed my chin. Might be time to shave yet. I swept my eyes from Pearl Harbor to Diamond head, looking out over what Keala called her "Domain." I could remember her saying that she liked to "look out over the South Shore like a bird, just looking down on everything and wondering what was going on down there." The look in her eyes when she said that was one of someone who had been orphaned to the world.

But at least way up here, it was her world. And that brought my thoughts to the picture of the mysterious Roxanne. It's an extraordinary image, really. The two of them, Keala and Roxanne, in the back of a limousine by the look of it. All faux fur, strawberries, and honest-to-god pink champagne. Roxanne, the New Yorker, the raver, a real knockout with heavy, sensual lips, dark flashing eyes, and a fountain of reddish-black hair. Roxanne. Yes, Roxanne. The woman no one really seems to know. The woman most dear to Keala. The woman whom Keala calls twice a day. Whom she sees in New York whenever she can. Whom Keala gives credit to "making me who I am today." I remember Keala, secretive of how they met, staring at the photo affectionately and saying, "Yeah . . . it took a woman to finally make a woman out of me."

It was Roxanne who got her out of surf trunks and t-shirts and introduced her to forward street fashion and nightlife and an uninhibited world where Keala was beautiful and special and accomplished. A hero behind the decks. A whole galaxy that was new and bright and warm and wondrous. A world beyond the crushing misfortunes of Kapaa High and the whole screwed-up male surfing world and beyond all the assholes who had ever given her the stink-eye in the lineup. Beyond all the male pro surfers who had ever muttered under their breath or uncomfortably shared a winner's podium with her. A world where Keala was fabulous and strong. A world where she gains more strength than she spends. A better world of smiles and laughter and friendship and understanding and love. A world that orbits her surfing like a radiant moon. A place of bright lights and brighter music and the brightest of all her friends. Roxanne. A woman Keala calls home.

I turned away from the window, pulled on a t-shirt, and walked to the kitchen table. A proud Keala has served breakfast. It looked like a spread from *Food & Wine* magazine. It didn't seem possible. Lying before me were all the cut fruit and warmed rolls and Hollandaise sauce and bacon and champagne mimosas of a full eggs benedict banquet. I could only raise my eyebrows.

"I used to have to cook for my brothers and my dad," Keala says, "after Mom, well, you know." And then Keala Kennelly laughed and so did I. And as I sat down to feast with the panorama of all Oahu before us, I thought of all the wonderful things that people don't know about Keala Kennelly. And may never. The stuff beyond the surf photos. Beyond the contest results. Beyond the rumors and the assumptions and the conjecture. Beyond the prejudice. Beyond it all. I think of the truth. That here before me is a woman. An independent woman. A real woman. At twenty-four years old, an accomplished woman. Whose courage, if nothing else, should never, ever be questioned. How many of us guys have that much?

Keala smiled at me and raised her glass in toast. And the champagne flutes in our hands rang softly as we held each other's eyes and took our first sips.

Her name is Keala Kennelly and she knows exactly what you all want to hear. But the day she reveals her sexual preference will be the same day some interviewer makes sexual preference the main issue in a Kelly Slater profile. The same day that all you guys make your sexual preference the dominant element of your very identity here on earth. Because Keala knows that the only people who are curious about who you sleep with can't handle who you sleep with. Hell, they can't even handle the people *they* sleep with. And those are a small people. And they have no place in Keala's life. Because until you guys put yourself in her shoes and walk that mile and give it a real good think, you will remain small. Because Keala Kennelly is a woman in the professional surfing world. And she will no longer be invisible. Because she sees and feels and loves exactly the same things you guys do. Because her journey has been long and lonely and trying. And you guys are mostly responsible. And all that really matters in the end is that when you turn to judge her, remember that when she touches the face of that rushing wave and pulls in deep and drives for the light at the end of the tunnel, she's just like you. The only difference is that she is trying to rise up in a male-dominated sport. Rise up and stand up and love and laugh and dance through life a champion. Now who could possibly hate someone, anyone, for wanting that? Remember this. Because her name is Keala Kennelly and no longer will she have a story that no man wants to hear.

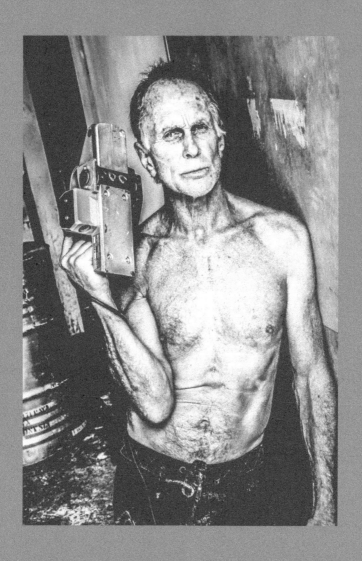

BYRNING HEART

THE LIFE AND DEATHS OF ALLAN BYRNE
TRACKS MAGAZINE, AUSTRALIA, 2013

Alan Byrne was one of those surfers who was always everywhere in history. His was a rare fame. Alan and I grew close late in our careers. Aside from his immediate family at his bedside, I was the last person to see him alive. It fell to me to write his story. —Mg.

July 28, 2013 — John Flynn Hospital, Tugun, Queensland, Australia

Allan Byrne had just died for the second time. This death was from staph. He calls me in Bali from his hospital bed in Australia. Tells me he's got two IVs snaked into the back of each hand. Tells me he's gonna be late.

I had treated Allen for injuries here in Bali during the 2011 Rip Curl Cup, where I was serving as both the contest EMT and broadcast commentary. Allan had a giant set of waves unload on him at a break called Impossibles. It drove him to the bottom. A nasty tumbling. The reefs are still alive around here. He'd made it in to the beach at Padang Padang and got himself to the first aid station. I'd patched him up. Ugly scrapes on his nose, elbows, and tops of his toes. No sutures. He took it in stride and promised that he would take care of his wounds. But like most of my surfer patients, I knew he wouldn't. He got nicked again on the ankle on May 15, 2012. He didn't look after that either. The *Staphylococcus aureus* bacterium that had built up in his system since 2011 jumped at the opportunity. Subcutaneous cellulitis infections erupted. Then the blood poisoning. Then the need for the hospital in Tugun.

The man really is a spectacle at the surf break known as Impossibles. The aptly named hell wave that rockets down the reef just north of the fearsome Padang Padang left on the Bukit Peninsula of south Bali. When it's big, no one goes near it. River current, shallow, too fast, ghost sets, no exit. But to Allan Byrne, it's a dream wave. His own private wind tunnel to test his wickedly sharp, wickedly narrow, wickedly channeled handmade superboards. To see him take off on that wave, on those surfboards of his, is like watching a space shuttle launch. He breaks the sound barrier on every wave. His board dropping booster after booster as he accelerates into the wild blue yonder. Even at sixty-two years old, he is easily the fastest surfer in the world. The only guy known to regularly complete a ride at Impossibles.

So now he is on the phone telling me that his latest bout with staph killed him for a few minutes. But the doctors brought him back. No white light at the end of the tunnel this time, or visits from old dead friends—just black nothingness for a bit.

"But it's not all that bad. Doctors said I should be out in a coupla weeks."

Jesus, Allan. Coupla weeks . . . How bad is it?

He doesn't answer me. He only expresses his regret that he was going to miss his invite seed into the 10th Anniversary Rip Curl Cup Padang Padang Contest. After all, this is the same sixty-year-old man who, during the 2011 event, scored a 9.5 barrel in maxing Padang Padang. Squinting through the afternoon glare, the five judges had thought the rider was twenty-four-year-old Ry Craike.

"So I'll meet you at the Uluwatu . . ." Alan stops talking on the phone. I wait a few seconds. Then I hear two code blue alarms go off. A nurse calls out in the background. The line goes dead.

The Superboards

The only other shapers in history so closely associated with a particular design are Mark Richards with his twin fin miracle and Simon Anderson and his "Thruster" game changer. But Allan Byrne's deeply cut, channeled surfboards are more like masterpieces. More than just a new board, the ownership of a Byrning Spear surfboard, Allan's private label, is a milestone in a surfer's life. These boards seem to be waiting for you. You and that one perfect wave. That one perfect moment you know a surfboard like this will find for you. Every great modern surfer has owned one. Or wanted to own one. Or should own one. And these sleek, specialized boards would never have existed if not for two wildly disparate influences. The first is Indonesia's close proximity to the Gold Coast of Australia, where for over thirty years, the perfect waves found on Bali's Bukit Peninsula served as Allan's hyper-charged test track. The waves that contributed to Allan Byrne's goal of creating a surfboard for one specific purpose: ungodly speed. The second greatest influence on these specialized surfboards was the science of aviation. Byrne's original concept for the boards was never so much F-16 fighter jet as it was the X-15 experimental aircraft—that half-rocket, half-airplane that shattered conventional aviation knowledge and took man to the edge of space in October of 1967. To give you an idea of how specialized this X-15 aircraft was, pilots were not allowed to fly it. You had to be a qualified astronaut. And that is where Allan Byrne comes in.

The Source

"The first board I ever touched was a board my dad made to paddle a big fishing set line with," Alan told me. "The line had about five hundred separate lines with hooks on them. Desmond Byrne. My dad. What a man. We were living in Gisborne, New Zealand, at the time. He used to swim five hundred yards out to sea to set the five hundred hooks by hand. After a while, some sharks got interested in what he was doing. So he decided to make a 13-foot long by 6-inch thick by 3-foot wide surfboard. He made it in our garage by looking at an ad for a Tom Blake paddle board in an old copy of *Popular Mechanics* magazine. My dad's only modification was a removable fin. Way ahead of its time."

Allan says his dad could make anything. A necessary skill when he once lived out on the edge of the world in the far South Pacific. Allan and his brothers used to flume the giant board down the river and into the surf. This was October of 1959. Allan was nine years old. By the time he was seventeen, he would hold seven New Zealand National Surfing titles.

He remembers his father's hands most of all. Hands like a pianist. But still Ocean hands. Agile and strong. The same hands that gave Allan his first pocketknife at five years old. The knife that set Allan free. Just like his dad, Allan started building everything for himself with that knife. Allan never saw a TV until he was fifteen, and by then, he wasn't interested. He was too busy building a catamaran. "New Zealand was just too much of an adventure to let it pass by in the living room."

In 1962, surfing swept over New Zealand like a tsunami. "We didn't skip a beat. We threw everything into it. All of it. Then this Aussie guy showed up, Bob Davey out of Cronulla. He decided he was going to make surfboards in Gisborne. I was twelve. My dad and I were walking along the beach one evening and we looked into this house, and in the front living room, there was a surfboard and a guy working on it. And he was taping a fin on it. Dad had to have a look. So we stepped into this stranger's house and said hello. Right away, Bob asked me to sight the fin while he set it. So I did. And then he came around and checked it, and the fin was true and straight. I can still feel him scrubbing my hair in thanks. There was really no turning back from that. In that instant, I became a lifelong surfboard builder."

Though Bob Davey was twenty-one at the time, he and Allan gravitated toward each other. Allan became his shop rat and what followed was years of what Allan remembers as a delirious blur of surfboard design, discussion, research, and construction. "Fin placement, rolled vees, hydrodynamics . . . man, I was involved. From day one, I could translate what came through my feet on a board while I was on a wave. Directly into my head. I could feel the board operating. We were slaves to our ideas. And I was my own test pilot."

Soon after, Aussie surfers Keith Paul and Russell Hughes dropped by Gisborne. Two of the fastest, most beautifully stylish surfers in history. "Watching them surf, I promised myself that my surfing and my boards and my life would always have an element of that speed involved."

The explosion of interest in surfing in New Zealand brought the master short board proto-shaper Bob McTavish to the shores of Allan's hometown. "With McTavish there, Gisborne had gone from zero to hotbed in a matter of seconds. And then the big bomb hit. *Surfing Holidays,* the movie. That was it. Pure progression. One day we were shuffling around on our boards, and the next day we were carving turns like maniacs." Bob McTavish took notice of Allan's carving and offered to make him a board. A fourteen-year-old Allan agreed. But only if he could help build it.

"I will never forget McTavish. He was so patient, just opening the treasure chest of his mind. I couldn't believe it. I wrote down so much that day, my hands cramped up. I remember I wanted a ten-foot board, but he looked at me and told me I was getting an eight-footer. Man, was I glad he did. That board ignited my life."

It was another movie that really got the hooks into Allan Byrne. This little homegrown movie from New Zealand called *Children of the Sun*, in which Allan was a featured surfer. Allan sent the movie and the entry fee of thirty-six New Zealand dollars to the organizers of the 1968 World titles, scheduled to be held in Puerto Rico, half a globe away. The organizers thought his entry so quaint that they gave him a spot. What they didn't know was that Allan had already surfed in the '66 titles in San Diego at fifteen years old. And got to the quarterfinals. He was so likeable in San Diego that he became an honorary member of the infamous Windansea Surf Club, a membership that he would maintain all his life.

"So, for Puerto Rico, I built a board that really worked well, and I managed to get some money off the New Zealand government, so off I went to Puerto Rico for the world titles. I showed up by myself. Now sitting there in the airport waiting room in Texas were five surfing Gods. David Nuuhiwa, Reno Abellira, Mike Hynson, Mike Diffenderfer and Nat Young. I'm sitting by myself, just shaking I am so star-struck. So, Reno came over and asked what I was doing. I couldn't speak. So, he walked me over to the guys and said I was one of them now. I remember it was my first look at those Brewer mini-guns. Sixteen inches wide. I had no idea what they were going to do on them. But it must have had a big impression on me because, to this day, my 8'0" is only eighteen and a quarter wide."

Two days before the contest started, Allan, who was living in a rusted-out abandoned car during the meet, hid his magic board in the upper branches of a nearby tree. It was stolen within the hour. So, he had to ride fellow countryman Wayne Parkes' board. Allan still did pretty well. Made it to the semifinals and onto ABC's *Wide World of Sports*. He was the only guy to beat Fred Hemmings in a heat. Hemmings went on to win the event.

"So, I went to the airport after the comp and there was Nuuhiwa and Reno and Hynson and some supermodel girlfriend from New York.

I wasn't sure who she belonged to. Maybe all of them. Surfers were considered rockstars then. So Nuuhiwa asked me where I was going. I said I guess I was going home. I was pretty downhearted. Stolen board and all. But they all said 'No, you're coming with us.' We all ended up in Los Angeles. I didn't even have a board. I was basically their driver. I had never even had a license. One of the first times I had ever driven. On what was, to me, the wrong side of the road. I might as well have been on Mars. I was seventeen years old."

It all culminated with a trip to Disneyland. Nuuhiwa's father, a fifth-degree black belt, was the head of security there. On the way to the park, David Nuuiwha asked Allan to drop this "funny little pill." Next thing Allan knows, he is peaking on acid on the Mad Hatter's Teacup Ride during a VIP tour of the place, surrounded by full security. "And I was thinking, *Wait, aren't I from a small town in New Zealand?* It was absurd. I can still recite the lyrics to "It's a Small World." It gave a whole new meaning to the phrase 'a trip to Disneyland.'"

At this point, enlightened and a bona fide insider of the progressive hippie surf scene, Allan bounced around as an itinerant shaper for a number of years. Building boards in New Zealand, shaping for Bill Caster in San Diego and for anyone at all who wanted a board while Allan was in Hawaii. And it was Hawaii that really put the second hook in him. He first showed up in Hawaii depending on his Windansea Surf Club membership for an in. He was picked up at the airport by some heavy Makaha locals and brought to the Waianae doorstep of Paul Yaki, Windansea Team Captain, Hawaiian chapter. Mind you, the Windansea Surf Club, with their strongarm tactics at surf contests, was one step away from a motorcycle gang. But again, Allan's irrepressible likeability played in his favor, and soon, he was a welcome figure over at Makaha with Chief Buffalo Keaulana and the boys who controlled the whole westside scene of Oahu. A throwback to the friendships forged between Windansea Surf Club and the sons of Makaha in the early sixties. Allan lived at Maile Point, surfed a spot named Green Lanterns, shaped for an outfit called Mystic Surfboards, and hit the North Shore whenever he could. But right around this time, despite his outward good cheer, Allan Byrne began suffering from a vague uneasiness. A sense of personal dread. Of meaninglessness. Something that he had to fight to put in the back of his mind. And nothing—absolutely nothing—could have prepared him for the epiphany that was going to take place. And once again, it was competing in the World Titles event that would change his life forever.

What is very little known about Allan John Byrne is that, at eleven years old, he tested at a genius level for complex mathematics, physics theories, and advanced engineering. He was very popular in his neighborhood. He could build or fix anything and make most things work better. His parents didn't make a big deal out of it. Being outdoors people, his family supported his passion for surfing. But it was this wellspring of knowledge in Allen that began really gnawing away at him as an adult. And it reached its zenith in 1970, when he was chosen by the New Zealand government and flown over from Hawaii to represent his country at the world championships at Bells Beach, Victoria, Australia. At twenty years old, he would be competing in his third World Titles contest. Yet for some "unexplainable reason," Allan arrived at the contest deeply vexed. "I had a very negative approach. Something that didn't even feel like me." Allan's observations on contemporary surfboards were the exact opposite of surfing's current zeitgeist.

"I was of the opinion that the short board revolution had turned into a bunch of crap. I saw Terry Fitzgerald and Nat Young and these guys struggling on these tiny little surfboards and I watched the surfing and it was just terrible. Rolf Arness, the American who won, wasn't a better surfer, he was just on a better board. It was 7'2" and narrow and kinda gunny. Nat and the boys, on their 5'4"s, looked like kids with bathtub toys compared to Rolf. They didn't have a chance on those little boards. You never go to the trough on a Bells Beach wave. You carve in the middle and hit the top. And that stuck in my mind. That speed that Rolf got out of it. I wanted to surf like that. I wanted to maintain that continuous speed. Speed, speed, man. Exponential speed. Always. All my life, I had pursued that in my designs. And at Bells, seeing all this crappy surfing, my life just seemed to come to grinding to a halt."

After a lackluster finish in Australia, a troubled Allan Byrne returned to his itinerant shaping life and his tiny apartment on the west side of Oahu. "Even though that apartment never seemed smaller, it became easier to hide from my mind there." Hide, that is, until that fateful night in December of 1972, when the last men walked on the moon.

The Moonshot

With more thrust and firepower than had ever been witnessed on earth, Apollo 17 blasted off into the sky within the dawning of a man-made sun. Lifting off just after midnight on Pearl Harbor Day, Dec. 7, 1972, the Apollo 17 mission was NASA's very first night launch. The fireball at the base of the massive 363-foot-tall Saturn 5 Rocket turned night into day as the long flames from its five powerful F-1B engines bathed a dark sky with a brilliant light over the Kennedy Space Center in Cape Canaveral, Florida. At the tip of these gargantuan boosters were three men. Three astronauts. Captains Eugene Cernan, Ronald Evans, and Harrison "Jack" Schmitt. Four days later, they landed at Taurus-Littrow Valley on the surface of the moon. Cernan and Schmitt remained on the surface for three days, the longest duration of any lunar expedition in history.

Before leaving the moon, Cernan proclaimed, "America's challenge of today has forged man's destiny of tomorrow. And, as we leave the Moon at Taurus-Littrow, we leave as we came and, God willing, as we shall return, with peace and hope for all mankind."

In that rundown apartment in Waianae, Oahu, a twenty-three-year-old Allan Byrne watched the whole drama unfold, from blast off to splashdown, with tears running down his face. "I sat bolt upright the whole time when I watched it, tears streaming. But not out of pride for mankind's achievement; it was out of sorrow for my own lack of achievement."

The Apollo 17 mission would be the last manned flight to the moon. And somehow, in one blinding moment, Allan Byrne, surfboard shaper, saw it as his last chance, too. "After feeling sorry for myself, realizing I was headed toward a nowhere life as a pot-smoking hippie shaper, it came to me that night how smart I remembered I once was. And I realized that with a little work, I was smart enough to be one of those guys on the moon. Smart enough to make real history. Be part of the big game. Be part of mankind. With my mind and my body and my engineering and my theories and, thoughts, you know? A bolt of lightning had struck me from the sky, and every cell in my body accepted it."

So Allan Byrne put down his planer, his bong, and his surfboard, gave away what little he owned, abandoned the apartment to some squatters, and returned home to New Zealand.

Where he promptly joined the Royal New Zealand Air Force.

The entire surfing world thought he had gone mad.

JUNIOR FLIGHT OFFICER ALLAN BYRNE, RNZAF

"I was going to get into the space program. I was going to be an astronaut. Thank God I realized that at twenty-three years old. I knew I was better than all this hippie shit. I had been watching the Apollo missions for years with a vague sense of dread. My inner vocabulary was Eagle lunar landing module, the Intrepid, Antares, Sea of Tranquility, Ocean of Storms, the Descartes Highland, all the lunar landing sites. But now . . . now I was actually going to do something about it and I don't think I had ever been happier in my life."

His entry aptitude tests were off the charts. On an official report, the Air Force listed his physical fitness as "Olympic." He was groomed for officer's school. With his keen, hungry mind, his new sense of discipline, and a burning ambition, Allan quickly rose in rank and got his wings as a Flight Engineer/Pilot in half the usual time. His superiors and peers looked at him as some kind of superman. To the enlisted men, he was a god. Soon enough, Allan was screaming through the skies over his home islands in the most sophisticated aircraft the nation had to offer.

"I flew the DC3. Orion's P3Cs. My holding station was the VIP squadron. We delivered all the important military personnel up and down the country. We did search and rescue. We flew the members of Parliament all around and through the South Pacific. I flew the Prime Minister of New Zealand. Name of Piggy Muldoon. We became mates. He designated me his private pilot."

Allan thought of his flying as "moving through molecules." And to him, the parallels to surfing were just too similar to ignore. "Water and oxygen are only different by two tiny hydrogen molecules. Oxygen was always just thin water to me, and I started making tracks in the sky that were very close to surfing."

Then came the news. A new secret program. Allan found himself a candidate. He was ordered to do an intensive eighteen-month course in advanced physics, secret avionics, and the meteorology of outer space. The New Zealand Air Force was grooming Allan Byrne for the next step into the unknown. He was going to become an astronaut.

"My favorite part of the advanced training was the top-secret wind tunnel stuff. I was fascinated. Smart trails, angles of attack, separation of boundary layers, how a foil relates to a medium . . . man, I got it all right away. I felt like a shaper again." In an ironic turn of events, it wouldn't be long until he was.

Three years into his twelve-year enlistment, Flight Officer Allan Byrne was busted for fraternizing with the enlisted men. Partying with the help, so to speak. Due to discipline standards, this is something that officers in any military are forbidden to do. Do not get too close to the grunts; the day might come when you will have to send them to their deaths.

"But the enlisted guys were the only guys I wanted to hang out with. They were cool. They drank beer and surfed. It made me feel like a surfer. That was still part of my energy. It stimulated my intellect. The officers were a drag."

This fraternizing bust was a serious infraction and began a slow slide to the bottom of the rungs for Allan. He had betrayed his officerhood. And the undermining began. He could see what was happening. The petty jealousies of his fellow officers started to wear him down. The politics. The maneuvering for his job, the surprise inspections, the more frequent performance reports, the scrutiny for any missed detail that goes on his permanent record. He had made powerful enemies with his brilliance and now they struck like vipers. The dog-eat-dog military culture of ambition had found Allan Byrne and had begun to break his will. His astronaut dreams were being torpedoed. And this was something that Allan just could not abide. He would not become a part of this ugly world. He chose not to fight it. He started dreaming of surfing again. Vivid, watery dreams that would come to him in the night: jet-fueled surfing, sky surfing, but always surfing.

"I just couldn't shake the feeling that all I was learning in the Air Force would blow the roof off surfboard design someday. And I realized that the Air Force had become invaluable to me when it comes to dealing with waves and surfboards. After the parade of surfing history that I had been a part of, the military and the dreams of becoming an astronaut seemed badly misplaced. I just didn't like the culture. It staunched creativity and bred petty, evil behavior between men."

Allan Byrne had winnowed all he was going to learn from the military. "Life is a wild animal. If you do not try to control it, it will steer you in directions where you belong. I now believed I was born to be this surfboard designer. And the energy of the world would not let me walk away from it, even though I tried my best to. It's as if my surfing life was looking for me and found me up in the sky and pulled me back down to the sea and asked me, 'Where the hell do you think you were going?'"

Facing more official charges, the New Zealand Air Force put an offer on the table. They would allow him to resign his commission rather than disgrace the force. After four full years of distinguished military service, Flight Officer Allan Byrne was allowed to resign his commission with honors and return to the beach.

HOT STUFF

Allan Byrne made his way back to the surfing world in March of 1977, a meteor of health, enthusiasm, and ideas. "I was thinking of these shapes as wings, not boards. The latent speed elements of these shapes came from the hybrid theory of Air Force aerodynamics combined with gravity-to-buoyancy hydrodynamics."

But first, he had to get married.

It just so happened that his resignation from the Royal New Zealand Air Force coincided with the inaugural 1977 Stubbies Surfing Contest held at Burleigh Heads on the Gold Coast of Queensland, Australia. On that first day at the Stubbies Contest, two fateful things took place in Allan's life. He met Jane, his future wife, and he landed a job with Hot Stuff surfboards. Allan immediately went to work on his radical Air Force theories and came out of the shaping bay with his prototype six-channel bottom board. Within the year, Hot Stuff team rider Wayne "Rabbit" Bartholomew would ride the design to a 1978 World Title. Quiksilver's young guns Gary "Kong" Elkerton and sidekick Chappy Jennings would pilot the boards around the world. Elkerton became world title runner-up on the boards in 1987, 1989, and 1993. Elkerton also won the Hawaiian Triple Crown on these boards in 1987 and 1989, establishing himself as one of the finest surfers that the North Shore's Sunset Beach would ever see, an accolade that rivaled a world title. All the while carving his channel-bottoms to victory after victory, providing the undeniable credibility of Allan's radical design. Everything about Allan's boards, from the fiery logos to the faded channel airbrushes, reflected the high energy, martial attitude of Allan Byrne. He surfed next to his riders on a daily basis, and though older, was considered a peer in the surf.

"Perhaps I had become an astronaut after all," he mused.

From this base, Allan Byrne prepared not only his surfboards but his own body for exemplary action in a highly structured Hawaiian surfing campaign. And the Banzai Pipeline became his new moonshot.

"I wanted to be scared again. At least once a year, I wanted to be scared. That's why I kept returning to the North Shore starting in October of 1977. Back to the island of my original military epiphany. I don't care how badass you think you are—in Hawaii, you are going to face death waves and call for your mum sooner or later. I really needed that again. So, I turned up on the North Shore and the first thing I see is Rabbit and Shaun and the new boys, and they were doing their thing and had just busted down the door on North Shore performance. They were doing this for years while I was flying around New Zealand in controlled airspace with Prime Minister Muldoon. Anyway, they all thought I was some old dreamer. They didn't know that I had lived there before. They didn't know that I had already done it all in my pre-life. I already had omertà with all the heavies. I mean, I was hitting the heavy waves at Sunset Beach with my mate, Derrick Doerner, and also longboarding over at Makaha with Buffalo. And so the new crew came to me like I was a grandad and said, 'Don't worry, mate, we'll show you the ropes.' And all I said was, 'Gee, thanks, boys. It's nice to have people looking after you at my age.'"

Allan Byrne launched his Hawaiian campaign with commanding performances on his new designs at Sunset Beach, Rocky Point, and finally, the Banzai Pipeline.

"I always used to go to Pipe before dawn. I would walk from Rocky Point and paddle out and surf Pipeline in the dark until the sun came up. Then the whole place would transform from cosmic to comic with the crowds. I wanted to know the place. Have a private relationship with her. But it was no love affair. That place kicked my ass over and over. But by the time I showed up for the Pipeline Masters in 1981, no one understood how experienced I was, how well I knew that wave."

In December of 1981, Allan Byrne stood on the beach with his secretly shaped 7'4" channel bottom under his arm, ready for blastoff into ten-foot roaring Pipeline. At thirty-two years of age—an ancient for the times—he had finally earned a spot into the Pipeline Masters based on his underground performances. And the fact that the contest organizers needed New Zealand's sole entrant: they were selling the thing to the ABC's *Wide World of Sports* as an international meet.

"Standing on the beach with that board under my arm, I could hear all those NASA transmissions in my head. All those historic words that men had said in space. That was my soundtrack. I was on a mission to the Moon, and by God, the Eagle was going to land."

Allan Byrne was unstoppable. He won every heat up to the semis. But what happened then remains the most controversial chapter in professional surfing history.

"It was pretty windy out there, hard to see on takeoff, and when Buttons [Montgomery Kaluhiokalani, an innovative Hawaiian surfer] accidentally dropped in on me in the semifinal and he got that interference call against himself and got knocked out of the contest, well, you know the North Shore; it's frontier justice over there. So the locals just went ballistic and wanted to kill me for ending Button's chances to be in the final. Somehow this was all my fault. There was a riot on the beach after the heat. 'KILL ALLAN BYRNE! IT'S ALL HIS FAULT!' It would have been funny if the death threats weren't so real. Buttons and Mickey Neilsen and Marvin Foster intervened and saved my life. It was all quite shocking to me because I have always had great relationships with all the Hawaiians. And I didn't want to call my mates over from the Westside, because that would have been a bloodbath."

The contest was put on hold. Angry locals demanded that Allan be replaced in the final by Buttons. The contest had degenerated into a very ugly scene. The judging tower was eventually rushed by the mob. Two judges actually leapt to the ground and fled for their lives to a nearby elementary school. The Offshore Clothing company, sponsor of the event, was horrified. The *Wide World of Sports* broadcaster was baffled.

"How can this be? This is like soccer fans of the World Cup overturning the score because they didn't like the result!" Organizers made a futile attempt to reason with the angry mob, but to no end. In fear of losing all control and facing the loss of sponsorship, ABC TV coverage, and the credibility of professional surfing in Hawaii, contest directors conceded to overturn the judge's decision and place Buttons, as an additional competitor, into the final.

Thus, the first, last, and only seven-man final in pro surfing's history paddled out into a blustery afternoon Pipeline. The finalists were Allan Byrne, New Zealand, Simon Anderson, Australia, Rabbit Bartholomew, Australia, Bobby Owens, Hawaii, Shaun Tomson, South Africa, Chris Barela, California, and Montgomery "Buttons" Kaluhiokalani, Hawaii.

The horn blew to start the heat.

"This was my vision quest. Looking me right in the eye. Whatever was going on at beach level, fuck it, I thought. I'm gonna win this thing!" Allan Byrne surfed the best heat of his life, pulling away from everyone but Simon Anderson, who was having a pretty good heat of his own. After the final horn sounded, the judges' score pads were immediately confiscated by the organizers. And the electronic judging machines, a first in pro surfing's history, were unplugged and the data erased to avoid a riot. But unknown to most at the time was that ABC had already filmed the broadcast footage and had collected the official scores from the computers as they came off the judges' panel. The broadcast footage, aired at a later date with the scores already on screen, indicated that Allan Byrne had actually won the event.

The highest-scoring waves of the finals told the tale:

Allan Bryne: 18, 18, 17, 18, 18 = average of 17.8
Simon Anderson: 18, 16, 16, 17, 18 = average of 17.0

But on the day of the event, the local organizers on the beach were terrified. There was no way that they could give the win to Allan Byrne. Not without a full-scale uprising from the local mob who had their pitchforks out for the man who "ruined Button's chances," local Hawaiian surfers being as passionate as any FIFA World Cup fans. Especially frightened was the ABC *Wide World of Sports* people that filmed the whole debacle. So in a hurried, nervous beachside awards ceremony, the first-place trophy and $16,000 dollars went to Simon Anderson. History was sealed. The beach was cleared. And everyone breathed a sigh of relief.

Everyone, that is, but Allan Byrne.

"Buttons and Simon and I were cool. Real cool. We didn't want any trouble. It was just the lay of the land. But there was no way in hell that the organizers would have been allowed to give me that trophy. That was set in stone before I even paddled out. I have never had any personal problems with the Hawaiians. I still don't. But still, I always wanted to be a Pipe Master. That was my moonshot. They let me try seven more times, up until I was thirty-nine years old. But it was never to be. The 1981 Pipe Masters was my day for that dream. And it became my nightmare."

BYRNING SPEARS

After the 1981 contest, a thwarted Allen Byrne returned to the Gold Coast of Australia and kept shaping and surfing. He was raising a family at this point. Wife and three boys. Inevitably, he broke away from Hot Stuff surfboards in 1986 to form a "self-defining incarnation" called Byrning Spears. The Gold Coast surfboard company that he had always dreamed of. More an experimental skunk works than a factory. With the finest surf Australia had to offer in his front yard, Allan's ideas and skills skyrocketed. He remembers the next decades as his most intense period of surfing and surfboard design. Something he calls his "Velocity Era."

"You don't fly an airplane; you strap it to your ass. Test pilots know this. Apollo 11? They strapped the lunar module to themselves. So in the same way, surfboards are attached to us by gravity and momentum. My board goes where my eyes tell it to go. If you are on the right board, you don't even think about it when you surf. It becomes part of your mind. Part of your thinking. I am not riding a surfboard. I am riding moving water. Like flying. I am not riding in an airplane. I am riding moving air. The true requirement of the surfboard is for it to not get in the way of our minds. Sometimes creators get hung up on their creations and they get hung up on one era. They do not evolve. And they stagnate. They have a moment in time and they stay there. The backwards movement. I don't want to be one of those guys making wall hangers for restaurants and museums and private collections. That's like grave digging to me."

The Heart of the Matter

In October of 2007, at fifty-eight years of age, Allan Byrne died for the first time. The initial heart attack happened in the surf. Fellow surfers got him to the beach and off to the hospital.

The heart attack lasted for five hours and required enough nitroglycerin to kill an elephant. Yet the doctors took a chance on death by nitroglycerin poisoning, thinking anything would be better than what Allan was going through. Finally stabilized—a miracle that the doctors chalked up to Allan's tremendous physical fitness—Allan then slipped into a four-day coma. Four days that Allan insists he spent surfing and chatting with his old pal Colin Smith from Newcastle, Australia. Smith had died of cancer some thirty years before. But it was this man who, near the end of Allan's coma, put his hand on Allan's shoulder and said,

"Time to go, mate." At first, Allan thought Colin was telling him that it was time to die. But according to Allen, that last goodbye in limbo was some kind of reward because of what he considers his "good karma."

Allan remembers coming to. A nurse fainted. The priest that was reading over him was so upset that he would require bed rest and observation for the next twenty-four hours. That's when Allan noticed a twenty-four-inch row of metal staples running the length of his body from belly button to his throat. He was now part of the infamous Zipper Club. The Surgeons had removed extensive blood vessels out of the inside of his right thigh and replaced the lines going into his heart. A radical surgery with very little hope for success. Six different bundles of metal wires were permanently wound in place inside Allan's body to keep it all together. Allan Byrne would set off airport security metal detectors for the rest of his life.

"I felt like I had just learned the wisdom of the ages. I felt so goddamned positive. I never loved my wife or kids or surfing or surfboards so much in my life. I felt like recommending death to everyone." Allan's recovery changed the professional destiny of the surgeon involved; the study of the procedure became standard curriculum at leading Australian medical universities. Allan himself became a vegetarian. He would be surfing the giant waves of Waimea Bay, Hawaii, by January of 2008. He would receive his first black belt in karate by June of the same year.

July 28, 2013 — John Flynn Hospital, Tugun, Queensland, Australia

I finally get back through to the phone by Allan Byrne's hospital bed.

He is as cheerful as ever. He explains to me that the emergency is over, nothing to worry about. No more code alarms. Something about too many antibiotics and not enough saline mainlining into his veins. He assured me he was going to beat the staph. That he would be seeing me in his Balinese surfboard shaping bay by mid-August. Enough of the hospital, he said; he felt like talking design.

So we did.

August 08, 2013 — Balangan, Ungasan, Bukit Peninsula, Bali

I stepped out onto my pool deck overlooking the Island of Bali.

Jimbaran Bay glimmered in the heat below. The airport was doing a steady business. The broad horseshoe of reefs at the end of the runway were fringed with waves, the offshore trade winds blowing the tops off of them like the manes of wild white horses. Mount Agung, the Holy Giant, the Balinese Hindu Center of the Universe, rose rampart 10,000 feet into the haze to the northeast. I breathed it all in and thought about my friend, Allan John Byrne. My friend who had departed the earth earlier that morning from a hospital bed in Kuta.

Two weeks previous, Allan had checked himself out of the Tugun Hospital against doctor's orders and flew to Bali. There was a perfect swell on the way to Padang Padang and Allan still had his spot in the Rip Curl Cup. It would make him the oldest competitor in any division of any professional surf contest in the history of our sport. He had showed up at the big annual kickoff rooftop Rip Curl Party his usual irrepressible self. I remember us together, arms slung over each other's shoulders, beers in hand, bent at the waist and laughing hard about the outrageousness of his upcoming competition. He was really getting a kick out of it.

That was Friday night, August 2, 2013.

It was in the early morning hours past midnight, in the soft light of a quarter moon, that Allan Byrne was found on the side of the road not far from Padang Padang. He had crashed his motorcycle. It was bad. Broken bones everywhere. Inter-cranial bleeding. Rushed to the hospital, he soon slipped into a coma. He never recovered. His family let him go weeks later.

So I now stood with Bali before me, thinking not about how he died but about how Allan had lived. Truly lived. At sixty-two, still doing all the things a man in his twenties would be doing. And with the same amount of glee. Allan not only didn't act his age, he ignored it. I thought about his formidable likability and the globe full of friends he was leaving in his wake. I thought about how tough Allan Byrne really was. About the similarities between he and Kelly Slater and how they had redefined age itself in our sport. Surfing in uncharted territory when it comes to the limits of the human surfing body. Its durability. Its endurance. Its longevity. And I thought about how Allan said that his whole life had been spent in the pursuit of velocity. Exponential speed. Always. All his life. I thought about Allan's boards, about his drive, about his vast skills and his vast intellect and about what he did with them all. What he made of them. And I thought about what surfing had done to him and about what surfing had done to me. About what surfing had done to us all. And I thought about how Allan Byrne's life would resonate through surfing's history forever. His stirring adventure. Resonating like the deep, final note of a piano concerto with the pedal held down.

POSTSCRIPT:

The United States of America has remained unaffected in a direct way regarding the desire for Intergalactic territorial expansion. After all her successful landings on the Moon, the United States has explicitly disclaimed the right to ownership of any part of the Moon.

As of this writing, NASA is planning one more manned flight to the Moon. Allan Byrne's friends are petitioning the New Zealand government to appeal to NASA to have his ashes placed there in a ceremonial urn.

.

FLESH AND BLOOD

THE ISLAND OF THE GODS EIGHT YEARS AFTER
TRACKS MAGAZINE, AUSTRALIA, 2012

Standing in front of the Bali Bombing memorial today, my thoughts turn to the forgotten afterlife of a sunken ship. Overtaken by sea life, the hole blown in its side, resting on a reef that has long recovered from the torpedo that killed it. A reef that is going about its business as it has for a million years. Just like here, the epicenter of the Kuta, Bali, tourist traps, where this bombing memorial rests today in the center of an endless, rapacious tourism district. A district that barely skipped a beat, going about its business as it will for a million years. Still, it is believed that the spirits of the dead walk on certain nights past the bombing site. And more than one tourist has felt the hair on the back of their necks rise as they pass. —Mg.

THE GHOSTS: PART 1
Kuta, Bali, Indonesia, 2010

With unblinking eyes, sisters Dimmy and Elizabeth Kotronakis smile and gaze out over the same brand of surfing's colonial irresponsibility that got them blown to rags in the first place.

It was at this very spot in Bali, at exactly 11:05 p.m. on October 12, 2002, that the first and only terrorist act in history perpetrated directly against surfers took place. It was here, in the tourist hub of Bali's Kuta Beach that catered directly to the hordes of visiting surfers, that two massive bombs were detonated within fifteen seconds of each other. One was set off by a suicide bomber and the other was set off by a cell phone in a nearby parked van carrying over two thousand pounds of explosives. In that last screaming instant, 202 souls were surrendered to history. The overwhelming majority of them being surfers. And the worst part of it all? The surfers had brought it on themselves. And upon innocents like the Kotronakis sisters.

Surfing is avarice by nature. Once a new, exciting wave is discovered somewhere in the world by an intrepid few, other surfers pounce upon it like a virus. Then, once the host is fully exposed, surfers from all over the world migrate to the site. Their numbers multiply exponentially, eventually killing the original uncrowded experience. Death by overpopulation. Then comes the next new discovery. And the surfers jump hosts again, leaving an overrun husk in their wake once again.

To witness what surfers, supposedly a peace-loving, green group of Ocean enthusiasts, leave behind, one need only visit Lagundri Bay on the island of Nias off West Sumatra. Once a dream wave set like a pearl in a pristine, shimmering bay, Nias is now referred to as "The Surf Ghetto." Dodge City with palm trees. A world turned upside down by the influx of visiting western Surfers. Local culture is buried under the weight of beachfront hawking vendors, warung restaurants, homestays, a brothel and a drug den. In the water, it's worse. Overcrowding has led to fierce territoriality from the local surfers, who once could only watch, but who now have reached a high level of skill on the cast-off surfboards left behind by the western visitors. Fist fights in the lineup are common. Not even a tsunami could change this state of affairs. With a bay like a catcher's mitt for waves, when that greatest of waves came steaming in like a fastball in 2004, it wiped the whole goddamned operation from the face of the earth. Sympathetic, surf-minded non-profits saw it as a chance to begin again, the right way this time. But this was not to be. It only took one short year for the local culture, with the help of the returning western surfers, to build it right back up into the sweat-soaked mess it had been, fueled by greed for the western buck and by the transient high of surfing. Its perfect wave continually pumping like a motherlode where everyone could extract their own desires.

There are other tragedies around the globe. In Mexico, Puerto Escondido is a deadly crime zone where a drug trade surfing mafia has taken control. There have already been two assassinations against offending surfers. "Cloud Nine" on Suriago Island in the Philippines is an environmental and cultural disaster. Costa Rica sags under the yoke of expat over-development, pollution and corruption. The list goes tediously on. But the biggest outrage of them all is clearly Kuta Beach, Bali, Indonesia. Where things got so out of hand that Islamic extremists took note and decided to slaughter a large international group of surfers for their sins against Allah.

Did a hell of a job of it, too.

Consider this. Kuta Beach, a sleepy Hindu fishing village on the idyllic isle of Bali, first catches the surfing world's eye with the 1972 release of Alby Falzon's surf film *Morning of the Earth*. Curious, but not tempted enough, most American surfers held off. The Australians, however, poured in. That is until *SURFER Magazine* nailed it to the American surfing consciousness by publishing their first article on Bali, "Uluwatu: Evil Waters" in 1975. The article claimed that these fantasy waves were in the South Pacific, but the truth had already escaped by word of mouth and in that one exotic image of Hawaiian legend, Gerry Lopez, surfing a new kind of Pipeline, combined with all the coverage of the international surf magazines, Bali became the mecca of a lifetime for every surfer on earth. The floodgates opened, and the great exodus began. With blinding rapacity, fueled by the lust for perfectly shaped waves, Kuta Beach's new colonization and subsequent tourist infrastructure was spearheaded by the world's keenest surfers. And that's where things started to go deadly wrong. Did these surfers bring their better angels to Bali? Were they doing any more than just emptying their wallets like junkies needing a fix? In their headlong rush for personal glory and orgasmic moments on the face of Bali's perfect waves, did they once stop and think about just what the hell they were doing?

By that night in October of 2002, surfing was an active invasion. A tidal wave of fanatic passion that had dragged in its wake rampant capitalism, graft, environmental disaster, prostitution, illicit drugs, and rivers of booze that quite literally ran from hundreds of bladders into hundreds of broken urinals, right down the naked streets, and directly into the very sea these surfers came to ride. By 11:05 p.m. on that October night, the "Hellzone" of Kuta had reached a zenith of decadence. Sodom and Gomorrah by the sea. Packed with sweaty western revelers feeding off the freedom of the place with a spirit not of joy, but of seedy exploitation. A turgid, sex-driven brothel. The Amsterdam of the equator. Not only a perfect example of the worst visiting surfers can bring with them, but a magnificent target for anyone who hated the west.

So, some Islamic extremists blew it from the face of the earth. Wiped clean by the wrath of their God. And Kuta Beach reeled in shock. And international tourism dropped 98 percent. But not for long. The surfing addiction was in place, and like re-schooling sardines after a Bryde's whale has plowed through them, surfers schooled and re-formed. The rise began again. Then, in 2005, in what were deadly maintenance ops, the extremists started blowing it up again. On surf shop row in Kuta Square and again on Jimbaran Beach, where the surfing jet-set go to watch the sunset and eat barbecued fish and drink red wine at white-clothed tables plopped right down to the waterline. A place so beautiful, so perfect for a vacation, that no one suspected anyone would want to destroy it. Which is exactly why the bombers did. And this time, Kuta Beach became a ghost town.

I first made my pilgrimage to Bali in 1984. The last year you actually had to walk a game trail into Uluwatu, the island's most renowned surf spot, whose name translates to "The Temple of the Last Stone." Today her famed limestone cliffs are crumbling into the Ocean under the weight of the rampant development, golf courses, condos, timeshares, pollution, run-off, greed, and corruption. Up on the Bukit Peninsula, a famous beach called Dreamland, a place world-renowned by photographers for its arresting vista and gorgeous quality of light, is now considered a tourist pit. A bus stop for Korean tourists who are herded like ducks into the hideous, enormous gray cement cliffside bar and souvenir shops selling cheap imitations of the Balinese culture all made in China. To then be herded back to the bus and on to the next express stop, liquored up, but no more enlightened.

I have visited Bali many times since 1984. Loved her deeply. But I'm no angel either. I brought the madness of a Hollywood film production to Bali in 1996. Doesn't get much more exploitative than that. And here I now sit in 2010 at the Bali bombings memorial with the Kotronakis sisters, looking out at the madness. I am pulling on a large Bintang beer just like everyone else, watching the phoenix of lust that has risen yet again from the 2002 ashes of the Sari Club and Paddy's Pub bombing. From what the Balinese call "The night of flesh and blood." Kuta is back. Might as well have tried to stop the tide. And don't think for one second the Islamic enemies of Kuta Beach haven't noticed. Newly installed CCTVs or no.

By the light of a neon moon, within a rock's throw, I can see five different mega surf shops, each blasting deep beats onto the street. Seven monster nightclubs are blaring away as well, inviting all comers into their howling, cavernous confines. I can see hundreds of people, hear hundreds of voices, feel hundreds of western souls blowing off steam, popping pills, smoking weed, snorting coke, gobbling mushrooms, drinking to insensibility, getting blown and laid and buggered and buggering by any means necessary, holiday-makers, hustlers, and dreamers alike. And surfers, you bet. Scads of them. Eighty out of a hundred.

And I can also see the Balinese people, serving them all. The waitresses, the bartenders, the street hawkers, the dealers, the crazy and the grim. And a steady stream of traffic that threads its way through the sweaty, sunburnt, beach-braided throng. Predatory taxis honking horns, and the hookers, sleek as blue sharks, cruising with sly inevitability. Out of the Bounty Club, six drunken, shirtless Australian surfers emerge from a semi-nude mud wrestling pit in a cloud of soap suds and vodka, and stumble over to the packed Espresso Club across the street, where freelance magician Terry Sheard is belting out The Doors' "Roadhouse Blues" with the local band.

. . . SAVE OUR CITY!. . . SAVE OUR CITY!. . .

I tip my bottle to the curled and faded photographs of the Kotronakis sisters. Photos that her family members had taped to the memorial in remembrance so long ago. And I tip my beer and I say to those photos of the Kotronakis sisters, "If only it was that easy."

THE NEW MYSTICS

"They're like new mystics to the Bali people," says Aussie Gary Roscoe, forty-three. We are both standing in the shade of a single palm, watching professional surfers Rob Machado and Bruce Irons rip into one of the newly discovered surfing waves on the east side of the island. Rob looks interested, but Bruce is surfing like he has a God-almighty hangover (but still ten times better than you can imagine). Little Baxter Woodger, fourteen, out of Coledale, New South Wales, is the only other surfer in the water. He is so excited to surf with two of the best surfers on the planet that he looks like he is going to pass out, even from shore.

Gary Roscoe, Baxter's uncle, towels off next to their rented scooter and goes on.

"Think of it, mate. These pro surfers show up, all they have to do is wander the earth like minstrels looking for waves and once they find them, they surf them like they are part of the Ocean itself. It blows the Indonesian people away. I reckon pro surfers are better thought of here than anywhere else in the world."

That may be one reason so many of them are moving here, I thought. Taylor Steele, surf filmmaker, who I could see out on the point behind his camera and tripod, lives here permanently. Jason Childs is here, *SURFER Magazine* staff photographer. Jason is a fourteen-year resident. Earlier, Jason and I visited Taylor Steele at Taylor's compound out in Canggu, the new expat Promised Land about a half-hour north of Kuta. Taylor sat comfortably in his spacious office overlooking the rice paddies and the nearby surf. He was distractedly editing his latest film, keeping one eye on the Ocean. "This is paradise. Inexpensive. A great people, healthy food, a great place for my wife and kids. Surf is good every day. All I have to do is visit California a few days out of the year and I'm set."

Seems the whole world is starting to get it these days. The Hurley clothing company has rented a big compound here next to Taylor's. Lately, that's where Rob Machado has been hanging. I sat with Rob in the compound's magic garden.

"Used to be Bali was just a transit stop for us pros on our way to the contest in Java," Rob said. "I must have been crazy . . . Bali is paradise. Perfect waves, perfect setting, perfect nightlife . . . definitely going to be a bigger part of my life from now on." Rob had recently borrowed a car and drove around for two and a half hours looking for Uluwatu to the south. It was the first time he'd ever driven in Bali by himself. But once he found it, a new love affair blossomed. His relationship with the wave below the cliffside temple, surfing's most picturesque wave site on earth, is now as sublime as Baryshnikov's relationship with the stage. There is even a hairy section of the wave named after Rob Machado these days, simple called "Rob's." The shallowest part of the whole live reef.

Top Australian pro surfers Joel Parkinson and Mick Fanning are building in Canggu. Hawaiian pros Bruce and Andy Irons are thinking about it. So are the other top pros. Luke Steadman and Jake Patterson have broken ground, Taj Burrow is rumored to be planning his own "Taj Mahal." Nathan Webster is in, Billabong surf clothing company is in, Quiksilver clothing is in, Rip Curl, the list goes on. What was once the gateway to adventure has become a gateway to retirement. We visited Hawaiian expat Mikala Jones's place too. A compound straight out of *Architectural Digest.*

"I think this is the way people were meant to live," says Jones. "My whole family is on the property in different houses. We have cooks, gardeners, and the Balinese people are the best daycare you can imagine . . . why live any other way?"

I mention this to Jason Childs, who is still shooting photos of Rob and Bruce. "Look, mate, pro surfers these days have to be adults. They finally make adult money and that allows them adult options. Marriage, kids, houses, retirement, it's a new world, mate. Best time to be a pro surfer in history. But is it the best time to be in Bali? I guess time will tell."

Just then, Aussie surfer Neil Hargreaves pulls up on his battered motorcycle, an equally battered 6'4" thruster surfboard strapped to its side. Here is a real Bali surf soldier. Countless visits, countless campaigns. Old as time, tanned and lean as jerky. Just north of fifty. To look into his eyes is to look into the history of Bali for a surfer on the other side of the cash. You can see the decades of cheap accommodations, cheap beer and cigarettes, the reef cuts, the infections, the scars, the malaria, the dengue, the failed marriage—all the elements of doing paradise tough. The thousands of waves and thousands of wipe-outs and the thousands of warm beers and thousands of red sunsets and the thousands of small rewards that add up to make it all worth it to what pro surfers call our "feral tribe."

Carved into the wood of his face, Neal's eyes, bloodshot sapphires, scan the surf. He cuts the engine, lights up a thick clove cigarette, draws deeply, takes in everything that's going on, then exhales a cloud, filling the air with its pungent spice. Bruce Irons takes off on a big wave on the outside, disappears into its interior, blasts out in a spume of spray, and then swings into a ten-foot aerial that he almost sticks. Rob Machado takes the next one, sculpts an impeccable series of hair-raising re-entries, and with elegance, kicks out of the wave. Neil just watches like a sentinel. We all wait. Finally, with a half smile: "Those blokes are pretty good," Neal says.

Gary Roscoe asks him a question. "Hey Neil, why do you reckon all these pros are moving over here?" Neil thinks about it for minute, grabs his board, and walks down toward the surf for the millionth time. But this time he stops, drops his smoke, kills it under his calloused heel, turns to us, and says:

"Poison snake bites you, you're poison, too."

THE IMMORTAL

You'll hear Christian Fletcher before you see him. It's not like he sneaks up on anybody.

And anytime he shows up, an ordinary day suddenly ends. This time he's tear-assing down crowded Poppies Lane, which is only about twenty feet wide and packed with vendors and holiday makers. He's doing about thirty kliks on his fire-orange, supercharged cafe racer with its bald back tire and crappy front brakes. Where he found the bike on this island is anybody's guess. His helmet has been fashioned into a terrifying, green full-face skull with Hindu symbols of perfection bleeding from the sides. The same symbols Hitler perverted into swastikas. The cops are in pursuit for the second time that day. Pub patrons roar as he blazes by. Balinese shopkeepers cheer. Two Aussie girls flash their breasts. He gears down, grabs an offered beer on the pass, kills it, and tosses it over his shoulder. Avoiding a cringing dog, Christian gets a little out of shape and starts to wobble, no back brake, so he throws the bike into a power slide, jumps the small curb and, trailing blue smoke, guns it into the darkness of Kuta's only punk rock bar and tattoo shop. The black-clad patrons inside help him hustle the bike into the storeroom and Christian is lighting a Marlboro red at the bar by the time the cops race by outside.

"I was named after a mutineer, after all," he says to me. He really is a sight. Sweaty, shirtless, barefoot, death tattoos. He is having his cranium turned into a speedometer above the skull tattoo that laughs at the world from the back of his head. And across his throat the new tat reads "PAPA GILA," Indonesian for "Crazy Father." Seems Christian's seventeen-year-old son, Greyson Thunder Fletcher, is over for a visit.

Good God.

I sit across from Christian and marvel at how he is still alive. A Californian pro surfer, thirty-six now and showing it, hailing from the mega-wealthy Hoffman family. Textile magnates who provide all the fabric to the world's surf clothing companies. Christian has never been anywhere near a job in his entire life. Quit school at twelve. Rumor has it the family has recently cut him off. Hence his assimilation into the Bali surf scene.

"You can hide in plain sight here . . . way easier than the States," he says in that whiskey voice with its unmistakably southern Californian accent.

I look down at his foot. Little toe mangled from his latest escapade. Christian Fletcher is always bleeding from somewhere.

"It's like an offering," he says. "If you aren't playing hurt, you aren't playing hard enough!"

The night before, Christian and I had a problem. I was supposed to meet him for our interview at The Balcony, a popular restaurant owned by Balinese surfing legend Rizal Tandjung. What with a full-moon party disguised as the Indonesian surf awards, things got all crossed up and Christian and I missed each other. Half-pissed, full-drunk, he's hammering on my hotel door at 4:00 a.m. telling me he's going to kidnap me and make me listen to him. I just put the pillow over my head and hoped the lock would hold. Then came the text messages, threatening to punch me in the mouth and stating that I owed him a hundred-dollar appearance fee. I handled that one first thing in the morning, hammering on his door this time. He was just coming to.

All he could croak was, "C'mon man, it's way too early for this kind of shit." My jaw unclenched. And we actually laughed. All was forgiven. I am a family friend, after all.

Seems Christian was surfing Balangan Reef most the night. Seems these days, he only surfs at night. With checkered Vans tennis shoes on.

I ask him about it, this night surfing thing.

"Vampires are cool, right? Think about all the waves they would be getting being able to see at night. So I just pretend I'm one of them. . . its working out great! Each night begins a new day!" Apparently, Christian has been existing in Bali for months now. Dark rumors sift around about how he is on the lam from Johnny Law back in the USA. Christian writes it off. "Just a possession charge. . . ...no big deal. It'll straighten itself out." Next thing I know, I am on the back of his bike, on a trip that could last anywhere from ten minutes to eternity. We are making our way to the Ku-De-Ta, a five-star beachside bar and resort where the expat intelligentsia, artists, and celebrities of Bali gather on Thursdays for their sundown gin and bitters. As usual, we've picked up two cops in hot pursuit. I look down at the speedometer and have to squeeze my groin not to piss my pants. One hundred klicks an hour into oncoming southeast Asian traffic. I just close my eyes and hold on to him like a lover and hope we get there before Christian starts seeing pink elephants. He'd just downed a six-bag magic mushroom milkshake. Enough to drop a large rhinoceros.

"I ain't doing nothing wrong, this shit's legal here!" In what is surely a miracle, we arrive alive. The cops couldn't possibly keep up. Hell, an F-18 couldn't. "I'm not crazy, I'm calculating," Christian brays. "Speed is the only way to stay safe around here. Everyone respects it and gets out of the way. It's great! That's the best thing about Bali: slowing down for cops is optional!"

We've arrived at Ku-De-Ta after dark. Christian's own private film crew arrives. I find myself relieved that someone is making a movie about all this. And considering Christian's pedigree, it ought to be a doozy. Surprisingly, Christian Fletcher is welcomed with open arms by the local staff here at what some would consider one the most contentious gathering in Bali. Soft candles, impeccable waiters, white tablecloths, chill music. . . and then Christian, shirtless, boardshorts, bleeding, body armor tattoos, bald, barefoot, sweaty and smelly, and thanks to the mushrooms, sporting eyes like a horse in a barn fire.

"Get me a bottle of tequila or I ain't talking!" he bellows like a bassoon. "Is Cameron Diaz here tonight? She was a few nights ago! She liked me!" The concierge smiles patiently and wiggles his fingers at a nearby waiter. That waiter smiles too and Christian moves through the crowd like an arctic icebreaker. He plops down next to a famous Japanese actress, grabs her cigarette out of her mouth, puffs it deep, and asks her if she wants to go for a surf. She giggles, not understanding a word he is saying. He launches into another story about himself. He loves telling stories about himself. "Ten-foot barrels, two-foot deep over razor-sharp coral and there I was . . . it was black as night . . . because . . . well . . . it *was* night." This time the actress titters, digging the attention from whom she assumes is a Hollywood celebrity. His conquest complete, Christian kisses her hand, puts the smoke back between her lips, jumps up, and says, "Hang on to that for me."

On a night of unexpected miracles, one of Christian's surfboards materializes, brought to him by a demure Balinese hostess. Apparently, Christian keeps a surfboard here under the beach stairs. Christian strips down to his boxers, trots down the beach under the moonlight, and launches himself into the shore break, camera crew in tow. Then, as if this happens all the time, the demure Balinese hostess trains a giant spotlight on Christian out in the water. No one is really taking much notice, as if this is all perfectly normal. The hostess and I watch Christian paddle out.

"Tombstones in his eyes," I say to her.

The hostess replies, "Yes...when Mr. Fletcher dies it will be with his eyes open."

And with a delicate smile, she moves away.

Which is exactly the point in Bali. Why a man like Christian can exist here. The Balinese respect insanity. It's part of their humanity. A number of their deities reflect it as a cleverness, a mischief, something almost holy. Because the Balinese are non-judgmental people. Because they are tolerant. Because they are resourceful. Adaptive. Understanding. Because they can understand Christian's madness and see a sweetness in it. Because there really is a sweetness about this guy. Because they can understand the madness of the whole goddamned world and see a sweetness in that too. And personally?

I can't wait for the movie.

THE KING

Sitting on the veranda of Rizal Tandjung's villa is about as close to heaven as one can get on the Island of the Gods. It affords an overwhelming view of Bali. Nusa Lembongan to the east, Mt. Agung rising in the mist due north, unobstructed sight from Canguu to the airport, and halfway up the Bukit to Uluwatu. A small palace. One that his surfing family has built. At thirty-four, owner of several surf businesses and still surfing like a teen, Rizal lords over the local surfing scene. Still winning surf contests, Rizal has started raising a family with his wife Chandra and son Verun. Another boy is on the way. With that winning smile, Rizal feels that he really is in his prime. And that despite all the progress and overloaded development, so is Bali. He explains that the Balinese believe in the balance of good and evil. And with too much of one comes the other.

"Before the bombs at Kuta, the spirits were out of balance," he says. "Too much greed, too much forgetfulness, so these terrible things started to happen. But look at the results: we all looked at ourselves and slowed way down. Many turned back to deeper beliefs. A few local surfers even became Hindu priests." Rizal goes on about the rebirth of the Banjar system, of how Kuta Beach is now divided into thirteen micro districts with grassroots watchdog groups. He describes a more aware youth, a more balanced youth who is being raised with more caution toward western influence. More in touch with not only the Ocean but with the spirits within themselves. Today, top Balinese surfers like Marlon Gerber and Made Widiartasurf in harmony with Dede Suryana, a Javanese Muslim and winner of the Quiksilver Open. And they are all looking forward to surfing against the big western pros at the upcoming Rip Curl Cup event at Padang Padang. Even though security concerns hang over the event like a thundercloud. As a restaurant owner in Kuta Beach, Rizal admits that nerves are still frayed from the bombings. Even after all this time. All it takes is a plate to crash to the floor to make everyone jump out of their seats. There are cops outside every major establishment; major hotels are like the green zone; satchels and bags are objects of suspicion and searched vigilantly, especially at night when the madness begins anew. And may Allah Himself help anyone who steps into a night club in Muslim garb with a backpack on.

Rizal, surf photographer Jason Childs, and I talk of the rumblings to the north at Medewi, the only Islamic enclave on this predominately Hindu island. It also happens to be home to a good point break. You have to go through three checkpoints each way these days to surf it. And then there is the anger over on Lombok, a neighbor island, home of the holy, immaculate surf spot known as Desert Point. Lombok, an Islamic isle, where there is evidence of Al-Qaeda training camps. Travel has changed dramatically for what used to be a milk run across the channel. Surfers are far more aware of exit routes and safehouses.

A quiet falls over our conversation. Rizal's son, little Verun, comes trotting out of the kitchen with a bowl of cereal laced with M&Ms for his dad. We all laugh at the sight, slightly relieved to be off the dark subject of bombings. Rizal lifts his boy up onto his hip and steps over to the edge of his veranda. In the distance, the tourist industry grinds away in Kuta. Multiple 747's chockfull of surfers are lined up like frigate birds as they silently float down onto the tarmac at Ngurah Rai International. And off the tip of the runway, a big set of waves moves over the airport reef, leaving a perfect triangle of whitewater in its wake. There is a peppering of small fishing boats near the breaking wave. There are sure to be at least thirty surfers in the water, getting their fix under the roar of the jets and the occasional misting of jet fuel that colors the faces of the waves with cosmic rainbows.

"Let them come," Rizal says quietly as he watches the jumbo jets land, knowing they are chockfull of yearning tourists. "Let them all come. The waves and the Balinese people have always thrived together. The waves will always be here and people will always come to ride them. And whether or not people leave this island in a body or as a spirit . . . that is up to the Gods."

THE GHOSTS: PART 2
Kuta, Bali, Indonesia, 2010

There is a lot of talk of ghosts these days. Apparently, they have been very active. People see them all the time. Especially here at the memorial. Plastered with photos of the Kotronakis sisters and all the other faded, dog-eared photos of the dead from that cataclysmic night. I'd heard two iron-hard Aussie rugby players discussing supernatural visitors in reticent, hushed tones just the night previous. Once you get off that plane, the spirit world is unquestioned here by Balinese and most westerners. The unexplained is commonplace. And as much as surfers like to think they happen to Bali, the truth is that Bali happened to them. Just like these ghosts. Though surfers have stamped their feet hard upon the earth here, Bali's beauty, her intrepid beauty, even here in Kuta at the memorial amid the tawdriness of a Friday night, her beauty is as undeniable as it has ever been. One need only to look up into the evening sky with its citadel clouds glowing seashell blue in their immensity, to hear the creaking of the bamboo grove outside your window in the dawn's misty light, to watch the gentle ceremony of the morning canang offerings, or, for a surfer, to see the ultimate dream: the view from deep inside a spinning wave as the sun sets over the whole show. This is the unaltered Bali. The question is not what you look for, but what you see. It will always be a matter of what surfers bring to it. Evil or saintly.

Hopefully—and a scant hope is all we have at this point—the balance of good and evil here will not tip in either direction. And the horizon will stay level and true and the ship will not capsize and break apart on the rocks ever again. Hopefully, we can all re-discover the beauty of Bali and help the ghosts keep her balanced with our better angels this time. Oh, it's possible.

Just ask the Kotronakis sisters.

Because beauty may never be enhanced by the discovery of it.

But it should be.

DREAMTIME

TRACKS MAGAZINE, AUSTRALIA, 2004
PHOTO CREDIT: MG COLLECTION

While I was covering this Australian surf festival, I saw this kid on the beach and around town a few times. Never said a word to him, but I could see his struggles. It inspired me to write about what can be the loneliness of childhood. —Mg.

Noosa Heads, Queensland, Australia

He is eleven years old and happy to finally be rid of the son of a bitch. Eleven years old and he knows a bad father when he sees one.

He can't reach his arm around it, so he drags his rented 9'2" surfboard by the nose through the sand and down to the edge of his new home beach. That's how he looks at it. How he has to look at it. Another new beginning for him and his mom. Fugitives from yet another bastard. The 9'2" surfboard is all beat to hell, but he rests it gently on the tide line. He watches the sea. His sunscreen lotion, hurriedly smeared on, is sour on his tongue and running from his sweating forehead and stinging his eyes. He feels the next hour's challenge. They're all here. Out in the shore break. The tanned, blonde local kids that have moms and dads and friends they grew up with at school. They are surfing on their brand-new Christmas boards. But they still make it look like a fight. Yesterday they called him a kook and splashed water at him.

A heat horn blares. He looks over at the fanfare of the big contest going on at the point. An announcer is booming over the public address system. A heat of grownups hits the water in colored jerseys. He watches them paddle. He envies their power and ease and strength. Going through waves like sharp knives.

Someday I'm gonna be that big. Someday I'll be eighteen, maybe twenty years old and surfing in a contest. Surfing in this *contest.* He looks back over his shoulder at his mom. Five days in and she's already in trouble. It has always been that way.

Eleven years old and he'd already had to call two different people "Dad" and some other guy, Gary, who insisted on being called "Gazza." He watches his mom through open eyes. Sees the smile on her face as a new suitor leans close and makes her laugh. She, all brown skin and flashing teeth, and all that beautiful hair and those brown eyes and those big breasts slung in that bikini that most teenagers wouldn't have the guts to wear. And next to her, the newest knight, wanting to win her scarf. He'd read something about knights and damsels in distress. This knight is lean, too young, t-shirt and trunks, a hungry posture, a surfer, sweating out last night's beer and last night's woman. It wouldn't be long. She'd take this guy home like the rest of her strays. She'd promised before she wouldn't, not this time, not this new start, but it always came down. She loved fucked-up men. That's what she called them after they left. After her fifth cocktail.

The boy purses his lips and lets his breath out of his nose. Gravity. Can't change it. He raises his eyes to the sky. He loves clouds. He watches a goshawk, glorious wings outspread, spin and tilt overhead. The shadow of it passes over his face. He closes his eyes and he can see what the great bird is seeing. He sees his own small figure at the Ocean's edge from above. The outline of his surfboard next to him like a stranded fish. He sees the tents and the fanfare of the contest. He hears the faint sounds of the announcer wafting up into the wind. He sees the surfers, animated dots, forming a crescent of surfboards along the edge of the sandbar and cobblestone point. Teal waves sweep in from the sea, white-fringed and bending to the contours of the coast and the white sands. He could see all humanity, from a place of near silence, aloft and hovering, and he could see how silly and small humans can be. Even his mom.

He opens his eyes and recovers. The blue Ocean is still there. He'd learned in school that the Ocean was the color blue because of heaven. Cloudy heavens, gray water. Sunny day, an invitation into an azure world. But he doesn't believe in heaven even though he's seen hell. He steels himself, picks up the nose of the board, drags it into the water. The big kid is there. It isn't going to go easy. He waits out a set of waves, then flops down on the deck of his board and begins to paddle out into the lineup. He joins the knot of little surfers out in the shore break. He has grown to hate rental boards. The big kid starts right in.

A heat horn blares again. He watches the next heat hit the water. He floats there and he watches and he dreams. Someday he would wear a jersey. A nice, bright blue one. And someday he would win a surf contest. And someday, someday surfing was going to be his ticket out. He squeezes the squishy rails of his rental. Someday he would have a real board. And it would be his magic carpet. His brown skin absorbs the sun while the big kid with freckles and sunburn scabs on his nose broils like whiting in a pan. There was a satisfaction in that.

He watches the really big guys out at the point again. One of his favorites takes off on a giant board with a big black triangle on the nose. The surfer, the one who wears the black nail polish and the cool eyeshadow and all the cool rings and earrings, dances to the front of the board. A perfect moment. The eleven-year-old closes his eyes and sees it. The glide. Hears the hissing of the wave. Sees before him nothing but a bending blue band, wind textured and stretching out before him. Magic carpet ride.

Forty-five tough minutes later, he drags the board up the beach to his mom. The asshole is sitting on his towel. His mom is damn near making out with the guy. The eleven-year-old lies to his mom, says he needs the bathroom. He knows this will remind the guy that he and his mom come as a pair. Then the eleven-year-old makes his move. Walking nowhere near the toilets, he walks instead straight toward the beach hotel.

The noise of the contest disappears behind him as he skips through the lobby, out the other side, and across the main drag, and catching his breath, he saunters into the surf shop like the man he will someday be. He makes for the surfboard rack. Moves toward the red board. The beautiful red board he has visited once a day for the last five days. He screws up his courage this time, steps over, and leans it from the rack. He runs his fingers up and down its rails. It seems to hum in his hands. He hugs it and smells it and closes his eyes. He sees himself in a blue jersey, older and on his own and wide-shouldered and long-haired, and he holds the trophy and check up high, and everyone in the world is there and they are cheering. Even his mom. And he can see his winning ride, his dance to the nose, and the bending blue band stretching out before him with the hissing clouds chasing his feet from behind. He can feel the power. The muscle of the wave. And he knows that this will be his way.

The big salesman steps up to him. The spell is broken. The salesman steadies the big red board in the eleven-year-old's hands and asks, *Can I be of any help, little mate?*

The eleven-year-old doesn't even look at him.

He just hugs the board closer.

WAR PARTY

SURFTIME MAGAZINE, BALI, INDONESIA, 2013

Most may not recognize the name Shapelle Corby. But in Bali and Australia, she's a household name, her notorious Bali drug bust having sent shock waves through the media on the far side of the world. As Editor-in-Chief of Surftime Magazine *in Bali, this was a very personal story for me. And in the end, it got me into all the trouble I asked for.* —Mg.

CHAPTER ONE
Off the Bukit Peninsula, Bali, Indonesia, 2013

Bernard "Ben" Panagian is part of our war party. He's calm. He paddles his stand-up board surely, but in a style I've not seen before. Legs close together, forward on the board, a shallow yet deceptively powerful stroke. If I had to describe his presence on a stand-up paddle board in one word, I would have to say "commanding." We are moving our way south in a pack of five, a quarter mile offshore the limestone cliffs of the famed Bukit Peninsula, south Bali. Home to the greatest surf on the globe and the main reason tourism exists in Bali on such a titanic scale. An exodus of surfers since the late 60s built this waterworld.

My brother Sam and I are part of an elite group that is being guided down the coast by Ben Panagian. We will put in at Padang Padang Cove, about a mile and a half ahead. It is just dawn. We put in at Jimbaran Bay in the dark. The sun's rays, just beginning to peer over the eastern horizon, are already hot enough to make you take your shirt off, a portent of the howling trade winds to come by 8:00 a.m. My brother is here, writing an article on stand-up paddling in Bali for *SUP Magazine*. I'm just shooting the photos. I live here in Bali. Have for some time.

This Ben guy. This cat was pretty cool. Knew what he was doing. Enjoyed it. Not so breathless and harried and scraping as most tour guides. This guy Ben spoke a quiet, informed sort of English. Not so much a whisper, but you had to pay attention or you would miss it. And you got the feeling from his voice that you didn't want to miss it. When we all reached the famed surf of the fearsome Padang Padang, it was small and playful. Ben Panagian was the first to swing in. Yep, he was an expert. And I live around experts. I also used to live in Hawaii, the birthplace of the sport of stand-up paddleboarding. And I can tell you one thing. Ben Panagian, all brown skin, body made out of solid oak—man, he rode beautifully.

CHAPTER TWO
Serendipity Bar, Kuta, Bali, 2014

If there's one thing I have learned, it's to never think you have seen the last of anything.

Ben and I had formed a loose bond since that morning on the Bukit Peninsula. Over the months following, I'd seen him around a few times. I would head out to Jimbaran Bay from time to time, to the beach center where he worked as a certified SUP instructor and as a guide for just about any water sport you could imagine. But stand-up paddling was his thing; you could always see that. I would take my friends out to his place on the beach. Ben was always a thinking man's host. The kind you would climb a mountain with. I will also never forget a quiet, painful conversation Ben and I had about trying to find him a sponsor for his professional stand-up surfing ambitions. He knew who I was. Me, the retired pro surfer, surfing journalist, once a feature surf film maker for Hollywood, connected. He knew. And yet it took a long time for him to approach me and ask for help. Could it be possible for me to help him find a way to step up, ramp up, and become a world champion someday? He knew he had it in him. And so did I. And I was flattered, so I took a crack at it. Got a resume put together, photos. Including the ones of him rescuing the passengers of an airline that had crashed short of the runway earlier that year in Bali. The plane had split in two on Ben's homeground reef. Ben was on the beach at the time. It's a good half mile out onto that reef and Ben was first on the scene. And to hear other people tell it, he was calm then, too. He rescued a half-dozen people with his board that day.

There was that command again.

I failed spectacularly in my attempt to get anyone interested in Ben Panagian's stand-up paddle ambitions. This is a traditional surfing town. Stand-up paddlers and body boarders beware. No one was interested. The same internationally. And I went back to a very hopeful Ben and gave him the news, straight up. I can still see it now. Feel it. He did not bow his head. He blinked two or three times, looking me straight in the eye, then he looked out onto the horizon. The slanting rays of the afternoon sun. The white fringing reefs. And he said to me—and I have it because I was recording our conversation for a future story—"It's the quiet I like. You can still find the quiet out on the sea here in Bali. Just the sound of the water. And being able to stand up on your board on the sea is different than sitting on a surfboard. You can see the whole world. You can hear yourself breathe and think clearly. I also think standing up on the sea makes you a friend of the things that live in the sea. I think they understand it more than surfing. And I think it makes you understand the sea in a different way. As a visitor and not a thief." It was the bravest expression of life acceptance that I had ever heard.

Which brings me to my point.

So I'm sitting in this bar called the Serendipity on a bashed-up back alley in Kuta. A place that would become your local haunt if you stayed long enough here in Bali. Nice enough place. Tall stools against a hardwood bar. Decent lighting. Cold beer. Couple of tables with boiled peanut shells scattered on them. The odd shot of warm whiskey. So anyway, I'm sitting there and here's this loudmouth Aussie drunk a few stools down. He's sunburned to all hell. I put his age around twenty-five. He wore a Newcastle Knights tank top over the beginning of what was sure to become a fine beer belly. The guy had been spouting off all night about his mushroom trips and his lurid antics with local prostitutes and more mushrooms and more drunken escapades—all the madness that comes with traveling—with beer in hand and malice in heart. And this loudmouth finally chimes in with, *Hey, did ya hear about that Ben guy? Yeah, yeah, mate, that surfer guy down at Jimbaran, the one that was supposed to be rootin' Shappelle? He just got busted for weed! Ha ha ha. Weed. Bloody hell, mate. How stupid is that? Fuckin Balos, they really don't have a clue, hey?*

My right hand tightened around my bottle of beer. Never mind that

Ben was from Java. I stopped listening to the rest of it. I thought about Ben. Not exactly my friend, but someone whom I had seen something in. Firsthand. Something great. And I was saddened. And I thought hard about what Ben Panagian was about and why he might get involved with all that. Maybe he wanted as much as the people he served—those people who come to Bali and empty their wallets like tap water. Maybe Ben Panagian wanted as much too. Being strong and handsome and smart, maybe Ben didn't feel like being a sheep. People hate sheep. People eat sheep. And I was thinking that Ben knows the feeling of being a servant yet still maintains his nobility on a stand-up paddle board, even though it's pretty goddamned difficult stuff to maintain when all you can think about is making it through the day. Ben knows that you gotta be rich to even think about anything but that. Ben Panagian knows that nobody can give you freedom; nobody can give you equality or justice or any goddamned thing in this world. If you are a man, you gotta take it. Take your freedom. Steal it if you have to, but take it. Maybe Ben Panagian knows the difference between kneeling down and bending over. And maybe he doesn't like either one of them. Maybe he knows that if you stay in the middle of the road, then you are going to get run over. Maybe Ben, with dreams of being a world-class athlete, felt like living as if he could look any man in the eye and tell him to go to hell. The same way he might have decided to take on Shappelle Corby, the most famous drug smuggler in Australian history, as a lover. So Ben gets involved with some weed on the side. I don't know. I don't know anything about it. But say he does get involved. Just to make ends meet and hopefully a little more. Just like any of us would if we had to. And if he plays his cards right, takes the risks that any man is expected to in this mean-hearted world, then just maybe, Ben Panagian would have half a chance to live the life of what I saw in his eyes. A world champion. But instead. He sits in jail. A murdered Mozart.

The loudmouth is still going off. The white guy with the money and the free time. The good life. The bricklaying job in Oz, the prostitutes here. The very same guy who comes to Bali and creates the demand for the fucking weed in the first place.

So I say to this guy, who was still going on about Ben and the ignorant

"Balos." I say to him, *Hey, asshole.* And that shuts him up. And he swings his bloodshot eyes around at me. And in his cracked-tooth grin, I could see the intent of every vulgar tourist in the world.

So I say to this guy, I say, *Guys like Ben Panagian aren't the problem here . . . you are.*

And we stepped outside and settled it.

THE HORNIEST SURFER ON THE WORLD QUALIFYING SERIES TOUR

KIDS THESE DAYS, HUH?
TRACKS MAGAZINE, AUSTRALIA, 2016

The World Qualifying Tour, the ticket to the show, is a twilight zone of unlikely ambitions and third-rate triumphs. But in between the tears, you find these young men, very young sometimes, chasing a carrot around the world with blinders on, oblivious of how extraordinary it is to perpetually travel the globe so young. Oblivious even to the effect it is having on their souls. —Mg.

He'd just turned nineteen. But he looked fifteen. And as I changed his bandage and checked the nine sutures I had sewn into his calf five days previous, he recounted a desire, an anticipation and a tale of experience that was so astonishing that I was glad to have had a witness. Otherwise, no one would ever believe me.

We had just made land along with an entire World Qualifying Series surf contest entourage, having just returned from a triumphant week on the Mentawai island of Sipora. One hundred nautical miles off the shores of West Sumatra, we had just concluded the most unique contest in the modern era with an honest-to-god live broadcast from the middle of nowhere in the best surf on the planet on that day. We now had ecstasy of an air-conditioned hotel room in hand.

The only other person in this hotel room was friend Nathan White, a WQS surfing judge, who was borrowing some toothpaste from me before he, too, became engrossed in what would be this young man's story of dark desire. In this manner, Nathan became the only other witness to this extraordinary encounter. As I picked loose and removed this young competitor's sutures, the kid exclaimed how stoked he was to be flying to Bali the next day in anticipation of the next contest.

"Oh," I said, "so you'll be training in Bali?"

"Hell no, I'll be fuckin'!"

There was a long pause.

"Come again?" I said.

"Fuckin', man. What parta that don'cha understand? The ladies, man, the hookers, whips and chains, you know?"

Well, as a man of my age, I did know, but I was nevertheless taken aback by not only this child's extraordinary statement but with the candor with which it was delivered. This kid didn't look like he would even know how to spell vagina, let alone have developed such a zeal for them.

"So . . . like . . . where do you meet these . . . ladies?" I asked.

"Meet them? Meet them? I don't meet them, they meet me!"

"Where . . . exactly?"

"Hotel rooms, man. I know one real nice place right on the strip, pool and everything, and the reception knows me and my girls so they let 'em by, like room service."

"Your girls . . . room service . . . I see," I said. "Am I to understand you . . . entertain . . . more than one of these . . . ladies . . . at a time?"

"Of course! You think I'm crazy? Better value . . . and if one needs a nap or some shit, you still got backup."

"Backup," I said.

"Yeah." And he said that looking me straight in the eye.

"Right," I said. "So . . . um . . . uh . . ."

"Yeah, man, I ain't leaving my hotel room for a week . . . unless I feel like going down to the Blue Moon."

"The Blue Moon?"

"Yeah, more ladies over at the Blue Moon Club. That place is crazy, man. Older chicks, yeah, but cheap. Crazy theme rooms. Pirate, Casbah, Barn . . ."

This stopped me. It really did. I could only look over my shoulder at Nathan, whose brow was knit and whose mouth was open. The kid looked puzzled by our reaction. "You two gay or something?" the kid said. And that busted the dam.

Once Nathan and I recovered from our fit of laughter, I had to inquire about the Blue Moon Club.

"Yeah," the kid said. "Be my second year going there now. Hot, man, I'm tellin' you. They really know what they're doing, these moms."

My god.

"Moms?" I said. "And these . . . moms . . . they don't ask you for I.D. or something?"

"What the fuck? These ladies *know* me, man. Most the other guys in there are fat, old Dutch guys, so the ladies are always happy to see me.

They're like older sisters . . . well. Not exactly . . . but you get the idea."

"Sure," I said.

"The music sucks, though. Parents' music. You know, Julio Inglesias, Foreigner . . . after a few sessions, I can't get that shit outta my head."

"Sessions."

"Yeah, with the ladies, you know . . . but fuck, man, I don't care what the fuck music they play as long as they keep bouncing those titties."

And at this point, the kid started singing.

"I wanna know what love is,

I know you can show meeeeeeee . . ."

The irony of these lyrics was not lost on Nathan and myself.

But it did give me pause later, when I was sitting near the same kid in an underground karaoke welcome bar that evening in Padang's China Town. This town was under Islamic Sharia law. Screwing around here could get you stoned to death in public. So anyway, I was watching the kid on his fourth gin and tonic, a lady his mother's age in his lap. They were both giggling and playing grab-ass. So I sipped my gin and tonic, which was the only drink the place served, and considered the WQS tour. I supposed it's a kind of home for these young traveling men. And that these young surfers are like orphan farm league wards to the world championship tour. The majors, so to speak. And these young squires were perpetually moving through one exotic world into the next. I supposed this could derail a normal sense of teenhood. I supposed it was only natural that, left to their own devices and with absolutely no guidance, a few of these kids would find the darker waters of the sensual world and swim in them, raised by the wolves of their unchecked desires. And, dare I say, considering all the competitive rejection and losses these guys suffer in these lonely foreign lands, I supposed they might find their own ways to deal with the need for teenage love. And passion. And romance. And copulation.

I looked over at the kid again. He and the woman were dancing now. She was a foot taller and had about forty pounds on him. The kid was on his tippy toes, attempting to grind his hips into hers. She was encouraging him. Cute-like. The way she would a chihuahua that could walk on its hind legs. They were dancing to a George Michael song. The kid had the lyrics down and was singing along in full voice.

"I'm never gonna dance again
Guilty feet have got no rhythm
Though it's easy to pretend
I know you're not a fooooooooolllllll . . ."

The kid had both his hands shoved up the woman's shirt, squeezing her enormous breasts like they were bicycle horns. Squeezing them like his life depended on it.

And at this point in his life, I thought, maybe it did.

BEAU YOUNG WALKS
ON WATER

A STORY OF MANHOOD
SURFER MAGAZINE, USA, 2001

The Australian newspapers got a hold of this one and, from countless Aussie Newsstands, the tabloid headlines blared, "SEPPO JOURNO BASHES NAT!" Meaning me, an American journalist, dared to look behind the curtain of one of their revered surfing heroes, Nat Young. To me, this is as close as I ever came to writing a biblical parable. —Mg.

January 05, 2001 — Lismore Aerodrome, Australia

"Some wounds never heal." I could still hear it as I buckled my seatbelt and prepared for the shortest commercial flight on earth. Lismore to Casino. Flight time six and a half minutes. During the seasonal floods, taking the Spring Grove road could take hours by car. If all went well, I'd just make the outback shuttle plane from Casino back to Sydney. I leaned over and looked out the window. Across the narrow tarmac, standing on the apron of the runway, shimmering like an apparition in the heat devils of the tiny airfield, was a man named Alastair Annandale. All fifty-plus, barrel-bellied, chain-smoking, beer-drinking, Aussie dinkum, six-foot-two of him. And right now, I figured he was just about the best friend Beau Young might ever have. I'd just spent a few days with Beau, our new longboard world champion, at his hometown in Byron Bay. Alastair Annandale, as I would learn, was a separate kingdom of Beau's life. Alastair had given me a lift to the local airport about twenty minutes out of town. Alastair wasn't waving from across the tarmac. He was just watching. He knew he'd given me something to think about.

Some wounds never heal. It was the last thing Alastair had said before tossing me my surfboard bag and sending me on my way with a raise of his left eyebrow. I assumed he was talking about Beau, of course. This was Alastair's answer to a question a lot of people had asked. A question that will haunt a father and a son for the rest of their lives. Why was it that while Beau's father, 1966 World Champion Nat Young, was being beaten nearly to death within three feet of him, Beau did absolutely nothing to help him?

A LEGEND SURFS INTO TROUBLE ON SHORE

From *The Sunday Telegraph* — March 26, 2000

"Surfing legend Nat Young may quit Australia after being savagely beaten by another surfer, it was revealed yesterday. The 1966 world champion is recovering in intensive care at St. Vincent's Hospital in Sydney after almost seven hours of reconstructive surgery to rebuild his face. The 52-year-old was beaten to the ground after an argument with another surfer at his home beach of Angourie. Young suffered two broken eye sockets, two broken cheek bones, smashed sinuses, a fractured upper jaw, and a severely bruised back in the attack. Witnesses, including Young's 25-year-old son Beau, claim the other surfer, an elder Michael Hutchinson, hit Young at least eight times, then kneed and kicked him while he lay on the sand."

I first met an eighteen-year-old Beau on the North Shore of Oahu in 1992, during his first serious trip to the islands. He rode short boards then. Beau was traveling with his father Nat Young at the time, but somehow, Beau and I ended up at some surf party at Sunset Beach, Hawaii, where bets were being taken on who would eat the biggest bug in the kitchen. Beau was just about the sweetest guy on earth. Courteous, low key, big smile, sipping on the one beer he'd taste that night. But still, even then, you could see the mechanical nod of his head when every single person he met would end up clapping him on the back and recounting a tale of Beau's famous 1966 world champion father. Fantastic tales of Nat Young, one sort or another. Beau would wait until they were finished and then smile and say, "Yeah, he's pretty incredible." But I'll never forget what Beau quietly said to me in the kitchen that night.

"I guess it's like growing up with any other father," he almost whispered, "as long as you understand that he's Alexander the Great."

I knew Nat. And I remember laughing a little too loud at that.

On January 2, 2001, I arrived in Byron Bay, NSW, Australia, to find Beau Young in love. His girlfriend, Kimberly, studying to be an ethnobotanist, was off in Colorado at the time. They had met in Ecuador while Beau was exploring for surf. Dead sick, feverish, and losing every ounce of fluid in her body from her nether regions, Kimberly had come stumbling out of the jungle after weeks of studying and ingesting medicinal plants with an indigenous tribe. For Beau, it was love at first sight. On our way to the surf, Beau proudly showed me a picture of her. Yep, she was a knockout. He looked long at the picture one more time before slipping it back into his pocket.

"I can't believe my luck," Beau said about his girl. "How could anyone so beautiful be attracted to someone who looked like me?" I could only smile. Beau seems to forget he was a poster boy for Ralph Lauren and that he was a muse of famed celebrity photographer Bruce Weber.

"It's all about being genuine," Beau continued. "I wouldn't be longboard world champion right now if it weren't for the love I have for Kimberly. I think love should generate a happy feeling inside someone and it should show in their surfing. That's why I find myself celebrating a wave more than just riding it."

"By now, girls were starting to figure in our surf program. Sex was, in fact, the main thing on our minds beside boards and waves. I remember well the first day we spied a prissy-looking girl getting off the bus in Collaroy. Dressed in a dark-green uniform of a girls' private school, she was plump in a nice, schoolgirlish kind of way and Henry, Westie, Belly, and I started to chat her up . . . after about a half hour of sweet talk, Westie got her into the casualty room of the Collaroy surf club . . . Westie had strategically positioned the girl so that she was lying on her back with her head facing away from the youthful group of lechers and so was able to give the nod over her shoulder.

As he slipped out, Belly slipped in, then Henry and I had our turn in the same manner . . . "The Grunter" as Westie called her, changed our whole perception of girls . . . The Grunter was really into group sex and we all greeted her with open flies every time we saw her getting off her school bus."

—Excerpt from Nat Young's self-titled autobiography, *Nat's Nat and That's That: A Surfing Legend.*

In early 1994, Beau Young was still a committed shortboarder who was making what he describes as a "half-assed" attempt at the pro tour. Despite an early family break-up, Beau still had grown up, in many ways, as "Nat Young's son." How could he not? Nat Young had always cast a larger-than-life shadow over Australian surfing culture, even on the cloudiest of days. Still, disenchanted with the whole shortboard scene, Beau decided to join his father and his father's protege, a teen longboarding prodigy named Joel Tudor, on a promotional surf trip for OXBOW Clothing through Europe. It didn't surprise Beau at all that his father had chosen to align himself with Tudor, the greatest young longboarder the world had ever seen.

"HE'S SO MUCH LIKE ME IT'S RIDICULOUS!"
—Nat Young on Joel Tudor from "Surfer's Journal Biographies," 2000.

"He's the king and we're all in his court."
—Joel Tudor on Nat Young from "Surfer's Journal Biographies," 2000.

One morning in Italy, waking up before everyone, Beau waxed up one of Tudor's longboards and slipped out into the tiny surf of the Mediterranean. Before long, he was inching toward the nose of the board and "moving with a bit of grace, and actually feeling what riding a wave was all about. At that moment, I fell in love with longboarding and decided to take a different path in my life."

FROM CONVERSATION WITH BEAU YOUNG:

Did you feel any jealousy toward Joel Tudor back then, knowing that your father was spending so much time with him, developing his career, gaining sponsorship for him?

Beau: Yes.

In Italy, did you feel any jealousy toward the relationship with longboarding that they both shared?

Beau: Yes. I very much wanted to be a part of that.

Have you? Become a part of it, I mean?

Beau: Well, I am the World Longboard Champion now and Joel is one of my best friends, so I guess . . . well . . . yes?

ALASTAIR and GRACE

The connection is still there. Flickering as sure as an old film on a new TV set. January 3, 2001. I'm driving with Beau up into the hills behind Byron Bay on an enchanted day. He and I were going to visit his horse. Beau drives and talks. He tells me he's grateful to his dad for introducing him to some of surfing's greats. The list of surfers Beau stays in touch with reads like the hall of fame: Wayne Lynch, Bob McTavish, Baddy Treloar, George Greenough, Miki Dora, Joey Cabell, and on and on. It's "one of the nicer privileges," he says.

The tires crunch onto a gravel driveway of a compound on top of a hill. Big snowy white geese scatter before our wheels in a flutter of feathers and grievances. Beyond the small farmhouse, a breathtaking view spreads out before us. The rolling hills of Byron that lead to its legendary headlands and its perfect surf, folding hollow and clean onto the talcum powder beaches of its crescent shores. Beau likes it up here on the hill, "on the farm." You can tell.

He's even wearing the hat for it. A perfect, floppy, felt replica of the hat his father wore in the classic 1971 surf movie, *Morning of the Earth*. Only two of these hats seem to exist in the world today. The other one was owned by Joel Tudor, Nat's young disciple.

The compound we've pulled into is a dead ringer for the one featured in *Morning of the Earth*. That early '70s groundbreaking surf movie shot in this very area. The one that reflected the pot-addled country soul of Aussie hippie surfing like no other film did or could or ever will. A film that featured, among other things, the empty surf of Byron Bay before the tourist invasion of the last twenty years. Before the Club Med, before the raves that bring 40,000 people at a time, before Paul Hogan's celebrity beer garden on the beach, before the designer shops and bistros and coffee houses and franchises and fashion outlets. Before it all.

But not before Nat.

Nat was the essence of *Morning of the Earth*. And it was his surfing and his lifestyle and his farm and his snowy white geese that were put on film. Not so much a time capsule as a time bomb. And no one has to shoulder that more than Beau Young. The film itself was actually the first thing I saw flickering on Beau's TV when I walked into his place down by the beach.

Getting out of his van here on the hill, Beau stretches once, looks at the view before us, and says, "Can't see the crowds from up here, hey?"

We walk across the country road, past the funky honor system banana stand, and down to an open pasture. Two horses are there. A roan and a big black. Beau, quiet now, carefully approaches the beautiful roan. It canters away into the middle of the pasture. Beau approaches again. It canters away. After a few minutes of this, Beau gets close enough and gingerly places a blanket on the back of the horse. When Beau puts on the hackamore, the horse's ears lay back, its nostrils flare, its eyes roll white. Beau freezes. He decides not to mount. He'll just walk her today.

Just then, two young girls come bouncing down the hill and join me on the fence. Judy and Jan, both thirteen years old. They look after the horses. Wordlessly, they watch as Beau and horse both nervously make their way over to within ten feet of us. That's all the horse is having. Its haunches and shoulders twitch and ripple under its skin. A lit fuse. One eye on us, the other on Beau. A tension hangs in the air. We all spend about thirty seconds watching Beau attempt to stroke the skittish horse's nose. You can see an attempt in Beau's eyes at some sort of connection to that old country soul. But there is none in the horse. The scene feels more like a re-enactment of *Morning of the Earth*. There was something false in the attempt that I couldn't quite put my finger on.

The girls sigh with relief when Beau turns the horse loose. Beau and I walk up the path, headed back to the farm compound. At the top of the hill, I look back. Judy is astride the roan, cantering about the paddock, pretty as you please. Jan is lunging the big black over some small jumps, both girls and beasts happy and comfortable with each other. Made me think about Beau. About false attempts and re-enactments. A horse knows when you ride them, you're just borrowing their freedom. Whatever Beau was looking for in that horse, emulating, past or present, that horse wasn't lending.

We cross the road back into the compound, as gorgeous a piece of land as anyone would care to dream of. Once there, I meet Alastair. He owns the compound. Having suffered a very private and very horrific loss of his own wife and child in a boat fire in Indonesia, Alistair loves Beau like a son. Knowing Nat, Alistair tells me he loves Beau like a son twice over. Alistair even offered Beau a piece of this land to build a place on, to live the country soul. But it didn't take. He lets Beau treat the place as his own though, whenever he likes. Beau opted for that luxury condo on the golf course in town. Beau lives down there in the hurly burly with his friend Dane Thomas, one of the hottest longboarders on earth, Dane's girlfriend, Amy, and from time to time, Beau's own girlfriend, Kimberly. It's a whole new kind of compound. A candle scent of country soul is still there, a few guitars, a flower box garden on the back veranda, but this time around, there's hot water, flush toilets, a microwave, and cut pile carpets.

Alastair and I both watch Beau out in Alistair's yard. Beau is washing his white van with the snowy white geese waddling and muttering about his ankles. Alistair, a Conradian figure of mysterious means rumored to have made his fortune in the "shipping business" of the East Indian Ocean, breathes in about fifteen years of pain through the burning tip of his peppery Indonesian clove cigarette.

"It's pretty simple," he says, not taking his eyes off Beau. "The hat, the horse, all this interest in a lifestyle gone by . . . Beau knows that time is over. He knows it's time for his own life. All this kid wants is a pat on the back. And that can only come from one place."

Later on, in the car, I asked Beau why his horse is so nervous around him. Beau concentrated on the road for a while. Then he replied softly, "Sometimes I think this farm life thing is somebody else's idea of me."

FROM CONVERSATION WITH BEAU YOUNG:

In April of 2001, Australian surf scribe Derek Reilly published an editorial in a prominent Aussie surf magazine indicting the resurgence of longboarding as the great evil of Australian surfing. This inflammatory essay begins with the words: "While every other boardsport progresses to radical new highs, surfing continues to crawl back inside a fetid cave of nostalgia. Read and weep."

Nat Young responded. "I don't believe in letting your surfing speak for itself. I think when you reach a certain status, it is your duty to defend your sport if need be. I called Beau and told him so. I believe it's his responsibility as world champion to speak out against this outrage."

Says Beau Young to me, "Everybody wants me to respond, but the piece is so ill-informed and profane that I'm not even gonna bother. I don't feel anger about it. I feel pity at the evidence of such a closed mind. Of a soul that will never break free, never love, because all it knows is that its narrow path is all that exists. I mean, the poor soul. He's out there trying to say that everyone who longboards is a kook and can't keep up. I can only shake my head at that. Longboarders have a much higher percentage of prowess. You paddle out at a place like Kirra, and it's the vast majority of shortboarders who are novices. Most of them are trying to ride equipment they have no business being on. I can honestly say that the best shortboarders in the world appreciate all levels of surfing. And that they are not close-minded. I believe in the courage of this kind of awareness. I didn't realize until I met these guys like Rob Machado, Ross Williams, the Malloy brothers—how cool they can be, given the chance. I dream of the day when shortboarders realize how cool longboarders can be, given the chance. Surfing is no place for bigotry. Derek Reilly should know that. He doesn't even merit a response."

"I did what any other Australian would have done . . . I hit him."
—Nat Young, from the *Australian Sunday Telegraph,* October 23, 1966, on the fight he got into over wave possession the day before his world championship effort in San Diego, California.

January 03, 2001 — Byron Bay, Australia

Beau's condo came pre-furnished, but over in a corner, on a small rough-hewn table, he's arranged a few of his things, altar-like, around an African kalimba drum. A book on Native Americans, an authentic peace pipe, recently used, and a dreamcatcher. I asked him what the connection was.

"When I was kid, whenever I saw a TV show or a movie about cowboys and Indians, I always saw myself as one of the Indians."

"Surfers regard Nat with a mixture of awe and uncertainty . . . He has a realistic idea of his own achievement and he's not exactly modest about [it] . . . Some people don't like him much. I'm just flicking through my phone book for numbers of all the people he's belted."
—World Surfing Champion Tom Carroll, from the article "Nobody's Happy When Nat Drops In," published in *THE AUSTRALIAN,* March 28, 2000.

January 04, 2001, Byron Bay, Australia

Byron Bay, despite the unbridled development, still feels like a one-horse town. Clouds like white wings drift through pink skies every dawn and dusk. You can still be arrested for foul language in public, the first baby born on the New Year gets a commemorative coin sent from the chamber of commerce, and glancing through the local paper, you'll come across an appeal to whoever stole little Margaret Underwood's new blue bicycle to "Please return it and take the punishment coming to you."

Tooling around in Beau's new white van, looking for surf, you get the idea the place loves him too. You drop by for a blown-out surf at Broken Head and on the way down through the trail to the surf, you see a dog smile at him. Honest-to-god smile. Sitting in a bistro on the main strip with him for his daily vegetarian fix, you notice a pack of cute girls staring and giggling, trying hard to get his attention. But Beau is too busy to notice. Instead, he is communicating with a young deaf girl who holds a small chalkboard in her hands, scratching her messages in pink chalk. She has come here from Germany to surf. She's not sure if she has brought the right equipment. Beau walks her over to the van and offers her one of his surfboards, and she takes it with a smile that could be seen a mile away. Things like that. His life seems to be in balance here.

Later on, walking across the sand back to the van after an evening session in cobalt blue water over sifted flour sand, I ask Beau what he thinks the main difference between longboarders and shortboarders is.

"The difference of growing up a longboarder is that there is a lot more emphasis on family and friendship. Of community, of belonging. Shortboarders grow up so alone. Aggressive, with little or no thought of sharing. Only two things can come of that. Trophies and loneliness. Just ask Kelly Slater." I let that hang there. He went on. "Plus, longboarding gives you a better relationship with the wave, and a better relationship with a wave will give you a better relationship with a woman. It's more tango than mosh pit. A woman sees you longboard and she knows you can move with something, not just up against it."

Back in the car, headed for a vegetarian pizza joint, I ask him if knows Kelly Slater very well. "Not that well, but I appreciate his genius. But I really relate to his brother Stephen, though." Stephen Slater, as most know, is a highly ranked professional longboarder. "I see a similar thing in Stephen and me. I relate to Stephen's bravery. It takes a lot to aspire to be a great surfer when there's already one in the family."

"*In situations where I've been under stress, I haven't always handled things rationally, but if I'm kind to myself, I have the ability to consider other people.*"

—Excerpt from Nat Young's self-titled autobiography, *Nat's Nat and That's That: A Surfing Legend.*

FROM CONVERSATION WITH BEAU YOUNG:

What is your take on surfing forever?

Beau Young: "I think it's all a matter of having a grasp of where you are heading. Twenty-five is the age you should realize who you really are. I'm really comfortable with growing older. I do trust people over thirty. And I hope I don't die before I get old. McTavish, Greenough, Wayne, Joey Cabell—I like knowing people who have developed a style with age, a solid way of being. Looking into their clear eyes, I find a lot of hope in that. I think that's what two-year-olds hope for when they look into their grandfather's eyes before they can speak. They see wisdom and style and soul and a lot of life."

"*I think Beau is such a beautiful, most graceful surfer. And I have seen some very special surfers in my time. When he surfs, you see what he is. Longboarding is the window to one's heart. As you surf is as you are.*"

—Marilyn Birmingham, Beau's mom, speaking from her beach home in northern Sydney.

January 05, 2001 — Casino, Australia

Landing in Casino after the six-and-a-half-minute flight, I stepped off onto the tarmac and made my way through a heavy afternoon rain to the small terminal. Due to weather, it would be hours before the air shuttle to Sydney arrived. I sat on my soggy duffle bag and unrolled a sandwich I had wrapped in a scrap of newspaper I had kept. It read:

[...] Young, 52, and Michael Hutchinson, 51, the man who reduced Young's face to pulp, are the dominant males in the water at Angourie point. The pair had been feuding for years before their animosity ended in blows on March 14. Angourie surfers said yesterday the two men hate each other, and former World Champion Nat Young is often overheard taunting Hutchinson whenever they share the water out at the point. Young's favorite term for Hutchinson is apparently 'Little Dick.' According to witnesses, Hutchinson and his eighteen-year-old son Luke were surfing when Young, his son Beau, and some friends entered the water. Using colorful language, Nat Young warned his friends about Hutchinson within earshot of Hutchinson's son, Luke.

"Luke said, 'What did you say about my father?'" said a witness who asked to remain unnamed. "And it just got worse from there. Nat said he gave Luke a backhander—believe me, it was no backhander. He grabbed Luke's arm, pulled it behind his back, and punched him in the face." Hutchinson was surfing nearby and was told his son had been hurt. (Luke later needed two stitches to close the wound on his nose.)

"Hutcho snapped," said a friend. "His son had blood streaming from his nose. What would you do?"

—*The Daily Telegraph,* Wednesday, March 2000

Reading that, I thought about how Beau and Nat's story ended up on the beach where Michael Hutchinson beat Nat Young nearly to death. With Beau standing right there, watching it happen. I remembered a last quiet moment with Beau. It was late the night before, and Beau was tired. He'd be flying out at dawn for another contest in Brazil. We were lounging around in his living room, plunking around on guitars, talking about love and family. At one point, he became quiet, thoughtful, as if he were really measuring what he was about to say. Then, just this side of a whisper, he said it. More than a confession, it sounded like absolution.

"It's been a pretty rough road with Dad and I. Our relationship always comes out looking extremely rosy in all the magazines, but it doesn't always smell like roses," Beau said. "I was really brought up by my mother, Marilyn, who is a beautiful, genuine woman, and by my stepfather, Kevin, who is a great guy. They are the ones who took me to all the contests; they are the ones that let me live my dreams. For all the times my father wasn't there . . ." He took a long, long pause. "Look, on the beach that day at Angourie, watching what was happening to my dad, that terrible thing . . . I realized that it was his path in life that had led him to this . . . his life, his way, not mine. And I'd just come too far to be part of all that." And with that, Beau led himself up to bed, his body looking as if a great weight had been taken from its shoulders.

Sitting there in Casino Municipal Airport Transit Lounge with that sandwich in my left hand and the newspaper in the right, that's when it hit me. That thing that Alastair had said when he saw me off at the airport.

Some wounds never heal.

Like father, like son, like hell, I thought.

Alastair wasn't talking about Beau, he was talking about Nat.

YOUNG SURFER A NAT-URAL

Herald Sun morning edition — October 10, 2000

Australian surfer Beau Young has finally emerged from the shadow of his legendary father. Young, son of former World Surfing Champion Nat Young, yesterday claimed his first world title victory in the Oxbow World Longboard Surfing Championships in Santa Catarina, Brazil. The 26-year-old defeated American Joel Tudor in the final with a display of traditional longboarding mixed with modern flair. Tudor said it was a relief to witness his close mate make his own mark.

"I'll have a beer for Beau," Tudor said, "now that he's not living under the foot of his father for the rest of his life.

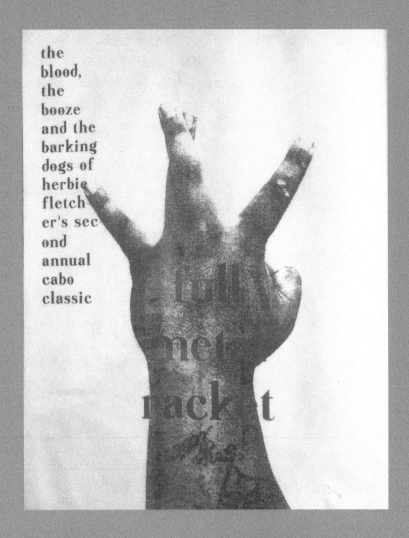

the
blood,
the
booze
and the
barking
dogs of
herbie
fletch
er's sec
ond
annual
cabo
classic

FULL METAL RACKET

THE BLOOD, THE BOOZE, AND THE BARKING DOGS OF
HERBIE FLETCHER'S SECOND ANNUAL CABO CLASSIC
SURFER MAGAZINE, USA, 1991

PHOTO: SURFER MAGAZINE

As mad as a surf contest gets. —Mg.

WHERE ANGELS GO, TROUBLE FOLLOWS

She didn't actually cringe until Christian Fletcher stepped on board. I think it was his Brahma bull nose ring that did the trick. I was watching them out of the corner of my eye, this young newlywed couple sitting across the aisle from me. She in her new sundress and perky straw hat, her new husband next to her in crisp vacation Bermuda shorts and black socks, fingering the new ring, taking account of what he had done. The flight was destined for Cabo San Lucas, Baja, Mexico. The newlyweds were the only people on the flight who were not involved with Herbie Fletcher's Cabo Classic surf contest. They had fallen into an uncomfortable silence shortly after coming aboard and discovering that some motley, long-haired, rag-tag group of young men had turned this flight into a party bus. Had she been counting, and I think she was, she would have seen close to a hundred tattoos ranging from Mickey Mouse in a space outfit to Madonna in the nude. Not one competitor still had a shirt on.

The flight had been delayed for over an hour. Squatting on a sweltering lesser runway of the San Diego airport. No air con. No water. No relief. No one knew what the holdup was. Thing was, nobody cared. I had seen real fear in the newlywed's eyes when the free Mexican beer had been passed out to settle the mob. Their fear had been well-founded since, that time, there had been two food fights, three moonings, and a belching contest. And just when the party had reached its crescendo, an extraordinary announcement was made by a terrified flight attendant. She took a deep breath before she let it fly. It seemed the holdup was that there were too many surfboards to fit into the cargo hold. She took another deep breath and then really dove in. Our only choice was to leave some things behind. Now what was it going to be, she gulped, our luggage or our surfboards?

I had never been in an aircraft that quiet. But it only lasted three blinks, really. That's when Robert Mahar stood up in his seat and yelled from the back, "Fuck the luggage, man. Surf naked!"

A cheer went up and the party resumed. I felt a tap at my elbow. It was the newlywed wife. She looked at me and asked in a trembling voice, "Is that what you people are? Surfers?"

I replied that, why yes, we were.

"Oh, thank God," she said. "I thought you were a motorcycle gang."

THE TIMELINE
DAY ZERO — 07/29/91

2:29 p.m. — Due to the surfers exchanging their clothes with the radio-sponsored rock bands on board, it's getting tough to tell who is who. But it has become quite clear that everybody present is just showing up for the party of the year. Including a sixteen-year-old Dan Steed, a starry-eyed youth on his very first surf trip. The law required that he bring a note from his mother giving him permission to be here. Signed and notarized by the Clerk of Orange County.

4:45 p.m. — Upon arrival in Cabo San Lucas, it is discovered that the sound equipment and instruments of the rock bands, along with Kelly Slater's and Christian Fletcher's surfboards, are still sitting on the runway in San Diego. The bands head for the airport bar to get trashed, Kelly disappears in a funk, and Christian blows off steam by going skateboarding with his infant son out in front of the terminal. Teetering atop the nose of the skateboard, Christian's son, Greyson Thunder, is seen clapping and gurgling at his father's every hair-raising move. It is also discovered at this time that Christian has tattooed his son's name onto the nape of his own neck.

6:00 p.m. — What seems to be 400 surfers now crowd the waves at Zippers, what is to be the contest site. In the last fifteen minutes before sundown, Shane Beschen, Kelly Slater, Christian Fletcher, Matt Archbold, and Vince De la Pena proceed to do the best surfing of the contest. Even though the contest has yet to start.

9:00 p.m. — Nathan Fletcher, 14, Christian's younger brother and lead guitarist for the band BLOODSHOT, turns his guitar up so loud that on his first note, he blows out the crude electrical system of the nearby bar where he has plugged every piece of the band's equipment into a single, spliced light socket. Everyone in the bar roars their approval.

11:00 p.m. — The owner of the bar realizes he has grossly underestimated the amount of beer that is to be consumed in the next four days. He takes two steps to remedy this. First, he sends his cousin into town in a military transport truck with orders to "fill 'er up." Beer, not fuel. And second, he fences off the entire perimeter with barbed wire and posts two hard luck welterweight boxers at the gate where it will now cost one American dollar for parking.

DAY ONE — 07/30/91

8:00 a.m. — Herbie Fletcher is nowhere to be found. It is rumored that he has gone surfing "somewhere up north." The contest is put on an unofficial hold for the day. Still, no one seems to care. Underground LA bands, clad from head to toe in black leather and chains, have begun to arrive for the Radio KNAC Battle of the Bands. Considering the beach temperatures are soaring to 105 degrees, it is generally agreed that these rockers are going to have to lighten up on the leather or die from heatstroke.

3:00 p.m. — Doctor Dorian Paskowitz, who lives with his wife at the contest site all year round in an RV parked next to the bar, has set up an impromptu operating theater on a picnic bench where he spends most the day, scalpel in hand, digging urchin spines out of everyone's feet. Before every operation, due to the bloody nature of the procedure, he asks every surfer one question: "Now be honest with me, son, do you have AIDS?" No one answers yes. Before and after each operation, the patient is offered a slug of tequila as anesthesia.

4:00 p.m. — The first fight breaks out. A drunken parking lot brawl between some local surfers and some impossibly sunburned white roadies for the KNAC Bands. The welterweights quickly run a book on the outcome.

4:10 p.m. — Everyone involved in the brawl is now down on the beach, drinking Doc Paskowitz's tequila, congratulating each other on their skills.

5:00 p.m. — Herbie Fletcher is spotted getting out of the water at Zippers. Kelly Slater approaches and asks when he thinks he will start the contest. Herbie replies: "Hey, man, chill out. Contests are just like bad colds, you just gotta let 'em happen . . ."

9:30 p.m. — The beach bar is packed. Four bands are slated for the night. The first band comes on. They look like vampires. They yell, "Fuck you!" and then crash into a metal maelstrom. Within seconds, a mosh pit is in full swing. It becomes apparent that this will be the music of choice for the rest of the week. Kelly Slater is heard asking Kaipo Guerrero what the band is so angry about. A local Mexican surfer, stunned by the screeching spectacle, describes the music to Shane Beschen through a translator as similar to "a car crashing while dogs bark."

10:15 p.m. — Young Dan Steed, permission slip from his mom in his pocket, is shoved into the mosh pit by his temporary legal guardian Brian Kane. Young Dan steps on one of the band's beer-soaked electrical cables that is buried in the sand. He is thrown ten feet by the shock. Brian Kane immediately runs over to young Dan, revives him with a shot of tequila, and offers him his congratulations. Kane then notices a gray patch of hair on the back of Dan's head. Dan will sport this gray patch for the rest of his life.

11:59 p.m. — The cops arrive.

DAY TWO — 07/31/91

8:00 a.m. — So severe are the hangovers that the surf of Cabo San Lucas, a glassy four-to-six feet, is empty of surfers.

9:00 a.m. — Herbie Fletcher, the host and organizer of the contest, decides to show up. Seeing the number of surfers who are sleeping on the beach in their clothes, announces that now is the perfect time to start the contest.

9:15 a.m. — Everyone is present and accounted for, and warming up in the water.

11:00 a.m. — Herbie enlists the entire Paskowitz family to run the contest. Two small judges' tents are erected. One is in front of the longboarding area, a hundred yards to the north of the scaffolding. The other is erected in front the shortboard area, a hundred yards to the south of the scaffolding. No one is quite sure how anyone is supposed to hear anything with the PA system on the fritz.

11:15 a.m. — Herbie enlists the lead singer for BLOODSHOT. He will henceforth be strolling up and down the beach and yelling out the times and information to the surfers in the water.

11:30 a.m. — The first heat hits the water.

11:34 a.m. — Head judge Dean Reynolds is heard asking Herbie where the flags and horns and heat sheets and clipboards and pencils and pens and timers and tabulators and spotters and all the other things one needs to hold a surf competition are. Herbie Fletcher is heard answering, "Hey, man, I can't think of everything!"

2:00 p.m. — The Cabo Classic is running like clockwork. Everyone understands the rules, wears their own watches, times their own heats, pays attention, and not one single dispute is heard. There is a crowd on the beach of locals and girlfriends and wives and camp followers who are enjoying their vacation. Cheers are heard after every ride.

3:10 p.m. — Mickey Munoz, who is a judge for this event, can't find a heat sheet as Kelly Slater hits the water. Mickey just shrugs and begins to write the scores down on his forearm.

4:15 p.m. — The last and favorite heat of the day hits the water. It consists of three snowboarders and the bass player for St. Elmo's Fire, who chooses to surf in a leather vest. Not one wave is successfully ridden.

7:15 p.m. — The second fight has broken out in the cantina. Same reasons, different guys. Jonathon Paskowitz, spiritual leader and resident philosopher of the contest, explains the phenomenon: "See, the locals, they start drinking 'bout noon. They get pissed off at the gringos 'bout dusk, then the gringos, after the fight, buy 'em tequila and they love them again. Now, the stinker is that just after midnight, the beers run out, see? So another fight breaks out and the whole cycle repeats itself. So if you want to have a good time at a Mexican cantina, just show up on dark and leave before midnight. Simple."

11:10 p.m. — In the middle of the fourth band's gig, a riot breaks out. Seems the dispute is over the "Chickenshit Game" taking place in the back of the bar. The idea is to put a live chicken on a piece of plywood that has a grid of numbers written on it. One then bets on one of these numbers. If, given time, the chicken shits on your number, then you win the pot. Problem was, young Dan Steed allegedly won the pot, and the angry crowd cried foul due to his age. His temporary legal guardian, Brian Kane, is reported to have thrown the first punch.

11:40 p.m. — The cops arrive.

DAY THREE — 08/01/91

10:00 a.m. — Someone reminds Herbie that most of the pros must leave by the following morning to join the pro tour in Europe. It is then calculated that there isn't enough time in the day to finish the contest. So Herbie announces that there will be four surfers in each heat and that the heats will be only twelve minutes. Another quick calculation reveals that under this new format, each surfer will have to catch and surf a wave every thirty seconds. This is physically impossible. When Herbie is informed of this, he replies, "Well . . . just surf faster, man."

10:30 a.m. — It is discovered that a mile-wide slick of stinging blue bottle jelly fish have moved into the lineup. Competitors are falling like flies. At Doc Paskowitz's sick bay, he is treating the wounded by having them urinate into a communal bucket and then splashing the collected urine over the welts. Young Dan Steed balks. Herbie Fletcher is heard to say to Dan, "Hey man, look at it this way: it's a bonding experience." When it comes time for Herbie's treatment, he refuses. "I may be crazy," he says, "but, man, I ain't stupid."

11:00 a.m. — Despite Doc Paskowitz's battlefield surgery, Herbie announces that, at all costs, the contest must go on. At that point, a gasping Kevin Billy staggers up to Herbie. Kevin is covered from head to toe with red welts from the stinging jellyfish. Kevin cannot speak. Kevin happens to be one of the head judges. Herbie regards him for a moment, then tells him he has permission to report to sick bay. Herbie then calls out to Kevin, "But make sure to send back anyone who can walk!"

11:55 a.m. — A devout Catholic, Vince Dela Pena, is seen evoking a prayer with a number of Mexican onlookers, imploring the powers of heaven to please make the jellyfish go away.

1:00 p.m. — The jellyfish have disappeared. Vince Dela Pena wins his heat and advances into the finals.

2:30 p.m. — To escape the heat, a number of competitors and officials go for a swim. Nathan Fletcher then crawls up on top of an exposed rock on the inside of the break and declares himself "King of the Rock" to all within earshot.

2:45 p.m. — No one is watching the contest. All eyes are on the battle for the "King of the Rock." Kelly Slater is thrown off by Matt Archbold. Christian Fletcher, going for broke, body slams Matt, leaving the title open. Soon, a battle royale has formed. Kelly, Christian, Matt, Nathan, and about five others are death-locked and struggling. Suddenly, a huge set of waves appears, the biggest of the day. As the first wave comes in, it soon becomes apparent that it is about twice the height of the rock. Suddenly, a dark form is seen body surfing this wave. This form is seen heading straight for the rock. It is Herbie Fletcher. Everyone stares as he body surfs the wave over the top of the rock, slamming into the entire contingent. When the water recedes, Herbie, bruised, hip scraped, but smiling, crawls to his feet on top of the rock, his hands held over his head in silent reign. When asked about it later, Kelly Slater is heard saying that, "Herbie Fletcher is easily the raddest surfer here . . ." Despite this fact, and a case of heat exhaustion, Kelly goes on to win the shortboard division.

6:35 p.m. — It was decided that the shortboard division awards were to be held in the cantina. For the sake of the Mexican press, the barbed wire is removed from around the compound. Since the parking is now free and there are rumors of a free concert, rock star Sammy Hagar and two hundred of his best friends showed up to catch the show. Unfortunately, the lead singer of top billed band The Exhumed, who had finally made it from San Diego with all the band's gear, took the stage stinking drunk, jumped off the top of the speakers on the first note of his first song, and snapped both his ankles. He was carried off to the airport and sent straight back to San Diego. It was told that he had to crawl onto the plane on his hands and knees. With Sammy Hagar in the crowd, the lead singer later claimed his self-destructive behavior was "just a case of nerves."

6:36 p.m. — Quick-thinking Christian and Nathan Fletcher narrowly avert another riot by picking up the band's abandoned equipment and rocking the hell out of the place. Christian on bass, Nathan on lead. Sammy Hagar was heard saying, "Man, you surf boys know how to party!"

11:15 p.m. — The cops arrive.

11:45 p.m. — At Sammy Hagar's invitation, the entire crowd from the celebration party moves to the El Presidente Resort and proceeds to take off all their clothes and go skinny dipping. Due to this development, the security guards decide to hold off a bit.

12:30 a.m. — Rocker Sammy Hagar, holding up the bar, is buying tequila shots for any woman that wiggles her breasts.

12:53 a.m. — The cops arrive.

DAY FOUR — 08/02/91

5:00 p.m. — Due to the difficulty of raising bail for a large number of competitors who were jailed the night before, the longboard division gets underway as the sun is going down. In two ten-minute heats, Chris Schlickenmeyer's timeless nose-rides take the open division. Dale Dobson wins the master's, going away with a series of standing 360s. Fellow competitor Les Potts is overheard leaving the water saying, "Pfft, 360s? Man, I got tired of doing those back in '71."

8:00 p.m. — With half the population of Baja back at the cantina for the longboard awards, a now thoroughly emboldened sixteen-year-old Dan Steed talks a group of young Swedish women from the hostel into a wet t-shirt contest. He puts up his Chickenshit winnings as first prize. The women agree. For lack of water, the girls are sprayed down with beer.

8:15 p.m. — A platoon of armed *Federales* are called in to control the ensuing riot.

9:01 p.m. — Like a plug pulled out of a socket and with the paddy wagon headed for jail with half the competitors in it, Herbie Fletcher's Second Annual Cabo Classic surf festival officially grinds to a halt.

EPILOGUE

Standing in line at the airport with the remains of the Cabo Classic survivors, I see the young newlyweds. They are laughing as a shirtless

Brian Kane, beer in hand, recounts to them last night's final adventure. Brian seems proud of his shiner and his fat lip. Story goes he got it from one of the Swedes. Just then, I was approached by young Dan Steed. He looked about ten years older, was horribly sunburned, and stank of last night's tequila. He lit a cigarette and then told me he just wanted me to know that he'd had the time of his life and that he was going to,

"Fuckin' surf forever, man!" Then he handed me an envelope and said, "I guess I won't be needing this anymore. I'm a real surfer now . . ."

I opened it up.

It was the note from his mother.

WATERWORLD

WHEN ISLANDS SCREAM
THE SURFER'S PATH MAGAZINE, USA, 2001

Smack dab on the equator, you feel the southern Maldives more than see them. Your eyes cannot believe what they are seeing. Low-lying islands, gin-clear water, an Ocean seething with wildlife. Islands whose grown adults are the size of children. It was time travel. Fitting, I suppose, since these islands have so little time left. —Mg.

Latitude Zero, South Huvadhoo Atoll, Maldives

THE FIRST MATE

With less than a fistful of air left in his lungs, the son of the Minister of Defense of the Republic of the Maldives lets the fishing line go, allowing his buoyancy to upend him. He kicks strongly for the shimmering roof forty feet above him. His eyes are bulging by the time he breaks the surface next to the boat he now calls home. He hangs on the anchor line at the bow, fattening his body with oxygen. He'd reach the errant lure on his next dive, he was sure. Big shiny lures with three treble hooks each were hard to come by in these waters. One of the Americans had forgotten to reel in his trawling line, and the lure had sunk and snagged on the reef when they had set anchor.

He could hear the giant surfers from Australia and the United States through the hull. They were amidships, excitedly pulling their surfboards out of their luggage and groaning at the airline damage. He noticed how it always seemed to cause them a physical pain, as if their boards were a body part. That made sense to him—he felt the same way about this boat. He heard one of them howl like a dog, so he glanced over to the reef pass. Another set of Ocean waves were rolling through, fringing white against teal, until they exploded in perfect symmetry and ground themselves out onto the shallows. The surfers were all howling now.

He had signed on as first mate of this seventy-five-foot Dhoni vessel a while back, much to the consternation of his father. It was his schooling in India that had driven him to be here, driven him to give it all up. Bright, creative, resourceful, he was at one time being groomed for a government post in his father's cabinet back in the capital of Malé. Then came the geography class that blew the lid off his life. It was there that he learned his islands were drowning. It was there that he learned that, within his lifetime, his country would be no more than ghostly pale blue outlines that would march toward the equator like underwater clouds. His country would only be able to be seen by air. His people would be forced to flee and assimilate into the stinking work forces of India, the Middle East, and Allah only knew where else. Being a race small in physical stature, it wasn't hard to figure out where they would find themselves in the natural order of things.

All this because of the man-made evils called "greenhouse gases" that were melting the polar ice caps and causing a tide that would never recede. His country contributed nothing to these evils. And yet it would be his country that would die first. No matter what he did or said, he knew someday even the stories of his country, the stories of planetarium skies, aquarium-blue lagoons, and warm white sand beaches would disappear from the lips of his descendants. After all, his country was no Atlantis. It, too, was small in stature in the order of things, and one can only tell ghost stories for so long.

Clearing his mind of such matters, he readied for the lure again. Breathed deeply. He was satisfied here. Satisfied to spend his life surfing, fishing, and motoring around his islands barefoot and alive. He was determined to revel in his country's existence while it was still around and not waste what little time was left in a corrupt government office in Malé. He didn't even plan to have children anymore. What for? What could he possibly leave them? Where would they go? What would become of their children? He'd left all that behind in India, along with a girlfriend and most of his Muslim faith. He was someone else now. He would live his life as if each day were his last. And in a way, he was right about that.

He took three deep breaths, held the last, upended, and began his descent down the fishing line. Above him rang a series of muffled explosions. He looked back toward the surface. The surfers were jumping off the railings of the boat, entering the water with their surfboards, one by one. As they plummeted through the mirrored surface, shrouded in clouds of white bubbles, it looked the opening barrage of some sort of attack.

And in many ways, he was right.

THE GUIDE

Coconuts were always clumsy cargo. He dragged a raft of them behind his surfboard as he headed out toward the boat. The coconuts would help the fish curry tonight. He smiled over his shoulder at the first mate and the cook, and they smiled back. He figured he was faring a bit better than them; the poor bastards were swimming their coconuts out. He was paddling his surfboard off the white-and-jade-green reef and out onto the indigo of the abyss. The boat was another hundred yards or so. He was twenty-six, a native of Caloundra, Australia, and he considered himself just about the luckiest sonuvabitch in the world. He loved being in this place. He loved its people who whispered more than talked, he loved surfing in tropical aquariums, and he loved being a guide for visiting surfers who had the guts to travel this far out on the edge for a few waves. This atoll was hard against the equator. Gone from the resorts to the north. He smiled at this thought. *If the boys back home could see me now.*

He looked out onto the reef pass; the latest batch of surfers were all out in the lineup, surfing well. He liked this bunch. They were easygoing and full of pranks. They were being paid to be here. *Extraordinary,* he thought. He had learned more about a pro surfer's life in three days than he had ever daydreamed about. It sounded pretty wild, what with desperate contests in bizarre places like Uruguay and Argentina and the endless parties and women with strange accents and long flights and creased, frayed passports. He always made a point to stay up with his guests, after the standard meal of fish curry and rice, drinking black market beer, rolling rag tobacco cigarettes, and talking into the night. He was naturally curious about other people's lives; he thought their stories were better than the movies.

The guide watched a set of waves pour through out at the pass in the reef. The three Australians lorded over the Americans in the water, their surfing ability on a higher, more aggressive plane. He could really relate to Trent Munro, an Aussie country kid like himself, quick with a smile or a laugh. His surfing was tight, hungry, and, like his life, simple and true. Luke Steadman, the boy of the trip, all toothy grins and flashy maneuvers. With something going on behind his eyes underneath all those goofy hats he wore. A mischievous intelligence, an acceptance of sore luck from time to time. Like when he paddled out into a lineup alone yesterday, only to find himself surrounded by hundreds of mating sea snakes. He looked a little older by the time he'd cat-scratched his way back to the boat. And Richie Lovett, the alpha male. The world championship tour surfer whose surfing, compared to the others, was in the slipstream. Speed, power, the right lines, a bundle of vicious grace. He surfed as if he knew exactly what each wave was going to do for him. Richie, who shared his scars, in his humble way, of close encounters with sharks and what it's like to get carried away by a tidal wave in the middle of the night in Java. Richie, slightly baleful, with a girlfriend of nine years, the only man the guide had ever come across on these tours who would go snorkeling by himself. The guide was slightly embarrassed of overhearing Richie in a private moment, questioning if there is any kind of place in the world for an aging professional surfer. But the guide soon forgave himself for eavesdropping. A boat is a small place and uncomfortable things are bound to happen sooner or later.

As for the Americans, they were easy to figure out. Jason Shibata, compact, efficient. A focused kid, with dreams of being the best someday. Even though he would never stand a chance. He just wasn't a surfer at that level. But he was an incredibly clean young man. The only surfer the guide had ever seen, the only *human* for that matter, who washed his clothes daily and meticulously cleaned his nails before and after each and every meal. Then there was Brandy Faber, loud and boisterous, hungry for conversation, who would patiently wait his turn in the lineup. And then Julian Sekon from Santa Cruz, Califonrnia. Well over six foot, all granite, and a private soul. Almost solemn. Julian was damn near arrested at the airport in Malé due to one of his surfboards being confiscated as pornographic material. Julian's girlfriend back home had ordered him to have this surfboard painted with a life-size nude portrait of her on the deck in order to keep him from straying. Out in the surf on a borrowed board, Julian was playing a different game altogether. He would wait forty-five minutes at a time for the biggest wave of the day and then make it look even bigger. The guide figured that must be the way they do it up in northern California.

The guide was going miss this group. They treated him like one of their own. And they had yet to complain about anything. The guide reached the boat and hauled himself, his board, and his sixty pounds of coconuts up onto the deck. He pulled the axe out of his belt and went to work on one of the coconuts. Three good whacks and he was drinking the sweet, warm milk. He repeated this two more times, letting the milk run down his cheeks. You could do that in a place like this; the water was never more than a railing away. He dove over the side and then clambered back up onto the deck to wait for his Maldivian crew. Brandy and Trent were paddling for the boat. The sky would set itself on fire in about fifteen minutes. He kept looking at that sky, remembering that there was no such word as envy or jealousy in the language of these southern Maldivian atolls. *Angels live here,* he thought. And he smiled at that. Generally, he smiled a lot. He loved the feeling of waking up each morning and finding himself in a dream.

THE COOK

Slicing the potatoes and flipping them off the blade of his cleaver into the coconut milk, the cook listened to the Adzan. The muezzin was calling the faithful to evening prayer on the island that they were moored near. The sound of the holy words competing with the grunts and groans of a pornographic film that one of the surfers was displaying on his laptop computer in the main cabin. The cook was devoutly Muslim and considered it revolting beyond imagination. Westerners carried their sin with them like a loaded gun, and like all sin, it wore most of them down until they became a part of it. The boat carried strictly Muslim-forbidden bottles of beer and whiskey on board, and he had seen the son of the Minister of Defense help open them every night. The rest of the crew were following suit. Evil was like that. It always came on slow. Like a tide. Sure of its result in the end. As a chef in the northern atolls, he'd learned all about tourism. In 1972, his country was untouched. By 1998, over 360,000 tourists were visiting seventy-six different resorts. The government hoped to lever that up to 1,000,000 tourists by 2010. *Human beings,* he thought, *are the only creatures on earth able to go anywhere they want in the world. That also have the capacity to bring good or evil once they get there. Why did they always choose evil? Tourists are worse than nuclear weapons,* he thought.

It was dark by the time the boat dropped anchor off the small pier that reached out from his home island. The cook was eager to serve the evening meal and then have the chance to kiss his wife and play with his six children for a few blessed hours. The cook sliced the last of the potatoes, fried them brown, and served them to the surfers with the rest of the food he had prepared. He then grabbed his prayer rug and rowed the dinghy toward shore. The sounds of the surfers on the boat disappearing behind him. He slid the dinghy onto the beach and moved toward the small mosque across the square, the pink coral of the path crunching between his toes. Overhead, giant bats moved like shadows against the stars. He wondered if, in the quiet, late at night, the surfers could hear what he could hear. He wondered if the world could hear what he could hear. He wondered if Allah could hear what he could hear. He wondered if anyone could hear that his islands were screaming.

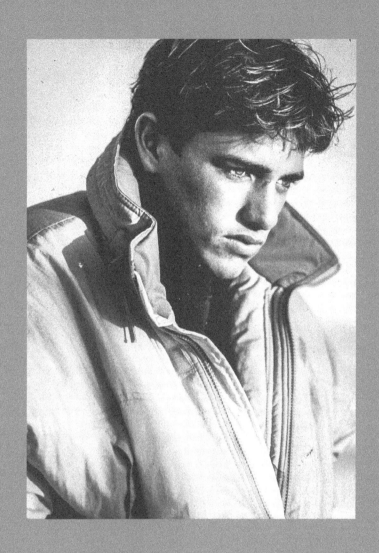

DON'T MESS WITH TEXAS

INSIDE THE UNITED STATES AMATEUR SURFING
CHAMPIONSHIPS
SURFER MAGAZINE, USA, 1985

You might still hear the braying about how our American amateur system created world champion surfers like Tommy Curren, Lisa Andersen, and Kelly Slater, but the truth is the other way around. —Mg.

The flight had been delayed. It would be another hour before we could board. Everyone got out of line and sat back down. Girls on one side, boys on the other, a couple grownups on patrol. Like a grade school dance. I took my place with the boys. We were all headed to the United States Amateur Surfing Championships, which were to be held on South Padre Island in Texas. A sandy barrier island known for the worst surf in the world. I imagined the same scene was going down in airport lounges all up and down both coasts of the country. Honolulu, too. A massive airlift, an enormous invasion force from every amateur surfing association in the USA, was deploying to this annual gathering.

I looked over the assembly in front of me, curious about this next generation of ours. It had been a long time since I was involved in the amateur side of our sport. All I remember were the Australians Peter Townend and Ian Cairn's glory days. Those two Aussies who were the first to take American amateur surfing seriously. Taskmasters, whipping our young American surfers into the same kind of competitive singlemindedness as their young Australian counterparts. A sort of saltwater *Boys from Brazil*. It would be interesting to see what had become of Peter's and Ian's legacy.

A couple kids, with sponsors stickers on their boards the size of dinner plates, were in the corner doing homework. In the girls' seats, a couple sunburned, straw-haired blondes were doing a brisk business in the candy trade. Snickers were going three to one. And the rest, every single one of them, were listening to their Walkmans, bobbing their heads to the beats of different drummers. This was definitely not the rowdy crew of surfers I was raised with. This was the Brady Bunch.

A kid sitting next me with a scabbed, sunburnt nose, was really stoked. About his Walkman, I mean. He was preparing a Duran Duran cassette with practiced hands. He appeared the perfect kid to ask what this contest was all about.

He just looked at me kinda funny and said, "I don't know, mister, sponsorship?" I thought about that one for a minute. Looking around, it seemed as if no one minded that we were traveling to one of the worst places for waves on the planet. So I turned back to my little friend and asked him what he thought the waves might be like.

He gave me that look again and said, "The waves? They'll be shit. That's how all these things are." And with that, he put his headphones on, flipped the tape, and thumbed the dial to ten. I could hear the lyrics, tinny and earnest.

Acting on your best behaviour,
Turn your back on mother nature,
Everybody wants to rule the world!

It was a pretty good night for an outdoor barbecue as the Gulf of Mexico goes. A clammy breeze was blowing in off the gulf and over the parking lot of the South Padre Island Holiday Inn. The twenty-two foldout tables were jammed with every surfing amateur walk of life—fifteen divisions' worth. Aside from the main event men's division, there was the over-fifties and the under-tens. There were things like the junior women's kneeboarding and Menehune's push-in, and every bodyboarding division known to man, which included something called the "Seniors Knee-ups." All of these divisions were busy tackling what looked like compost heaps of food that they had piled willy-nilly on their paper plates from the Tooter's Lunch Wagon Buffet. Buck-fifty a pop. Most kids paying in quarters from Ziploc baggies. I could only imagine the amount of rubble from all those busted piggy banks. As for the food, the Californians didn't understand the Cajun hush puppies and Jamaican jerk grits being served. But that was okay—the kids from Louisiana made up for it.

Soggy paper plate delicately balanced on my palm, I was leaning up against one of the gulf's sea barrier walls that stretched off into the distance. A sort of surfers Great Wall of China, but built to defend the gulf coast from the tides and storms that lay in ambush to scour the island raw. South Padre Island, a summer hotspot for surf bathing Texans, was winter deserted. Businesses were boarded up and dutifully graffiti-smeared with anatomically challenging human mating positions. Concession stands were hasp-locked shut, stolidly awaiting the inevitable storms and the freak tides and the spring break party arrests. But for now, the Ocean was brown and foamy and the beaches were empty. A visual that seemed to shout at us, *Y'all outta yer minds?*

Maybe we were. The surf had been dumping ashore at a weak one-to-two feet and blown to bits by the onshore wind. I was told this was good, since Texas depends on onshore winds for any kind of waves. Out on the horizon stood hundreds of giant oil rigs with flotillas of shrimp boats weaving around them, headed for the barn. The rigs were all lit up and winking like Macy's Christmas trees dumped overboard and left to bob on the swell. Except for the one on fire. That one looked like Armageddon itself.

I mentioned to the Texan surfer kid next to me that at least we had some decent onshore winds for the waves. He looked up from his gumbo, up into the sky, and he took its measure.

"Yeah," he said, "but it's gonna have to get a lot uglier before it gets any better."

Contest director Dave Brown was standing in the gravel of the parking lot off to the side of these proceedings with a microphone in his hand. Lawn grass is impossible to grow here. Wicked barbed sawgrass does great, though. Some of the kids had already learned that the hard way. Dave was welcoming everyone and going through the protocols. With the gummy wind and all, you could hear about every third word. He stood next to a small stage that had been set up. What for, no one knew. The stage, I mean. If you squinted your eyes and thought real hard about it, the scene resembled a washing machine giveaway in the parking lot of some rez casino. Just then, moved by the spirit of the evening, eleven-year-old Nathan Fletcher finished off his third corn cobette and beaned the former Junior Champ Ricky Shaffer with it. Hell of a shot, too.

So after the food fight was over, with everybody smelling like barbecued orange rinds, we found out what the stage was for. There was to be a fashion show. The Beach Boys erupted over a fuzzy speaker and a pack of exotic dancers took to the stage in lingerie, whirling through a single spotlight. Judging from their bored looks and their triple-X moves, these would be the women moonlighting from The Whipping Post, a gentlemen's club a mile down the causeway. The only business, by the way, open twenty-four hours on South Padre Island this time of year. Actually, I heard it was open *all* year, even Christmas. Anyway, most of the kids watching the stage were confused. On my left, little Sally Winkler asked, "Is this for us?"

Two concerned mothers were already moving like icebreakers through the crowd toward the stage. Knowing they had lost the attention of their male counterparts, the young girls help clear the way for the moms with glee. A smoke machine, stage right, was going gangbusters, but with the onshore wind, all it really did was make it look like the cars in the parking lot were on fire. The dancers were game, though. The older boys, once over their initial shock, were now encouraging the dancers. Shrewdly, a home-room mother had captured Nathan Fletcher and his cache of corn cobs and was holding him out of range. The turgid dancing on stage increased in fervor as the Beach Boys reached a crescendo. So did the older boys' encouragement. Perspiration began to form on the foreheads and upper lips of the dancers.

"They smell like Double Mint!" cried a fifth grader. And as if on cue, that's when the whole right side of the stage caved in and two of the exotic dancers took headers into the front row. Another dancer, the "big un," as she would later be called, gamboled into the icebreaker moms, knocking the breath out of them. The music slurred to a halt. On stage, the spaghetti-strapped survivors gazed on in horror. With one hand on her bare left breast and the other protecting her thonged nether regions, one of the hoofers was heard saying to another, "Oh my gawd, Sapphire, that could've been me!"

The wounded were borne off on litters through the smoke, and the wreckage was cleared. A two-man band took what was left of the stage and ripped into *Wooly Bully*. Twice. Nathan Fletcher shook loose and, using the empty baked bean pot, got enough Kool-Aid to drench the bodyboard team from 'Bama. More moms were alerted and they waded in and evac'ed the victims with fireman carries. Most of the dads, and strangely there weren't many, stood in a knot, hitting a flask and looking on with amusement. They were busy holding their smokes over their heads, yuckin' it up. *Atta boy, Luther!* I ducked over the seawall with a few of the giggling girl competitors to wait it out. From this point of relative safety, I could see that some pregnant storm clouds were moving in. I wasn't sure in the dark, but out there on the Ocean, it sounded like the surf had dropped a foot. Here at the opening banquet of the United States Amateur Surfing Championships, things were looking up.

It *was* getting uglier.

The Finals

Taking a head count on the day of the finals revealed not one spectator. It had been that way all week. Wait, I take that back; two days earlier, I counted twelve. High schoolers. But they were more interested in their beachfront tailgate party. Playing horseshoes with real horseshoes, drinking highballs, and smoking cartons of Pall Malls. You are allowed to do that in Texas as a teenager, drink highballs and drive your parent's car on the beach and smoke cartons of cigarettes. Looking at the station wagon they had managed to drive down a half mile of sand, I could only hope someone had taught them what tides were in whatever high school they were ignoring. I myself was sitting in the passenger seat of a grownup's rented economy car that was stuck to the axles. We were all enduring the third complete weather change of the day. Through beating windshield wipers, I was watching as the master's division bodyboarders ran, flopping in their swim fins down into the hissing two-foot surf . . . backwards.

To my right, the scaffolding had long been abandoned. Lightning warnings were in effect. The officials sat in the sand, exposed to the elements. They were all wearing Hefty garbage bags.

Junior kneeboard division finalist Barry Dengis had just come in. He braved the back of the scaffolding to check the posted heat sheets. The sheets were wet and streaked and he had to turn his head to make sense of them. His left cheek was all swole up where one of the thousands of jellyfish that came in with the tide had zapped him. There was one good thing about the jellyfish, though—they made the sea lice look like sissies.

Barry wasn't the only one suffering from the local sea life. I could see another competitor, his cries lost to the wind, trying to wrestle his way out of his wetsuit with one hand while clutching his groin with the other. The rain had shorted out the PA, but no one had noticed. I stepped out of the car and almost got hit with a golf ball. One of the kids had got his hands on a sand wedge. I walked down to the water's edge. It didn't look like any Ocean I had ever known. And I looked real hard.

Behind me, the wind sheared off three 8-by-10 plywood sheets from the scaffolding that bore the contests' sponsors' names. The plywood, scythe-like, was dashed to the sand with all the drama of a disaster movie. It nearly took out the entire boys surfing finalists who, lightning be damned, had a dollar ante blackjack game going under the scaffolding. The contest didn't skip a beat. It couldn't afford to. There were so many divisions of competition that twelve-hour days of surfing were scarcely enough. Some freelance roughnecks were attempting to put the plywood back up, but it was tough. Nail guns and lightning were an unpredictable cocktail. And what was the point? Who would see the sponsors' ads? The only photographer on the beach was a father with a handicam filming his little girl's heat. He was knee-deep in jellyfish, shooting through a plastic bread bag to keep the thing dry. Still, up on the high steel of the scaffolding, orders were barked and the rescue of the structure continued. It seemed imperative to save the scaffolding at all costs. Without it, there might not be any contest at all.

I walked over to the National Scholastic Surfing Association's pup tent. It looked like a sandy igloo. I thought I would strike up a conversation about the contest with a few of the National Team members. Upon my summons, a couple of them made their way out of the tent like released prisoners, t-shirts wrapped around their heads, turbans against the slashing wind and sand. It was hard to tell who was who; they all looked like Tuaregs. But it didn't really matter because they asked not to be identified. They told me something had gone wrong with the system. It used to be a big deal to be on the National Scholastic Surfing Team someday. If you kept your grades up, you just might have a shot at the big payoff. The almighty professional contract. But after shining stars Chris Frohoff and Kelly Gibson got busted for fraud—remember, they were both falsifying exemplary junior college records while not going to school at all—it drove NSSA leaders, Australians Peter Townend and Ian Cairns, from the temple . . . and . . . well . . . that just shot the National Team thing all to hell. And while it was at it, the Olympic dream, too.

"That dream died awhile back," said one team member in the same tone as a scientist might break the news of a mass extinction. "But don't quote me on that." Jesus. These kids were serious. Left behind, lost at sea in the dissipating wake of Peter and Ian's fabled juggernaut. Done in as sure as the Titanic by the icebergs Froholf and Gibson.

Two hours later, after a short break due to a third lightning strike on the scaffolding—which, by the way, was practically glowing at this point—the Menehune division was out in the water, chopping around in the slobbery surf. They looked cute in the contest jerseys that were too big to fit and had to be worn like Pancho Villa's ammo bandoliers. Menehunes is the favorite division of this contest. A chance for parents, tears in their eyes, to watch their hatchlings in mock battle. Whether they were tears of pride or tears at the thought of the long drive home was never clear. And so, the contest staggered on. "Getting itself over with," said one of the parents who also asked not to be identified.

If there was a highlight, it had to be the boys' division final. One reason: Kelly Slater. For the first time all day, headphones were removed, golf clubs set down, and everyone lined the beach to watch Kelly win yet another national title. It made me think back to the same phenomenon that surrounded little Tommy Curren. The fact that Tommy was never just *in* a contest, he *was* the contest. I asked a mom next to me what she thought of Kelly.

She looked offended. "You mean the Kelly Slater show?" she said as she watched Kelly rack up five times more points than her son. "We shall see . . . We shall see . . ." It made me wonder if she had something planned. Especially because she asked not to be identified.

The United States Surfing Championships didn't really end. It just stopped. A wispy cheer was raised and carried off on the soggy wind.

The weary officials and judges slipped themselves out of their garbage bags, balled them up, and tossed them into the sawgrass. The NSSA tent collapsed, and a pickup truck full of the faulty sound equipment drove off down the sand toward the Holiday Inn just visible on the western horizon, at this point not so much a beacon as a safe house. Trailing behind in the deep tracks of the pickup was everyone else. Officials, judges, moms, dads, and the competitors. Afoot. Like exhausted infantry. We were told that the trophies would all be "handed out" at 7:00 pm. And they were. Not so much awarded as handed out. After all, they were in the dozens. And just how long can a pre-teen applaud without their hands going numb?

I awoke at dawn the following day. It was Thanksgiving. I was lucky enough to have a rental car with a half-tank of gas and a ticket on the last flight out. Everyone else was stuck. There was only one rental car left in the region, but it would be a long walk down the causeway to the Whipping Post. Seems a local councilman had been arrested there for drunk and disorderly, and the girls were offering the government sedan left in their strip club parking lot to the highest bidder. Other than that, after this past week, most parents agreed that a Greyhound bus station was way too much to face.

I walked downstairs, through the lobby and out to take one last look at the gulf. The weather had been gnawing at everything all night. The temperature had dropped fifteen degrees. The waves had dropped too, ragged rows and rows of them hissing like a den of Texas diamondbacks. I propped myself up on the sea barrier. To my left, through the sea mist, I could just see the scaffolding in the distance. A wild high tide had undermined it. The scaffolding was listing hard to port. It wouldn't be long. It was rumored that, since everyone was stuck here anyway, that they were going to hold the trials to select the team for the World Titles coming up in Puerto Rico. Hold them *here*. In front of the Holiday Inn. In the shadow of the burning oil rig. I wished to god they wouldn't, I really did.

I gazed back at the scaffolding, worse than the Tower of Pisa now. And maybe I was a romantic, but it seemed to me that the USSC, the highest pinnacle of amateur surfing in this great nation of ours, should be worth just a little more than this. I mean, it wasn't the kids' fault. A lot of them could be world class. Kids like Kelly Slater, Jamie George, Pete Rocky, Scotty Blake, Walter Cerny, Nea Post. The list goes on, sure, but didn't we owe it to them to provide a more decent forum for their youthful ambitions? And how about the others? The unblessed. The ones another mom told me she was just "trying to keep off the streets." Didn't they deserve at least as much as the Cub Scouts? Didn't we owe it to ourselves? It would take more than two Australians to try and make it right, but who would be the next to bother with it?

I shook loose from that thought. I knew someone always would. Bother with it, I mean. Because that's what it seemed to be these days, a bother. I stood up, found my rental keys in my pocket, and turned to go. One last look. I could see a waterspout off in the distance on the bruised sea. The smoking oil rig. More rain was sweeping our way. It didn't really feel like Thanksgiving. It felt like a funeral.

Down on the beach before me, tilted forlornly against the wind, was an overfilled garbage can, bearing the official anti-litter slogan of Texas on its side.

The slogan read: **DON'T MESS WITH TEXAS**.

I took its advice.

I got the hell out of there.

THE ART AND SOUL
OF ROB MACHADO

SURFER MAGAZINE, USA, 1996

I spent a week with the very thoughtful twenty-year-old in his family's home. Rob was poised right on the edge of real manhood. The big surprise to me was that he was a master potter, spinning beautiful pottery by hand beneath the family deck. —Mg.

CARDIFF BY THE SEA, CALIFORNIA, 1996

Rob Machado is weeping quietly. He sits on his parents' back porch, gently holding his eyes in the heels of his hands, his head bowed. On the table before him is a small portable stereo. He is listening to Beethoven's "Moonlight Sonata." I stand, looking out at him from inside his parents' house. To my left, from out of the kitchen and onto the porch, walks Corrina, Rob's longtime girlfriend. She goes to Rob. He looks up. I can see her eyes and they look into his. There is an understanding. She sits on his lap and enfolds him in her arms, slowly rocking him. I glance down at a piece of paper in my hand.

> The sky turns blue as the
> sun reflects off the sea
> the trees that once stood tall
> stand in peace around me
> the winds blow as if it were its last day
> as I watch the clouds drift further and further away

It was one of the Rob's poems that he gave me as a gift. I reach down, pick up my bags, and head for the front door. And for a few moments, I understand.

I had arrived days earlier at the Machado compound and was invited to stay while Rob and I worked together. Like most houses in Cardiff, California, the place was an open affair. Up on the hill. A back deck, a big backyard. Outdoor jacuzzi, no pool. Coastal cool. Lots of trees and plants that had been there long before the house was built. The kind of place in the kind of neighborhood where locking the doors when you went to the market wouldn't cross your mind. I was to spend a few days with Rob during the pro tour break before his Hawaiian campaign. It was a much-needed rest period for Rob, having charged his way into world title contention once again over the past year. He was going to spend it re-energizing with his family. Despite owning two houses of his own nearby, Rob still stayed here with his parents when he was home. After seeing how close-knit the Machado clan really was, after seeing how warm and loving they are toward each other, I didn't blame him one bit. Rob and I fell into a rhythm. Surfing when we felt like it, dinners with the family, a few errands here and there. By the time I was headed north on the interstate for home, I had learned that his was not as secretive a world as most people currently thought. I had learned that it was just a quiet one. And steeped in the aspect of a deep thinker. In the isolation of a poet. In the loneliness of a musician and the ambitions of an extraordinarily gifted athlete, with no choice but to prove it all. I also learned that great music of any kind could bring him to tears.

On the way to his band practice:

Surfing: sport or art?

"What?"

Surfing, is it a sport, or an art?

"It's a sporting art."

So where is the art to be found at your level of competition?

"You don't have to look for art in the Ocean; it's already there. I just go out and become a part of it."

Beneath the wooden backyard deck of his parents' house, I see Rob Machado finding peace. It is midnight. A single bare light bulb lights his way. He sits on a gnarled wooden stool, kneading a three-pound piece of clay. Rolling it, spindling it, getting the air bubbles out of it, getting it perfect. He picks it up and throws it down on the potter's wheel in front of him, quashing it. He looks at it for a few moments. A few moments more. The he flips a toggle switch and the wheel begins to spin. With strong, practiced hands, he cups the clay in one hand, and massages it with a wet sponge held in the other. He has no idea what will become of it yet, but here in his small, cramped pottery studio under the stairs, he begins to create. He knows that the key to throwing pottery is keeping the clay centered on the spinning wheel. Keeping the mind loose and rhythmic and calm. Letting the clay take its own shape with a minimum of predetermined thought, a minimum of guidance. I see that this is also the key to being himself on a wave. Letting the wave guide him. Center him. Contorting him into a graceful moving sculpture.

Rob remembers well the first time he rode an Al Merrick shaped surfboard. It was on the East Coast during the US Championships a lifetime ago. His friend Kelly Slater gave him the board. Rob remembers that by his second turn on his first wave, he knew he would be riding Channel Islands surfboards for the rest of his life. But a dilemma arose. There was someone else to think of. Back home, Rob already had a surfboard shaper. A local Cardiff shaper who had been supporting Rob's surfing from the very beginning. All the way back to when Rob weighed about seventy pounds, back when Rob, already lithe and bone-lean in teenhood, was known as "Mouse." Returning home from Florida, Rob knew that something had to be done. This local shaper was his good friend. A family friend. Rob had an idea and talked it over with his dad. A month later, the Machado family threw a birthday party for this local shaper. The birthday present? A brand-new surfboard shaping room that Rob and his dad had built in their own back yard for the man. A soundproof shaping room that they told this local shaper would be his for the rest of his life. To this day, the low buzz of a planer can be heard coming from the shaping room five days a week. This family leaves no man behind.

Rob took me to a soccer game. It seems that Rob was a bit of a soccer prodigy in his younger days. He keeps in touch with it in his own way. The game was an American Youth Soccer Organization affair. Rob's team is known as the Blazers. I say "his" team because he plays the part of an owner. He sponsors and outfits the whole team out of his own pocket. The average age on the team is ten years old. While on the back of other jerseys there are such sponsors as ABC Plumbing and Johnson's Locksmith Service, the back of his team's jerseys simply read: ROB MACHADO. The day we watched, his team won.

It made me wonder what other pro surfers do with their money.

Waxing up our surfboards at Cardiff Reef:

What do you think of your own surfing?

"You pick up a guitar and it has six strings and twenty-two frets and that's it. But consider all the possibilities for different sounds. All the different songs we hear throughout our lives, throughout history. An instrument like the guitar is suddenly transformed, in the right hands, into an instrument of the soul. With infinite places to go. You'd think that one day it would all come to an end, that all the chord changes would be used up. But the end never comes. The strings just keep playing whoever's heart's into it. That's how I feel about my relationship between my surfboards and the waves. Infinite amounts of interpretations for an infinite amount of moments. I'm just one soul and I'm just out there riffing."

In a small, dusty room in a huge t-shirt warehouse in Carlsbad, I watched Rob's band practice. His four-man band is called Sack Lunch. A group of local Cardiff surfers. Close friends. One of Rob's side projects. It's mostly ragged punk, but man, they all play like they mean it. That day, Red Eye Records, a local indie label, released Sack Lunch's CD. Rob and I later went into the local record store to check it out on the racks. Rob just smiled when he saw it there.

He didn't pick one up, he didn't even say a word. He just went over and bought a CD of Beethoven's *Sixth Symphony*.

While checking the surf:

"I don't surf on nerves; I surf on instinct. It's important to surf as who you are. Otherwise, it's just an act. I don't want to be remembered as some guy who tried super hard and was all edgy. And I don't want to be remembered as a guy who won such-and-such contest. I don't think I want to be remembered at all unless it is for being a stylist."

I drove on, working my way home. And my strongest impression was one of a vague loneliness that I felt coming from Rob Machado. It's behind his eyes. It's not that easy growing up a prodigy. Being special. Everything Rob has ever tried to do, he has been great at. He's been a champion athlete, a great friend, a wonderful boyfriend, a loyal family member, a respected teammate, a straight-A student, a successful competitor. All his life, he's been exceptional. And he has been responsible for it and responsible with it. Testing himself and reaching potentials with a quiet classiness. And in all this self-responsibility, I think, lies the separation for a man who has just turned twenty-three. The loneliness he feels inside. That pressure that comes with being exceptional. The above-ness. That loneliness of that lofty perch that drives someone like him to seek a connection with normality with his friends, with his family, with the world. It's just that his extraordinary talents that get in the way. He will always be special, and considered special, and it does not sit comfortably under his skin. I am reminded of surfers like Rolf Arness, Tom Curren, Tom Blake, Phil Edwards, Dave Parmenter—a DNA pool of exceptional talent, geniuses really, but painfully introverted. They all walked away from the limelight in one form or another. Although far more personable, maybe Rob's headed that way too. Maybe that's what all the music is about. Maybe that's what he was trying to say in that last conversation I had with him out on the porch before the Beethoven.

Rob spoke of the pro tour. "Sometimes it just feels like a circus out there. A traveling circus. The circus is supposed to be fun, yeah, but underneath, there is that scary thing. That unreality. The greasepaint. I remember being in Japan and the contest was on hold, and I thought, *Well, the lions won't be fed today.* I mean, pro surfing just doesn't mean that much to me. And competition as a surfer—well, it's disjointed. A wave for a surfer is not to be thought about, or judged; it's just supposed to be ridden. I mean, when you get tight with the Ocean, really tight, you get tuned into its mystery. That's why surfers can feel sets before they are coming. You're paddling out and, all of the sudden, you just move to the right and a wave comes right in there at you. Or when you take off and you can feel what the wave is going to do before it happens. It's a mystery. A mystery that we are all a part of. I just don't see where that relates to competition most the time."

He spoke of the pressures of the Hawaiian leg of the tour. "I don't even know where I am rated right now. World title? I try not to pay too much attention. If it happens, great. If it doesn't? I'll still have all my real friends."

He spoke of a crossroads in his life. "Right out of high school, right out of amateur surfing, I was offered a great contract by one of the top surf companies. And I wasn't sure what to do. I took a lot of long walks by myself, spent a lot of time alone, you know? Asking myself, do I really want this? Do I want surfing to be an employment? Or do I turn my back on it? Live a normal life and go to school? Like my best friends, you know? They went to school; one of them is a math genius. I could have gone that route. I was prepped for college. It was a real hard choice for me. After a lot of thinking, I believe I made the right choice. I believe I will someday be able to return to a normal life after this is all over. I mean, I still want to learn a different language. I love mathematics, history . . . there is just so much to do. I guess that's what my connection with Cardiff is all about. I know that someday, I will be able to come home."

We ended the conversation with a discussion of what it must have been like to be Jimi Hendrix. To have so many thoughts in your head behind a cool exterior. An implosion of the soul. That's when Rob gave me one of his poems. "To get a better idea of what I am about," he said. And he gave me something else too. His favorite quote.

Man did not weave the web of life, he is merely a strand in it.
Whatever he does to the web, he does to himself.
—Native American Chief Seattle

Later, much later, I pulled into my driveway in San Clemente and shut off the motor. I just sat there. Listening to the ticking of the cooling engine. Not yet ready to go upstairs and slide into my own bed with my own girlfriend. I could still see Rob and Corrina on that back porch.

I could still hear the pottery wheel and the Beethoven and see the tears.

GOING BACK: KAHUKU, OAHU — DECEMBER 1995

Kelly Slater, Peter King, and Rob Machado sat before a packed crowd in a small club in Kahuku, Oahu, playing their guitars. They were well into their acoustic set, finding their groove. Kelly on vocals, Peter on lead, Rob on rhythm. This auxiliary band of Rob's didn't even have a name yet, but a wild rumor about some giant record contract for the three of them had been circulating. I watched and listened and thought of Rob and Kelly and of how odd, but of how beautiful, it is that they have intertwined their lives like this. Kelly, the most fiercely competitive human being on earth, and Rob, Mr. Sunshine. They had been battling it out all year. Rob had plastered Kelly in perfect surf in Western Australia;

he had also beaten him in slop at the US Open at Huntington Beach, California. An extraordinary day for Kelly, that. Kelly had finally reached a place in his career where the crowd was cheering for the underdog and booing the great champion. Kelly heard those boos for the first time in his life. And he had lost and come in looking dazed. What had just happened? And it was Rob who had handed that to him. I watched the two of them up there on stage in Kahuku, friends, bandmates, playing together. And I wondered what kind pressure competing squeezed into their relationship. Three days later, the whole world would find out in a single moment that ended Rob's run at a world title. He would never get another.

It was a moment at the Pipeline Masters when Rob Machado came flying out of a Pipeline barrel, and Kelly, who was paddling out, raised his hand in a high five. In the spur of the moment, Rob weaved over to him and slapped Kelly's upright hand in solidarity. And in that moment, the world title slipped between Rob's fingers. Rob was ahead on points at the time, and all he needed to do to win the world title was kick out of the wave and skedaddle back outside the break to establish priority position for the last few moments of the heat. In this way, he could of blocked Kelly from getting a final wave. But instead, he weaved over to Kelly for the high five and in doing so, handed Kelly the opportunity to race outside the break and establish the priority that should have been Rob's. Kelly took off on a beauty in the final seconds of the heat, and that was the end of it. Yet in a moment that most would deem tragic, Rob Machado announced his very different arrival on the North Shore's vicious competitive scene. Making a statement that the act of surfing and the camaraderie it brings are more important than the trophies. It was an extraordinary, confusing, and magnificent moment and one that will be remembered longer in history than had he become the world champion. It was Rob Machado being Rob Machado, letting the joys of surfing guide him. Not the accolades.

Up to that point, Rob had been surfing Pipeline with a grace that was being compared to the masterful Gerry Lopez in his prime. Most were surprised, especially the Hawaiians. Unlike Kelly Slater, Rob's presence on the North Shore is not one of total domination. Rob would quietly go about the business, surfing outside the main arena most of the time. "It's not that I don't like big waves; it's the crowds I can't stand," he had said at the time.

For the number-two surfer in the world, Rob is almost invisible on the North Shore. But no one gets to a world title shot at Pipe by holding back. Rob was once again taking responsibility for his talents when it really mattered. Two surfers, two friends, perfect nonstop waves. "I mean, in the first ten minutes, there were three ten-point rides between us," Rob had said. "That's when it snapped in for both of us. I mean, you know that feeling after a really long barrel? Kelly and I were just riding that buzz the whole heat. It's no wonder we high-fived in the channel; all three elements, the Ocean, Kelly, and me, were in perfect sync. That heat taught me about something in my life. I think it has something to do with synchronicity in this world."

CARDIFF BY THE SEA, CALIFORNIA, 1996

Later that year, I was driving up after a surf trip to Baja and I pulled into Cardiff to visit Rob for an hour. I found him sitting on the porch railing of one of his new homes that overlooked his beloved Cardiff Reef. He was playing his guitar as the sun set. It was a funky little California two-bedroom with a single royal palm and a welcome mat and a small front yard that drank in the splendor of the California dream. I sat in a lawn chair on the porch. Inside, I could hear his girlfriend, Corrina, patting down homemade tortillas. Rob had decided to make his stand here. He had moved in with his gal and they were just setting up shop. Corrina was ecstatic, running about, talking about the paint and the pictures they would put up on the walls. Out in front of me, Cardiff Reef's waves were folding over, giving a local pack of bodyboarders the rides of their lives. The sunset went all the way to heaven. A herringbone sky that extended a blood-red finger to the deserts of the east. The kind of sunset that makes you crook your neck and look straight up.

It seems the rumors of Rob and Kelly and Peter's band were true. Rob told me all about it. About the last few days that he had spent in Los Angeles at Epic Records, signing the deal. Six figures, maybe more. About being in the studio with T-Bone Burnett, the legendary producer.

It was T-Bone's guitar that Rob was playing. A gift to Rob because it seems old T-Bone loved the way Rob surfed in the Western Australian Billabong Challenge contest video.

Before long, a small gathering was underway. Rob's Sack Lunch bandmates had shown up with the beer, and two of Corrina's girlfriends pulled up in a red convertible Stingray with some champagne. Rob played on, considering the surf, pausing and smiling from time to time when some bodyboarder pulled into a suicide tube. He laughed once after one such ride, shook his head, and whispered, "Beautiful."

Rob had recently cut off all his trademark long, electric-curls hair. He looked like a completely different person. I asked him about it. He replied, "That's funny, I don't feel any different." And that was that. The sunset deepened to a desert wildflower purple. As we sat out on the porch, he asked me if there was anything I would like to hear. On a whim, I asked him to play me something lonely. He smiled at me and looked back into the house at his friends and at the little piece of the web of life that he had chosen. Then he looked back at me and winked.

"Loneliness is good sometimes. It keeps you pure," he said.

Then he played. An original. His lyrics went like this:

Drifting amongst the clouds
From today until yesterday
The sun shines brightly upon us
As if it were its last rays
The world is full of strangers
One, which I am myself
Yet ones who find me strange
I find they, too, need some help
The clouds, they move through the sky
But only on a breeze as the days go by
Someday it will be me

The last note of the song hung there. He looked at me. I looked back and nodded.

"Yes," I said. Satisfied, he squinted out at the horizon and breathed a deep lungful of air. Just then, Corrina came out onto the porch with a flute of champagne in her hand. Rob raised his eyebrows at her and carefully leaned his gift guitar up against the railing. Then he and Corrina walked across the front yard and crossed the small street. The two of them stood arm in arm on the bluff overlooking the train tracks and the surf below, and they watched the last sliver of sun drop into the sea. Inside Rob's new house, I heard the pop of a champagne cork and a cheer was raised and someone called out to Rob to come join the party.

But Rob stayed right where he was.

THE GREAT
NATIVIDAD
SNAKE HUNT

SURFING MAGAZINE, USA, 1995

This story seemed to be written before we even took off from Brown Field in San Diego. All it took was one look into the eyes of a customs agent. —Mg.

Lichanura trivirgata saslowi is a secretive creature. It is a subspecies of the desert rosy boa and is one of the rarest constrictor snakes in existence. It is a smooth-scaled, burrowing animal, pale cream in color, with three bold, black stripes running the length of its body, one along the back and one on each flank. *Lichanura* spends its day hidden in burrows, under stones and debris or simply buried in the sand. It emerges at dusk to forage for its prey of small mammals and birds, often climbing into low-growing bushes in search of the latter. It is a powerful but inoffensive creature, due largely to the fact that it rarely reaches the length of three feet. There are only two places on the planet where this snake can be found. Both are small islands standing side by side few miles off central Baja. One of these islands is called Cedros. The other is known as Isla Natividad. There are only two groups of people who are aware of these snakes: herpetologists and United States customs agents.

OAKLAND MERRILL LYNCH COMPLEX, OAKLAND. CA
JUNE 13, 1995 — 11:30 A.M.

John McMahon Jr., vice president of the Oakland California's Merrill Lynch, didn't want to think about all the money people were making on this day. He didn't even want to think about all the money he was making. Not anymore. Ever since the bell went off that morning, trading had been brisk. The headset he'd been wearing all morning was beginning to give him a headache. He had been working at a hysterical pace. It was always this way with new IPOs in the works.

John punched the mute button on his phone console, leaned back slowly, and took the headset off. He stood, rubbed his eyes, and stepped to the giant picture window of his twenty-fourth-floor office. The entire panorama of the San Francisco Bay spread out before him. He glanced back at his phone console. Every line was winking.

John turned back to the view out over the bay. He could make out the Golden Gate Bridge. He knew what was out there, beyond that bridge.

He knew that twelve days previous, a giant tropical storm had ripped around from the Southern Indian Ocean into the Pacific and settled itself off New Zealand. He knew that, for three days and three nights, it measured 800 by 600 miles with sustained winds of sixty knots or more. He knew, because of that big gray spot on the weather map, that ships had been re-routed, planes grounded, and that the southern shores of Tahiti and Hawaii had been clobbered by the biggest south swell most would see in their lifetime. It made him think of how long it would be until the surf spots of Alaska were lit up. And of how he would have to hear about the whole show while he sat here with his headset on, making money for everybody.

John put the phone on speaker, hit a speed dial button, and stepped back to the window. His friend Jeff Kurtz, a bush pilot who specializes in Baja, came on the line. John asked what it would take to fly him and his friends to a tiny island named Isla Natividad about halfway down the west coast of the peninsula. In just hours, the surf there would be tremendous. Jeff Kurtz explained that no planes were available, what with the way everyone had gone mad over this swell. The only possible way to do it would be to set up a ferrying system where Jeff would drop his customers off at Magdalena Bay, fly back to the Palomar Field in Carlsbad to pick up John and his friends, and take them to Natividad. After that, Jeff would have to pick up his customers at Mag Bay, drop them off at Brown Field in San Diego, and then return to Natividad to pick up John and his crew. But, Jeff explained, that would be crazy. Because first, they would have to leave from San Diego within the next twenty-four hours, and second, the price of all this flying around would have to be picked up by somebody. And the cost would just be too much. Way too much.

John looked down at his wingtips for a second and scrunched his toes. Then looked out through the Golden Gate. He knew then that he wouldn't be putting his headset back on.

"Too much?" John said over his shoulder. "And just how much is that, Jeff, exactly?"

FREELINE DESIGN SURF SHOP SANTA CRUZ, CA
JUNE 13, 1995 — 7:00 P.M.

Professional surfer Peter Mel locked the door of his family's surf shop and stepped over to the register to deal with the receipts. The evening shift had just shown up. The phone rang. It was his surf brand sponsor telling him that a last-minute flight to Isla Natividad had been arranged to meet the big south swell. The rub was that if he wanted to go, he'd have to be at a small airport in Carlsbad by daybreak. Carlsbad, California, was 427 miles to the south. Peter hung up the phone, tapped the receipt roll on the register a couple of times, figuring things, calling up the map of California in his head. Eleven-hour drive . . . *easy*.

Peter put a rubber band around the receipt roll and stuck it in the cash box. He told his employees to grab some dinner, then he locked up and pushed the keys through the slot. Let his dad figure it out from there. Peter knew that flying down to Carlsbad was out of the question. Too late now. He'd have to do this the Santa Cruz way. He went over to his girlfriend's place, borrowed her truck, and loaded up his boards. An hour had passed by the time he eased out of town, headed south for Salinas, where he'd pick up the 101. The tape his girlfriend had been listening to was still in the stereo. He listened to it twice through as the moon rose in the sky. Fleetwood Mac. Her favorite.

ABOARD THE JUNO, SIX NAUTICAL MILES OFF ISLA NATIVIDAD
JUNE 13, 1995 — 11:30 P.M.

Craig Finch called for his sixteen-year-old son, Sage. The kid came up from the galley where he was finishing the dishes and took his place on deck. They were readying for their waypoint tack. His boy had got into trouble with the law recently and Craig had taken him on this trip to straighten things out. The thirty-six-foot islander sailboat eased around smoothly and ran with the big, even swell toward the small fishing village, whose lights were winking in the distance. Three months out now, they were working their way back up the Baja peninsula, bound for Ventura and home. Two days earlier, off Cabo San Lucas, the pair had learned of this swell. Craig had caught his son poring over the charts for no real reason and later saw him waxing his surfboard board up on deck. He knew without asking what his son was thinking, and they had set the new course together.

Craig looked at his son now, up on the bowsprit, checking the trim of the jib and riding the swell on the bow of the Juno. He saw his son ride out a large set of waves that moved under the boat, staring at the moonlit humps of the swell, timing them and moving with their power.

There was just enough light for Craig to see his son's teeth. Craig realized that his son was smiling for the first time in weeks.

SAN DIEGO MEDICAL GROUP BUILDING, SAN DIEGO
JUNE 14, 1995 — 5:00 P.M.

Surfing Photographer Aaron Chang could feel the doctor tugging at the surface of his left eyeball. Aaron lay there on his back patiently. He'd been through this before. For the second time in his life, he was having stitches removed from one of his eyes. The operation days previous had been deemed a success. Pterygia were just another on-the-job hazard for Aaron; that and getting run over by surfers while the whole Pacific Ocean was caving in on him.

Aaron relaxed and breathed shallowly, trying not to move too much. He thought of Mike Castillo, a pilot and surfer, who was airborne right now with Peter Mel and Chris Brown on their way down to Isla Natividad. Castillo and the boys just couldn't wait another day for Aaron to get his stitches out, so they'd bolted. Aaron would hitch a ride with Sparky, the sandal-maker, in the morning, doctors' orders be damned. Aaron had been studying the weather maps for weeks. He knew what was about to happen down there. He'd been there before. Aaron found himself tensing up, so he allowed himself a deep breath and eased the muscles in his neck, his mind now a jumble of film speeds, f-stops, water housings, and millimeters. The doctor leaned a little closer and the tugging on the surface of his left eye continued.

8100 FEET OVER THE PACIFIC OCEAN, OFF CENTRAL BAJA
JUNE 14, 1995 — 6:30 P.M.

Chris Brown was drowsy from the thrumming of Mike Castillo's 206 single-engine turboprop Cessna. He looked over at Peter Mel, who was sleeping with his head against the airplane's window. Peter looked terrible. His marathon drive had done its work. Chris was reminded of a giant day of surf at Mavericks near San Francisco that he and Peter had spent together. It was a couple of days before Mark Foo had drowned there. It had been a sunny day and the giant icy North Pacific waves were perfectly horrifying. That's about all Chris remembered about it. He'd operated on nerves alone that day, and that'll do things to a man's memory.

Chris looked out the window. There was a lot of water between them and land. He shut his eyes and tried not to think about it. Flying was always an edgy thing for him. He fell asleep then, his face twitching, dreaming of crash landings and of putting his hands behind his back inside the long spinning barrels of breaking waves.

Mike Castillo, in the pilot's seat, looked back to check on his passengers. He always did this when he reached this spot in the sky. Sixty miles from everywhere, he called it. Sixty miles from San Carlos, sixty from Cedros, and sixty from the mainland to the east. Any trouble with the engine now and it meant a long swim, if you were lucky. Mike went through the checklist in his head. First, look for a ship to set the bird down next to, and make damn sure you fly right in front of the bridge so they see you. If no boats are around, then take a heading of 110 degrees and work the glide ratio. That heading wasn't exactly straight toward land, but you'd get more mileage using the wind that way. You'd have about fifteen minutes until splashdown. Get everyone to put their wetsuits on. Stuff power bars and crackers down their wetsuits and loosen up a surfboard or two. Grab a couple gallon jugs of water for drinking at first and for flotation later; someone was bound to get banged up. Then take the doors off and let them go. Then jettison anything that wasn't bolted down and strapped in. With the stall kit he'd installed, Mike knew he could turn her into the wind and hit the drink at about thirty knots. It would mean going over the bars and coming to your senses upside down and underwater, but if the seatbelts held, you stood a pretty good chance of being conscious. Then it would just be a matter of getting everyone out before the thing sank.

Mike checked his manifold pressure and flew on.

"You got to think about them things," he said out loud. Then he looked back at his passengers. He figured they were dreaming of sugar plums.

Oh, you lucky sons of bitches, he thought to himself.

MONTGOMERY FIELD, SAN DIEGO, CA
JUNE 15, 1995 — 1:00 P.M.

The mechanic had his head under the cowling, working a stripped nut with a vise grip. This little Grumman Tiger was always running hot. Real hot. The gauges were screwed up, the navigation system spotty at best, the radio intermittent . . . the list went on. The wrench slipped and the mechanic split the skin of two knuckles on the bolt. He cursed the two surfers waiting on the tarmac for him to finish with the overheating problem. The mechanic knew they had no business hedgehopping down into Baja, Mexico, with this aircraft. No business at all. He'd told them all the problems with the aircraft, but they'd been rushing him all morning anyway, keeping at him, a real couple of terriers. He knew they were going, no matter what in the hell he was saying about it. *Maybe it isn't any of my business,* the mechanic thought.

Two hours later, Sean McNulty helped his friend Kevin Billy cram the last of the boards in. The little plane was packed as tight as a can of tuna, the surfboards stuck in between the seats and pressed into the instrument panel. They wouldn't be seeing each other's faces for the duration of the flight and would have to yell over the boards to be heard. Sean and Kevin climbed into the cockpit. Sean, left seat and an inexperienced pilot, went through the checklist. He taxied out onto the runway and ran his engines up, checking the pressure, the heat. Too early to tell yet.

Giving them their chance, the tower gave them clearance for take-off. The sun was beating mercilessly through the clear bubble canopy. Their scalps were dripping sweat off their hair and onto their faces. Sean pushed his sunglasses back up the bridge of his nose and pushed the throttle forward. Kevin crossed himself and grabbed his seat with both hands.

The mechanic had stepped out of the hangar to watch them take off, figuring it was his duty. *All things considered, a beautiful takeoff,* he thought, listening for the engine. The mechanic closed his eyes and listened to the drone of the engine until he couldn't hear it anymore, making sure. When he opened his eyes, the thing was gone. That's when he realized that there was something beautiful in what these two surfers were doing, taking chances like this. The mechanic sucked his bloody knuckles and turned back to the hangar. Work to do.

1SLA NATIVIDAD AIRSTRIP, BAJA
JUNE 16, 1995 — 7:00 P.M.

Guillermo loved to watch the planes land. Loved the noise of it, the spectacle of all the dirt flying all over kingdom come, and of the men getting out of the machines with looks on their faces as if they were never going back up again. He shouldered the rifle and looked over at the surfers' encampment. There were four planes over there. He'd watched them all land, crabbing in against the howling wind that had pulled at his hair as long as he could remember. He'd watched the planes, one by one over the past few days, taxi to a stop way down by the sand. And he'd watched the surfers pile out. And as the big waves pounded the beach, he'd watched as the surfers danced and jumped and howled and yipped like the coyotes on the mainland. Guillermo had seen this ritual a hundred times before. A lot of surfers had come to his island over the years. But never like this.

He'd spent the last two days down here at the end of the airstrip, just being around the energy. Five airplanes full had turned the end of the runway into a village all its own. A couple of the surfers had even sailed in here, one of them not much older than he. The only other place Guillermo had ever seen this kind of energy was at a carnival his family once went to on the mainland. That had been three years ago. He was eleven now.

Over the past few days, Guillermo had caged a few stickers and a t-shirt and a couple of candy bars, surfers always being a soft touch. He'd watched them cook the fish they'd caught with shiny fishing poles and spearguns and seen them range from tent to tent, yelling, laughing, and drinking cans of beer as the sun disappeared. He'd seen a couple of them hike up to the lighthouse to spend the night. He'd seen a couple of them poke around the old abandoned church. He'd seen three of them walk up to the cross that overlooks the main village and he wasn't sure, but he could've sworn that one of them said a prayer. He'd even snuck down at night after the dance that was held in the warehouse of the fish processing plant and heard them as they all crawled into one tent and drank more beer and listened to music and told raucous stories late into the night.

On this day, he had been down at the beach at the end of the airstrip, looking for snakes and shooting seagulls with his dad's .22 caliber rifle. He'd catch hell for taking the gun while his dad was out fishing, but this boy had caught hell before, plenty of it, and had learned just about the most valuable lesson in his life: catching hell wasn't all that bad. Some things were worth it.

Guillermo walked up to the small cliff and watched them surf again. He'd never seen waves so big. He thought about how harmless waves were out in the Ocean when he was fishing with his father. Harmless like lumbering cows in a field. *But,* he thought, *let them reach shore, and waves put their heads down and charge, like bulls with sharpened horns, looking for something to gore.* Guillermo saw one of the surfers paddling for a wave. The wave caught the surfer and he bounced along until the wave swallowed him in its mouth and chewed on him for a while. The surfboard came up first. It was in two pieces. Then the surfer's head appeared, a black dot on a field of white. Guillermo let out a breath he hadn't realized he was holding. The other surfers over at the camp were on their feet, howling again. It was a happy sound. The surfer in the water raised both his hands over his head triumphantly.

As he watched the surfer swim to shore, it seemed to Guillermo that surfers knew the same things he did. That things like fighting bulls and shooting seagulls with your father's gun and riding waves were things worth catching hell for. He smiled at this.

BROWN FIELD, SAN DIEGO, CA
JUNE 18, 1995 — 9:30 P.M.

She stood outside the wardroom door and looked up at the sky, thinking of snakes. From time to time, her face would be lit with an orange glow as she pulled on her hand-rolled cigarette. She adjusted her gun belt from where it was digging into her hip and stuffed a bit of her shirt tail down there to pad it. She liked this time of night and she liked Sundays. The air traffic was heavier with weekend warriors coming back from Mexico. She looked over at the tower. Someone up there was smoking, too. She dropped her cigarette and ground it out underfoot.

It was not the most glamorous job, her first post as a customs agent at Brown Field, San Diego, but at least it was close to the action. And her parents and her little boy were proud of her. She figured that part of it was all in the gun. Things just worked out that way sometimes, she thought, simple things like that. There had been nothing much going on this day, except for the snakes. There had been seven different flight plans filed for an island called Isla Natividad last week, and some genius, knowing that the place wasn't a drug drop, had figured out that a rare snake lived there. Maybe an exotic pet-smuggling operation was in the works. A standard alert was issued over the wire. She had gone over the information twice through. She thought boa constrictors only hung from trees in the Amazon and ate donkeys. She was glad that the suspects she was looking for only grew to three feet and weren't poisonous. She'd searched three planes that day from Isla Natividad, every one of them packed full of surfboards and unshaven, sunburnt surfers. The surfers smelled of campfires and sweat and three-day beards. It was a damned sexy smell, she thought.

She hadn't found any snakes. She knew just walking up to the planes that she wouldn't. She had intuitions that way. They were a handsome bunch of men, surfers; that much she gave them. Robust and square-shouldered. Courteous, they always took off their sunglasses when she addressed them. And cheerful too, almost giddy. As if they shared some big secret. Her little boy had recently started to surf out in front of the stucco apartment they rented over in Imperial Beach. It was all her boy talked about now, surfing. And his eyes had brightened because of it. For the better, she thought, considering what the two of them had been through. Her son was curious about something again, looking for something, and that could only be good, surely.

She always thought she might guide her son toward the military, but if the men she saw today were what surfers grew up into, well hell, there were worse things. At least they seemed to be dealing with something bigger than themselves in this life. Nothing like the slob she and her son had fled from back in Toledo.

She rolled herself another cigarette, lit it, snapped her zippo shut, and drew in deeply. She emptied her lungs slowly, completely, watching the smoke twine its way up into the heavens.

And she thought of snakes and of surfers and of her little boy.

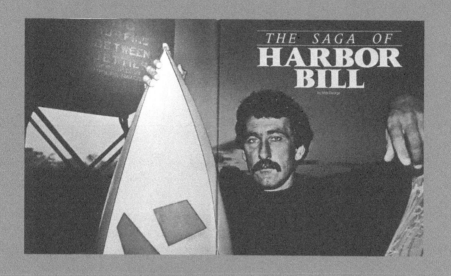

THE SAGA OF
HARBOR BILL

SURFER MAGAZINE, USA, 1985

I couldn't wait to write about this guy called "Harbor Bill," a sort of Robin Hood character who would surf the Santa Cruz Harbor mouth during big swells. Surfing there was illegal, with surfers considered navigational hazards. Which was ridiculous to all of us because it was always surfers who saved the boaters when they foundered in the big surf that used to close the harbor. When I filed my story, I was asked by the editor to supply his full name, which I did. Little did I know, his last name was the most closely guarded secret in town. It caused no end of trouble. Twenty-five years later, the local Santa Cruz newspaper caught up with a self-exiled Harbor Bill on the island of Kauai. The last line of the three-page story read: "The now gray-headed Bill, at home in Hawaii, had little to say about the SURFER Magazine reporter who blew his cover, preferring only to turn to the camera and produce the middle finger." —Mg.

THE PROBLEM

Harbormaster Steve Scheiblauer leaned against his office window at dawn, steaming coffee mug in hand. He had a problem. A big problem. Its name was a shadow known only as "Harbor Bill." This Harbor Bill had moved to the forefront of the ongoing battle between the Santa Cruz Harbor Patrol and the surfers who illegally rode the waves at the harbor's entrance. Scheiblauer had the Army Corps of Engineers to thank for that; it was their construction blunder, years ago, that caused the dramatic shoaling off the west jetty in the first place. For the surfers, the resulting sandbar meant a perfect winter wave. For the boat-owner, it meant a recurring winter nightmare. A gauntlet of Ocean violence to be run at every significant swell. That or the sandbar would barricade the entrance completely, damming the entire harbor. Great for the surfers, sure. But all that didn't matter now. Laws had been passed. Scheiblauer had a job to do. He must arrest Harbor Bill for surfing the entrance. Breaking the law. Pure and simple.

The harbormaster tested his coffee and eyed his jurisdiction—a quaint California harbor setting—and for a moment, wished there was a way for everyone to cooperate. Being a surfer himself, he respected a great many of them as good watermen and had an understanding of their "independent nature." Indeed, their knowledge of the Ocean had resulted in numerous saved lives at the entrance when inexperienced boat owners had foundered and become helpless in the surf. Scheiblauer had seen it with his own eyes. But cooperation was out of the question now, so was any real communication. He'd tried both and the surfers had blown that tactic all to hell. It had come time for the harbor patrol to do their duty. For him to do his duty. Uphold the law.

It bugged him a little that this one guy, this Harbor Bill, had been so elusive and had escaped arrest so many times. This guy was the obvious leader. Bust him and the house of cards might just fall. But this Harbor Bill character had a following, like some surfing Robin Hood. Apprehended surfers staunchly refused to give his name, and civilians had gone so far as to cheer and aid his escapes on a number of occasions.

Scheiblauer dumped his cold coffee in the office sink and considered the daily duty roster tacked to the corkboard. He considered which of his own men were going to help him.

THE GREAT ESCAPES

The excerpt from a Santa Cruz Harbor Police crime report stated: *"Deputy Morley and myself responded to the entrance of the harbor channel in the patrol boat. The park rangers took positions in their vehicles on the east and west side beaches. Subject known as Harbor Bill continued to surf defiantly and continually displayed the middle finger at us. Harbor Bill, at one point of a profane exchange, challenged both Deputy Morley and myself to 'come over and fight me right here. Name the time and place, you chickenshits. I'll be there.' Neither Deputy Morley nor myself responded to those challenges."*

From a private discussion with Harbor Bill: "Well, I had a few words for them, I guess. All's I tried to do was say, 'Let's have a gentleman's agreement and duke it out at the local gym; you name the place and I'll be there.' I mean, what could I say? I was sick of this. I came to go surfin', not to threaten people. So the other guys out there saw this and just scattered. The beach and cliffs were just crawling with rangers; it was a damn free-for-all. It was getting pretty hot out there. One guy actually hopped in the water and dragged some kid in by his wetsuit. So about this time, I had to make up my mind. So I took off on this wave, flipped the harbor patrol the bird, and lit out. By the time I hit Black's Point to the south, everyone was after me. So I went in and started to climb the cliff, and then I saw the rangers comin' down. Well [laughs], about this time back at the office, they're booking this little kid, buddy of mine, and he can hear over the dispatch all the rangers saying, 'We got Harbor Bill, we've got him! He's trapped!' And this kid starts yelling, 'No way! You'll never catch him! That's Harbor Bill!' So anyway, I just turned back and hit the water and started scratching through the waves back out to sea. Everybody on the cliffs was cheerin'. I didn't hit the beach again 'til Santa Maria's, and there, some old granny and grandpa said, 'Hey! Give us your board and run for it!' Can you believe it? All the people were trying to help me. Just then, the rangers pulled up, so I had to keep my board and hit the water again. And by the time I got to 26th Avenue, it was getting pretty dark. Outside, this big set was comin' in towards me and at the same time, the Harbor Patrol boats was zoomin' in to get me [laughs]. So I just paddled in a little bit to watch the show, and sure enough, this big set of waves moved through and those guys sure got out of there in a hurry. I guess local knowledge really paid off on that one . . ."

Excerpt from Santa Cruz Harbor Police crime report: *"The two state rangers, Officer Morley in a patrol boat, and myself in a patrol boat chased the subject in the water where we aborted the chase due to manpower shortage and water conditions too hazardous to continue in boats. However, at 26th Ave. I was able to come in close to the subject and I told him that if need be, we could outlast them and why don't he make it easy on all of us and just paddle in. The subject, who we suspect is Harbor Bill, told me to "go fuck myself." With wave conditions worsening, I broke off pursuit and drove the patrol boat away as the subject continued yelling the same kind of profanities."*

THE REAL ARTICLE

Harbormaster Scheiblauer shook his head slowly. There had been so many other times. They lost Harbor Bill once when he ran down the beach and paddled out under Stearns Wharf into huge surf. Another time, he had buried his board in the sand on the beach and casually walked past the very officers who were looking for him. And there was even some wild rumor that he had hid among a rookery of seals off Steamer Lane until the coast was clear. The public loved that one. Hell, they loved him. Who was this guy anyway? Did he even have a name?

Scheiblauer turned from the picture window and sat at his desk. It was early yet, still time to skim the morning mail. A surfer himself, he was thrilled when he saw the new issue of *SURFER* Magazine had arrived. Positively elated when he found that it featured an article on Santa Cruz. Then suddenly, as he turned to page 83, he froze in his chair.

The paragraph read: "Or maybe the harbor mouth, that million-dollar wave courtesy of the Army Corps of Engineers, and the kind of place where legends are made in a day. Pat O'Neill's frighteningly late drops are still talked about, and 'Harbor Bill' Mulcoy's local knowledge of the place allows him heroism five times a day."

There it was in black and white. His name. "Harbor Bill" Mulcoy. And a snatched city directory provided all that was needed for the arrest. Scheiblauer sat there and looked at it again. In one instant of sheer chance, the thorn in his side had been cleanly plucked. And it wasn't until he had sat back and calmly finished his coffee that Harbormaster Steve Scheiblauer reached for the phone.

At exactly 3:50 p.m. on June 14, 1985, William John Mulcoy, 37, golf course groundskeeper, husband, father, surfer, walked into the harbormaster's office to, as it states in the official report, "face the music." After fourteen years of pursuit, the game was up.

THE MAN

From a conversation with William John "Harbor Bill" Mulcoy: "After all the trouble I've had out there and after all the escapes and the chases, I was really expecting a much more exciting bust. Considerin' my commitment, you know? I've surfed that wave for fourteen years. Gone through a coupla' harbormasters. It's my break, boy, and me and the harbor go way back. When I was a kid, I saw a picture of it when I went into this store down there to buy a candy bar. And I knew then that I was goin' to ride it someday. Sure enough, I got to know it all right [laughs]. It suited what I like about a wave, 'cause what could be more challenging around here than riding someplace like the harbor? Taking off in front of tons of cement and pulling into barrels that are a live-or-die situation, and once you tap into whatever it is out there, once you tap into that, well, shoot! It's like being buried alive and then somehow livin'. Now how are you going to explain something like that to normal people? I set up my whole life so that I could surf that place whenever I wanted to, and now they're going to try and screw all that up. I guess I got somethin' to do here. I won't plead guilty. I'm just a surfer, you know? Shoot, if I ever want to get a little peace of mind and be able to surf the harbor again without being some outlaw, I'm just gonna have to fight it. I guess I'm carryin' the ball now. But all I ever really wanted is for everyone to just leave me alone and let me ride deep 'til I hit the jetty someday and can't ride no more."

EPILOGUE

William John "Harbor Bill" Mulcoy was charged with violating section 131 of the Harbor and Navigation code. Interfering with the navigation of vessels by obstructing a navigable waterway. And section 148 of the penal code: resisting arrest, threatening officers of the law. Mulcoy and his lawyers plan to contest these charges and submit the idea of having the harbor mouth break declared as a recreational surf resource for the citizens of Santa Cruz. As of June 6, 1985, the decision is still pending.

THE BEAUTIFUL
ISLAND

OLD BONES AND NEW SIGHTS IN TAIWAN
SURFTIME MAGAZINE, BALI, 2011

About a year into my tenure as Editor-in-Chief of Surftime *Magazine in Bali, we sent our first contingent of Indonesian surfers over to Taiwan, "the beautiful island," to look for surf. On return, Javanese Surfing Champion Dede Suryana told me of a playful encounter he'd had with an old Taiwanese woman who had watched them surf. Talking to her through a translator, Dede discovered it was the first time she had ever seen surfing. Dede also said she smelled like booze and pinched his ass as he turned to walk away. —Mg.*

She is a Taiwanese woman and very old. Bent in places and stooped and feeling every hard step of her years in her bones. The weather is no help. Neither is her husband. Two years gone, now. Next year would be her turn, she was sure of it. But the Kaoliang was helping, the good stuff; 140 proof. Pure grain happy time. She tips her thermos to her lips and a fire roars into her gut, canceling the cold air for a few seconds before it comes rushing back. These walks were her consolation prize of her bent-over life. She could walk and nurse her thermos and be alone with the sea. She was surprised as anyone that she could still walk at her age. But then, she had been going for long walks next to the sea all her life in this place. She found the chaos of the sea comforting. Like a tiger pacing back and forth, about to make a decision. A strange, impulsive power to it all. And it was this thought in her head, bowed against the wind as she was, that she saw people surfing for the first time in her life. A soft cry left her lips, lost on the wind. Stopped in her tracks, she did not know what to think. She could see that they were young men on the sea, clad in black bodysuits, like seals. The young men seemed to be doing the impossible. Making sense of the chaos. She could tell they were not of her place. Dark-skinned, tall, dancer strong. And proud and free in what they were doing. Daring the Ocean, playing with it, bobbing in it. She could see an exuberance. She moved to the railing of the tsunami barrier and hung on to the railing. Damn the cold steel. Astonished and a little frightened, she watched the young men hunt the waves and jump to their feet and ride like circus acrobats. The only way she could tell how long she had watched was when she began to shiver. Another gulp from her thermos took care of that. She kept watching. Eventually all three of the young men made their way in and picked themselves across the cobblestone beach to the wall. They clambered up onto the promenade and began walking her way. They were all handsome and strong beyond her imagination. All three of them smiled broadly at her and tipped their faces as they passed. Close enough for her to smell the different country they came from. Smell the sea that was dripping from their hair and their eyelashes. Jet black hair and great, clean white teeth. The rubber suits they were wearing like a second black skin. As they passed, she could see their tightly bound muscles roiling beneath the surface of the rubber like corded ropes. And despite the obvious masculinity below their waists, she knew that these men were in love with something unearthly, something unlike human love.

She still had enough woman in her to know that.

MARLON GERBER:
GOING DEEP

SURFTIME MAGAZINE, BALI, 2015

It's not easy growing up with mixed blood in Bali. Despite the "Eat, Pray, Love" reputation of the island, straddling two cultures can be brutal here as a kid. Half-Swiss, half-Balinese pro surfer Marlon Gerber, brother-in-law to the great Rizal Tandjung, was a sensitive boy and the chiding he suffered in grade school affected him deeply. He went on, of course, to be one of the greatest surfers the island has ever produced. He still is. Handsome, wealthy, introspective, and lovelorn, this surfer is considered one of the most eligible bachelors in Indonesia. He helped me lead a team of surfers on a freediving trip for the magazine. Being underwater for long periods of time suited him.
—Mg.

The night sky is pregnant with rain. A rare quiet has fallen over the tourist town of Kuta on the island of Bali. A foot-long tokay gecko kicks off its mating call from high in a tree, and you can just hear the hushing sound of the surf down at the end of side street alley. And if you find yourself sitting across an outdoor table from the Balinese professional surfer Marlon Gerber, and you listen, really listen, you will learn much. If you sit with him on the front porch of his wooden house within the balcony restaurant compound and share a cold beer with him, he will speak in his soft way to you. In that comfortable yet watchful voice. This is a very private man, a solo act defined by an aloneness, an apartness. Of mixed blood, Swiss and Balinese; perhaps this separates him, too. He will reserve his charming smile, looking like an intense warrior one second and a happy child the next. The effect is unsettling, how quickly he can change. Like a camera coming in and out of focus. And it's that focus that you learn the most about on this November night.

He will speak of how, at thirty years old, he feels very young. Better than ever, he will say. And that he is happy with his surfing life and that his dreams have all come true. Because he has always believed in his dreams, and in the power that his dreams have held. He will also tell you that he does not consider himself a competitive animal. That his 2011 Indonesian Championship was for himself, to prove to himself that he could do it, to prove to himself that he was a good surfer, not just an average one. That he didn't want to beat the other guy, and that to him, there is no other guy. That the championship was within himself and all he had to do was bring it out, and that he did.

And he will speak of his obsession with F1 racing. How he once was serious enough to go to driving school and how he found himself in the pits with the Mercedes team in Singapore and how it blew his mind. A metaphor for himself, he will say, in that there is a lot more going on at an F1 race than meets the eye. And that that is how he relates to it, how he loves the technology of F1, the precision, the focus. And you will hear his passion for this racing in his soft voice.

Then he will sit and think a bit, twisting a strand of his long dark hair, and then he will tell you of how he felt when he lost his professional surfing sponsorship a few years back. The company had gone bankrupt. How he thought he was done for, that he would have to go back to school, learn something else. Go to Holland or Amsterdam or Zurich to study something. Maybe hospitality, manage big resorts here in Bali. How, at the time, that was his plan. And he will speak about how his brother-in-law, Rizal Tandjung, saved his life for the second time. The first time was when he first took Marlon surfing at twelve years old; the second time was when Rizal, who is the director of the surf brand HURLEY for Southeast Asia, told Marlon that he didn't need to go back to school, because Marlon Gerber was going to surf for the Hurley brand now. And Marlon will speak of how he had no idea how big the things were to come, and that he has never been happier in his surfing life or with the surfing that he plans to do for the rest of his life.

Marlon Gerber will then tell you of his first surfboard, the one that is still in his front yard, the one his old man picked up for him for three dollars; once red, now faded pink and moss-covered. And he will also speak of what it means to be of mixed blood. How tough it was growing up between two worlds. How he was never really allowed to feel Balinese by the island's kid culture, how he does not feel Balinese to this day, even though he was born and raised here. How it would feel wrong to think he was Balinese, and how he sees himself as something different. Even though he is fluent in Balinese and that all his good friends, whom he considers brothers, are Balinese. But he will say that doesn't give him the feeling of being Balinese in his heart, how his biggest challenge in life was being considered a mixed kid growing up, how the caste system on Bali is brutal to a mixed kid. That he is not Hindu. That he finds his happiness in being half-Indonesian, not half-Balinese.

And Marlon will keep twisting that strand of hair and speak of heartache. How deeply he has felt it in his life. How, at one time, he was so down he felt true hopelessness, and he will speak of the lesson he learned from it. That the mistake that people make when they are so in love or so heartbroken is that they think they are the only ones in the whole world feeling it. Whether they are in the shithole or the cloud nine of love, Marlon will say that you must realize that you are not alone, that you just have to realize that it is your time to hurt. And that it happens to everybody, that the survivors are the ones who move on and heal the wounds of love patiently.

And then Marlon Gerber will go quiet for a bit and a misty rain will start to hiss through the trees and he will look up at it. Letting the small droplets collect on his lips. And that is when he will speak of his freediving, of being underwater, of how much it meant to him to train recently. How he felt so very calm thirty meters below the sea. How he imagined it would feel the same on the surface of the moon. That aloneness. How that hovering down there in the blue deep with just a lungful of air made him feel irrelevant in an exceptional way. Just another speck in the Ocean, cut off from everything that has anything to do with being on land. How the whole world just shuts up. And the noise is replaced with a feeling of belonging to a different place in the world and of being not so alone after all.

THE NORTHING

A JOURNAL OF CLOSE ENCOUNTERS
SURFER MAGAZINE, USA, 1997

At the time, I was writing a column for SURFER *called* Echoes. *Recollections and snippets of things that would not make a complete feature but were good for spread breakers and columns next to advertising pages. I was restless and decided to take off for a month by myself and just drive the West Coast. The result was a series of columns that, when strung together, formed a quirky-sounding map of the top two-thirds of the state of California.* —Mg.

So I headed north. Planning a surf trip that would start from the northernmost point of California. Then I would make my way back home to Santa Barbara. It wasn't about getting waves; I already knew where to find those. I wasn't even sure what I was looking for. Which was probably for the best. Because in the end, it found me.

PART ONE: CALIFORNIA/OREGON BORDER INSPECTION STATION, SMITH RIVER, CA.

I didn't have to go very far to find the northernmost surfers in the state. It was one o'clock in the morning when I crossed into the California state line into Oregon. Then I spun a U-turn to start my California journey from north to south officially. I pulled out of the fog and into the yellow glow of the California border station lights. There were no other cars in sight. The place looked abandoned. It was freezing out. I pulled up to the booth and rolled down my window. An older, uniformed guard appeared behind the round silver speaker, looking out at me from the warmth inside. He smiled and surprised me by putting on a beanie and stepping out of the booth to walk up to my car.

"Are those Channel Islands boards?" he asked. "Al Merrick made 'em?"

"Uh, I mean, yeah, sure, go ahead, check 'em out," I said. Turns out the border guard was a surfer and so was his workmate, who also emerged to check out the surfboards that were strapped to the roof of my truck. We all got to talking and before long a couple of those orange highway cones are set up behind my car and all my boards are on the hood of my truck and I'm in the booth with the both of them, sipping on some hot chocolate with mini-marshmallows floating in it. The guy's name was Rob Bryant, and he and his work partner, a quiet woman by the name of Deanne Parks, were in charge of the graveyard shift here on the northern border. Deanne was a surfer from Santa Cruz. Rob was from San Diego. He told me he still rode single fin surfboards.. But he used to shape surfboards and always wanted to check out some Al Merrick designs. Rob had some history. Seems at seventeen he even entertained thoughts of competing in the 1966 World Surfing Championships when it rolled into his hometown.

"You know, the one that Nat Young stirred up all that trouble at?" he said.

"Yeah," I said. "Yeah, I've heard tell of it."

Rob Bryant joined the Navy instead. Ended up a crew captain on a gunship in Vietnam assisting special forces black ops. The hairy shit. Said that once he was there, all he wanted to do was get home and surf. He made it back to America with three bullets in his leg from friendly fire during a VC fuel dump raid.

"No one could see shit that night," was all he said about that. "First thing I checked into when I got home was surfing," he said. "I dunno, everything had changed by then. The whole scene was different. Different crowd. No one seemed to know where their heads were at. Lots of drugs. I didn't even understand it anymore. I got the feeling that if I would've gotten back into it, stuck with it, I probably would have ended up in jail or dead or . . . worse. So here I am."

Deanne listened. I don't think she'd heard the story before. We talked a bit more, lightening things up. Before long, a car pulled up and we all had to pile out of the booth to get my truck and the cones out of the way. I said my goodbyes and thanks. They both wished me the best of luck on my long drive and said I'd really need it. It made me feel as if they knew something about my trip that maybe I didn't. I pulled my truck through and then Deanne helped me put my surfboards back on the racks. She did this confidently, perfectly. That's when I could tell she was an experienced surfer.

"I like the late shift," she said looking out into the dark toward the Ocean. "We're close enough to the coast here to hear the waves"

It was the first time I was conscious of it.

"They always seem louder at night," she said. She closed her eyes and took five seconds to listen. Then she opened her eyes and looked into mine and held out her hand and I shook it. She nodded once and then turned and walked back to toward the lights of the booth. I can still see the gun bumping against her hip. The braided holster. The mace and the cuffs. Rob Bryant was right.

The far north isn't the kind of place that surfers go. It's a place they end up.

PART TWO: EUREKA MOMENTS

The Ocean is nobody's friend up here. It's tombstone cold. Mean old man cold. Deep, glass-of-ice water cold. Solid, gray, and heavy. Hovering around forty-nine degrees come Christmas. I was rapping with some of the guys from Eureka, California, and they called the water up here "the enemy." They had a few bits of information for me.

a.   Best to turn off the heater of the car and roll down the window before you get to the beach. That way your brain can get used to the cold so that the ice-cream headache won't be so bad when you push through your first wave.

b.   Out in the lineup, you should say your ABCs out loud every twenty minutes. That way you'll know when the hypothermia is setting in. Your speech will slur.

c.   Always have your car keys attached to a big key ring. That way you can use the key ring for leverage when you're trying to get the key in the car door with your frozen hands.

d.   Once, a couple of guys on the beach were so desperate for firewood after a surf session that they burned their own surfboards.

e.   One guy used to get the ice-cream headache so bad that he went to see his doctor about it. Doctor told him it was like a temporary seizure. The doctor's prescription: stay the hell out of freezing cold water. The guy couldn't very well do that, so he just started paddling out with a stick in his mouth to bite down on instead.

Now I'll tell you why I believe every word of this. Next morning, I found that I had left my wetsuit outside the car. Woke up to find it in a mud puddle. Wasn't till I tried to pick it up that I realized the mud puddle was frozen solid. I had to pee on it to get it unstuck. Then I wrestled into it and paddled out, trying to keep my hair dry. The shore break threw me around underwater. Did a good job of it, too. When I surfaced, I just sat there on my board, gripping the rails, wondering why my hands were on fire and trying for the life of me to figure out who hit me in the head with a baseball bat.

Then I vomited. Twice.

PART THREE: THE BULL, CRESCENT CITY, CA.

Head out past the Pelican Bay Prison, hang a right on Route 22, and look for the redwood burl stand about five miles in. These directions, that I'd scratched into the side of a Coca-Cola can with a flip-top, had been my only guide. You won't find the house of Greg Noll on any map. Greg Noll of the striped jailhouse shorts who, in December of 1969, rode what many at the time believed to be the largest wave ever surfed. Greg Noll. If ever a legend existed in surfing, here it was. The man who rode the biggest wave ever imagined and then walked away from the sport forever.

It was sheer luck that I'd found myself sitting in his backyard on a crisp fall night, overlooking the white hiss of the Smith River. In my hand, I was holding one of the strangest objects I had ever seen in my life. It was a man's whole thumb, hacked off at the base, entombed in a chunk of surfboard resin. The famous thumb of Ricky James the surfer. The one Ricky had accidentally cut off while sawing surfboard blanks at the old Greg Noll surfboard factory in Hermosa Beach, California. The story goes that Greg found it on the floor of his shop. Doctors didn't do that kind of surgery back then, so Greg decided to preserve it for posterity.

"All it took was a dixie cup and real hot batch of resin," Greg had told me.

I rolled the gruesome thing between my hands and thought back over the events of the last few days I'd spent at the Noll's. I had always been curious to see just where Greg Noll had gone to ground. The Greg

Noll outfit made some surfboards for my dad and my brother Sam when we lived in Hawaii. I was ten when Greg rode that giant wave not far from our house. I had always kept loose tabs on Noll's life ever since. I'd loved those boards.

I had been met at the gate of Greg's compound by his two giant dogs. The dogs were pretty excited; they'd just chased a black bear off into the redwood forest that surrounds the Noll place. The bear had been trying to get in at the dog food. The dogs saw me to the porch with what looked like pride in their step. Greg struck a prideful figure himself as he met me at the door. What with his six-foot-three, bare-chested frame propped up on some straining crutches. He was wearing only a down jacket, open to the waist, a pair of surf trunks, a cast on his lower right leg, and that famous ear-to-ear smile of his. I was reminded of the giant bass in that old story, when a little boy lands an old bass that has the scars and marks of a thousand great battles with fishermen on its body. And still has the hooks and lures of a few of them dangling from its mouth. The story goes that the boy was so moved by the sight that he cut his line, letting the bass go.

Greg grabbed my hand and pumped it; I was lucky to maintain my balance. Seems he remembered me after all this time.

"Oh, shit ya, I remember you! I got a memory like an elephant! Look like one too, these days! Age is bitch, man. Come on in! Come on in! My wife's making lasagna!"

He led me in and sat me down next to him on this huge bed he'd set up in his living room in front of the TV. He propped up his injured leg on a pillow.

"Busted it," was all he said about it.

Later, I learned Greg had broken his leg while trying to get at some old redwood. He'd been using the redwood to make antique surfboard replicas, an old hobby of his. If you can call it that, his replica's go for fifty k a pop. He'd been laid up for a while, but he'd laid up pretty well, surrounding himself with his needs and loves close at hand. Like the aquarium that bubbled at his elbow.

"I just really like fish. When you really think about it, they're a pretty neat deal!"

"Uh . . . yeah," was all I managed at that. Magazines like *WOODWORKER'S JOURNAL* and *COMMERCIAL FISHING QUARTERLY* littered the floor. Over the roaring hearth hung an enormous trophy trout that his youngest son had caught. There was also a gun rack that held a loaded 30.06 rifle.

"Just in case that stupid old bear comes back," Greg told me. "Just to scare him away; shit, I wouldn't wanna hurt the greedy bastard." Other than some fishing poles, that was about it. I didn't see a single surf photo up anywhere.

Only then was I introduced to the family as I sat on Greg's side of the bed. His wife Laura, his younger son Jedediah, and his daughter Ashlyne. His oldest son, Rhyn, had already moved out. Then Greg hauled himself to his feet and took me for a tour of the grounds. It was an impressive set-up. Out in the driveway, he had a couple of boats. One for his river guide business and another for those hairy coastal jaunts. Pacific Northwest waters kill humans regularly. In his backyard, he'd installed a koi pond and a lawn that overlooked a most picturesque view of the Smith River. He winked that the fishing wasn't too bad either at this particular bend in the river. The whole place felt less a home and more a lodge. Dug in.

The next couple of days I spent with Greg and his family. It turned out that his oldest son, Rhyn Noll, was the owner of the local surf shop and the builder of most the boards in the area. They were beautiful things, too.

"You know why?" Greg asked me of his son. "Because he's one of the last of the craftsmen, man. He shapes, glasses, and builds those sunzabitches from start to finish, just like I started out. It's the only way."

Ryhn had set up a corner of his retail surf shop as a museum to his father's career. Here were the photos, enshrined, the mementos, and yes, even those famous black-and-white striped trunks of his father's. The one's as famous as Waimea Bay itself. Rhyn had even kept the same sticker on his boards that his old man had used way back when.

I was shucking my wetsuit off on the cliff above the local break, watching Greg standing in the middle of the street, leaning heavily on his crutches. He had a look of glee on his face. He held in his hands the controls of Jedediah's miniature dune buggy and was maneuvering it wildly against a gravel berm. Jedediah, or "Pinch" as he is called by his father, was still in his wetsuit, capering after the thing, shrieking out directions to his dad. Rhyn was still out in the surf, all by himself. Greg's daughter, Ashlyne, playing hooky from high school, sitting on the hood of her car with a fellow truant. They had a transistor radio. Top forty countdown. The sun had come out for the first time in weeks. At that moment, I think all was well in the world for Greg Noll. A crisp slice of heaven. Later, I crouched down by Greg's koi pond and swirled my hand around a bit. A big orange one swam up and sucked on my finger. It was a quiet night out, still and fogless. Greg and I had stayed up late, just talking, picking at the leftover lasagna. He had just stumped off to bed on his crutches and I was considering the stars through boughs of the redwoods.

You know, to look Greg Noll in the eyes, late at night, in front of an outdoor wood fire is to look into the eyes of a spirit. I've seen this kind of thing before in my travels. I've seen it around sunset on the face of African Maasai chieftains, old pilots, and retired mountain climbers. On the face of World War II veterans, astronauts, grandads, my sister and other wise women. It's as if the soul finally surrenders the most honorable spirit that a person has had to call on so that it can be worn on the face like a mask. As if the deepest part of the soul remembers itself. As if it retires from where it was once needed so completely and so deeply within the heart, only to rest itself on a creased face for a few brief moments of wisdom.

The spirit Greg wore? The one I saw resting on his older face, that tired face? The most honorable our sport can offer. The spirit of courage. A spin-around-and-take-off-on-a huge-smoking-wave kind of courage. A drop-in-blind-on-a-monstrous-wall-of-water kind of courage. A bust-your-eardrums-held-underwater-till-you-choke kind of courage. Surfing's courage.

I looked up into the night sky. It was moonless, but softly lit by the mist of the Milky Way. The monolithic redwood trees around me sighed and held their secrets and I just kept rolling that weird chunk of resin around in my hands, trying to imagine all the wild waves that Greg Noll must have ridden in his lifetime. I don't know quite what it was about that night. Maybe it was a relief to know that places like this can exist. Little Valhalla's at the end of the road where our tribal elders can rest their spirits. Or maybe it was the vague feeling that my eyes had seen something. That my heart had brushed up against some holiness that exists in surfing. I don't know. Maybe it was just the fact that I still had both my thumbs. But I'll tell you this, ever since then, ever since that night, I've always believed in the afterlife just a little more.

But that it can only be found right here on earth.

PART FIVE: THE FOG

Damp, thick, pull-your-car-over-on-the-side-of-the-road-because-you-can't-see-shit fog. It affects every aspect of life up here. From being the reason redwoods are so goddamned big to the fact that fashion does not exist here. Down jackets, cableknit sweaters, Levi's and boots. That's it. The fog gets so thick that surfers get lost in the lineup. Have to wait for a set to wash them into the beach. Fog so thick that it's impossible to tell what time of day it is without a watch. Fog that can end daytime an hour and a half early. At a vista point overlooking the surf at Klamath cove, I came across the world's most optimistic description of fog. The placard read:

> *GROUND CLOUDS*
>
> *Literally earthbound clouds, fog is the pervasive weather phenomenon that sustains the redwood forest and dramatically alters your perceptions of the natural world. As the fog obscures your vision, explore exciting new ways to see. As the sea disappears behind the mists, find it again by listening. Welcome fog as an opportunity to cultivate a new and more intimate involvement with the world around you.*

Now go and try to tell that to some poor guy with a stick clamped between his teeth while he's waiting for some freezing-cold wave to blast him, hoping it will wash him up on the beach like a piece of driftwood.

PART SIX: ARCATA, CA.

Imagine what surfing would be like in a Lewis Carroll novel and you might get the idea of what it's like in California's logging country. Every surf a jaunt through an enchanted forest. Trees that tower so impossibly high that they make paddling out on to the Ocean a Lilliputian experience. It's the kind of place they bus in underprivileged inner-city kids just to blow their minds at the size of the things. There are redwood-bordered corners of the coastal highway here that have never felt the sun.

"Monarchs of the mists" they call the redwoods up here. Of course they've made it easy for the tourists to enjoy them as well. You don't even have to get out of your car. They've got trees you can drive through; they've got coin-operated chainsaws and logs aplenty to hack at, thirty seconds for a dollar. I even had one burl coffee table maker tell me that redwood would be the way to go if I wanted a real surfboard. I didn't have the heart to tell him that he was about a thousand years too late for that. So he just tried to sell me his life-sized redwood sasquatch instead. Couldn't really blame him. Not too many surfboards around these parts. Not too many surfers for that matter, either.

My brother Sam had joined me on my journey for a bit and we were in this diner called Babe's. So my brother orders a stack of flapjacks for breakfast. The menu called them "saddle blankets."

"A stack?" the white-haired waitress had said with a wry smile. "You sure about that, hon?" Puzzled, my brother said yes, of course. While we waited for our breakfast, I took a look around at Babe's decor. Someone had thoughtfully hung up a number of serving plate sized paintings depicting the mightiness of America. You know the type. Portraits of the John Wayne and Elvis, a bald eagle, a Harley-Davidson out on the open road. It took me a moment to figure out that these were not ivory plates at all but worn-out buzz saw blades. The folk art of the modern lumberjack. I also finally put it together that this joint was named after Paul Bunyan's blue pet ox.

The saddle blankets came short order. They were, quite literally, the size and thickness of competition frisbees. The stack of flapjacks stood almost a foot high and hung well over the blue plate, resting their edges on the bare table. Sam had ordered six of them. Apparently an order of one was the standard. Sam could only stare out from behind giant griddlecakes at the waitress. His hand had somehow managed to find the sticky maple syrup bottle. He just sat there holding it. The waitress didn't move. I didn't move. Nobody moved. The whole restaurant was looking at Sam waiting to see if he really would dig in. Just then, a real live lumberjack regarded us. His t-shirt read:

Run out of toilet paper?
Then go wipe your ass with a spotted owl.

Then he leaned over to Sam and said, "You ain't from around here, are you, son?"

PART SEVEN: THE SAN ANDREAS FAULT, BOLINAS, CA.

My heart went out to the kid. I used to hitchhike to the beach myself. Me and my brother, on rotten days just like this. Raining, wet, gray, cold. Yeah, the kid reminded me of myself standing out there in the middle of nowhere with his thumb out, hitchin' a ride to surf that resembled nothing that was in the surfing magazines. His board in a soggy, wax-spotted board bag cocked under his arm, a surf leash as a shoulder strap. I pulled over into the mud and the leaves and helped him put his board up on my racks.

"Name's Dale. I cut school," was all he said as he hopped in. I put him at about fifteen years old. I wheeled back onto the two-lane highway, winding my way down towards Stinson beach. He was pretty stoked to get out of the rain. Just to start conversation, I asked him where he was from. He told me vaguely that he was from somewhere "over the hill" and that I'd "never heard of it anyways." Then he asked me where I was living. And I told him. And his eyes lit up.

"Really?" he said. "Santa Barbara, really? Do you know Tom Curren?"

"Yeah," I said. "Why?"

"Huh! Why?" he said. "Well, maybe cuz the guy's the best surfer in the whole wide world!"

Dale went on from there to tell me he'd been "studyin'" Curren's technique. That he had his board colored like Curren's, had all his pictures up in his room, and that he wanted more than anything to be the world champion "just like Curren" someday. Dale was on a roll now, telling me of how he was "gonna start competin' and shit." How he was "gonna move to Santa Cruz someday, because you gotta make it there or you'll never make it." He told me he had never even been there yet, but he'd "seen all the pictures and shit." I listened. The kid had a dream, no doubt about that. We wound our way down into the town of Stinson beach and I made to pull over to a beach break there. Dale wouldn't have it.

"Listen, mister," he said. "You don't want to surf here. I know a better place; keep driving."

So I drove on. About ten minutes up the road, I pulled over to a small local market to pick up a sandwich. The kind of market with a creaking wooden floor from decades past. Dale came in with me. I saw him grab an apple, take two big bites out of it, and then put it back. He also ate a banana, stuffed another one into his windbreaker pocket. He opened a bag of potato chips, had a handful, put it back. Oreos the same. I saw all this by watching Dale in one of those big dome mirrors that little wooden-floor grocery stores have up in the rafters. I turned to the butcher behind the counter and told him to make that two sandwiches.

Dale actually bought a Snickers bar after pocketing another. I noticed he paid for the Snickers with quarters and dimes and that he took the three cents in change. Back in the car, I offered him the sandwich and a little carton of milk. He said he couldn't take it, couldn't pay for it. I told him that was all right.

He said, "Well . . . " and wolfed it down in silence. We drove on.

"Thanks, mister, that was good," he said. "Lot better'n we get back at the house."

There was something about the way he said it.

"The house?" I said.

"Yeah, the state house," he answered. "I live there with the other kids, guys like me, don't have no parents . . ."

He left it at that. So I did, too.

We made our way around the lagoon and through the small town of Bolinas. It had stopped raining and a dull sun was out in the evening cool. Dale directed me down to an old boat ramp at the end of town. We parked and hopped out to check the surf. It looked okay.

"See? What did I tell ya!" Dale said. "This here's the Patch. Been unreal ever since the earthquake."

"The what?"

"The earthquake," he said. "The San Francisco earthquake . . . you know, a while back. See, this here's where the fault line runs out into the Ocean. After the quake, that right peak out there started working . . . " And with that he ran back to the car for his board.

The kid was right. I was standing smackdab on top of the San Andreas fault in the exact spot where it leaves land and stretches out into the sea. I looked out onto the oddly shaped surf. Swells would hump up here and there, feathering, threatening to break, and then they'd back off. But one spot seemed shallow enough and sure enough an occasional swell would cap over it. I walked back to the car. Dale was already in his wetsuit. It was old and worn and he had outgrown it, the legs of the thing ending long before his ankles started. He crammed all his clothes back into his wet backpack and then shoved it all under a hedge by the car. He threw a handful of leaves over it.

"Hey, thanks, mister," he said. "For the ride and the sandwich and all. See you down in Santa Cruz someday." Then he pumped my hand once, said, "Later . . ." and ran off toward the surf. And as he ran off, I think I saw him for the first time. The tattered wetsuit, ripped up to one knee. His dinged-up board, once a single fin, now a backyard three-fin thruster. And he'd told the truth. His board was colored just like Curren's. Except that anyone could tell he'd done it himself with a magic marker. The scene made me think of some of the surfers his age that I knew in southern California. Kids with new boards, Astrodeck, leashes, the latest wetsuits, the latest magazines, the latest videos, nice parents who give them rides to the beach, the high school surf teams they belong to, warm water, better surf, the easier lives, and all the modern dreams and gilded promises that go with it. And then I watched Dale paddle out into the freezing surf in a wetsuit that couldn't possibly be doing him any good. I thought of how far he'd hitchhiked to be here: about forty miles. Of what he'd had to eat that day. Of what he was going home to afterwards. And of how he was going to get there. It made me think of what his chances were of making his dreams come true, the long odds.

Then I thought of how many other surfers were out there up against the same kind of odds. Born under a bad sign, picking this world up by the feet and shaking the coins out of its pockets, three cents at a time. Trying their best to ignore the meanness of it all. Trying to get something going, trying real hard, doing whatever it takes. And all the while living on the fault line of their own dreams. Dreams that, at any moment, this mean old world was likely to shift and shake and reduce to rubble.

Out in the surf, I saw Dale spin and start paddling for the first wave of a set. He dropped in and bottom-turned and sped down the line. He wasn't half bad. And I found myself smiling.

May the great spirits bless the survivors of this world.

They're all we'll have in the end.

PART EIGHT: OCEAN BEACH, SAN FRANCISCO

The personal ad in the San Francisco Chronicle read:

GWM'S SEEKING THE SAME FOR THE SAN FRANCISCO SECRET SOCIETY OF SURFERS (SFSSS). Meetings will include fun, sun, tan dudes, and perfect tubes. Goofy-foots need not apply. (Only kidding guys, don't be shy.) Send photo of surfboard.

I was in San Francisco for the week so I took a polaroid of one of my boards and slipped it into an envelope, explaining that I was a writer for *SURFER Magazine*. I dropped the envelope off on the front desk of the *San Francisco Chronicle* newspaper. I got a call back the next day. The voice said his name was Dick.

Right. So I explained who I was again and that I was interested in hearing what his secret society of surfers had to say. No, I assured him, there would be no photographs taken, nor anything but first names used. He said in that case, it would be a kick to be in *SURFER Magazine* and that he and his group would be glad to meet me and go surfing. We agreed on that afternoon.

I parked where I said I would. Through my windshield it looked a dreary day down at Ocean Beach. The fog started about three stories up, the sidewalks were wet even though it hadn't rained, a flock of pigeons were battened down behind the seawall, and there was some guy with a cardboard hat on his head peeing in a garbage can off to my left. An old Chinese man, holding a straightened wire coat hanger and big plastic bag full of cans and bottles, waited patiently for him to finish. I could see a small group of surfers out on the water, black wetsuited dots bobbing on a frigid, slate-gray sea. The surf was small and ragged, the beach abandoned. I looked at my watch. I was early. I stepped out of my car, walked across the parking lot to Mustard Mike's kiosk, and bought his last Louisiana hot dog. I sat eating it on the hood of my car. A powder blue 1980 BMW 320i coupe, with a surfboard strapped to its roof, pulled up next to me and out of it stepped a man. He was about six-foot-two and looked like Jim Morrison's younger brother. It was Dick, except his real name was Devlin. Devlin was thirty-two years old and a greenskeeper at the Golden Gate Golf Course. Devlin and I paddled out together. I met the rest of the crew out in the lineup. There was Gary, lawyer; Steve, waiter; Carl, schoolteacher; Christopher, cop; Danny, antique dealer; and Joshua. He was seventeen, unemployed. When I asked him where he was from, he said the place didn't exist for him anymore. I stopped prying. We all surfed together, trading waves for about an hour or so before the fog set in earnest. Then we all headed back up to the cars and got dressed in the parking lot and everybody agreed on a coffee shop they all dug. I observed that a few of the men had brought Joshua some things. A new backpack full of food, a t-shirt and some new jeans, an envelope of what I assumed was money. A short while later, I'm in the Castro district of San Francisco with an Irish coffee, a tape recorder, and a slice of raspberry pie in front of me. We rapped for two hours. Mostly surf talk, who was the best ever and all that. But my day with the San Francisco Secret Society of Surfers, which I was recording, ended exactly like this:

MG: So, why was the society formed?

DEVLIN: Brotherhood. It was started about two years ago by a guy named Alex. He just wanted to get a surf team together.

CHRISTOPHER: Yeah. Yeah, I mean being a surfer makes you different anyway, right? So with us we just thought we'd add to that by getting together.

MG: Discrimination out in the surf?

DANNY: Are you out of your mind? [Laughs all around.] Do you know how many gay surfers there are in the world? Thousands and thousands. [Mocking Boris Karloff.] They're everywhere!

GARY: That's one of the good things about surfing. Out in the Ocean, it just doesn't matter. Everyone's having a good time. Everyone's happening, just digging on the energy. Gay, straight, crazy, the Ocean's a place it doesn't matter.

MG: What do you think straight surfers would think if they knew who was gay and who wasn't?

JOSHUA: They'd probably be a bunch of jerks.

STEVE: Oh, I don't know about that. Surfers are cool.

JOSHUA: Not that cool.

MG: How do you mean?

JOSHUA: Look how they treat women.

DEVLIN: Yeah, but that's just the macho element.

JOSHUA: What other element is there, Dev? Alex fought that one for us more than once.

CARL: [Quietly] Yeah. Sure did. [To me.] You said that surfing's closest relative is bullfighting. That's a pretty macho relative.

DANNY: The macho thing is one of the reasons I was attracted to surfing in the first place. The guys are fun-loving, in great shape, hip, handsome . . . I think it's got something to do with the saltwater. Makes your teeth straight or something. [Laughs all around.]

DEVLIN: This club of ours isn't about outing anybody. Never was. And were not in the closet either. This is only a small group of us. Our membership is up to about twenty-five. We're not here to make some political stand. We do enough of that on our own. Danny and Carl and Steve here are ACT UP [AIDS Coalition to Unleash

Power]. The rest of us are involved politically. But this surf club is about relaxing. Letting our hair down. Going surfing. Just gettin' some waves together. [Murmurs of approval all around.]

JOSHUA: Say something 'bout Alex, Dev.

DEVLIN: Yeah, Alex. He is the inspiration. A great surfer. Older than all of us. And he's tellin' us to keep this thing going. And to protect it. Not to expose it for everyone to ridicule. And not to turn it into some bathhouse thing either. He just told us to get together and go surfing now and then and to feel good about it. He says that in the end, that's all that really matters, feeling good about things. About ourselves.

MG: Where is Alex? Could he join us?

At this point the table goes silent. Everyone is looking at Joshua. Joshua slumps his shoulders and hangs his head. Carl puts his hand on the back of Joshua's neck in comfort. It seems to be Joshua's job to answer the question.

JOSHUA: [Speaking to the floor] No, Alex can't join us today. He . . . uh . . . doesn't surf anymore. He . . . um . . . he's in County. The Hospital. County Hospital. (Pause) Fuckin' virus. It's taking so long with him. Why is it takin' so long with him, huh? Answer me that!"

Silent moments pass.

Then Joshua shudders and begins to weep.

I reach over and turn off my recorder.

PART NINE: PACIFIC GROVE, CA

It looked a lonely place to die. A lonely way to die. The coldest, cruelest, most horrifying way any surfer has had to die. I gazed out over the kelp beds, oily and wet under a bruised sky. Great rafts of the brown kelp, pungent and graceful, undulated silently, as if serpents were roiling around beneath them. The swell was blown out, chunky, about six foot at the reef. No one was out. It would be a long, spooky paddle out to the break. For Lew Boren, it was his last.

You remember Lew. If you don't, you should. Lew Boren was the surfer who, on December 19, 1981, paddled out by himself at this very spot. He never made it back in. Later, when his surfboard washed up, it was confirmed that he had been attacked by a great white shark. A mammoth shark. Judging by the bite radius found taken out of his board, it may have been the largest white shark to have ever attacked anyone in recorded history. Twenty foot. Maybe more. A submarine with teeth. Imagine that.

I did. As I stood there looking out over where Lew Boren was eaten. I could remember the national uproar it caused, the sensational press. Every major paper and TV station in the country covered the story. I'd always remembered the feature story in ROLLING STONE. I could even remember the artwork that they ran with the article. It was, more than any photograph, more than any movie I'd ever seen, the most chilling depiction of a shark attack I had ever seen. I ripped it out of the magazine and pinned it up on my wall. It was an artist's underwater head-on view of a monster shark cruising slowly, perfectly, through some nighttime kelpy shallows. It was a sinister, image that made you remember these giants are pure, malevolent silence. You could make out the shark's shadow on the sand just inches below its belly. Pale moonlit shafts shot down from the surface and dappled its great, broad back. And it might have been called a beautiful painting, if not for the gore and blood, diluted pinkish by the sea, streaming from its gills and then down alongside the gray of its body. So disturbing was the image that my girlfriend, upon seeing it, ripped it down and burned it over our gas stove.

I have often thought of that image since then. Being here brought it back. Along with the thought that the magnificent, deadly creature that had Lew Boren was still out there. That there was a pretty good chance that tonight, it would be cruising silently through the shallows, perfect and unknowing of the horror in its wake, uncaring, shafts of moonlight dancing on its back.

I remembered reading somewhere that boxing was considered the last mighty sport on earth, the last great primal sport because it is the last arena where murder is legal, where one man may beat another to death with no reprisal. And that boxers who have died in the ring should be exalted for belonging to such a rare breed of man. Blessed with ultimate sacrifice, peered only with the honored dead of soldiers and sailors.

Well then, what is to be said of surfing? The last sport on earth where it is possible to be eaten alive by a sea monster? By a great, powerful, stealthy descendant of dinosaurs, out for blood and meat? How mighty does that make a surfer? How primal our sport? And how should we exalt those who have died in our arena by our ultimate sacrifice? What about our honored dead? Surfers like Lew Boren?

I found myself staring glassy-eyed out over the tide pools. I had to shake my head to clear it. The fog was rolling in now, clinging wet, lonely wet. A chill was setting in. Out there somewhere, the first foghorn sounded. I turned and walked back to my car.

I felt like I'd just visited a graveyard.

PART TEN: WILLOW CREEK, BIG SUR, CA.

There is a group of ex-Woodstock hippies who live in a psychedelic school bus and travel up and down the Big Sur Coast. They make their way by hanging out at tourist vista points, offering to paint people's faces. They do this during the winter months, the renaissance fairs and Grateful Dead concerts being back in spring. If you're cool, they'll sell you one of their edible hashpipes made out of Starburst candies. If you're even cooler, they'll turn you on. And if you're cool but don't know it yet, they'll share their lunch with you and turn you on without you knowing it. If you accept their invitation to dine, you will have no choice because they put psilocybin mushrooms in the macrobiotic salads they eat two times a day. If this happens to you, you will come to about five hours later and find yourself lying on the ground next to their magic bus with your shirt off, and your chest and face painted with zebra stripes, stars, and sunbursts. Red unicorns will be painted on the top of each of your feet. The hippies will then all smile at you. You will feel as if you've just stepped off a flying saucer. I know this because it happened to me. This band of gypsies calls themselves "The Ocean People." And every one of them surfs.

Naked.

PART ELEVEN: MONTANA DE ORO STATE PARK, LOS OSOS, CA.

He had about ten pounds on me, but he was younger so I just slapped him. His one friend stepped back, looking shocked, and said, "Whoa . . . " The guy I'd slapped just stood there with a surprised look on his face. I stepped by him and continued down the trail to go surfing. My whole surf session was ruined, I knew that, but I had to go out and catch at least one wave, just to prove my point if nothing else. How much I hated territorialism, localism, in surfing.

"Hey, asshole, you live around here? You don't live here, you don't surf here, man," was all he'd had time to say to me. *Slap.*

What the hell would he know? He hadn't survived the range wars of the mid-seventies around these parts like I had. He wasn't the real thing. I could see that plain as day in his eyes. He'd just heard about it somewhere, so he figured it was cool to pop off. A pop-culture local.

I was enraged. I'd lived through all those years in this area when localism was at its most toxic. And even then I'd learned that surfers are just a bunch of mice that roar. Chest-thumping about, threatening violence, posturing like zoo gorillas. But when it came down to it, when it really came down to it, nothing ever amounted to much more than a few flattened tires, cowardly done while no one was watching, and a few boards being kicked at one another in the surf. Surfers just ain't that bad. For all the braying I'd heard, I'd only seen two surf-related fist fights in the years that I lived here. One was between two brothers, and the other was because this one guy didn't like the way this other guy was talking about his ex-wife.

Californian localism. What a paper tiger. I wonder what we would find if we took a consensus of just how many violent acts, due purely to localism, have ever taken place. I'd like to put that figure up against the wide scale intimidation that thousands have felt and take a hard look at just what the hell we're really up against. Not much, I'd wager. Let's face it. We're not killers.

I paddled out and caught my wave. Made my way back up to my car. Just as I'd finished changing, the kid I'd slapped stepped up with his friend again. I guess he figured he was going to take another crack at this localism thing. I could smell that his friend had goaded him into it. Now, I ain't that bad either, God knows, but I'd really had a belly full. And I didn't know what this guy had, but I figured it was worth the chance. So, without giving him a chance to say anything, I spun quickly and made to belt him in the mouth. I stopped just before I hit him. He had jumped back, surprised again. He stood there, not sure what to do. He didn't come in at me. Didn't say anything either. I shook my head at the sight.

"I thought so . . ." was all I said. Then I threw my wetsuit into my truck, stepped into the cab, and drove off. Once I'd pulled away to a safe distance, I heard him yell:

"Fuck you! LA kook!" I looked in my rear-view mirror, saw him bend down, pick up a rock, and whip it at me. He missed by a mile.

On purpose.

PART TWELVE: JALAMA STATE PARK, CA

We lay in a bowl of sand. That warm wind was still coming out of the inland valley and pushing against the surf. The waves were lime-green and white-fringed and anyone who caught one was envied. You could mind-surf all of them. But we'd already done that. And we'd already surfed since noon, Steve Hansen and myself. We'd just walked back from up the beach and plopped ourselves down on this berm overlooking the carpark beach break. Steve and I decided to just hang for a bit, no particular hurry to get home.

I'd known Steve. We were both there on the cusp when pro surfing was just coming home to California. 1979, 1981, somewhere around there. We were both on the same track at that time, both wanting to be professional surfers so bad we could barely sleep. We were getting there, too. Passion like that never goes unanswered. Steve got his answer sooner than he thought he would. It wasn't the one he wanted. Five days after taking fifth at the Stubbies Trials in San Diego, five days after signing a sponsorship deal with O'Neill wetsuits and Channel Island surfboards, it all caved in. Steve was running back to get his wetsuit out of his backyard, having heard that Rincon was firing, when the old redwood fence he was climbing over collapsed beneath him. He couldn't believe his eyes when he crawled out of the wreckage and looked at his arm. Two bloody bones were sticking out of it just behind the wrist: the ulna and the radius. The ulna had a divot of grass hanging from it. It took him a few seconds to realize that they were his own bones. That it was his own forearm. That he had suffered a severe compound fracture.

The doctors said he was lucky. At least they had saved the limb. I asked him about it now in the quiet, now that we were both older. I had been around the world surfing professionally. He'd become a landscape gardener. He and I had never talked about that much.

"My arm made all my decisions for me," he said. "I lost years on that, lost my sponsorship, everything. Had to go back to college, finish my art degree." The thought trailed off and I let it go. He brought it back after about a minute. "It's just one of those things I block out. I'm not bitter about the injury. I guess I'm just more bitter about not having any guidance through all that. Once I got hurt, I was on my own."

Steve had always kept surfing. He graduated from college and went on to become a mixed medium artist of some renown. His work was seen in a major LA gallery called, ironically enough, The Marc Richards Gallery. Change the C to K and you have an art gallery with the same name of surfing's legendary four-time world champion. Steve always laughed at that. Over the years, he had also become a wistful observer of the Santa Barbara surfing scene. I asked him if I'd missed much since I had been gone the last few weeks.

"Nah, not really. Same old problems. What's wrong with Santa Barbara surfing is what's wrong with Santa Barbara in general. It's just too nice a place to live."

I thought about that for a minute.

"Look, it's like this: the younger generation around Santa Barbara has just one place to go, and that's down. These kids grow up with perfect surf, perfect weather, beautiful surroundings, beautiful people, wealth . . . most people work all their lives to have that and these kids are burned out on it by the time they graduate from high school. It softens 'em. There's no ghetto urge to keep climbing when you got it all in the palm of your hands. When it comes to ambition, paradise just isn't that great a place to come from . . ."

What about our world champion, Tom Curren? I asked.

"Perfect point," Steve said. "Comes a time in Santa Barbara where you either break out or shut it down. Tommy came THIS close to being a casualty. If he didn't have that machine behind him, his mom driving him around, and Channel Islands and Al Merrick guiding him and giving him boards and all, he probably would have shut it down. And then he got smart. He split. And he ain't never coming back. But you know who Tom Curren's mirror was? A guy named Tim Smalley. Perfect example. Tim Smalley shut it down. He's still here, doing God-knows-what drugs. It's a tedious story. And I always thought that Tim's surfing was better at the time than Tommy's. A lot of people did. And Tim threw it all away. All this comfort around here and niceness just fragments these kids' passions. Too easy; nothing to fight for. Yeah, Tom Curren was real lucky to escape this. It took more than just his talent to get him out of here, it took guidance . . ."

Guidance from where? I said.

Steve paused and I got the feeling that maybe I'd brought up the subject of his arm again. Steve was fiddling with some sticks in his hand that he had fashioned into a cross and stuck in as a center piece in a small pile of pebbles he'd collected. He finished it, looked at it, and then turned the cross so that it faced the surf. It stood about twelve inches tall and the whole thing, honest to god, belonged in an art gallery. He looked out at the surf, scratching the itch of his pink, lumpy keloid scars on his forearm, and said, "I don't know . . . from the Universe, maybe . . . "

We sat in silence. I was thinking about all he said. I agreed with every word of it. I was also thinking about all the things he didn't say. And I agreed with all that too. I felt for my friend. Looking at Steve Hansen made me think about all those guys out there who once had everything it took to be one of the best. Everything, that is, except luck, or a roll of the dice, or guidance from the Universe, or whatever it is that a young man needs to chip a flint spark into tinder and flame. I thought about them all, out there, working away at whatever jobs life had shunted them into, whatever lifestyles, whatever marriages or kids or careers. Working away with that little bug in the back of their heads that whispers to them now and then at the most unexpected times . . . "What if? Can you imagine what it would have been like, if only . . . if only . . . if only . . ."

I looked over at Steve again; he was staring out past the surf at some far-off place that didn't even exist anymore. I could see the dusk sky reflected in his sunglasses. Made me wonder if that little bug would ever get any easier for him to live with. I hoped so.

But I doubted it.

PART THIRTEEN: LEDBETTER BEACH, SANTA BARBARA, CA

She told me her name was Seraphim. "My mother named me that, after the highest order of Catholic angels, you know." She certainly looked the part. Radiant smile, a barefoot five foot ten, lovingly formed. One couldn't help but notice, what with the Brazilian bikini. I had met her in the shore break when I'd swam in for my surfboard. She was, quite literally, rolling around in the sand. She told me she loved to come down and just lie in the surf at sunset. Just to remind her that she had actually made it.

"I'm an American dream," she said. "A living, breathing Bruce Springsteen song."

That made sense too, once I heard her story. Seems she was originally from Waukesha, Wisconsin. Grew up Midwestern, dreaming of making it out to the West Coast one day. She wanted nothing more than the California dream.

"I had surf posters on my walls. I dreamed of warm sand, palm trees and lifeguards, just like in all those movies."

Her chance finally came the day she turned twenty-one. It was the day she'd set for her escape ever since she was a little girl. She saved up all her money from babysitting for single mothers and from her graveyard shift as a security guard at the Waukesha Savings and Loan.

"I helped guard the Brinks trucks. You know, those big things full of gold bars?" She told me, "The kind you can't touch? It was like working in hell, I guess. So close to freedom and you can't even think about it."

She had made her way out west by bus with a single suitcase. "Just like in all those movies. Kansas City, Amarillo, a real Route 66 type thing." The bus she was on had a final destination called Santa Barbara, California. It sounded good to her. "Though at that point, any old beach would have done." Fresh off the bus, she got a job the same day at an ice cream factory. The manager even rented her a room out back. "And here I am," she said. I asked her what she thought of it all.

"Well," she answered, "I thought the water was going to be a lot warmer, that's for sure. And I thought the beaches would be more crowded and I thought all the surfers would be bigger, you know? Like in all those movies or something. But they all look so small to me, like little kids. And not many of them are that blond. I thought there would be more girls on the beaches, too, but that's okay, I like it here just fine anyway."

I asked her if there were a lot of people like her where she came from.

"Oh, sure, plenty, but not all of them have got the guts to come out here," she said proudly. "Not hardly any of them got the guts."

I asked her what she was thinking of doing.

"I'm not sure," she said. "It's like all those songs I've heard; it's just a destiny thing at this point. I'm just rolling with the punches. Seems like everyone in California just wants to be rich and famous. Me? I'd rather be famous. It really is the land of opportunity for pretty girls like me; that's one of the things that all those movies didn't lie about. I figure I'll get around to all that. Maybe writing or modeling or acting. I don't know, depends." She left it at that. But she told me she'd been writing some poetry. I told her I was a writer.

"Oh!" she said. "Are you famous?"

"Not really," I said.

"That's okay," she said. Then she asked me if I'd like to read one of her poems. I said I sure would. She pulled a notebook out of her beach bag and showed me the poem she'd written after swimming in the Pacific Ocean for the very first time. It read:

> A gritty sensation
>   cups my back and rear
>   as the lines of my body mold the sand.

Waves of blue salt
  kiss my toes, then retreat
  over and over again.
Rhythms, like that of two lovers,
  touch me repeatedly
  then evaporate, leaving a salty residue.

She watched me read it three times in a row. She asked me if I liked it. I answered yes, very much. Then I asked her if she had had a chance to learn how to surf.

"Not yet," she said, raising one eyebrow, holding me with her eyes. She was very proud of her audacity. And I smiled back, proud of it, too. And then, in the final golden glow of another California day, we both turned and watched the sun go down.

Just like in all those movies.

PART FOURTEEN: RINCON DEL MAR, CA.

There is a low stone wall out on the point at Rincon Del Mar where a Santa Barbara surfer can watch his world wake up. I went there very early the next day. I took off my backpack, set down my surfboard, and hopped up onto this low stone wall that retained one of the many billionaire houses that line the point. They hadn't let the dog out yet. The dawn was blushing pink on the horizon. The surf was absolutely perfect, brushed gently by a land breeze that tailored the dark, marching walls into a tumbling magic. The crack of a lip, the hissing of whitewater, the rumbling of the polished stone rubble on shore as each wave washed over them. The smell of the sea at dawn, like no other. That crispy, secret smell. And dawn light, the candlelight of surfing, casting a spell on it.

I watched another set of waves approach. A herd of surfers, looking like marauding seals in their slick, dark wetsuits, were already out in the cold. I could feel them all paddling for the approaching waves. Feel it in my shoulders. I really could. I silently urged one of them into the best wave of the set. He didn't make the drop. I reached down and started to get my wetsuit right side out. I had returned to Santa Barbara two days before, ending my journey that took me from the northern border of California over what felt like a million miles of coastline and people and life to this very spot. My home. My home surf break. I couldn't feel as if my journey were over until I'd come here. To this little stone wall that had witnessed so much of surfing's history at one of the greatest surfing breaks in the world.

Another set of waves pumped through. The sky was yellowing now. It wouldn't be long before the warmth would come and the mystery of the dawn would slip away. Already a steady stream of surfers was jogging up the point, throwing themselves into the Ocean one by one. I looked up from my wetsuit to see my older brother Sam taking off deep on a wave. I watched him surf it all the way to the inside of the break, the tips of the spray from his maneuvers reaching into the yellow sunlight. I took my time getting into my wetsuit. Then I stuffed my backpack under some driftwood, put my board under my arm, and stepped down onto the rocks to paddle out to join him. And the moment the water rushed up over my knees, my journey was over. To be honest, I didn't feel like a surfer. I felt like a tired priest.

Too many confessions.

SAM GEORGE, TOM CURREN, AUTHOR; SUMMERLAND, CA

THE PRIVATE
WORLD OF
TOM CURREN

SURFER MAGAZINE, USA, 1985

One of my earliest features, and it shows. But from the first second I saw Tom surf, I knew he was going to become a world champion. We all did. And in the end, he bagged three titles. Through the years, my friendship with Tom has been, at times, both loving and strained. The blurred lines of being a friend and a surf journalist is always shaky. I like to think we got through it. This was my first feature on Tom. I would not write another profile on Tom for over thirty years. —Mg.

January 29, 1985 — 6:02 p.m.

The horizon is swallowing a late January sun as a small gray truck pulls into Rincon Del Mar's deserted upper lot. The sky is aflame. The truck door opens and a twenty-year-old man, wearing only worn sweatpants and a watch, steps out onto the gravel. Arms akimbo, he looks east towards the Santa Ynez mountains. He stares at the hills. They look like giant waves, frozen in green and black. He begins walking west across a scrubby lawn towards the cliff stairs, rubbing warmth into his arms against the chill. His hair is a tousled dirty blond. He is barefoot.

Down on the beach, he and the dusk are alone. Feet crunch through the low-tide sand crust as he paces out a hundred yards. A simple line is drawn with his heel. Then three deep breaths before he crouches down into a sprinter's start and stares at that piece of driftwood 100 yards away. He is leaving for Costa Rica in the morning. He is going to see his dad for the first time in more than two years. Tomorrow, Pat and Tom Curren, father and son, will be out in the left-breaking waves of a private ranch point, both doing what they do best: surfing. Together. Again.

BANG!

He explodes up and out, forcing himself into the rhythm of his first sprint. He's breathing. Six seconds, seven seconds, breathing, nine, ten, then the last effort and the warmth of winding it down. Tom comes to a stop, shakes it all off, feels pretty good, and readies for his next. He crouches.

His wife Marie will be with him this time in Costa Rica. *Thank heavens she and Dad get along,* he thinks. *And no wetsuits in the middle of winter down there. That's good.*

BANG!

Three seconds, four, five, six, seven, breathing, stepped on something, nine, ten, pain, eleven, TWELVE. He takes it down. He checks his heel. Piece of glass. Not bad though. He picks it out. Dime-sized blood. No problem. There is a song playing in his head. The Who. *Sparks*. Live version. He air-drums along.

Dark dusk. He readies for sprint three. He has yet to surf the giant waves of Waimea Bay in Hawaii. His father has. Plenty. Became a legend for it in the late '50s. It was different for his dad. It was physical, the equipment crude. But it took some glorious dedication to massive waves. Chuck Yeager territory. Tom remembers what his father said it took to ride the hills: "a lot of rail, and a lot of guts." Chasing that demon out in the thin air, all the right stuff.

BANG!

Three seconds, four, breathing, seven, eight, breathing, legs pumping, ten, eleven, twelve, thirteen, FOURTEEN. He gulps at the air, lousy start, a look at the watch. A slow one. Can't allow that. Number four. He crouches again into a start position and remembers. The first glimpse he had of his father surfing Waimea was with popcorn in his hands staring at *Goin' Surfin'* flickering across a veterans' hall too-small screen. Pat Curren footage. It looked impossible.

BANG!

Sand flies from the pads of his feet, three seconds, four, breathing, five, six, breathing, eight, nine, ten, ELEVEN. Fast stop. He plops down and drinks the air. He recovers quickly. Better, good. Tom stands up, looks out to sea. Crappy surf for two days now. A marginal left-breaking wave crumbles in. Tom imagines himself surfing it. It closes out. He turns to toe the line. This is number five. Six more to go. Then home. He readies himself. Thoughts. Costa Rica.

The estranged, world-wandering, peasant dad. He looks at his toes for a time; eyes fixed, he raises his head as the answer forms: take it as it comes.

BANG!

It's dark now as Tom pads his way up the stairs and over to his car.

He feels better for the sprints. A glance at his watch puts a hurry in his step; another glance, a jog. Tom, twenty years old, has just remembered something as he hops in the truck, and it gives him a good excuse to spin the tires and punch it. A newlywed, his wife Marie will have dinner ready by now. And he was going to be late for an interview.

February 15, 1985 — 7:02 p.m.

American Tommy and French Marie, both still twenty, are back from Costa Rica. They have invited me over for dinner. It will be our last chance to talk before they leave for Australia. My last meeting with Tom took place on the eve of his trip down to Costa Rica, and it was a bit odd. Over the years, I had never seen him nervous. That night, his gestures were quick and the music was never quite right; Tommy was preoccupied with the cassette tapes. Springsteen, no, Sade. Wrong again. The Who? Forget it. He finally decided on nothing.

Then something curious. Later on, when we were walking to my car, I asked Tom if his father had taught him how to surf. The answer came slow.

"Well . . . uh . . . no. I taught myself about fourteen years ago. My father was there, though. He just sort of stood back and watched."

He just watched?

"Um, uh . . . yes . . . I like to think so . . . Listen, uh, let's talk when I get back from Costa Rica; I'll have more answers then." More answers? I had been wondering what he meant by that for twenty-six days.

This time, we're sitting in Tommy's brand-new condominium, bought with his latest sponsorship money. All three of us are sitting at the new dinner table and eating Chinese take-out. We are having fun with Marie's recent win at the Rincon Classic Surf Contest. A quick look around reveals a cozy affair: Tom's first real home. The surf influence is understated. Thoughtful photo art hangs. The Empire State Building. A couple Henri Cartier Bresson classics. The famous Steve Bissell shot of Rincon Del Mar, a gift from the photographer from the housewarming party depicting the long lines of a big Pacific swell warping in around the point of the famous surf break. A break only seven minutes away by car. In the open kitchen, the refrigerator enshrines surfing. Cute little magnets pinning up cut-out photos of Tom's more recent exploits. The whole place, from overstuffed bookcase to lived-in kitchen, doesn't exactly shout that it houses one of the world's greatest surfers.

Tom is his old self tonight, like an intelligent puppy in a constant state of curious orientation. His mischievous side surfaces when I ask him how he thinks he will fare Down Under. He fingers a plastic-wrapped fortune cookie thoughtfully.

"Well ... let's see ..." He rips the thing open with his teeth. He opens just about everything with his teeth. Drives Marie crazy. Tom pulls out the fortune and looks perplexed. He hands it to me. LUCK IS COMING YOUR WAY.

It is easy to see that the most important thing in Tommy and Marie's life is each other. In 1981, a cute little French surf girl, visiting friends in America, literally bumps into Tommy Curren at the Channel Islands surf shop on State Street in Santa Barbara, California. They are both sixteen. They go surfing. They fall in love. But by this time, Marie has to go home. This launches a two-way international campaign of letters, phone calls, and jet-set visits to France and Hawaii. It lasts for two years, backlit by Tom's mercurial rise in the surfing community. It all leads to 1983 and, in Tom's own words, "the most difficult phone call of my life. I had to call Marie and tell her that I was a professional surfer now and going to Australia again and that I ... um ... well, probably wouldn't be seeing her for a long, long time. At 8:00 p.m., I called over to France and told her. Then at 9:00 p.m., I called her back, told her to forget everything I just said, and asked her to marry me. I was nineteen. Two months later, I won the Australian Grand Slam and married Marie in Australia. It was ... well, a pretty good year." They both tell the story, often checking facts with each other in French. Tom learned the language as a gift. It affords them the luxury of privacy in certain crowds. And this privacy, I sense, is paramount.

During a private moment with Marie in the kitchen, she says to me, "Everybody thinks Tom is so mellow. That the competition isn't important. That it just happens because he is so good. But that is not true. Tommy is intense. He gets up early and goes to the playground to jump on and off the merry-go-round just to strengthen his legs. Things like that. He wants this. He wants to be the best in the world."

When the conversation turns to surfing, Tom gets thoughtful and Marie puts a stop to his nail chewing. He weighs each word carefully, pausing frequently. "It goes way past recreation. It's as close as you can get to living a primal scream. Good surfing is all a matter of channeling the wave's energy to your board, using your body as the conduit. " He cites 1978 World Champion Rabbit Bartholomew as an early influence and the originator of his patented right-arm, follow-through re-entry and "double pump" bottom turn on the face of a wave. Employing this technique "allows power with style." Tom's starting to warm up a little. "I've always appreciated the radical and I get as vertical as I can. It's just that I . . . believe that a little control and a touch of class goes a long way. Aerials are not a functional maneuver, yet. It's the barrel roll that has potential. They are definitely in the future, along with the . . . well, the refinement of re-entry controls." He talks like an absent-minded professor, playing with his toes, tossing a coin, and sometimes thinking out loud in French. Surrounded by his quiver of surfboards, Tom Curren's words become a metaphor for his surfing. Thoughtful, radical, original. All borne on the undercurrent of a remarkable intelligence and a strong sense of the aesthetic. It's a different Tommy than the media has depicted. Here on his own ground, you begin to understand the inner workings. The passion, a drive. This man, who in the media is described as "low key," "enigmatic," "a man of few words," is, in reality, a man on fire.

On the pro surfing tour: "Keeping it together is the responsibility of the surfers themselves. Not the other way around. In some countries, say Australia, it is better to depict surfing as a competitive thing, like tennis. But in other countries, like France, the carnival atmosphere goes down better. I think that the organizers and the surfers should recognize this and work together as sort of an adaptable traveling festival of events, music, competition—you know."

On the Hawaiian scene: "I think that there has always been an animosity there because most everyone goes to Hawaii in full force, just stomps all over it, and then leaves. That is wrong. My father didn't do that. I certainly never will."

At this point, Tommy and Marie are curled up in the corner on an inflatable guest room mattress. All his words are spoken carefully. There isn't a trace of anger or force in them. These are, to him, simple matters of fact.

On his Christianity and personal history: "It's a simple, private belief within me. It's based on strengths, not weaknesses. I was twelve and a half years old and going down the wrong street in life. My mom got me out of that. From there, it was a pretty standard history for a competitive surfer. WSA, NSSA, World Amateur Title, going pro. Then I took Shaun Tomson's [1977 world champion] example and waited for a strong sponsorship that would afford longevity. Al [Al Merrick, owner of Channel Islands Surfboards and quasi-manager] and I finally decided on Op, Rip Curl, and Bucci sunglasses. It's what I always wanted . . . real sponsorship. Professionalism."

On happiness: "Oh, well [sitting up, kneading his right shoulder— this demands real attention], I have definitely found what I want, what I always wanted in my personal life, definitely. Marie, the travel, and the, you know, financial stuff." He thinks for a moment. "But no, I am not satisfied with my surfing yet. I am looking to improve my Hawaiian performances and [difficulty, then pushing on] will be looking for the title several times over." Is he going after Mark Richards' four-time championship record? His brow knits. "I don't think about it that way."

I am walking out to my car with Tom. This time, he is not preoccupied. Some sort of personal purge has taken place. He knows his time has come. Tom Curren's genius in his surfing has always been that innate sense of patience for just the right moment. About his career up to now? He's just been going to school.

One last question. *Tom, have you ever felt that you had a legacy to fulfill with your dad being who he is?*

This prompts a deep breath, exhaled through a small smile, and a wistful look to the left that I have never seen in all our years as friends. "Um . . . well, yes, once I felt that way. But after the Costa Rica visit, I understand that his was a different way. He is off on his own trip. Always has been. Some dads are distant. I get it. They leave it up to the kid to do it for themselves. Just like they did. So . . . now it's time to do it my way."

January 26, 1985 — 6:16 p.m.

On another empty stretch of beach, just south of his beloved Rincon Del Mar, Tom Curren has just finished stretching out. Australia is for tomorrow. It was illuminating to see his father again after all that water under the bridge. A lot of answers. Tom grabs some sand and sifts it through both hands. His father had his time and made his mark, and now lives a simple existence in a foreign land. Now it's Tom's turn. He knows his father is quietly impressed by what he's achieved in his career as a pro surfer, but that his father scoffs at the obligations that come with it. And that his father has never paid any attention to money. Not the way Tom has had to, raising himself. Making his own luck.

Tom stands up and walks over to his starting line. Highway 101 roars to his left, the Ocean answers to the right. Tom crouches down. Deaf to it all. Ready. His plan is simple: a definite structure towards the world title in 1986, a decade of competition, and then take Marie, move to France, and live happily ever after. Have his time, make his mark, and then live a simple existence in a foreign land.

A legacy fulfilled . . . Tommy Curren's way.

BANG!

Two seconds, three, breathing . . . breathing . . .

DREAM ON

CASTLES IN THE SKY AT THE TRESTLES BILABONG PRO
SURFING MAGAZINE, USA, 2000

Professional surfing seems in a perpetual state of emerging from childhood. And never is this more evident than when sponsors attempt to emulate the great importance of our sport by throwing lavish welcoming parties at surf contests. Especially around the year 2000, which was another make-or-break year for the sport as a profession. Today, despite the million-dollar contracts and wave pools built in the middle of nowhere, surfing still falls short of its dignity when it tries to emulate the golf world. —Mg.

THE BOOZE CRUISE

Nothing in a surfer's life will ever show them more than the Ocean will. It shows us not how or why, but what it takes to dream. I considered this as my eyes swept over a room full of dreams at the media kickoff party for the Billabong Pro 2000 at Trestles, San Clemente, California. The elite, among surfers and industry alike, had set sail at dusk in the Dana Point Harbor aboard a giant motor yacht. Sumptuous banquet, with silver trays of hors d'oeuvres and foxy waitresses to carry them. You know the type. The hors d'oeuvres, I mean. Frilly little bite-size savories made of all manner of salmon and capers and rye squares and onions and cream cheese and water crackers and jellies and cherries and kiwis and nothing that any surfer in their right mind would eat on dry land. And I say "set sail in the Dana Point Harbor" for very good reason. A south wind had kicked up, so the contest organizers were taking no chances of any maritime disaster that might await us out in the big blue beyond the Harbor's jetty walls. Seasickness topping the list. No, we cruised at a walking pace back and forth between the dock and the harbor entrance. Hawaiian contender Vincent Sennen "Sunny" Garcia loved it. Not a lover of boats, he said it was like always heading for port.

I stood, pondering the proceedings with six-time World Champion Kelly Slater and female champion-in-waiting Keala Kennelly. Kelly loved the irony of the whole shebang. "The best rough water swimmers in the universe are on this boat," he deadpanned. "If this thing went down, the Coast Guard would show up and we'd all be bodysurfing."

As it turned out, we only ran aground twice.

THE PRESS CONFERENCE

Topside, coupla beers later, the longshots and sure things were clearing their throats behind a table of microphones, facing a crowd of what was supposed to be the esteemed members of the press. Except that everyone knew each other, so it was more like a Thanksgiving dinner. Sunny Garcia brooding with his winner's podium face, savant Mark Occhilupo whimsically amused and smiling at private windmills, Shane Dorian calm and focused, CJ Hobhood looking shocked that he was sitting alongside these knights of the round table, Luke Egan nervous as hell, Rob Machado mellow as hell, and Kelly Slater looking downright retired, a king waiting for Donovan Frankenreiter's band to set up so he could sit in with a guitar.

The pace was set by the first question. What was that alluring fragrance Shane Dorian was wearing tonight? That busted us all up. Shane explained that it wasn't his scent at all, that it was his girlfriend's. Luke Egan looked a little disgruntled. This pro surfing thing was serious, man! Rumor had it Luke was pissed off at Billabong for letting an off-tour Kelly into the contest as a wildcard. This close to a world title between Luke and Sunny and you gotta throw in a spoiler like Kelly? Sunny, the leader, intimidating, pressed his advantage, made a mean call.

"Let them try and catch me," he said. "I just want to win this thing, go home to Hawaii, and eat a plate lunch."

Kelly bared some teeth, commenting that Sunny might have to let that plate lunch wait a while. They stared each other down. It was a dead heat until Occhilupo stole the show. "Occy" explained that he'd been lost earlier in the day. That he'd mistaken the Upper Trestles surf break for the contest site at Lower Trestles and had been surfing the wrong spot all week.

"I went surfing with Luke today," Occy explained, "and I stopped at Uppers to put my wetsuit on. Luke kept walking south and all I could say was, 'Where ya going, mate?'"

Things fell apart after that. Then Donovan's band crashed in. That brought out the dancing girls. The girlfriends and wives, I mean. I found myself over on the port rail next to a thoughtful Rob Machado, who was staring at the stars and looking like he could really use a hit off a joint. As everyone howled in on Donovan's cover of "Brown-eyed Girl," I looked out over the cavorting crowd of the world's best, all singing full volume, and I thought about dreams again.

There was Shane, Grey Goose vodka tonic in the palm of one hand, super foxy girlfriend in the other. I thought of his dreams. Shane's building a ranch on the upper reaches of the long mountain volcano on the big island of Hawaii that will stand sentinel over his hometown of Kona. Complete with a skyway that will lead to a freestanding glass outdoor shower. Shane demands honesty from himself and his guests, if nothing else. He dreams of "keeping it real." Shane is, in the end, very real. Surfing has, and will, give Shane these dreams. He would go on to defeat Kelly in the losers' round in the closest, highest-scoring heat of the contest.

Over by the starboard railing, Sunny Garcia was ignoring the music, slow dancing nose to nose with his magnificent wife, Reina, to their own music. She is the absolutely stunning daughter of Joey Cabell, Hawaiian surfing legend and Chart House restaurant mogul. For Sunny and Reina, there was no one else on the boat. I thought of his dreams. Sunny dreams of this: the love of a beautiful woman. Of his many children whose names are tattooed across his mighty chest. Of home. Of community. Of a lush, tropical island that's his, all his. He dreams of never being dirt-poor again. No matter what. He dreams of motorcycles and big black trucks and money. He dreams of the good of pain. If you don't have pain in your life, he has said, you're not doing all you need to do. I heard this from him as he was getting two needles full of cortisone jacked into his hip right before one of the biggest heats of his life. He dreams of love someday quenching the rage in his soul. And he dreams of a peace. The kind of peace he finds when one of his boys rides on his shoulders. Or when his daughter slips her soft, dry, tiny hand into his and squeezes. He dreams of being a world champion. Surfing will give Sunny these dreams. Sunny would make it to the quarter finals, virtually ensuring him the 2000 world title.

I searched the crowd. Conspicuously absent was Andy Irons. Probably passed on the party for a good night's rest. He knows what it's like to win. What it feels like to win. He'd like to win again. More than winning, Andy Irons dreams of respect. Self-respect. Of a self-esteem that has eluded him. He dreams of the respect that seems to come so easily to his more handsome, extraordinary younger brother Bruce. Andy dreams of gaining this respect through competition. Through never, ever backing down from the gnarliest tubes on earth. From pushing himself over the ledge at Pipeline and Teahupoo again and again. From not just *trying* radical things and getting his photo taken for it, but by successfully completing radical maneuvers and finishing his waves. His are the dreams of a bullfighter, not an ice skater. There is no room for error in his brand of radical surfing, only grace or gore. Only creative perfection. He dreams of the look in strangers' eyes that don't worship, but understand. He dreams of the look in his peers' eyes that won't question so much as let him know he belongs. Andy dreams of the day that he won't have to face fears that most people don't even see coming. When that happens, on that day, he will be able to tell his brother Bruce something he has never been able to say: *I love you.* Surfing will give Andy these dreams. Andy Irons would go on to win the event.

Mark Occhilupo stood in the middle of the throng, one hand up in the air, head down, eyes closed, like a preacher man. He wasn't listening to the music; he was feeling it. He surfs the same way. I thought of his dreams, and it came to me that Occy doesn't dream at all—he lives in one. A man-child at play on the surface of the sea. Naive of greed and ambition and hate and killer instincts and rage and boastful pride and inner demons. He just surfs, like an animal feeds. He loves, he laughs, he surfs. But he doesn't dream. He's our current world champion. At thirty-four years old. With a house on a hill back in New South Wales and a wife and child and all the waves he can ride and all the boards to ride them with. And he's not done. Not yet. Occy would go on to eventually find the proper contest site, but not before badly spraining his ankle on the Flowrider, an artificial standing wave at an amusement park. At thirty-four years old, this would be the first injury of his entire career.

Over by the punch bowl, Keala Kennelly was hopping up and down to the beat inside a circle of her girlfriends. She looked so pretty in glitter, gown, and grin. I thought of her dreams. Keala Kennelly dreams of being a DJ. An honest-to-god, master-MC, club-thumping, in-the-house DJ. She also dreams of the day when, at contests like these, the women will not have to surf in a WQS event five miles up the coast. In shitty waves where a Jumbotron screen would pipe in the men's action live from Trestles so that during her heats, she would no longer be constantly reminded that the men were getting better waves, and that half the crowd where she was surfing was watching the TV and not her. She dreams of the day when she doesn't have to swallow the bitter pill of knowing that, in an event like this, thirty-third place in the men's division earned seventeen hundred dollars, and twenty-fifth place in the women's division got you fifty bucks. No matter; on her best days, Keala dreams of deep barrels and of music that can heal the soul and of a musical beauty that will save the world. Surfing has and will give Keala these dreams. Keala would go on to win the event and three thousand dollars. Five times less than the men's champion.

I saw Kelly step off the dance floor and over to the railing next to his friend, Rob Machado. They watched the band together. Not singing, not dancing. Just watching. Perhaps remembering their own moments in the sun, on stage. I looked at Kelly's eyes, volcanic-green and tired. I thought of his dreams. Kelly Slater dreams of golf. And of miracles. He speaks of Payne Stewart, the famous golfer who died in that bizarre plane crash. And how regardless of how catastrophic the crash was, the only things that survived were Payne Stewart's "What Would Jesus Do" pendant and bracelet. Kelly speaks of seeing that pendant and the bracelet with his own eyes as he played golf with Payne Stewart and his wife and son. For Kelly, there's salvation out on those fairways somewhere. It's just a matter of finding it. Like Michael Jordan's baseball stage, our great champion, Lord Slater, dreams the dreams of those who have achieved everything. The dreams of achieving more. Like a ferocious gladiator, Kelly has fought his way from the slavery of borderline poverty to a freedom beyond the Colosseum. From Cocoa

Beach to Hollywood, from a scrutinized affair with Pamela Anderson to six world championship trophies, from hometown newspapers to the cover of Andy Warhol's *INTERVIEW* magazine. Yet at the core of all his extraordinary success, Kelly still has the instinct to know that with this brand of success comes the wings of Icarus, and that flying too close to the sun will bring ruin. This was evidenced by a dream he shared with me.

"I dreamed I was standing on Canaveral Pier and the surf was six-to-eight foot, and I thought to myself, in my dream, *Fuck! I wish I was at Sebastian Inlet! The waves would be way better there.*" Kelly Slater will always dream of being a surfer. Kelly would go on to lose his first-round heat to an unknown Armando Daltro. Shane Dorian would then beat Kelly in the losers' round. Kelly would then go golfing.

It was eleven o'clock in the evening now. Way past bedtime for the dawn contest start in the morning. With the music still ringing in my ears, I walked the gangplank onto the dock, thumbing through the official Billabong Pro Press kit. I came across this item:

Now Lower Trestles hosts the most important surfing competition to ever grace its shores. Who will add to the cherished history of the one break in which every A.S.P. surfer has always wanted to compete! And now at long last will? Come down the footpath, or through the parking lot, and look for the perfect peeling waves with the world's surfing maestros unleashing their greatness!

Through the parking lot, unleashing their greatness? Oh, what the hell, sponsors can dream too. I stopped up on top of the dock to watch the disembarkation of the world's surfing maestros and to say goodnight and good luck to my extraordinary friends. It was a beautiful harbor night—a dusting of stars overhead, the clink-clinking of sailboat rigging, the snubbing of boat fenders against old, waterlogged wooden berths, the smell of life just beneath the inky waters.

It's pretty simple. With all its foibles and pitfalls, the best thing about the pro surfing machine is that surfers can fight their way out of the ghetto. Young men and women who are generally born to poverty and broken homes. Who, through their own iron will, life-risking courage, and physical blessings, are given the opportunity to travel the world while young and beautiful and strong. To become young heroes and stuff their pockets with enough cash to build their own, better worlds. To make their own dreams. And to surf. And surf. And surf. This contest would be over by the end of the week; at least that was certain. Ratings would be adjusted, mortgages paid, wedding rings bought, gifts given, and children born. The contest in Brazil was next, then Hawaii, where this old world would keep turning, to be sure. And waves. Lots of waves would be ridden.

I turned to go home, stopping once to look back. That's when I noticed the name of the boat that we'd been on. Emblazoned in relief on her stern were the words:

DREAM ON

I laughed out loud. I really did.

CHEYNE HORAN'S
RAINBOW BRIDGE

SURFER MAGAZINE, USA, 1986

A fiercely competitive top surfer, Cheyne Horan, was a real controversy at the time. Never a man to do anything halfway, in complete incongruity to his competition fervor, Cheyne had adopted a sexually ambiguous, macrobiotic vegetarian hippie lifestyle. Complete with a private all-male commune home in the hills behind Byron Bay, Australia. A 180-degree turnaround from the "Aggronaut" rep he was known for. And with the confusion surrounding his "Winged Keel fin," co-designed with the America's-Cup-winning keel designer Ben Lexcen, I was dispatched to go get to the bottom of things. I lived with Cheyne at his commune for a week. —Mg.

Goonengerry, NSW, Australia — Dawn

I awoke with a start. Disoriented. My neck and chest wet with sweat. The room took a few of my breaths before it stopped spinning. It had been an atrocious dream with lots of spiders. I was relieved to be still alive. I focused as best I could. Birds chirped. It had to be dawn soon. I was lying on a soft, woven Indian rug on a wooden plank floor beneath two Indonesian batik sarongs. Waking up on the floor of the backcountry Australian commune lodge, where Cheyne Horan had decided to live. I was surrounded by six sleeping dogs. One's warm flank served as my pillow. Another was staring at me with bloodshot eyes. I smiled, it smiled back, then we both lay our heads back down. The dog went back to sleep. I just lay there, staring at a snarl of hand-sized huntsman spiders on the wooden beams of the ceiling. I couldn't take my eyes off them.

I had arrived the previous morning at the Coolangatta Airport with a lot on my mind. Mostly Cheyne. He and I had been acquainted since 1980, and on occasion, as is true with all who fall into the currents and eddies of the Pro Surfing Tour, we had actually had times of camaraderie. Yes, I recalled as I stepped off the plane, Cheyne was a friend of mine. Having heard the allegations against his descent into weirdness, I was curious to see what the real story was. The general contention was that Cheyne was emotionally broken after having a record four runner-up finishes despite his burning world championship aspirations. Cheyne reportedly refused to speak the name of Mark Richards, our four-time world champion who had dashed Cheyne's dreams four times in a row. Cheyne could only refer to Mark Richards by his initials, MR. I intended to find out Cheyne's side of the story by coming to live with him for a while. After all Cheyne had contributed to surfing and, I dare say, to a lot of our lives as one of the best surfers ever seen, to be understood—he deserved that much, surely.

I could smell Cheyne before I could see him. I turned from the baggage carousel and there he stood at five-foot-ten. Barefoot, sweatpants, no shirt, carrying a burning stick of cherrywood incense. We laughed and embraced. It seemed a perfectly natural thing to do. And I am no weakling, but the physical power and girth of the muscle on Cheyne's upper body was staggering. Had I not held my breath, his embrace would have popped me like a balloon. We loaded my boards and backpack into his car and took off, headed south out of the Gold Coast of Queensland and toward a place called Goonengerry in New South Wales. We caught up on some memories, some glory days. South Africa, Brazil, early Stubbies contests at Burleigh Heads, Bells Beach, and an odd little excursion that straight-edge Dave Parmenter once took us on, out to Rottnest Island, off Western Australia. I think Cheyne was on acid for that one. That or mushrooms. I remember Cheyne brought a box of organic carrots for lunch.

Headed for Goonengerry now, I was jetlagged from the thirteen-hour flight from San Francisco. He offered me some rainwater he had collected in an old bicycle bottle. He said it was filled with energy from falling through the atmosphere. He said it would help. I drank deeply. It was warm and tasted like water from an old bike bottle, but at that point, I was a believer.

Slowly, carefully, Cheyne drove his souped-up Holden coupe through the south end of the Queensland's Gold Coast, notorious for cops seeking scofflaws fleeing across the border into New South Wales. Cheyne seemed at peace with everything, not talking much, passing the cherrywood incense under his nose now and then. It wasn't until we crossed the border into New South Wales that Dr. Jekyll showed up. Cheyne threw the incense out the window. He had some room to move as the roads became rural once over Tweed river bridge. He told me we would take the back way to Byron Bay; it was faster. That must have contributed to my nightmare. Shedding his tranquility, Cheyne drove like a parolee with the hounds of hell on his trail. Hunched over the wheel, he buried the needle. Gravel roads, mind you. Where, when it comes to bends in the road, the emergency break becomes more important than the steering wheel. Things got real quiet between us. He was intent on the back roads that spun below us on ball bearings. On one long straightaway, I had the white-knuckled composure to ask what he felt about the public's opinion that his time as a contender was over. I had to shout the question. Trying to slow him down.

He sped up.

"Mate, like, I'm twenty-six, right? Twenty-six! A lot of people put me in that era with MR and Shaun Tomson and Rabbit Bartholomew. But when those guys were actually happening, I was still a grommet reading about them at school! I've never felt a part of that era, but I feel like I got dragged into it. When everyone saw MR fading out, they figured I had to go with him, since I dueled with him for so fucking long. And I've had to handle that. I mean, I can see why MR has faded out; he drinks fuckin' Coca-Cola and hangs out in a coal mine called Newcastle. I'm into health and fitness and yoga, mate. I reckon I'm in the Tommy Carroll era. He and I have been competing against each other since day one. I'm not through."

At that moment, like a bounding boulder about to go over the edge, I was sure Cheyne and I were through. The curve up ahead was too much at this speed, I knew that much. And even if we pulled it, I was convinced the panel van tottering toward us in the opposite direction would finish the job. Cheyne hunched forward, downshifted, threw it into a slide half-off the road, stiffened his hands, and, arms at ten and two, fought the pull of the boggy shoulder, threw up a six-foot rooster tail of mud and grass, knocked a fence post out of whack with the back end, rocketed by the van by three millimeters, and swung it back on track just before a drainage ditch that would have answered any questions about eternity. My heart hadn't resumed beating before Cheyne shifted up. And floored it. We gained some more speed. "That was heavy, mate, but you always gotta accelerate out of turns or you lose."

This was the Cheyne I remembered. The boy wonder with the heavy moves.

Now I had woken up with the dogs. His lodge was silent and sparse. Big, wild zen pillows, no chairs or tables. This was a ground living affair. No one was up yet. Cheyne lived here with the friends most of us on the outside had heard so much about. I'd met two of them the night before here on arrival at what Cheyne described as a "four-man commune." Kerry, early forties, tall, leonine, shirtless, colorful Bali sarong tied daringly low around his slim hips. He told me he didn't own a shirt. With baleful eyes and graying curly-haired temples, he resembled a Greek God on a carrot juice diet. He didn't really fit the description of the evil Svengali he'd been painted as. Next was Brad, probably sixteen. A runaway. A dark, beautiful boy with piercing blue eyes and full, sensuous, henna-outlined lips. The third, whom I hadn't yet met, Paul, was down in Sydney, doing . . . well, that was all I knew. That Paul was down in Sydney. It had all been explained to me by Kerry, the languid spokesman of the commune, which they'd all voted was to be named "Solarfarm." Where they all four lived together in "human possibilities stasis." And that their latest interest lay in the possibilities of manufacturing futuristic solar habitats. And that the four of them and their six vegetarian dogs, Matilda, Jock, Matey, Astro, Cindy, and Cocker, were a "group of the sun" committed to changing the world through Kundalini yoga, macrobiotic food, and "global enchantment."

Where they were going to get all the money for this was anyone's guess. Aside from Cheyne Horan's dwindling sponsorships and endorsement monies, Brad was too young for unemployment checks and Paul "supplemented things around the property" with his Australian welfare checks. Kerry just took care of the organic gardening and was the "overseer of the political ramifications."

I was too jetlagged to ask. I figured we'd get into all that in the morning. So, after a garden meal of organic tofu and wheatgrass cud,

I collapsed on the floor, where Cheyne had very thoughtfully made up a place for me. He had actually tucked me in with the Bali sarongs. I undressed beneath them after I was encouraged by Kerry to sleep in the nude. That way, he noted, my Kundalini points would be easier to pierce as I dreamed. So I took off everything and placed them in a bundle next to me. It seemed the courteous thing to do. Kerry really was a charmer. And then the dogs had gathered around me, sniffing my ass in turn, the stranger with the capitalist's scent. I hadn't showered since America. I screwed my eyes shut, as if I was sleepy, letting Cheyne say goodnight. Through my slitted eyes as I feigned sleep, I saw him pause on the porch and look back at me for long moment. Then he looked out into the night's insect symphony for a full minute. Then half smiled at the night and moved off to his room.

Next morning. I stood up, stretched with the dogs, tugged on my jeans. Feeling that disquieting feeling one always has when awake and alone in a strange house before anyone else is up. I took a look around. This place was isolated, all right. Tucked right up on top of one of the rolling green foothills behind Byron Bay. It was a simple structure. Like a big Swiss ski patrol hut without the snow. All wood. Solid. Three bedrooms, wrap-around ranch porches, and an open chalet-style living room. Picture windows floor to ceiling, each framing lovely bush country views. You didn't just look at these views, you breathed them.

The open kitchen was one of the larger areas. A bunker of vegetables, fruit, burlap sacks of oatmeal, and battered cookware. All the organic food moved through there and then through their bodies, I was told. When I agreed that peristalsis was indeed a miracle, I was met by blank stares. Moving on, Kerry explained their exhaustive feeding process, and how it offered stage keys to open the mind's doors to performance. Exactly what kind of performance was never made clear. All the washing of vegetables and rinsing of tofu and shucking of legumes and skinning of grapes and chopping of apples and peeling of carrots and boiling of basmati rice. All of it keys to doors. There were six wooden cutting boards that I could see. I was told it took hours to prepare a single meal, but only if love of body was in the air. Yet the result of this process was always the same communal salad with pressed sesame oil dressing in a basketball-ball-sized stainless-steel bowl. Help yourself with a wooden spoon. Even breakfast. All of its contents raw and at room temperature. Remarkably, recycled wooden chopsticks from a Chinese take-out were also to be used as utensils. I was told by Kerry that modern metal forks and knives interrupted the vibrations of our heart's electrical impulses when we swallowed. Magic mushrooms and chives were optional to a visitor. I had to keep an eye on things, or I'd be flying above the compound by noon.

I crept up to the overstuffed bookcase, trying not to make any noise, and plucked at some of its readings. *The Seven Pillars of Ancient Wisdom* by T.E Lawrence, *The Secret Teachings of All Ages. Jesus: The Evidence. Esoteric Astrology: It's real! The Penguin Book of Homosexual Verse. The Underworld Initiations of Sinful Styx.* And then, dog-eared copies of *The Warrior Athlete* and *The Warrior's Way.* On the top shelf was Cheyne's certificate of merit from the Australian surfing Hall of Fame, for "The Development of the Winged Star-Fin Concept with Ben Lexcen." It was dog-eared, too. Ben Lexcen of America's Cup fame. And the "star fin," Cheyne's answer to Mark Richards' proven twin-fin design. Cheyne's stab at the same kind of design revolution that was doomed to be a misguided footnote in surfing's history. The design never surf-valid enough to be translated from a sailing hull to the dynamics of a surfboard belly. A left turn of thought, a knee-jerk reaction. Many assigned the blame of Cheyne's losses of a world title to his belief in this heavy, bizarre-looking rudder on the bottom of his new heart-shaped surfboards he named the "Lazor Zap." Cheyne seemed the only man on earth who could saddle these broncs. And he did. Despite the design. He even surfed fifteen-foot waves on one at Waimea Bay in Hawaii. It seemed more a stunt than validity.

I am at the bookcase again. Something else was missing. There was not one of the countless trophies that Cheyne had garnered in his twenty-six years. You would have had to count them by tonnage. Including the one I saw him buy an extra seat for on a Qantas flight from Brazil, where he had won one of his first pro contests. The Championship trophy was as tall as he was. Cheyne had brought it home to Australia in that separate seat as proof to himself and the hometown media that he had done it for all of them.

Posters were tacked up the walls here in the lodge. One of Buddha and the sixteen Arhats, one a pro contest poster featuring Cheyne at his best. One poster was a unicorn leading a procession of monks through the fog. Then the classic Rick Griffin blacklight of Jimi Hendrix with the Medusa head. And over by the weight-set and military press bench, torn from the pages of magazines, was a kind of shrine to assorted musclemen and rippling frog-like bodybuilders. There was no furniture, just rugs and those wild pillows and milk crates waiting for any kind of use.

But then, on that one desk with the one small lamp, was a brand-new Macintosh desktop computer. Cobwebs attached it to the wall.

"To plug into the global brain," I was told later by Kerry. During my entire stay, I never saw it turned on. A massive stereo system dominated one wall. "To provide our soundtrack." From Kerry again.

The TV was a nice color job. But there were cobwebs on that, too. And in the middle of this communal room, on the floor, was the real entertainment center. A scattering of all their paraphernalia for what they called "herbal enchantment." A veritable head shop, as neatly arranged as a surgery. I risked picking up a traditional wooden opium pipe. It smelled like a layover I had once in Guangzhou.

Still waking up, absorbing all that had happened in the last twenty-four hours, I stepped out onto the veranda and took the morning in. The dogs, barkless but mad with hunger, were hunting rabbits before their herbivore masters awoke. The sun had yet to burn open the horizon. Diaphanous folds of tulle fog had filled in all the valleys below, leaving only ranks of the lime-green hills that marched off to the sea. The Ocean was black and still in the distance, and the lighthouse on the distant headland was still washing the countryside in its silent intervals. The few birds starting their day only added to the quiet. I watched, feeling a long way from home, just standing there, arms crossed against the dimpling chill, gazing upon an awakening world from the porch of Cheyne Horan's Mount Olympus.

Dusk. Same spot. Two days later. Brad, Cheyne, and I had been spending our days surfing the Lennox and Broken Head surf sites. Two classic Australian point breaks which were suffering from not-so-classic conditions. Cheyne had been riding his "star fin" keel fins. Brad would ride whichever board Cheyne wasn't using that day—Brad apparently owned nothing but the few coins in his pocket. Cheyne referred to these surf sessions as "Nirvanic, a soothing balm for the bruises gained while on the pro tour." Yet he also considered this "sanctuary surfing" as a heavy R&D training period. Every time we paddled out, it involved at least three mock twenty-minute heats that Cheyne would attack with a vengeance, even though Brad and I were his only available adversaries. Brad was a beginner and I was no Mark Richards. Cheyne had lived in competitive rarefied air since he was twelve years old, and was once Australia's Junior Skateboard and Surfing Champion at the same time. Cheyne's onslaught was relentless against Brad and myself. Every time Cheyne took off on a wave, it was as if the wave were sucking all the energy it could out of him, transforming him into a surfing B-17, dropping bombs on the unsuspecting. Cheyne's was a mad, violent union with the Ocean, incongruous with the womanless, ambivalent life on Solarfarm. Also interesting was the fact that Brad could barely manage to make it to his feet. I just stayed out of Cheyne's way every time he paddled for a wave. And Cheyne won every heat and was pleased.

This was Cheyne's behavior. Driving like a maniac one moment, then quiet and reserved the next. Fiercely competitive during a game of beach cricket, then later passive, observing the peaceful doctrine of "the group." Speaking of improving his relationships with some people on the pro tour one minute, then vehemently explaining how to mash his competition. I found myself confused. I could only imagine how he felt.

In town and out in the surf in Byron Bay, Cheyne is clearly regarded with awe. In a region that is considered a national preserve for alternative lifestyles, Cheyne's commitment to his commune lifestyle has gained him the status of deity. The shock of blond hair, the freckled, sunburnt nose, the bizarre boards and star fins, and his powerful animal aura. He walks like an Olympic wrestler. He's impossible to miss wherever he goes. But I didn't see one other short board with his star fin on it, though about five longboards in the lineup sported them. I brought this up to Cheyne. He just smiled and said, "Yeah, I gave them to those guys, the star fins are unreal for noseriding."

In the afternoons, after the blow-out winds, Brad, Cheyne, and I, despite the interest our trio garnered from the girls behind the cash registers of town, would head back to Solarfarm alone, with bulging recycled paper bags of the day's fresh vegetables. Cheyne paid for every dime from the bottomless dollars in the pocket of his boardshorts. I tried the same, but Cheyne would not have it. I was a guest. Brad would just show up with his favorite ice cream bar and a bag of organic cashews, wave them at the cashier while squeezing by Cheyne, and wait outside on the sidewalk, finishing the ice cream before the sun got in at it.

Later, with our haul from the market, I would pitch in to fix the evening meal. The pressing, grinding, shredding, chopping, squeezing, peeling, slicing, bunching, washing, wringing, and mashing. What it was all based on was rather hazy to me. Yoga, I was told by Kerry. Though for all the talk, I had yet to see a single downward dog. But what the hell. I'd seen a lot of unhappier households in my time. So I just relaxed and gave them their space. Kerry, now confident that he had my ear, seemed to spend his days reading homosexual prose and pondering infinity as a nudist on the sun deck. He tried surfing once. Twenty years back. Didn't like it. And Paul, who had mysteriously arrived sometime in the dark hours of the morning, was back from Sydney with a plastic bag full of green "tips" from his transient gig as a waterfront bartender at the famed Bondi Beach.

Apparently, Paul, staggeringly handsome, body by Bowflex, had ambitions to be a high fashion model. Paul was a nudist as well. A rather proud one, I might add. He had managed to bring back plenty of "herbal enchantment." And his stash was handled like the sacrament. Supplies had been running low, I was told by Kerry with a wave of his hand. He went on. "These natural herbs are the key to all that we're doing here. It opens all the doors. Beers are rude. Whiskey numbs. Smoke is ceremony."

By this time, I was ready to open a few doors myself, so I sat down with Cheyne for an on-the-record interview. After spending a few days surfing with him and after the "family" had screened Cheyne's self-produced surf movie for me, *Scream in Blue* (a startlingly well-crafted, brutally honest documentary of Cheyne's worst year ever on the World Tour), and after hearing some vaguely outlined interests the group had in things like solar shelters, environmental protection, and making this cruel world a better place, I just wanted to talk to the man.

But we weren't to be alone. We never were. All eleven of us sat in a circle. You had to include their band of vegetarian dogs in every meeting of minds.

"It's only fair," said Kerry. Even the dogs waited patiently for Kerry to properly prepare the herbs, slip in a Van Morrison CD, and then begin the enchantment ritual before they dug into their wild carrot salads. The pipe was lit and the whole bunch of us smelled like skunks in about twenty seconds. I wasn't smoking, wanting to get all this right, but this explained the dogs' bloodshot eyes in the mornings.

With a hoarfrost exhalation of blue smoke and a stately wave of his hand, Kerry gave me the stage. I began by asking Cheyne just what the underlying purpose of this lifestyle was. What was the message he was trying to get across to the common man through his surfing? There was an eruption of opinions from everyone but Cheyne. Kerry said it was a holistic message of unification. Paul said something about it being bits and pieces that can be singled out and made whole. And Brad said Cheyne was a disciple of health whom others could incarnate. I hadn't taken my eyes off Cheyne. Again, I asked him what he thought. He just smiled softly and replied, "I reckon all that is right."

Well, I asked, if you are trying to set an example of what a lifestyle like yours can achieve, what about all the competition failures you're experiencing? Don't those hurt your cause?

"Yeah," he said. There was another eruption after this. Cheyne stared his friends down. He'd handle this one. "I try not to get caught up in all that stuff, the winning and the losing." Nods all around. I wasn't buying it, and Cheyne knew it.

"Well, I mean," Cheyne said, "I'm still going out trying my best moves and trying to win, right? But I'm not that attached to winning anymore.

If you're attached to winning, you feel down if you lose. And if you win, you feel elated. They're each as bad as the other." When Cheyne spoke, there were murmurs of encouragement from the group, like a Martin Luther King speech. Then a reverent silence fell. More herbal enchantment was drawn into lungs, including the dogs', who got it through the nose from human exhalations.

Then Brad, in a brave act, chimed in with, "Someone has to set that example for other people. Winning and losing isn't everything. You don't have to jump off a cliff or become a heroin addict if you lose. You know, maybe people will see how to modify themselves when Cheyne loses."

More enchantment all around. Blown into the heavens through cotton-mouthed lips. Even those spiders in the rafters must have been high by now. But I waited it out. And then I said, simply, *Cheyne? You hate losing.*

Before he answers, there's just the music.

"Yeah. I know it. But I'm changing. You gotta change. You gotta become a better person. You gotta evolve. You can't stay a leaf all your life, or a stem; you have to grow into a flower, or the best thing you can be."

Kerry rocked back and forth at this statement, beaming an approving smile while loading another round of Paul's Bondi waterfront bounty. Before it all went really south, I asked Cheyne, *What is the best thing you can be?* He sighed and smiled. "Happy, peaceful . . . content."

Not a word at this.

Kerry changed the music to Joe Cocker's greatest hits. Cheyne began again, "Yeah . . . you know, mate, I'm still just working on credibility with the contest judges. I think the whole way they judge competitions should be reviewed." This got Kerry to raise his head and push his ringlets out of his eyes. I noted that Kerry's voice rises at the end of each sentence, making it sound like each statement is a question.

"Well," Kerry said, "I think what it is? Is that there is something new developing here? In surfing? And surfing is part of it? I reckon we should be careful not to squeeze it into the old bottles and shove it into the old trips? Especially when we try to adopt the American way? What they inherited from Europe? Capitalism and commercials and all that?

That's where I reckon they've made a mistake in surfing? Like, it was growing, okay? You know what I mean? Then they said, 'Aww, now let's go back to America and do it their way? Get an American Champion and get money for the sport? And then it will really grow?' I reckon they're wrong?"

I asked Kerry just who "they" were.

He replied, "The magazines? The clothing companies? It's a conspiracy?"

I wasn't going to touch that one with a one-inch roach. Especially since he was using a sharpened chopstick to clean the pipe. Instead, I changed the subject. I asked Cheyne what the ultimate success of the group would be.

Kerry answered: "Self-transformation? Like, if the group could devise the way for people to transform themselves? That's the original yoga goal? As a group, maybe we could transform society a little bit? Transform the planet within the time that we live? But, it starts with yourself? If you fix yourself up a bit first? You can fix up others and then the world?"

At this point, I was thinking I would never, ever record over this cassette tape. Not for all the whiskey in Ireland. Kerry, Brad, and Paul were all hugging their knees, staring into the center of the circle. Most the dogs had gone hunting again; it seemed they had the munchies. Cheyne sat cross-legged, bolt upright. More enchantment was inhaled. From the stereo came Joe Cocker singing "Feeling All right."

> "Seems I got to have a change of scene
> Every night I have the strangest dream
> Imprisoned by the way it could have been
> Left you on my own or so it seemed
> I got to leave before I start to scream
> But someone locked the door and took the keys"

I asked Cheyne what he would transform the world into. What exactly needed this fixing-up.

"What needs fixing-up?" he said, surprised. "Well . . . people are starving, we've got a nuclear threat hanging over our heads every day—there's that paranoia. There's fuckin' shit in the Ocean, and after all that is fixed up, that'll clean up the vibration and then the relationships between leaders can be fixed up."

What kind of fixing-up do leaders' relationships need, Cheyne?

Cheyne takes a breath and comes down a bit. "I reckon just harmony, basically."

Feeling a threat to the household for the first time, Kerry, the philosophical paramedic, comes to the rescue. It startled me. I thought he had already passed out.

"It's like yoga is sort of an integration? You know that in the body, there are seven centers?"

I said yeah, sure there were.

"Well," Kerry said, his second wind coming on, "the Kundalini? Which is the yoga we practice here? Is sort of a male-female bond of that multi-structure? And the idea is to awaken it and pierce all those centers in the middle of your body until it hits your head? Enlightenment and all that sort of stuff?" Kerry went on to explain that everyone is split into two polar poles. North and south. Male and female. The problem is that no one has this figured out. The answer is to seek a way to even out these male and female polarities, the yin and the yang, so they can cancel each other out and transform the individual into a more complete, balanced person. We apparently must fix this up first before we fix up the world.

Does this fixing-up require a bisexual lifestyle, then? I asked. Dead silence. The music had stopped. Everyone was waiting for Kerry to field that one. Seems we had to wait for the next song to come on.

"Okay, we're a yoga group? And at the moment, we're a celibate yoga group? Everyone has to handle their sexuality in their own way? But we're a Tantra Yoga group too? Tantra Yoga involves centering yourself through touch? It's actually through touching or using sexuality as an engine to find the Kundalini centers? It's a high and advanced yoga?"

I pondered this. Even Astro the dog, apparently returned from the field for more enchantment, seemed to ponder this. I turn to Cheyne and look him in the eyes. *Cheyne? Is that the way you feel about all this, too?*

Cheyne hesitated. Answered. Gently. "Yeah, that's right. That's, um, that's how I feel about it, too."

Paul had dozed off with a strategically positioned throw rug over his ample groin. Brad lie sprawled out next to him, tapping his index fingers against his chest to the beat of a song that had a different beat than the music that was playing. Kerry had begun explaining just how easy it would be for the world to be harmonized. And Cheyne? Cheyne turned and remained cross-legged, still bolt upright, staring deeply into a full-length mirror that was propped up over by the barbells and the bodybuilders. Cheyne's posture was so intense, so sure. Yet the look on his face as he peered into his own eyes seemed so naive. Twenty-six years old, I thought.

Twenty-fucking-six.

Cheyne and I were sitting up on the chimney rock that overlooks The Pass, Byron Bay's famous surf break. Cheyne was in the process of dropping me off in town for my afternoon train down to Bells Beach, Victoria, Australia, for the next surf contest. It was time for both of us to start thinking about getting down to the Bells Beach competition. We had an hour to burn and went to check the surf. It was sparkling in at two feet, pipe dream perfect, with a raft of silhouetted figures moving about in the lineup's diamond field reflections. We were flanked by the enormous verdant headlands and the valleys that led up to Cheyne's commune. The utter beauty of the scene right there, right then, was astounding. We were alone. It was a place for honesty. A place without Kerry.

"I'm not a homosexual," Cheyne said out of nowhere. "That's not the way it is." I nodded. He continued. "A lot of this prejudice I get on the tour is just people and their assumptions. I've been treated as a homosexual, but that's not me. I love women, have loved women. I'm just into modifying my sincerity right now, learning about myself. That's why I'm celibate. And without women. Because when I choose someone to love, it will be because I am complete and able to touch and share with purity."

He met my eyes.

"I know people get uptight about my new trip. My yoga, my friends, my ideas. I just take that as it comes. No one really knows me. My mystique is there, because I'm still out there battling on the front lines of misunderstanding. Still surfing against the best in the world on my own terms and I just won't go away."

A bigger set of waves moved through. We watched it tumble in, the whole six waves. When it's over, I said that maybe there had been a lot of assumptions because Kerry does a lot of talking for him.

"No . . . no," Cheyne said. "He just makes things a lot clearer than I can make them for people. I'm practicing the stuff. I'm in an initiation stage and he's the leader of the group. I have my own voice, but it's an internal voice. It's not a struggle, either. It's like an understanding. And one of the things I understand is that I don't care what people think of me. I know me. That's enough for me, I think."

We considered that for a minute. Then I asked Cheyne what was coming up for him, short term. "Well, yeah," he said, "my extremism has got me on the edge with my sponsors right now. If that doesn't get any better, I won't have any backing. You can't do anything without backing. I'll be a . . . Look, I love pro surfing, mate. I wish I could be mentally and physically able to compete until I was forty-six."

Why that number?

"Because it's even," he said.

Forget forty-six. At twenty-six, this was the second year in a row that Cheyne's top sixteen seeded position in the pro ranks was in desperate peril. What would happen, I asked, if he did not qualify. If he dropped out of the top sixteen seeded position? At this, Cheyne turned his head, brow furrowed, stared down at his feet. He picked at his chipped toenails. Another set of waves moved through the point below. He didn't watch them this time. He just waited a bit, then suddenly looked up at a seagull pinwheeling overhead and said, "I can't even imagine that."

Two weeks later, Bells Beach, Victoria, Australia. The Rip Curl Championship. The most prestigious possible win on the tour—and the most important heat of Cheyne Horan's life—was going badly. Gary "Daffy" Green, a cheerful pixie of a surfer with a third of Cheyne Horan's talent, was plastering Cheyne out in the surf on a conventionally designed board. A cold, wet drizzle, driven by a stormy onshore breeze, had run everyone out of the parking lot contest area. The Public Address system had shorted a while back. Except for the heat horns and sweater-bundled officials and the judges in the double-decker bus on the cliff, the place was a ghost town. Where once, thousands of people cheered every time Cheyne paddled for wave, I was now the only spectator interested. One minute remained.

Outside the break, Cheyne took off on his fourth wave. He knew he was down on points. He poured it on, fighting his bizarre board and its bizarre star fin. Like an aquatic dowser, he ferreted out some power spots on the funky wave face and made some moves despite the struggle with his equipment. A cutback, a low-bottom turn, off-the lip combo. During these moments, his center, his balance, his strength would flash so purely that it was like watching a memory. Moments that not only reminded you that Cheyne was still one of the greatest surfers on earth, but that convinced you of it. I knew that more than just one judge was praying that he would get back on standard-designed surfboards while he still could.

The heat ended at the flat blatting of an air horn. Gary Green rode to the beach the silent victor and headed straight for the pub without even taking his wetsuit off. The officials and judges bolted, and a work crew started dismantling a few advertising scaffoldings that were catching the wind. A swirling, soft rain moved in. Though the heat was over, Cheyne was still outside the break, all by himself and staring at the horizon for another wave. He looked lost and adrift on a confused sea. I felt sad for my friend out there. For all the effort and commitment he'd put into his journey, his search for meaning, for belonging, he seemed to deserve more than this. Earlier, Cheyne shared with me that he had embraced a number of new beliefs. One being of the California Chumash tribe's belief in the "Rainbow Bridge." Of being able to walk on a rainbow as a bridge to reach a new world. A metaphor for the spiritual connection between life and death. Cheyne had "modified" it to fit Kerry's maxims. Based it on "personal attempts at mixing one's own energy with the cosmic forces of nature. To create a synergy that would leave you and the world enlightened." It was all so bewildering to me, coming from one of the most gifted athletes Australia had ever produced.

I pursed my lips. Out there in the water was a surfer who had always had the guts and creative power to take his ideas to the end of the line. The trouble was, just as this contest site was abandoned, so had Cheyne lost his audience. And by slipping into the morass of the lower rankings of the pro tour, perhaps even himself.

From where I stood on that lonely, windswept cliff, it appeared that Cheyne Horan's Rainbow Bridge was evolving into his own Bridge of Sighs.

BEASTS OF BURDEN

CARRYING THAT WEIGHT IN PANAMA
SURFER MAGAZINE, USA, 2001

I applied for a permit to travel through the Panama Canal. I ticked the box 'Small Pleasure Craft' because I planned to travel through it on my surfboard. When I showed up at the Port Authority, there was some confusion. I almost pulled it off, until one guy brought out a scale from the bathroom and had me stand on it. Apparently, there is a minimum weight of vessels allowed to travel through the lochs. I was too light by a ton and a half and two grand in fees. So I joined up with some surfers and wrote this feature in an homage to my favorite book on the Vietnam War by Tim O'Brien. —Mg.

To Panama, Joe Curren carried his heartache. The suppurating wounds of the lovelorn. He carried her every pound in his eyes. Her every ounce. Cuts so deep and infected you could see it in the way he held his hands. His hands didn't care about anything. Buttons were left unbuttoned, a surfboard bag zipper unfastened, careless gestures, dismissive gestures. Hands that would wave "I don't know" and "Figure it out for yourself," when he knew the answer all along. Hands that would reach for booze he knew wouldn't solve a goddamn thing. Hands that fought the urge to hold his head between them and scream like an animal. Hands that would help load everybody else's boards onto the van, help an old Panamanian woman across the street; hands that would lend anybody all the money in his pocket; hands that left his luggage poorly packed. He didn't care where you put his surfboards. Bottom of the pile was fine. Fuck it. He carried the Curren genius, the Curren melancholy, the Curren wit, that private wit that is mistaken for inarticulation. Some call it mystique, but it all comes down to a broken heart.

With him to Panama, Joe carried the Curren talent. Surfing comes so easy for Joe that he doesn't know what to do with it half the time. He does more surfing on one wave than most people do in a lifetime. Just like his older world champion brother, Tom, who Joe carries around like a tattoo. Locked under his skin both in awe and confusion. Like his belief in Jesus Christ. Joe also carried with him to Panama three forest-green Channel Islands surfboards with thick glass-on black fins. He carried the need to be hugged in reassurance and the aura that wouldn't allow anyone to do it. But he carried her most of all. He carried the echo of her laugh, the five years of love. Gone now. Like all the Curren men, he carried the brand of imagination that tortures. A knowing of too many things. The shortcomings of those you love.

Joe carried a camera to Panama. He could be seen shooting photos of flowers and footprints in the dirt and puffy clouds sailing like clipper ships against an endless cornflower sky. The only time he pointed his camera at the sea was to photograph two children who were playing at last light in the shore break of a village. When asked why, he was heard saying the words, "They don't know yet." Like his surfing, he didn't understand his photography, the power of it; he was just good at it, that's all. Maybe he wasn't paying attention to anything. Maybe that's why he ended up getting rolled for his wallet by a razor gang in Panama City and then frog-marched back to the hotel by the cops. Fuck it. In his mind, he wasn't in Panama at all.

The things the entire crew carried on this mission to Panama, the "Cup of Gold," depended largely on where they were from. The Santa Barbara boys Ryan Moore and Brian Aresco carried security and savvy respectively. Matty Liu from Haleiwa carried a sex drive that could launch the space shuttle. Matt Gilligan from Wrightsville Beach, North Carolina, carried a fuel to surf that can only come from the necessary fantasies of the East Coast crappy wave lifestyle. But, regardless of origin, they all carried one thing in common: the knowledge that these are the days of fashion shoot surf trips. With perfect waves and perfect lighting and perfect timing, tailor-made to spray a water photographer so that one could justify things like dwindling sponsorships and inspire things like getting laid. Skate park surfing. Man oh man, were they in the right place for it. Twenty-four-hour-a-day offshore winds, a perfect reef, constant swell. Great food, and boats, boats, boats, to take them to the Jurassic offshore islands anytime they cared. Prefabricated, set-up, guided, simple, easy. Just add water. Perfect for today's farm league surfer.

Matty Liu, former Hawaiian champion, movie star, carried attention deficiency disorder. Matty's life had always been about distractions. He carried a skill of surfing that can only be forged on the North Shore. He carried fearlessness. Memories of giant waves at Waimea, tow-in surfing behind jet skis at Jaws on Maui and friends drowning around him. And yet, Matty remained. His surfing talent on tap, but never uncorked. Long ago, distracted by dreams of fame and game and girls, he'd tugged himself over to Hollywood. And he'd done all right there. But still, every time he picked up a surf mag and saw bitchin' photos of his friend Shane Dorian, he reeked with the scent of a road not taken. Matty also carried one and a half pounds of assorted pots and creams and personal grooming products to Panama. He carried a large bottle of his favorite men's perfume, a favorite deodorant, hair product that could shake its fist at any weather. He carried tweezers, nail clippers, emery boards, dental floss, toothpicks, toothbrushes, Q-tips, his favorite soap, and an array of incredibly clean and neatly folded trunks and t-shirts and brand new, perfectly laced white tennis shoes. He also brought a couple of surfboards. But they matched his wardrobe perfectly. Mornings weren't about simply waking up for Matty. They were about showers and mirrors and decisions. He carried a deep hatred for perspiration. Here in Panama, he was in a world of hundred-degree noons with half-hour walks out into the surf over a volcanic griddle that made you stink and drip and wilt while those black bastard buzzards wheeling overhead hoped you'd drop where you stood. Matty carried a hatred for the sun. A constant complexion variable that could foil even the most meticulously applied sunscreens. He called Panama the "Red Planet" because it reminded him of a sci-fi movie where the sun burned everybody up real good.

On Coiba, the remote offshore prison island and the world's best black marlin fishing hub, he found a beautiful blonde. A remarkable feat in these waters. After a year in the tropics, up to her knees in heatstroke and fish guts, she was astonished at Matty's monumental cleanliness. A Casanova in cologne. This woman was from Houston, foxy, stacked, and the girlfriend of a guy known only as "Sausage Finger Tom." Sausage Finger Tom was from Houston, too. The biggest, baddest marlin fishing guide in all of Panama. This woman had to walk around with Sausage Finger Tom's stomach-ripping 130-pound Rottweiler named "Mephisto."

The beast was a prophylactic against any potential prison break and to ensure the respect of the island's prison trustees that served the marlin fishing fleet. But there had never been any trouble. Coiba was an island, after all, and the only prisoners there were the handpicked ones that couldn't swim.

All day, and most nights, Sausage Finger Tom was out killing big fish with rich white Texas oilmen and CIA types from Panama City. But Matty was blinded to the danger he was in. Because even Mephisto loved Matty. On the night that Matt Gilligan threw a secret vodka stag party for the prison trustees, Sausage Finger Tom, night fishing with the CIA operatives on R&R, called ship to shore and heard all the commotion going on in the background. Understandably, parties are unheard of on prison islands. Figuring it was those slippery-looking surfers that had shown up, Sausage Finger Tom motored for port at flank speed and found Matty and his girl in the corner of the open pavilion, a little too close to each other and deep in conversation. Sausage Finger Tom's hands were big enough to pop Matty's head between his palms. But, smelling of fish guts and spattered with marlin blood, he saw his only real defense was to drag this woman away. "We wasn't even doing anything," said Matty. Later, when asked about what he and the woman were talking about before the Sausage Finger Tom incident occurred, Matty replied innocently, "sports bras." The only thing that wasn't a mystery to Matty was that he was in some place Van Halen once sang about. Even though Matty didn't know that the song was about a stripper named Panama that David Lee Roth was hunting down in Vegas.

Distractions. Matty carried that.

Brian Aresco carried, above all other things, a math book. A shrewd survivalist amidst the mega-rich of Santa Barbara, California, he carried the responsibility of knowing the score. A landscaper's son who had learned long ago what side the bread was buttered on. Brian, from the class distinction known as Carpinteria, California, who had gained a foothold in the affluent society of Montecito, California, by kissing and remaining faithful to the daughter of a very, very rich man. He'd grown up in the shadow of Santa Barbara's royalty as the son of a man who made rich people's gardens look good. He knew the nobility in his father, a father who, when all was said and done, could paddle out at crowded Rincon and ride any wave he chose without dropping in on anybody. Local knowledge, they called it. And patience above all. Brian carried this all the way to the volcanic reef of Catalina, Panama. He'd wait for the set waves, taking off deep behind the pack. Then, as they were forced to pull back out of sheer decency, he would methodically work the wave over like a surgeon. Cutting and stitching in all the right places. His father had taught him this. How to make little things grow into bigger and better things. Brian Aresco carried back-breaking work of soil and manure under his fingernails amidst a lazy generation of peers who worshiped the airbrushed fantasies of music videos and Victoria's Secret push-up bras. Brian knew that college, and not surf endorsements, was the answer to it all. While the others hunkered down with tepid beers under the crushing noonday furnace here in Panama, Brian could be seen swinging in a hammock, math book in hand, pencil in mouth, fingering the thing page by goddamned page. By the time he was done with the school thing, a degree in advanced economics, Brian's rich girlfriend's banker of a father would no longer call him "that boy." Her father would call him Brian. Brian could wait for this moment. He carried this patience with him, how to make things grow into bigger things. Like the math book.

Ryan Moore carried a quiet calm and a quiver of five absolutely perfect boards, handcrafted by his dad. Ryan also carried with him, twenty-four hours a day, the electronic gate key to the exclusive estates of Rincon Del Mar, a hop, skip, and a jump away from the working class in Carpinteria. He'd stolen the key. Off some drunk girl at a party down on the point who had dropped it in the sand and staggered off out of her mind on GHB. Ryan cared about the surf break at Rincon. And he carried that care to Panama. He had to. He and his father own the pink slip to Rincon. And a good boat-stake in the Channel Islands offshore. He and his father also owned the coolest surf shop in Carpinteria, and the best lifestyle that the town has to offer. Ryan loved his outrageous birth luck. Loved it. He loved living with who he was. Ryan carried the most important thing one can carry back home at Rincon, and he brought it here to Panama. Ryan carried style. Waves were like instruments to him. One didn't play them; they played you. Sapping power out of your muscles and contorting your movements into perfect notes. He carried the wisdoms. In the tube, keep your eyes on the horizon. In offshore winds, drive down the face, follow your board. Seek the seamless drama. Let the wave, not your board, do things to your body. Waves were the symphony, all he needed to do was play in key. Play to the sea. Ryan carried this. The security in himself. He slept without dreams, woke up early, and surfed hard and beautiful all day long. And because of this, he carried few burdens.

Matt Gilligan carried the chip on his shoulder of being a right coaster. Not as wave privileged as his glamorous counterparts and less of a surfer because of it. But more of a surfer because of it as well. Five-hour sessions under the incendiary noon sun were not a problem for Matt. He also carried the guts of an opportunist. He carried, in his eyes and in his surfing, every infrequent swell that crept in over the murderous continental shelf off his hometown back in Wrightsville, North Carolina. Hang it all. Take life by the ankles and shake the coins out of its pockets. The future? Hang the future; worry about Saturday. The swarms of Brazilians out on the reef at Santa Catalina here in Panama? Hang 'em, surf around 'em. No girls around? Hang it, a night cap of warm tequila, dream about a bunny, then take advantage of your morning glory. Matt carried the strength of being the palest blond-haired human in all of Panama. And a physical strength that came from carrying the worst sunburns on earth as part of the job. A surfbilly counterpart to his elegant West Coast surf mates, he carried a toughness. The guts to ignore biting insects and sweat in your eyes and scorpions in your shoes and buzzards in the sky and blistering black sand and the hot beer that goes along with it all. Hang it. Don't like it? Drink the tap water, take what's coming to you. Let the enlightened leave behind monuments. Matt knew all he was ever going to leave behind in this world were moments. Like when he went fishing for three hours without a bite. Hang it. He bought a twenty-five-pound Mahi Mahi and a couple bottles of prison vodka off a trustee and returned triumphantly to camp. Even threw a party for the trustees, poor bastards. He carried the ability to make stuff like that happen.

Coupled with Matt Gilligan's savvy was a sensitivity buried deep within. It served him well. Unlike all his counterparts on the trip, he was the only one whom Panama actually touched. Honest to god touched. On the far side of the prison Island of Coiba, after a great surf session with everybody at some unnamed rock-strewn left break, Matt paddled to shore from the boat and up the river a ways to rinse off in the cool, pristine fresh water. His sensitivity drew him farther up the river. His self-reliance. That, and a total lack of fear. He'd been punched in the face before, nothing much worse to fear than that, Hell with it. Let things unfold. Take what's coming to you. He paddled farther. Around a couple of bends. A couple more. The sound of the Ocean disappeared behind him. The sound of mankind disappeared. He kept paddling. He came to a silver sand bank that, when he stood upon it, sunk him up to his calves. He could hear the jungle growing. The distant howl of a white-faced monkey. A red bird with fluting wings, skimming the deep green surface of the shallows for gnats. He stood in dripping surf trunks, enduring a stinging, sunburned neck, and listened to a world as old as life itself. He stood alone, as enlightened as anyone who had ever walked the face of the earth. And he closed his eyes and lifted his face to the sun and disappeared into it. And more than all the other surfers put together, he carried the guts to know how to do that.

He carried that.

ICE BLUE EYES

LAYNE BEACHLEY KNOWS HER NAME
SURFER MAGAZINE, USA, 2000

Layne Beachley's courage has never been questioned, but to me, in this fragile moment, I saw a courage in her that went far, far deeper than any of her athletic feats. —Mg.

Layne Beachley and I once held hands on the far side of the world. It was in the shade of a coconut palm a lifetime ago. She and I sat on the sand of a Mentawai Island beach, one hundred nautical miles off West Sumatra, waiting for the offshore wind to pick up at a surf spot called Hollow Trees. We were surrounded by a covey of Mentawai village children. The kids would mimic our every move, hour-glassing handfuls of sand, hugging their knees and burying their feet and toying with the small hermit crabs that peppered the beach.

The kids were fascinated with Layne's ice blue eyes. Through sign language, they were saying that her eyes were the color of the sea and that the sea must be inside her. I remember thinking that was just about the truest statement I'd ever known.

The soft land breeze was made for conversation, and Layne was trying to share something with me. I had never seen her so uneasy. It was about her mother. Her biological mother. The woman whom she had seen for the first time in her life just two months earlier. After years of searching, she had finally met up with her mother at San Francisco International between flights. There, they'd spent the only two hours they would ever spend together. In that two hours, Layne's mother tried to explain a few things. Layne learned that her mother was a teen gang-rape victim who had become pregnant with Layne as a result of the attack.

"And being a single mother in Australia in 1972 wasn't fashionable," Layne said. "Fortunately for me, neither was abortion." Left behind in a Sydney hospital, born six weeks premature, Layne survived, alone. Her mother had fled to New Zealand, and then on to the United States, where she disappeared from the face of the earth. Twenty-seven years and four marriages later, this woman met Layne at an airport bar in San Francisco just to tell Layne how proud she was of her daughter's achievements. This woman had secretly followed Layne's life from afar.

Following through surfing magazines and Australian newspapers and whispered favors from trusted friends back in Oz.

Layne told me that this woman's name was Maggie.

I knew a time when Layne had to hold two jobs to support her surfing career. Surf shop by day, barmaid by night. A lousy apartment. Out on the pro tour, she had to stay in rundown youth hostels, sleeping with all her surfboards leashed to her ankles, ready to clash with anyone who tried to steal her boards. A time when she was vilified by the men on tour, made to feel freakish and repugnant. They gave her a nickname. "The Beast." She couldn't get a date to save her life. She went for four years without being hugged or kissed by a single soul. Four years. In the prime of her life. It was her loneliest time in a lifetime of loneliness. Stressed emotionally, financially, and physically, Layne was diagnosed with chronic fatigue syndrome and ordered to take months of bed rest. She didn't. She couldn't. She had to fight on. And she went on to become the best female surfer the world had ever seen.

"All I'd ever had was my backbone to lean on," she said. I remember sitting in the quiet with her on that exotic beach after hearing her story, thinking about the miracles that the surfing life can perform. About the places it can take you, about the adventures it affords. About the hope it can give and the lives it can save. Lives like Layne Beachley's. That was Layne to me at that moment. Only her backbone to lean on. Imposing her will on the world against long odds. As we sat there, she was twenty-eight years old and on her way to her fourth world title. The woman sitting next to me on that beach seemed to bring with her, wherever she went, all the history and hopes of every powerful woman who has ever existed. Plenty achieve trophies, but only a few achieve royalty. A queen to Kelly Slater's king and all Aussie pride. Despite the challenges of life, Layne was the irrepressible spearhead of surfing's suffragette movement long before it was cool. The very movement that would eventually alter the entire surfing industry and alter the way every one of us would look at women in the lineup. And considering the fact that Layne is a woman who stands only five-foot-four, and considering the fact that she would eventually go on to tow into sixty-foot waves, and considering the fact that she would go on to be the only woman on earth searching for the hundred-foot wave with the rest of the Billabong Odyssey boys—considering all that—I believe, at that time, I was sitting on the beach with the most courageous surfer on the planet. At that time, Layne held the Holy Grail—multiple World Titles and that which all women pray for: respect. Still a sufferer of chronic fatigue syndrome, yet pound-for-pound, one of the physically strongest athletes in the world. Unlike other heroes who have come and gone, the woman sitting next to me on that beach was more than a woman; she was a symbol. A tattoo on surfing's history. The living personification of the only three things that will ever make an athlete great, that will ever make the world great: strength, wisdom, and achievement.

"I learnt my real birth name from her, though," Layne said. Snapping out of it, I could only raise my eyebrows. Layne waited a minute, arranging the seashells at her feet. Then, softly, she said, "My real name is Tania Maris." And this was when the tears began to well in the corner of those magnificent ice blue eyes. And that is when this powerful woman next to me, this sporting icon, was alone in this world all over again. And that is when I gently reached out and took Layne's hand in mine on the far side of the world. I could feel her racing heartbeat through her palm, urgent as a captured bird. And we sat quietly among the children and the seashells and the hermit crabs, staring out at the surf, waiting for the offshore wind.

THE FATHER, THE SON, AND THE HOLY SPIRIT

AT HOME WITH MICHAEL, MASON, AND COCO HO
SURFER MAGAZINE, USA, 2008

Once you have lived in Hawaii, it never leaves you. Especially if you lived there as a barefoot kid. In 1967, my father was stationed at Pearl Harbor. At Waikiki, my brother and I became surfers for life. I remember watching a surf contest at Queens surf break and watching this kid, not much older than me, win the Menehune division of the State Championships. Little did I know that our fates would be entwined and that I would someday be writing about his sense of fatherhood. —Mg.

The Throne
February 4, 2008 — 3:16 p.m.

Michael Ho is going to live forever. Though we will never know him at all. This time, you find him at the Banzai Pipeline, sitting on the Ronnie Burns Memorial Park bench under the old hau tree, surveying the greatest stretch of surf on the North Shore of Oahu. A domain that has been his birthright since he was seventeen years old. He sits alone, the park bench his throne. This is a community understanding. It is late afternoon and, like an aging lion, Michael Ho sits on this bench, surf fit, barefoot and trunks, no shirt, one leg tucked up under himself, watching his cubs at play out in the ragged small surf of Ehukai Beach Park and the rough trade surf of the nearby Pipeline surf break. His teenagers, Mason and Coco, are out there in mock battle with the rest of the young pack, developing the skills that, with a little luck, will allow them to survive in this hungry world. Allow them to live forever, too. At least that's the plan.

So I walk up to Michael Ho, all five-foot-five and 145 lbs of him, and I shake his hand and feel more than a strength in it—I feel life. We both walk down onto the beach for a closer look at the kids, and soon, we are sitting on the berm and sifting sand through our fingers and watching his Coco surf. Her older brother Mason is down at Pipeline with the big kids. Dusting off old memories, Michael and I realize how long we have known of each other. I first saw Michael surf in 1968 at Queens Beach in Waikiki. I was nine years old. My old man was stationed at Pearl Harbor at the time, and his idea of daycare for me and my brother was setting us loose in Waikiki at dawn and picking us up at dusk. My dad paid the beachboys to look after us with six packs of San Miquel beer. My brother and I had Waikiki as wired as any white Navy kids ever would. Still, it was a transcendent experience to hang out at the State Championships at Queens that year. Being within earshot of Hawaiian surfing royalty. Michael Ho won the Menehune division that day. I can still see him on the winner's podium. He had that island cool, that Hawaiian touch of menace, a young prince. Already enigmatic at eleven years old.

Looking into Michael Ho's eyes now, forty years later, I am fascinated. The body has thickened, the hair is gone, a smear of pterygium tugs at his left eye, but that enigma, that island cool, is still there. Where once was a prince, now sits a king. He is comfortable on the beach, but uncomfortable with scrutiny. It takes the both of us a while to reach equilibrium. His last profile for *SURFER* was written by his neighbor, Hawaiian great Reno Abellira, in 1977. There was little in it. He tells me he has preferred it that way. That he is now only cooperating with it for the sake of his children. And I think I know at least one reason why.

Surfing's appetite for heroes has always been keen, but the image of the gentleman pro does not always satisfy us. The dark Hawaiians have long been an intrigue within pro surfing. They have always had a razor's edge. An aloofness, an entitlement that comes from actually living in the place we all need so badly. The North Shore of Oahu and her monumental waves. The place that holds court over all of our reputations, saints and sinners alike. The Hawaiians are the only surfers in the world who can tell us how to behave during our pilgrimages to the North Shore and still have the juice to back it up. Hawaiians like Michael Ho and Dane Kealoha have always maintained the aura of sanctioned badasses. Living lives that oscillate between aloha, risk, and predatory gain in the surf. A role which, though the bane of many professional annual visitors, garners the general public's adoration. Forever sympathetic toward the Hawaiians' three finest qualities: daring, sincerity, and unquestioned physical courage.

So, I dust off some old memories with Michael Ho. South Africa, Brazil, Australia. Campaigns of long ago. And again, I am struck with just how unique this man before me really is. How he has forever been right in the pocket of surfing's historic pageant. Hoisted into the surf by his old man Chico in 1960 at age three, rising to US boys champion at Huntington Beach, California, by 1970. Fifth place at the 1972 World Championships at Ocean Beach, California, at a skinny fifteen years old. The same year he started charging the heavies at Sunset Beach, by now squire to Eddie Aikau, Jeff Hakman, Gerry Lopez, Reno Abellira, Barry Kanaiaupuni, and the entire pantheon of '70s Hawaiian greats. Michael Ho was a full-time professional surfer by high school graduation, long before the world champs Shaun Tomson and Rabbit Bartholomew ever busted down any doors. By 1975, Michael Ho was runner-up at the Duke and the Pro Class trials. Relentless on the international pro tour 1976 through 1988, rising to third in the world rankings. He and Dane Kealoha were the Hawaiian spearhead for all the world to see, ripping from J-Bay in South Africa to Bells Beach in Australia to Nijima in Japan. Michael Ho has been a five-time Pipeline Masters finalist. In 1982, winning the Masters with a cast on his right arm from a bar fight, he invented the grab rail "pig-dog" backside approach to, at the time, the world's heaviest wave. He owns thirteen Duke Kahanamoku Surf tournament trophies, is an eight-time Duke finalist, and won it in 1978 and 1981. He is a four-time winner of the Xcel Pro, two-time Triple Crown champ, and George Downing says he will not hold the Waimea Bay Eddie Aikau Memorial contest without Michael Ho in it. Michael being one of the few contestants to whom Eddie was a close friend. Remarkably, at forty years old, Michael was the runner-up at the 1997 Pipe Masters, defeating Kelly Slater in an earlier heat. Michael won the World Masters Championship in France in the year 2000. In 2003, at Makaha Beach on Oahu, he brought tents over to the homeless in Nanakuli and stayed with them for the duration of the contest, and damn near won another World Masters' title. And now, right now, in 2008, fifty-one years old, he is preparing for another World Masters' title and the Eddie contest at Waimea Bay—where they don't hold the contest unless the surf is enormous. All this while busy fulfilling his role as "Uncle Mike," ferrying and mentoring the next generation of the North Shore's golden children, including his own, around the globe, passing the torch to the modern age.

All this and yet, we hardly know him.

Michael's eyes are drawn to the surf. His daughter, Coco, has swung into a three-foot left and is working it over with precision. Michael and I watch in silence. Coco surfs beyond her years, generating speed, finding power spots. As the wave closes out, she rockets into the lip and, of all things, you are reminded of a young former world champ named Martin Potter. It's a world-class ride. I see a young John John Florence hoot at her moves on his way out into the surf. And I see that this puts a smile on Michael's lips. And I find that I am relieved that Coco is such a good surfer.

"Gives a whole new meaning to 'soccer mom,' yeah?" says Michael.

He looks out at his daughter and she can feel it. She waves to him. He smiles and waves back and then looks down at his feet, putting his ten fingers between his ten scarred and gnarled toes. I don't think Michael Ho even owns a pair of shoes. Then he surprises me with a direct question.

"Can you believe how old we are, Matt?"

I answer no, I can't. And then I ask a direct question. *How old would you be if you didn't know how old you were?* I see Michael squint and think about it. He takes the question seriously.

"Twenty-five."

The sun falls into the sea beyond Kaena Point. It is the golden hour here on the North Shore and the teenaged golden children of "Da Country" are shaking off their third surf session of the day and making their way up the sand to backyard outdoor showers and home-cooked meals.

Coco Ho, a glowing bundle of pure giggling delight, bounces up to us. It is the first time I have met her. Here in this light, it is impossible to not think of her as some sort of divine being. She wins me over in an instant. So open is her smile, so invigorating and clean is her energy, so happy and enthused is her spirit, that she seems to float, even on dry land, all dripping blonde hair and clear eyes and gleaming white teeth. She could have gossamer wings at this moment and I wouldn't bat an eyelash. Her father is as smitten as anyone.

"You surfed good," Michael says to his treasure.

"Really, Dad? Really?"

"Really," says her dad.

It's enough to send her bounding up the beach to the showers. Michael Ho watches his daughter until she is out of sight. Then he looks back out at the surf.

"Nah, bruddah . . . I don't want to be twenty-five," he says. "I like it right here."

The Palace
February 5, 2008 — 5:02 p.m.

Dino Andino, Michael Ho, and I now sit on the back porch of the Billabong house that overlooks the break at the Banzai Pipeline. Dino's boy, Kolohe, and Michael Ho's boy, Mason, are out in the lineup. The Pipeline Pro is on hold with rumors of it having to be run the next day because of permit issues. Michael is eager to watch how nineteen-year-old Mason will do in the high-pressure lineup. Dino, a former Californian champion, is more relaxed. Michael's eyes are locked on Mason out in the Pipeline scrum. A set of waves come through. Mason, Clay Marzo, Kolohe, and Sean Moody scratch for it, five others in hot pursuit. At the last second, it looks like Moody will prevail. Michael Ho stands up on the porch, stamps his feet, and waves his arms. He just can't help himself.

It reminds me of the two times I have seen this behavior in Michael before. Both times involving world champions. There was the time in 1985 when Michael was running up and down the side of the wave pool in Allentown, Pennsylvania, calling his younger brother Derek into waves during a final heat against Australian World Champion Tom Carroll.

And then there was that time in 1996. I was sitting on this very same porch with Michael Ho, watching him jump and prance and wave his arms to brother Derek once again. Derek, by then the 1993 world champion, was surfing against another world champion, this time Kelly Slater. I remembered how Michael willed Derek into perfect wave after perfect wave in exactly the same light as now. And even though Kelly took the final, you remember thinking that maybe Michael had a magic about him. That the only time he loses his island cool, that privateness, is when he is willing the ones he loves toward success. And I saw a real beauty in that.

I watch now as Mason pours it on at the last moment, pushes himself past Moody and Marzo, drops in over the ledge and into the concave blue of a perfect Pipeline wave. He drives down the line, clean and true and alone. I watch this competitive spectacle here at the unofficial colosseum of our sport, and I see that Mason's will be a harder road to stardom than his little sister's. Coco only has to surf better than a handful of other women. Mason's foes will be legion.

After the ride, Michael Ho sits back down, exhales. Dino Andino laughs.

"You can't do it for 'em, Mike," Dino Says. "That's what I'm learning." Michael smiles at his old friend. He knows that Dino is in the same boat with his son. Two fathers stuck in the role of having next-generation sons vying for the brass ring. A brass ring that has swollen tenfold, in both money and complexity, since their own time in the ranks. I sense that it is bewildering for the both of them. These fathers are navigating in unknown waters. A balancing act between father and manager. Trying to make sense of this mega-monetized new era. The brave new deals.

Out in the surf, Mason is into another one: a beautiful cobalt hump. He drops lightly, carves a deep bottom turn, pulling a bio-luminescent contrail into the tube with him. Then emerging in the spit, then the cutback, then the re-entry in the shore break. That wave could be a heat winner tomorrow. Maybe a contest winner. Mason kicks out. Michael Ho exhales. Dino laughs again and shakes his head at Michael. And I find myself relieved that Mason is so good a surfer, too.

Lei Lei's Restaurant
February 5, 2008 — 8:06 p.m.

At the five-star Turtle Bay Resort, Lei Lei's golf course restaurant is the one choice of surf industry bigwigs by default. As they sit on the porches of their winter big-surf-season rented villas, sunburned and tired after a day of pulling the business strings of the North Shore, the drinking establishments of Haleiwa, five miles to the west, can seem a world away. So agents, managers, captains of industry, parents, and surfed-out pros alike congregate here at Lei Lei's. The adults to discuss bottom lines and the children to discuss bottom turns, at the most expensive joint on the North Shore. Just two tables over, I can see the twenty-member Billabong B-team is diving into their thirty-dollar entrees under the watchful eyes of their handlers. They eat like wolves.

I am also currently looking at the incomprehensible sight of Mason and Coco Ho inhaling four hundred dollars' worth of sashimi, coconut-crusted and seared Ahi with garlic-roasted mash, Macadamia nut chocolate milkshakes, and green tea ice cream in eleven minutes flat. I see that the wait staff is so familiar with the Ho family, and so enamored with Coco, that they feel no need to drop off menus. And that so often is the Ho family courted here by the industry nabobs, that they never need think of paying for anything. The Ho triumvirate are now a cash-producing corporate acquisition. With two young world-class surfers and a surfing legend as a coach in one package, before this family lay not dragons, but a yellow brick road.

And Michael knows it.

It is here that Michael Ho sits at the head of the table, their regular table, the one with the best view of the bay and the swaying palms. Dino Andino, manager of the Billabong team, is across from me, and Pipeline Pro event promoter Paul Taublieb is to my left. It feels like the ultimate school lunch on parent day. And despite my attempt at probing questions to Mason and Coco, the only telling moment in the whole scene comes in a glance. At one point, I ask the adults whether or not it is wise for parents to manage their children's professional careers. Dino and Michael freeze for a moment. And then Michael answers.

"Well, there may not be as many zeros on the checks at the end of the day, but at least I know where my kids are and who is dealing with them." I notice Mason has stopped with a forkful of Mahi Mahi halfway to his mouth. I see that he is looking at his father, his brow creased, thinking of all those extra zeroes. Michael notices his son's look and levels his gaze right back at him. Mason gently puts down his fork, sits back, and stares into a middle distance. After a few seconds, he picks up his fork and returns to his meal. Eating a little slower.

Later, two members of the wait staff, clearing away the licked-clean plates of the kids' sashimi and Ahi platters, are bringing Coco her second desert. A heated chocolate chip cookie the size of a pancake, with a dollop of melting vanilla ice cream laced with chocolate syrup. Coco digs in with a fork, never skipping a beat, knowing that despite how many zeroes there might be on any checks in the future, right now this surfing thing is the crime of the century for a just-sixteen North Shore girl. Then she looks at me and sees my grin and realizes that we are thinking the same thing. So she forks in another cheek-bulging bite, closes her eyes in smiling bliss, and shivers with delight. She knows that my expense account is paying for the whole evening. And that the chef knows how to make her desserts *just* so.

The Compound
February 6, 2008 — 4:06 p.m.

At the end of a cul-de-sac on Sunset Beach Point is the Ho family's classic two-story plantation house. It is a surfer's place. Surfboards and trophies reign supreme. One of Michael's many Duke Kahanamoku Contest trophies, perhaps surfing's most prestigious trophy, serves as a doorstop. The house smells of surfboard wax and fiberglass and sand and shells and salty, wet grass welcome mats, and of a total worship of, and a complete belonging to, Sunset Beach. The great bastion of surfing's history, where the Ho name will live forever. A shaggy three-legged dog holds sentry, but the doors are open to all. Surfers of all ages and renown flit in and out of this house. Surf legend Tony Moniz and his beautiful daughter, Marvin Foster's kid, visiting Australian Junior champ Clay Marzo. It is safe and comfortable and cool here in this house. I sit with Mason Ho out on the porch as he carefully waxes a new surfboard board for tomorrow's contest at Pipeline. It's easy to see he's got the same poise as his old man, right down to the compact power, the wary grin, and even the new mustache. I chat with him for a half hour and realize that, just like his old man, he has very deftly avoided saying anything too personal. I point this out to him and he surprises me.

"You've see that that tattoo on my dad's ribs?"

I have. *Kaohelaulii.*

"It means 'new bamboo chute,'" Mason says. "Strong, unbreakable, unstoppable. It's also my middle name." I take this in. Mason stops waxing his surfboard. Not grinning this time. "My dad is ten feet tall . . . and I intend to live up to that. How's that for personal?" And then he goes back to waxing his board.

Coco has a middle name, too. Hapaikekoa. It means "the carrier of strength." Seems everyone in this house has names to live up to. Underneath her sparkling demeanor is a fluttering of seriousness and hope and pain. A single-parent home, her estranged mother's prom dress hangs like a ghost on the outside of her closet in her bedroom. I also see all her stuffed animals have been thrown into a kiddie blanket that has been tacked completely out of reach to the upper ceiling corner of her room.

"Like in a cloud," she says. "They're all safe up there." I can hear in that statement the echoes of a house that has lost a mother. And perhaps not under the most pleasant of circumstances.

Any conversation with Coco swerves all over the place. Oddly mature and then childlike in turn. We're talking so she yells at Mason and his friend Clay Marzo in the next room to turn down the their music. And they do, immediately. This brings me up short. Coco, now the woman of the house. She is also the only one who is eager to talk of the meth epidemic on the that has been whittling away at her community and its dignity for years. Apparently, this is her nemesis.

"Drugs?" she says. "They are like torture! Growing up here? It's only a matter of time before you get offered a crack pipe! Watching what it does to people? That sucks! That's the funny thing about all this pro surfing stuff, they throw money at us, but they never ask us about drugs and stuff." She squints for the first time. "Don't they have all the power? The surf companies? Can't they do something? I'd be glad to help!" And I see that she means it.

Coco quiets for a moment and then she begins to tell you of many things, of the special road she would like to see built around Oahu so that the kids could all get themselves to the beach in bumper cars. She speaks of sunsets and seashells and, perhaps most poignantly, of how much she loves the North Shore and how the sound of the surf is like a sister to her. She makes you close your eyes and listen to it for a full minute and it feels like you are hearing it for the first time. Such is her presence in this house. Such is her belief in this life that is spreading out before her like a banquet. I look at her gazing out toward the surf and in that moment, she turns to me with that knowing smile on her face and I'll be damned if I don't feel like I am being blessed.

We step out of her room and I find Michael Ho alone at the family dinner table, tired from a day of riding hard. I sit with him. He watches Mason waxing another surfboard and his beloved Coco feeding their three-legged dog one of the many dog treats she keeps in her pocket. Michael exhales the doings of the day and rubs both his bloodshot eyes with his palms and tells me that despite the whisperings of his children's future greatness, it is ultimately up to the mercies of fate. Just like his was. He's just doing the best he knows how with them.

A soft, fragrant trade wind blows through the thin floral drapes of the kitchen and across the dinner table. A folded paper napkin lifts an edge and then settles. Michael Ho is quiet. And he closes his eyes, raises his chin, and breathes in deep and holds it. He seems to feel the wind and lose himself to it. And there is such a dignity in this moment.

And looking at him like this, at his family like this, I am struck with the thought that the vague promises and theories of a spiritual eternity could, after all, be just a ruse. That the truth could be that, strive for greatness though he will, any man's real forever can only be found in his children. His blood that is now their blood. The blood of legacy, the blood of the future. And if lucky, these children and their children and their children's children will carry this blood on and on and on through time and time again. Carrying a man's forever through the pageant of the ages. Carrying the blood of a man like Michael Ho.

So, sitting at his table, it's my turn to look at the three of them. The Father, the Son, and dear Coco, the Holy Spirit. And I can't help but marvel at the fact that Michael Ho is going to live forever.

Though we will never know him at all.

MP AND THE
FAT MAN

PLAYING THE LONG ODDS AT THE
QUICKSLIVER PRO 2004
TRACKS MAGAZINE, AUSTRALIA, 2004

Surfing unhinges certain people. The sport is peppered with stories of surfers going off the rails. None more famously than the great Michael Peterson. A paranoid schizophrenic, it is remarkable to me that he got as far as he did. That says a lot about the amount of tolerance the surfing world has for eccentricity. There were times when our eyes met, Michael and me. First at his brother Tommy's house where I was playing chess with World Champion Rabbit Bartholomew. And once, years later, Michael Peterson stared at me from across a pub for about seven seconds, straight into my eyes. Like he was trying to tell me something. Like I would understand. For me it was like staring into a volcano. So I wrote my contest report like this. —Mg.

The Superbank, Snapper Rocks, Queensland, Australia
March 12, 2004 — 2:05 p.m.

In the upstairs VIP beer garden of the old Snapper Rocks Surf Lifesaving Club, fifty-two-year-old Michael Peterson, schizophrenic, ex-heroin addict, ex-con, shock therapy survivor, several-time Australian Surfing Champion, and one of the greatest competitive surfers who ever lived, sits silent and inert at a fold-out plastic table on a fold-out plastic chair. The annual Quiksilver Pro Surfing Contest is unfolding before him, and he is an honored guest. It's a little cooler in here with the VIPs than down on the beach with the surf contest rabble. And the VIPs, out of respect, are less likely to ask for his autograph or try and strike up a conversation with him. He's through answering questions and through talking to anyone other than Dottie, his sister and full-time caretaker. She sits next to him now, protective and wary of the other surfers in the room who are stealing glances at what remains of the great Michael Peterson. In his right hand, Michael Peterson holds a paper cup of Coca-Cola gone warm. There is a slight tremor in that hand and he is staring not at the live action on the TV, but out the window to his left at the undulating Ocean up the coast. Having spent his entire life lean as a flintlock, tanned, shirtless, and in shorts, he is now sallow, double chinned, and wears a childlike wardrobe that defines his current special needs. Brown baseball hat pulled to his eyebrows, brown t-shirt, black jeans that are too short, white socks, cheap white running shoes with velcro laces, and the extra hundred and sixty pounds he'd put on since the Thorazine took hold of his life two decades previous. Michael Peterson, once both lightning bolt and rod, now a reclusive survivor of life's countless beatings, speaking only in whispers to himself. With voices rolling around in his head like a marble on an uneven plane.

Listen.
Can you hear that?
The droplet of water.
That first droplet of water that falls and becomes the river?
Can you hear that? It is here.
It is only twelve inches from the head to the heart, but it is the longest journey in the world.

His eyes do not move. He blinks only once a minute.

Listen.
Do you hear that river? There is water coming from somewhere and going somewhere.
It has flowed on a set course for thousands of miles. It is not only getting away from something, it is moving toward something. It is getting away from the mountains and it is getting to the Ocean.
That's the way a man's life ought to be.

In a way, Michael Peterson is home. Before him, beyond the raucous crowd, beyond the beer-soaked carpeting of the bar, beyond the veranda, beyond the contest's tent city and the fanfare, out there underwater are the sands that he has sped, skittered, and carved over so beautifully countless of times before.

Otherwise, there's just no purpose. A man is right to get away from evil, from trouble, from things that are bad for him. But he can spend all his life running away from them. What he should do is pick something that will better him, that is good to him, and try to join it. Or let it join him. Then he's running toward something and not away.

See what I mean? It took all those years to find it out. And now it's too late to start doing anything about it.

Michael Peterson is now watching a surfer on the big screen. A surfer shaped somewhat like he himself is now. Mick Lowe, the keg with legs. Michael sees that Mick has the shine. Sees that Mick has the answer to the waves today. The last storm has carved a hole in the Superbank sand bar. The waves are still amusing, but there will be no famed tube rides today. So Michael sits and he watches for more sign from Lowe. At a table behind sits Phil Jarratt, the former editor of *Tracks* surfing magazine. Phil is sitting with Paul Neilsen, Gold Coast legend, and a Yank journalist who is laying long odds on Mick Lowe to win the whole contest. Apparently, this Yank could see Lowe's shine as well. Michael hears the naysaying from the Aussies: *No way. He'd have to beat Kelly, Andy, and Taylor Knox to do it. Christ, but you're a mad seppo,* they say. *Put your money away.*

Put your money where your mouth is, Michael hears the Yank say. And they do. And Michael can hear the handshakes and backslapping all around.

Out in the surf, desperate now, Kelly Slater takes off outside, generates some wild speed, and jacks a suicide aerial. The crowd bellows. Michael's eyes do not move from the screen.

What was it that drove a man to the Ocean, to this kind of life and kept him at it? Nomadic instinct? Each wave a new life? A sense of some inborn irresponsibility? The same thing that made a fighter want to keep coming back after he has lost time and again?
Whatever it was, it was there. There inside a man. Not be denied because it could not be explained.

BAP! Michael Peterson hears a balloon pop. It does not move him or his eyes in any way. The room goes silent for an instant. Then Michael sees Rabbit Bartholomew laughing and follows his gaze to where Rabbit's son, Jaggar, sits on the floor in a knot of children, showing them how to pop balloons.

That's the way, little one. Pop balloons. Pop as many as you can find. Find your way through noise and confusion and embrace it and do not be afraid or surprised by it. Pop balloons, find your way, find the Ocean, and get out there and pop balloons.

Underneath the brim of his cap, Michael's unblinking eyes go back to the screen. Quarterfinals. He watches Mick Lowe uncork a series of backsides off the lips. Looking for balloons to pop. Kelly Slater sits outside. Mick kicks out. Fresh from his perfect heat before, Kelly now sits, helpless to the crowd's roar. Kelly slaps the water. Michael's catlike eyes squint slightly. He shifts his bulk in the chair, a bullfrog of a man, bloated with past vices and medications and hellish and heavenly memories of an Ocean that once made love to him. He thinks of his book signing the day before. The place was as packed as it was now. He had sat at the same table. Sister Dottie at his side, paper cup of Coca-Cola in hand. The tell-all ghostwritten book. His life and times. There for all to see. Michael Peterson, fatherless, product of a brutal, forgotten gang rape, drowning survivor, genius surfer, inventor of the modern cutback, greatest competitive surfer of his time, heroin addict, paranoid, schizoid, jailbird, fugitive, insane asylum resident, tube-rider, med-taker. It was all there.

It was all here.
Let the winds blow.
Let the swells billow.
Let them wash the soul of so much pain.
Let time hide me, let heaven and Ocean swallow so much shame.

The sounds of the beer garden are rising with each beer tipped. Boisterous shouting laughter reigns. Michael's eyes do not move from the TV screen now. Surrounded by a world he was instrumental in creating. Surrounded by the captains of the industry. The fat cats, the players, the soon-to-bes, the champions, the ex-rivals. All mates now. They were never the enemy. His enemy was within. He wished they'd all be quiet. The semifinals are in the water now. He knew it was no quieter in the water than it was where he sat. It just sounded better out there. Wind and spume, whistling barrels, hissing rails, spilling water. He watches closely as Taylor Knox spins down the line. Michael knows exactly where Taylor is going to fall off. And Taylor does. Taylor falls off like a junior and Mick Lowe soars again. There is raucous laughter from the gamblers behind him. He hears the words, *"It ain't over yet, mate; he still's got Andy Irons to see."* But Michael Peterson knows something more. He knows it is over. The Ocean is Mick Lowe's today. The crowd around Michael roars. The scores are in. Michael remains still. He feels his sister squeeze his arm gently. Letting him know they have stayed long enough if he wants to leave. He doesn't look at her, but he feels that squeeze all the way down his spine. It reminds him of the only real lover he ever knew. He remembers her waves and her jade-clear water and talcum powder sands and her dolphins racing his own shadow down the line.

What you have done to me was give me your one kiss, and we discovered all the love in the world and we gave it to one another. But then my mind betrayed it all for a poison girl, didn't it? No way around that. Well, the one who hurts, cries. I once went to the ends of the earth with you and for you, and you folded me into your womb and comforted me. Because I had cried enough and I deserved someone who loved me the way I loved you.

Michael Peterson watches Andy Irons surfing against Jake Paterson. The second semi-finals heat. Andy will win the heat, he sees that. But he also sees that Andy is beatable now. And by the most unlikely candidate of the day. Mick Lowe. Michael looks around the room without moving his head. Former world champions Martin Potter and Tom Carroll are deep in conversation, their eyes glued to the screen. Former World Champion Rabbit Bartholomew and his wife are tending to their newborn baby, Keo. Pneumatic bikini girls parade, applying sponsors' temporary tattoos to anyone who'll have them. Local surfer and brawler Bruce Lee is talking them into applying one to his forehead. The girls are laughing. The beer is flowing in gallons. Despite the air conditioning, everyone is wet with sweat. The heat is what a lot of this is about. The heat drives all animals to water. Michael Peterson knows this much. All kinds of heat drove him to it once. He remembers the details more than the scope. He remembers the Ocean tugging on his hair as he pushed through her swells, he remembers the showering spray of the offshore winds on his back as he punctured her dimpled faces, the crisp, breathing silence of her spinning tunnels and her warm, itchy salt drying on his back. He hoped all these people in the room felt the same. Beyond the lust for competition. He knows there is more to all this than what meets the naked eye. Riding a wave meets the naked soul. He knows that even though most of these people do not realize this, he knows they are drawn to it.

They are here because she is here.

How far I am from the place of my birth.
Memories visit me like a jester.
Seeing myself so sad, so alone in my head, so alone with land, my enemy.
So without my lover.
After all this time and all her waves.
I wish I could cry. I wish I could die of such emotion again.
Land of the sun, sea of joy, I fight to see you, to remember you not so far away.
After you, I lived without light, without love.
And I live now in between.

Michael Peterson watches only the first wave of the final. Mick Lowe scores an 8.17 out of 10, fanning a flame that he can see will consume Hawaiian Andy Irons in a conflagration of Australian patriotism. He sees it in Andy's world-champion, slumped shoulders. And Michael decides he has seen enough. In one silent motion, Michael Peterson stands. He turns to another table, finds the Yank's voice, and then finds the Yank's eyes. The Yank stops collecting his winnings for a moment and they hold each other's gaze. The whole table is watching this. Michael then gives the Yank a congratulatory wink. The Yank doesn't move. Nobody moves. Michael Peterson then allows his elbow to be taken by his sister, and she guides him slowly, carefully, from the room. And everyone in that room, even the little kids, watch as Michael Peterson shuffles toward the door, carefully steps through as his sister holds it for him, and vanishes into the outside world.

AUTHOR AND THE DAY AFTER.
PHOTO: JOSH SYMONS

SAVAGE BEAUTY

THE OTHER SIDE OF THE MENTAWAI
TRACKS MAGAZINE, AUSTRALIA, 2011

PHOTO CREDIT: JOSH SYMON

This was the second tsunami for me. The surf resort's main building had lost its first two floors. We were tearing around by boat, delivering emergency supplies and performing first aid. We came across this woman in a tent with her foot half-torn off. Myself an EMT, I chose to operate with the help of a fellow surfer. We sewed it all back together the best we could. They would arrest me for doing that in America. Years later, I lost my board at Silabu Bay and swam in over the reef to get it. There she was. With children all around her. A basket of fish on her head. A big, ugly scar ran halfway around her foot. She nodded at me once with a scent of a smile. Then she turned back and sauntered into the jungle with the kids in tow. —Mg.

The betrayal was complete. A roaring wall of Ocean water bursting through the jungle in the darkness of night. A sea where there should be no sea. Her child ripped from her arms, her husband found mangled and reeking in the debris two days later. She still could not bear the thought of what had happened to her sleeping infant. Below her left ankle, her foot had been half-severed from her bones after a tumbling nightmare through the grove of palm trees, tin rooftops ripping against the night like scythes. Here, on her home island off West Sumatra, she walks and remembers all this. She will always remember.

A lot of her died that night. And it had all started in the very church that was supposed to be her salvation. She remembers the long hours of that night, the bleeding, unable to move, waiting for the sun. At dawn, she'd fashioned some palm fronds around her knees and hands and had crawled to a makeshift hospital tent down by the small bay where the great waves had come from. She lay in a sweltering tent for another twenty-four, trying not to look at her swelling foot. *Wait for doctor,* she was told. And then the agony and the fear returned in the form of a sharp needle. Pushed into the meat of her foot many times over and over. A wicked-looking needle. And not by a local doctor, but by strange-smelling white men wearing rubber kitchen gloves. The searing bite of the injections was a deep, nervy pain. Childbirth pain.

She remembers. Though she wished she wouldn't. There had been more pain after that. Her eyes had swum before her as a big, hooked needle entered her skin around her raw wound. Her foot was now a swollen, bleeding pumpkin. She had passed out at the sight, awoken hours later. It was quiet. The white men were gone. She had stared at the top of the tent for hours. A hot rain had begun to fall. She had no idea what to do. She was afraid to sleep. The nightmare would return. That hoarse, steady roar of the Ocean, the screams, the entire village running past her home, that last wild look at the impossible sight behind her as she dove with her child into the safety of the small church. Then the explosion of wood and water and pews and prayer missals and hymn books and tin roofing. An ungodly force ripping her little girl from her arms forever. The tumbling eternity underwater. Lungfuls of it. The vomiting. And then the jungle silence.

And then that dawn had come. She had seen it blushing pink to the east. Still on her back, tangled in debris, she remembers searching the sky for answers. The clouds were beautiful. Unconcerned. The bald stalks of coconut trees had eventually come into focus. She'd tasted sand and sea and blood on her swollen lips. And she had started to crawl and crawl. Hours of it. Eventually, she found the tent. And so the tent had become her life. Everything else was gone. All that was left then was the taut, angry lines of black thread that had held her foot to her body. She walks and remembers.

Married late, she knew what was ahead. Too old to start over. A village tragedy. She would trudge into old age and become that mad, toothless fish woman. And people would shake their heads and pity her and pity themselves, for she would be their burden. Her husband dead, she would have to beg from them. She remembers a last thought that she'd had when she'd finally sat up and looked out of the tent. Staring out over the bay, ravaged and brown and choked with debris, the Ocean confused. She remembered, in that moment, everything had changed inside her.

She had reached up to her throat and ripped the cross pendant from around her neck. Now, she walks and remembers much.

Twelve nights after the surgery, the white men were back. The giant centipede of black threads was removed from her ankle. The white men were pleased. She was told she would walk again someday.

The next morning, a group of women who had lost their children and a group of women who had lost their men had come to her for help. They were to all to form a sort of orphanage. She was asked to be the headmaster. She was already holding another woman's infant to her left breast. As her milk flowed into the tiny creature, the sparks of a new connection to her island were formed. But this time far different than before. This time not with the enraptured sky of her abandoned religion, but with the mud between her toes. Because she could feel this suckling baby's heartbeat through her nipple. A faint, pulling whisper.

She had her secret. A new belief. The village women had told her not to worry. That Jesus Christ, in all his wisdom, had planned this all for them. It was a test of faith. Their doorway to heaven. The women had spoken of the Lord and his mysterious ways. That Jesus Christ was hope. He would provide. She had fought back a frown and nodded. Because she had a plan of her own now.

She would whisper the truth. In the orphanage, she would whisper the real truth into the ears of the young. She would whisper to them to never trust the phantoms of the sky ever again. That no thick-bearded God, no old white man, was sitting on a throne in the clouds and waiting for them with milk and honey. She would whisper to them that their world would always be here. In the mud. A world of bone and gristle, of blood and sand and more blood and jungle steam and the malevolent sea. And that nature would truly scream again. And that it would have nothing to do with Jesus Christ. *Be ready,* she would whisper into their small ears. *This is your home, no one else's. You must know how the Ocean can betray you.* And she would whisper these truths. She would tell them that in their world, they would find no peace from hardship. That theirs was a world of savage beauty. She would tell them.

She walks, sweating in the jungle heat, and remembers all this from the years before. She had kept her secret. Kept her promise. She had whispered to the children and they had understood. Magical tales of magical beings and magical lands that await the obedient were just that, magical tales and no more. Their lives were here and not up in the sky.

Now there were more white men around. Anchored in big boats in the greater bay not far from her jungle home. They were here to play in the Ocean and they needed more food. She carried a large basket of fish and fruit and eggplants and palm sago balanced atop her head. As she walked, a band of village orphans scrambled about her feet on the narrow trail. The moist jungle opened to the beach, its coral sands white as flour and dry as bones. And the greater bay spread out before them. A number of big boats were at restless anchor near the reef's crashing waves, and she could see the dots that were the white people playing in the Ocean. They would catch the waves on their small surfboards and stand up on the waves and shoot across the faces of them over the reef and into the deep channel. It looked like a kind of merrymaking. And that made her wonder if they knew, really knew, just how vile their playground could become.

The children who had followed her fanned out into the sun and sand, marveling at the shells and the hermit crabs and the bone dryness. The open dome of the sky, unobstructed by the jungle canopy. Full of all the possibilities of reality. She could see a sea eagle soaring above the greater bay. And she thought about how lucky that creature was. To be able to fly from harm in an instant. If only she could have flown away that night, her baby in her arms.

A smaller boat from one of the bigger boats had seen her and was coming her way. So, she put her burden down to wait. The kids were excited, knowing the white men would bring sweets and sugar drinks for them, as they always did.

She remains standing. She never sits near the Ocean. Not anymore. Not ever. She feels the soles of her feet rooted to the ground, able to run, feeling her regrets from that night long ago. If only she would have had warning. So she stands and sweats in the heat and watches the beach and the sea and the white men on the sea. Then, as she always does, she squints her eyes toward the undulating blue horizon. Wondering when. Never trusting. Never again. And a shiver runs up her spine.

WATER FROM THE MOON

SURFING THE SEVEN GHOSTS OF SUMATRA
SURFTIME MAGAZINE, BALI, 2011

PHOTO CREDIT: MICK CURLEY

Though surfers have always found and ridden tidal bores, there was something about the newly discovered Bono River tidal bore deep in the Sumatran jungle that took our breath away. The size of the wave, the color of the water, the crocodiles, and the tiny village that had lived with the phenomenon for so long. It was also an unnatural disaster. The silty deposits, which the wave broke over, are the result of the runoff from the horizonless tracts of surrounding land that had been leveled to make room for immense palm oil plantations. Still, the image of a surfer riding on the effects of the gravity of the moon and sun will always be our miracle. —Mg.

The Bulan

You are four billion years old. Old and battered and pockmarked. Yet you march on. Hung like a glowing bauble between heaven and earth. You are hurtling, wobbling, spinning through the freezing, lonely expanses of black space, forever held in orbit, being tugged at and broiled by the sun. And being loved and dreamed about from the earth, 384,300 kilometers below. The creatures below see you rise above the seas and disappear beyond it with wonder. You have made it possible for man to exist. With your tides that have risen and fallen for millennia. It was these tides, scouring the surface, leaving small pools of life, giving water in their wake, that allowed life to spring forth like a fountain. You shine full and round upon the lands with your ghostly glow like white candlelight, making faces beautiful and magical. Or you shine dim and hidden or as thin as a bent quill. Unlike the sun, you allow man long lofty gazes at your light, and in that moment, he transcends. And all the while, your mysterious power heaves the Oceans about as restless as the winds. You impose your will upon the seas, upon all waters, pulling a great mass of liquid in your wake. And the waters, they listen and heed your word.

The Lunatics

As the young Sumatran woman pushed the needle through his ear for the fourth time, James Hendy winced. That one hurt. Having one's half-torn ear sewn back on always does. Still, things could be worse, considering the caper that he had just pulled off. A helicopter, jet skis, boats, cameramen, surfers, all here in the middle of the sun-steamed West Sumatra jungle, quite literally up a creek without a paddle. And all to meet not so much a wave as a phenomenon. James and his crew all came in search of a rumored tidal bore that, pulled by the moon's power, created an upheaval, an imbalance on the planet, that resulted in a great bulge of water moving the wrong direction around the twisting bends of a remote jungle river with tree-snapping strength. On their last day, things had gone terribly wrong for James Hendy as he tear-assed around on the jet ski. The great force of nature, this moving mass of water at the mercy of three planetary gravities, had caught him and eaten him, and by the time the tangled wreckage cleared, a propeller had sliced his ear half off.

The young Sumatran woman pushed the needle through his ear again. The rubbing alcohol hissed. But James sat as still as he could, taking it. He felt like a completely different kind of surfer now. Remembering that the waiting was the worst. You could set your watch to this wave. You heard it before you saw it. Chewing up the riverbanks like an approaching dragon. And then it's there, in the distance, something impossible to believe. You blink your eyes. Squint them. And your mouth goes dry. And there is no paddling around it. No duck-diving it, no escaping it.

It is an advancing army. So you put yourself in its path and you pray. Hopelessly outnumbered.

Cosmic Children

In a discovery as wild as the Seven Ghosts tidal bore itself, are the toys that the children have adapted for themselves in the village of Teluk Meranti in Central Sumatra. The little boys who design, shape, and weight their own miniature surfboards. Then, after the tidal bore floods their village, they place these tiny surfboards, with their tiny riders attached, in ankle-to-calf-deep water. Then, mimicking the Bono River tidal bore, they shuffle their feet through the shallow water, creating a pressure wave before their legs. This allows them to surf their miniature boards with their miniature riders down the main street of town. By manipulating their legs, they have figured out how to create left- and right-breaking waves and control the size, speed, and power of these waves. They have favorite sections in town, outcroppings, sand mounds, and channels. They are going to start creating their own underwater contours out of rock-filled tin cans to create little mini barrels for their little surfers, and to use the wakes of the scooters that rip through town to set up their own miniature surf spots. And that each spot will have a name.

And the posture of this play is fascinating. Like the moon itself, which looks down upon their village from on high, so do the children look down upon the waves that they are creating. Their minds encased in their skulls are providing the science of this act, moving like Titans through their world, affecting all the little things that dare stand in defiance before them. If the subjects on their boards were actually human, they, too, would be looking up at a great globe that creates the wave they ride upon. And in the end, beyond all the science and imagination, is a reminder to us all. That surfing is a form of play. A simple, childlike act of gumption and play. And even here, on the far side of the world, deep in a primordial Sumatran jungle, surfing has found a people. And despite the violence of their wave and the fear of it and the lore of it all, it has still inspired the village children to invent an entirely new form of it.

A form created from the wonders of the celestial heavens and the eternal wonders of kid world. With both as mysterious and filled with perfection as the other.

THE COMING AGE OF
MARK OCCHILUPO

SURFER MAGAZINE, USA, 1987

For a man who has had his name misspelled all his life, Mark Occhilupo maintains a very familiar and happy place in our hearts. His 1999 World Championship remains one of the all-time greatest comeback stories in sports history. Even though all he really wanted to be was a lounge singer. I think this feature is a portrait of a very simple young man wrestling with what he was about to become. —Mg.

Mark Occhilupo and I sat waiting on the white-cliffed Ocean's edge of Cronulla, perched on a boardwalk railing. There wasn't much daylight left. We had just strolled down to look at the surf for the third time that day and found it the same as the first two checks. The moist, blustering onshore breeze was still pressing against the headland's surf, tattering it.

Mark had been gazing into the tidepools, softly smacking his lips to himself. He was somewhere else. He is always a little somewhere else. During the last couple of days, a time he had deliberately spent away from his professional surfing career, much had occurred. Mark continued to stare at the rocks and into the small mirrored bowls of low-tide sea life. As a row of foam swept in, erasing a hundred identical images of the sky, he shared a secret.

"Sometimes when I'm surfing, I look at my reflection on the surface of the water and . . . well, mate, I mean, it just seems . . . this reflection . . . it's like a second person staring back at me from the Ocean." Mark stopped there, perplexed, and then smiled. "But it is me, isn't it?"

I was silent. The thought just hung there, tapping its foot for a bit, until it was dismissed with a shrug and a chuckle from Mark. But this tiny scrap really stuck with me. As we walked back up the hill toward his place, I wondered who or what was going to answer that question for him.

Seven stories above the streets of his hometown, Mark Occhilupo stands on the balcony of his new penthouse apartment, showing me the view. A startling after-dark panorama spreads before us, stretched like a glimmering blanket from the glamour of Sydney, a half-hour train to the north, all the way back to the hustle of blue-collar Cronulla below our feet. Pieces of the night song floated up to us. Someone yelling for a friend across the main intersection of town, the squealing tires of a car in an underground garage, the loud hiss of the Ocean two blocks to the east. We could see clusters of people making their way through town, drawn like moths to the brightest place on the main drag. A muffled thumping coming from a windowless, dangerous-looking cinder block bar called Northy's Pub. We'd be headed there ourselves as soon as Jenny, Mark's girlfriend of two years, was ready.

Mark stood there with his hands clasped behind his neck and stretching as full as a cat. Earlier in the day, the '86/'87 pro tour had ended for him with a loss to Tom Carroll in the semis of the Coke Contest up in Manly. It was already being called the best heat of the Australian season. Mark seemed unaffected—hadn't said a word about it since I'd arrived. Probably because this had been one of the first opportunities he'd had to enjoy his brand-new digs, having bought the new condo sight unseen while he was in Hawaii earlier in the season. The place was sparsely furnished. One couch, a TV, and a couple of bedrooms. One he called his "boardroom," where twelve surfboards of varying sizes leaned up against a bare wall. There were windows everywhere, three plants, one cheap framed poster of some flowers, and Mark's Pipe Masters Samurai Kabuki Helmet trophy displayed on an end table. Not bad spoils for a twenty-year-old surfer kid who had yet to shave. He just stood there, taking it all in, slowly shaking his head back and forth with that faint smile of his.

"I know, mate . . . I can't believe it either. I can't believe I'm standing up here, woweee!" There was a genuine surprise in his voice, mixed with his chuckle. He was wondering just what the hell he had done to deserve such luck.

The elevator descended with just the three of us inside. Mark and the very pretty, very blonde Jenny were arm-in-arm, a picture of youthful ardor, cooing and teasing.

"Mark, look at you, you're such a slob," Jenny said as she poked at his arm. I had to admit, he was a sight. If there was any single description that fit Mark's general appearance in life, it would have to be "wrinkled." Tonight, he sported a long-sleeved shirt, one sleeve pulled up, the other not. He had too-big corduroy pants on that he had to hang on to by their belt loop, and he'd finished with blown-out, low-top sneakers and no socks. One shoe was untied. His hair was longish, a palm pushed through it its only grooming.

Mark answered simply, "Yeah, but Jen, I'm comfortable like this." Jenny fussed her best to straighten him up.

The elevator halted with a thump and opened. "Street level," a recorded voice said.

"Wow," said Mark. "Like a spaceship!" This luxury condo living was all new to him.

Across the elegant lobby stood the double security doors and a guy in a uniform. He opened the door for us as we neared.

Mark went to help him.

The three of us accepted the attention when we walked into the notorious Northy's Pub and took a place in the corner. The whole town had turned out for "Church," local slang for the Sunday-night rager at the North Cronulla Pub. The smoke-choked dance floor was dominated by the Black Uhlans, a heavily bearded biker gang. The band on stage, name of Bandana, crashed through "Sweet Home Alabama" as the Uhlans soused them with beer. The bikers all bellowed "Cro-nulla" instead of Alabama. Got a real kick out of it, too. A mob of boozed-up clubbies, the local lifeguards, had staked out a good portion of the bar, each with a different silly hat on his head. Seems it was Silly Hat Night for them. All the bricklayers and the rest of the working force, still wearing the cement and paint-stained t-shirts, had taken most of the "leaners," or standing tables. Over in the corner, where I had stood with Mark and Jenny, the local surfers had established a perimeter. The whole place stunk of burning cigarette filters, beer-soaked carpets, and the promise of bloodshed. The ghost of surf legend Robert "Bobby" Brown was in the room too. Back in 1967, Bobby, like Mark, was also a Cronulla surfing prodigy. A sure thing for the world title. Except that Bobby was killed in a bar fight with a broken beer bottle to the throat just up the street at the Taren Point Hotel.

Mark leaned over, sloshing a little Tooheys Gold beer, and yelled into my ear, "I always used to fit in as the young grommet, you know? I used to get patted on the head a lot, that kind of thing. But now that I've grown up a bit, I can walk into this pub and just be one of the boys. That is the best feeling. I have a strong blood tie with Cronulla. A strong tie for sure. For what it is."

The madness continued to swirl around us as the evening gained momentum. All girlfriends had long since given up on their men and now just schooled for safety. Gary Green and Kiwi Champ Ian Buchanan showed up and bought another round of bourbon, raising their glasses to the day's competition, a distant memory at this point. Mark's presence was a quiet one, almost sleepy, and he spent his time observing the proceedings through half-mast eyes. Once in a while, someone would bellow, "Good onya, Occy!" and clap him on the shoulder. He'd throw them a smile. He seemed a simple object of pride to this wildcat town. But in Cronulla, a town that's steeped in the lore of its underground heroes, the admiration is pure Aussie working man's soul.

As I returned from the bar, Mark spoke again. "Even apart from the surfing world, I'm beginning to feel like life is starting to happen. I've got a flat, a girlfriend . . . well, mate, it's unbelievable, really." There was that surprise in his voice again.

WHAM! Two figures in a violent embrace suddenly smashed into the cigarette vending machine we were leaning against and bowled down onto the floor, where both combatants began clubbing each other with their fists. "Oh God," said an exasperated Jenny, "not those two again. Don't worry Matt, they're brothers. They do this every Sunday." At this new development, Mark, Jenny, and I slipped over to the bar, out of harm's way. A circle was forming around the fight, the Uhlans roaring their approval. The evening had finally broken wide open. Down here at Church Street, the first official fight of the night was on.

Much, much later, I found myself standing on a curb out front of Northy's Pub with some new, very drunk friends of mine. Everyone was milling about, finishing off their smuggled beers and optimistically planning tomorrow's surf before drifting away. Mark and Jenny had left an hour or so earlier, and from where we all stood, if you wanted to, you could see Mark's new luxury apartment. The lights were on up there. Bluey, I think his name was, Cronulla Boardriders Club captain, had been staring up at Mark's balcony for a long while. When he was done, he saluted and then he mumbled "Oh, lucky bloody you, Occy." The salute put him off balance, but he recovered nicely. Then Bluey finished his beer with a dramatic belch, turned back to me with a thumbs up, and walked off toward the darker streets of Cronulla with his arms crossed against the chill of the night.

The next afternoon, Mark, his sister Fleur, Jenny, and I were bunched in the family compact, waiting to pick up Mark's father at the train station. From there, we would all be going to dinner at Mark's family house. We'd had a great day of surf at one of Mark's secret spots down the coast. A stunning, beautiful beach. A natural coliseum of verdant Australian bushland that faced a snappy five-foot beach break. The session had been all-time. Mark, "set free," as he called it. Had surfed hard, working over the lefts with knee-buckling efficiency. Powerful, full-on, full-rail. Raw exuberance.

I remember one moment from that session like a photograph. I was paddling out as he dropped late, skipped down a six-foot face, and didn't quite beat the lip to the bottom. It had blasted into the back third of his board, burying his legs. But instead of trying to recover, he somehow crouched into a bottom turn so extreme that his board shuddered, fins humming. An instant later, he was gasping for breath deep inside a beautiful barrel, perfectly trimmed. It smacked of genius, doing what he loved. Outside the surf, in between sets, he had told me how lucky he felt to be blessed with his body and how this had inspired him to care for it better. Vegetarian diet, yoga regimen. Somehow, by pure and simple chance, Mark Occhilupo had been born with a frame perfectly suited for modern surfing; 150 pounds, the ideal weight, five-foot-nine, the ideal height, counterbalanced by a low center of gravity, anchored by power-plant thighs for rotational fireworks. All this is connected to a slighter, more lithe upper torso that allowed for artistic expression and follow-through. He has never been injured, ever, and doesn't think he ever will be.

"I'm really comfortable physically, mate; no worries." He said that even his hair was part of the deal: "It can really affect my performance. Sometimes I like it long so I can feel it throwing the water around, and other times I like it short and . . . fast." Afterward, he, Jenny, and I had basked nude in the hot sand. You can do that in Australia and nobody gives a damn. Mark said it felt like a vacation. Jenny had to remind him that it was.

I told Mark I was going to turn on my tape recorder again. I told him he could talk or not.

In Australia, surfing comes naturally, like in Hawaii. Oz is this huge continent, you know? Like a Motherland, you can still live off the land here. You can still feel all that. Surfing's a part of this, I reckon, living off the land.

I don't care if there are people watching, I love to tap into the Ocean. I'm having my very best session when I'm blending with the Ocean.

When I compete, I feel like . . . I become animalistic. When I'm in front of a big crowd and all that hype, I love it. I love to fan out and flash and bring everything to a climax. I reckon that's the right thing to do . . . same like with a woman.

I'm really lucky. I can talk about a dream wave that actually happened. I got in this giant tube at Pipeline, right in the ultimate power point, so far back that my board came up and was actually floating on the inner explosions. It was like a magic carpet ride. I was in complete tune, in another time zone; it got to the point where it was really weird in there, with me looking out, and . . . it's hard to relate . . . Jeez, people will be out there thinking I'm crazy. But crazy is what makes dreams come true, reckon?

The train finally arrived, twenty minutes late, and emptied its harried commuters. Mark hopped out of the car, called out once, and then met a man in the street you would never guess was his father. A tall, dark, very Italian-looking man with jet-black, neatly oiled hair. Mark hugged his father briefly from the side. His father only used one arm. Then Mark opened the passenger door for him before walking around to get behind the wheel. I was in the back seat with Mark's sister, Fleur. As I met the head of the family in the rear-view mirror, it became clear that he'd had a long day. We drove for a while in silence, headed for the outskirts of Cronulla toward the township of Kurnell, where the family home is. There was a viscous air of respect for the patriarch Luciano Occhilupo, the "civil engineer." He sure didn't look like a civil engineer to me, with his beefy square shoulders squeezed into an impeccably tailored Giorgio Armani suit. But I'd be damned if I was going to ask for a resume. Occhilupo, in Italian, does translate to "eyes of the wolf."

Mark jumped in. "So, Daddy, what did you think of the contest yesterday, eh? I was on the news, hey?"

His father replied in a thick Italian accent. "But how come you fall off with that Tom Carroll many times?"

A cloud crossed Mark's brow. "Aw, yeah . . . I know. I fell off on the easy parts, too, eh, Daddy?"

"Yes, you deserve to lose twice for that."

His sister Fleur came to his rescue at this point, asking Papa Luciano about his day, but sneaking empathetic glances toward her brother. Despite this, the tension remained on Mark's face. Mark was quiet after that, smacking his lips softly and keeping his eyes on the road, driving slow as a grandmother. He always drives slow as a grandmother.

The dinner was marvelous. A vegetarian feast. Except for Luciano. He had four big meatballs in his pasta. And Italian Chianti from a straw-wrapped bottle. Mark's proud mother couldn't look less like his mother. She a petite, very white-blonde New Zealander with blue eyes. Who also happens to be a living relative to Sir Edmund Hillary, the first man to climb Everest. It was easy to hear where Mark got his distinctive high-pitched voice. Mark is the youngest child, the only boy, and is treated with unabashed child-like adoration from his mother, Fleur, and his other two older sisters at the table. I had expected them to break out into baby talk. I could tell this female mollycoddling rankled Luciano, who, at one point, made it clear that he would have preferred Mark be a great skiing champion like Italian Alberto Tomba. Mark remained preoccupied throughout. Later on, during the drive back to Cronulla, Fleur reached up from the back seat, placed her hand on Mark's arm, and said, "Don't worry, Mark; that's just the way he shows you he cares." Mark smiled vaguely at this, and drove on in silence, his eyebrows raised.

By 1:00 a.m., Mark's apartment was still. I was spending the night, at the couple's invitation. It felt like a slumber party until we all corked off. Having rolled off the couch for a drink of water, I now stood alone in his darkened living room, close against the picture window, looking out to sea. Standing there, nose-to-nose with my own reflection, made me think of what Mark had said down by the Ocean's edge. It seems that until recently, life had just happened to Mark. He'd simply played the cards he'd been dealt. That would explain his feelings of disbelief as he stood surrounded and baffled by "the benefits that have been given to me for surfing well." And that it was all so "unbelievable, really." But now it felt as if he were on some personal threshold.

Mark's incredible natural talent had afforded him wealth and potential greatness in this world. Perhaps for the first time in his life, he'd begun to question that. *"But it is me, isn't it?"* Maybe at twenty years of age, Mark Occhilupo was finally losing his famed innocence. No longer considering that fate was his stage manager. His passion for surfing waves is sincere and something he's only beginning to articulate. His world championship goals and the motives behind them, that much seemed to fit. But something was still missing. I could feel it tonight. He seemed unsettled, dissatisfied. As I looked around at some of the evidence of his success, the Pipe Masters' trophy, the new home, and its Camelot view over the surfdom, it made me wonder why. What more was he trying to figure out?

The dentist's drill had been whining steadily for over an hour before Mark Occhilupo came staggering back into the waiting room, his mouth half-stuffed with a tater-tot sized cotton wadding. I asked him how it went in there. He just plopped some strange objects into my hand: two blood-stained molars the size of large grapes. They looked prehistoric. He'd just had two new fillings, too. Mark Occhilupo loves his candy and soda pop. Since the surf was flat that morning, he'd decided to get the choppers taken care of while he could. He was taking all this in pretty good stride, considering the anesthesia and what had just happened to his skull.

We returned to his apartment and he stretched out on the couch, making jokes about the pain in his jaw. The sunlight spilled in as we lounged around, entertaining thoughts of a possible evening glass-off surf session at the small Shark Island despite the mouth sutures.

Out of nowhere, Mark piped in with, "Hey, mate, pretty heavy with my father last night, eh?"

I agreed, yes. Very heavy.

"It's really funny, you know?" he said. "How sisters don't understand the shit between a father and son. How we feel like we can never satisfy them."

I agreed again. Yes, it would be funny if it wasn't so fuckin' tragic.

He continued, "Well, I'm glad you were there to see all that. It really gives me a chance to say something I've wanted to say for a while now, and I think it has a lot to do with all these things that are happening to me."

He sat up and finger-hooked the bloody wadding out of his mouth, squeezing it in his right hand. Drops of blood fell into the new carpet, but he didn't give a shit. "Well, mate, I'm sure you noticed that my father is a very Italian-looking man. In this country, they have a name for that. They don't like immigrants. They call them 'wogs.' I guess it's like calling a Black person in America, well, something terrible, you know? Well, I really used to be embarrassed about that, that I was a 'wog,' you know? I used to hide in school, wanted to change my name and all that. I think my dad knew."

He took a deep breath here, collecting himself. "Well, the Coke contest was the first time my father has ever come to watch me surf. And when I saw him there off to the side, all of a sudden I didn't feel that way anymore. I didn't feel like a wog. I felt Australian. I have done some things now, and I was proud of family, my immigrant heritage. My dad has done a lot for me in his way. Pushed me. Helped me understand what's at stake for wogs. I mean, I carry my dad's name and I am just seeing what it means now. Nobody knows this, but my real name is Marco Jay Luciano Occhilupo with a C, Marco, and I reckon that's who I am now. It is me. Isn't it."

I could only say yes, of course it is.

And with that, Marco Jay Luciano Occhilupo, twenty-year-old pro surfer, son to a difficult father, adored brother to his sisters, and beloved son to his mother, laid back onto the couch, staring at the ceiling and looking satisfied with himself.

Then he blinked once, twice, and by the third, he was fast asleep.

IN ANOTHER
COUNTRY

GYPSY DREAM IN PORTUGAL
SURFER MAGAZINE, USA, 1991

If any sport is closely related to surfing, it has to be bullfighting. The maintaining of grace and control under deadly pressure. Against an adversary a million times stronger than you. Get as close to the horns as possible. To prove the theory, I went to the bullfights in Lisbon. —Mg.

It was the smell of blood that first reached into me. Metallic, heavy on the flat of my tongue. Like a dirty coin. The powerful bull was staggering around the ring, its breath rattling, blood streaming from its nostrils and back. Red spittle tattooed the sand with each of its snorting exhalations. Six barbed picador spears hung from its shoulders. Across the ring, the picador himself, who had just executed a two-handed two-speared thrust into the bull's massive shoulders, was still receiving the adoration of the crowd. The picador rode on perfect horseback, hands held high, dressed in impeccable sequined garb. He and his horse had been untouched by the bull. The crowd was wild for this picador, the applause stomping through the stands. One man threw his shoes into the ring—a gift to the brave bullfighter. The picador's job was through for the evening. Much would be said of this man's efforts in the morning papers here in Lisbon. And still, the great black bull paced its angry circle, awaiting the onslaught of toreadors, the men who would face the beast on foot. The picador scooped up the last of the roses and the shoes and made a grand exit.

The trumpets blared as the toreadors made their entrance. The bull stopped, measuring them. The beast seemed to be saving his strength. I watched from the box seats of the mezzanine level. It seemed fitting to me to spend my last night in Portugal at the bullfights. As the players moved into position within the ring, I thought back over the misadventures I'd had.

Lightning. Stark and icy on the horizon. A set of waves approaching through the gray downpour and towards the reef. I keep paddling out,

squinting my eyes against the stinging rain, tasting its fresh water on my lips. The clouds black, swollen, low. My friend, Josh Klein, traveling with me from Santa Barbara, is the only other surfer in the lineup. He is outside, paddling for the horizon. At the last second, he spins around, paddles once, and jumps to his feet, airborne. I wriggle my way up the face, not five feet away from him. Just before I try to push through the wave, a bolt of lightning cracks and overexposes the scene. For a brief instant, frozen unnaturally in the blue light, I see Josh connect with the face of the wave and gain control. His own face, open mouthed, is filled with surprise. On the peninsula, jutting out in the distance, an image of an old, tiled farmhouse lashed by the rain. There is a tractor and a cart full of hay tipped over beside it. Two horses are feeding on the hay. The lip of the wave has me now. I push into the blackness. Then comes the sickening tug, and I know I'm going back over the falls. I blink my eyes once.

Blackness.

In Portugal, they fight the bull by hand. A group of men take to the ring and stand in single file. The first in line walks up to the bull and taunts it into charging. The idea is for the man to test his courage by standing his ground in the face of the bull's charge. The man must then place his body between the horns, absorb the blow, and hang on as his friends jump on the bull and wrestle it to the ground. It is far more difficult and horrific than it sounds. This night, the entire stadium fell silent when the toreadors faced the bull. There was something about this bull. The picadors, the privileged gentry who fight so elegantly from magnificent horseback, are supposed to tire the beast so the toreadors, usually young peasants from an outskirt city, have an easier time of it. This bull did not look tired. It seemed to ignore the spears in its back, the taunts of the crowd, its own blood pouring from its throat. The men formed a line. The first man approached the bull slowly, taking half steps. The bull waited. The man got within six feet of its horns before it charged.

Christ, who the hell were these guys? Bandits? Trying to roll some white guy in a rental car? The girl in the seat next to me cried out in Portuguese, "Mother of God! It is my brothers! Drive fast, very fast. I will tell you when to turn!" I mashed the accelerator and lurched through the medieval cobblestone streets. I missed the first turn, took the second too fast, caromed off a stone wall, staving in my door, throwing sparks. I was driving straight for the castle gates. Within the walled city of Foz de Arelho this late at night, no tourists were about, thank god. I glanced at the rear-view mirror. The car chasing me had slammed into the wall and pinched its front fender against its front tire. One of the madmen was outside the car, pulling on it. I swung a suicide left and sped off into the night. We took the back roads south to Peniche, the small fishing village where she lived. I parked the car on the point, behind an abandoned house that stood all alone.

"Here they won't look for us," she said. We walked out onto the point and watched in silence as the fishing fleet came into the harbor. It was midnight. Her father would be on one of those boats. "You understand that each year, surfers come here. They are very charming boys," she said. "The girls here sometimes lose their hearts over them. Always the surfers promise. But they do not always return."

I nodded. Said I understood.

"No, I do not think you do," she answered. "Portugal boys are very proud. You see, if my brothers would have caught you, they would have cut your throat. Thrown you away with the old nets."

The first toreador took the blow like a ragdoll. The bull looked so much bigger now that a man hung from its neck. The man clawed for a grip and found the bull's eye socket and tore its eye out. With a short jerk of the bull's head, the man went flying off to the side, landing heavily. The bull scattered the rest of the men, each of them diving over the wooden barrier as the bull cut a path through them. The injured toreador lay motionless on the sand. He was smeared with the bull's blood, his right hand covered in gore. I could see the man breathing. He waited until the bull paced to the far end of the ring before he got to his feet and tried to make the barrier. Crawling the last five yards, he made it just before the bull slammed into the barrier, leaving a kite-size smear of its own blood. The fellow toreadors gathered around their comrade. There was heated discussion. Then the toreadors opened a gate and entered the ring once more. The bull watched them through its remaining eye. The crowd roared and stomped their feet. The stands shook. Even the police were waving their helmets. This bull was strong. Perhaps unbeatable.

I was completely lost. We'd left the villa over an hour ago. Fabio, our host, was having his brother take us to a secret spot that he knew of. Fabio's brother, Carlos, was motoring before us on his souped up 50cc scooter, picking his way through the dirt trails as they snaked through open country. Carlos would stop and look for something recognizable now and again, then race off in another direction. I had been in Portugal for a week and had never heard Carlos utter a single world. One of the trails came to a dead end. Carlos just looked back, smiled, and turned off his bike. Fifteen minutes later, Josh and I were following the brothers through more fields, boards under our arms. Thirty minutes later, we scrambled up a dirt cliff, up out of the valley we had been navigating. Soon, we were all standing on the edge of a dizzying white stone cliff, looking out at the Atlantic. The Ocean's surface was groomed smooth by an offshore wind. The water was aquamarine, indescribably clean. Fabio pointed out a reef that fingered its way into the sea. The water was so clear that the reef looked as if it were floating in mid-air. From the deep green, a series of waterbands moved towards the reef, warped around it, and turned into a set of perfectly breaking, top-to-bottom, six-foot, right-breaking waves. The waves foamed and hissed and spit, then disappeared. The reef seemed to float up again, waiting for the next set, the water perfectly clear again. As if the waves had never been there at all. Our mouths had gone dry.

At that moment, Carlos stepped up to me, clapped me hard on the back, and uttered the first words I had ever heard him speak. He then grabbed a rope augured into to a boulder and lowered himself over the cliff's edge. It took me a second to recover.

"What did your brother say?" I asked Fabio.

"He says, 'What is the matter, your tongue has been taken by the cat?'"

I heard a girl scream as the man died. The bull had charged head down, but at the last second, it feinted left and swung right, catching the man in the gut. It was over in three seconds. The bull split the man's chest open, tossed him, and then ran him over, breaking the man's twitching legs. The other toreadors scattered as the herders came in with tang poles and drove the bull out of the ring. I saw one man spit on the bull as it staggered down the chute and into the holding pen. He was yelling at it as it passed, *"Diablo! Diablo! Diablo!"* Four men in white entered the ring while carrying a canvas stretcher. They tossed the body aboard and carried it off without ceremony, a red-stained sheet pulled up over the man's face. The crowd took its time quieting down. Then, as at the end of some reverent mass, the stands began to empty. The shuffle of feet or an occasional murmur were all I could hear. I joined the crowd, jumping into a river of dark skin, a thousand colognes and oiled black hair. It carried me out into the street. Yet hundreds of the hungry hung back, waiting for the slaughter of the bull that would be butchered and its meat distributed among the poor.

It was one o'clock in the morning in Lisbon. I made my way down the main boulevard, past the exhausted-looking hookers in the park, the prowling cabbies, past the old castle. I had heard surfers even younger than myself argue that the spirit of travel surfing is dead, that it all has been discovered, and done. I have heard them speak of how travel surfing now is only about yuppies and surf camps and photo ops and touring pros. Safe and sane. Of how the concept of surfers as global wanderers, as a tribe of adventurers, will be forgotten by a new generation of Nintendo players. By a generation that is satisfied with fifty-seven channels of TV even though there is nothing to watch.

As I walked by the huge cathedral, an old gypsy woman appeared and offered me a goblet of wine and said I could drink it if I paid her to tell my fortune. So I sat on the cathedral steps with her and I drank the rich-tasting wine and she held my hand in her withered palms and closed her eyes. Then she began to speak in a type of English. She spoke of the future. Someday, she said, I would have two children. That I should avoid travel by ship or by camel for the next year. She also said I would always find what I was looking for, because I would always be looking for so many things. So many things, indeed. Her words. As she continued her incantations, I just sat there, holding her hand. Here I was, sitting on the steps of an old cathedral in Lisbon, Portugal, at one in the morning, hell and gone from home, having my fortune told by a wizened gypsy woman. I believed in that moment. Felt then that the spirit of travel surfing is not dead at all. It will always survive. The marvels and the memories. They're still out here for the harvesting. These days, it's just a matter of how hard you're willing to look. I know this for a fact.

Because a gypsy saw it in the palm of my hand.

OSCAR WRIGHT AND THE FEAR OF FALLING

FREE SURFING'S RESIDENT ARTIST COMES OF AGE
SURFER MAGAZINE, USA, 2002

ART CREDIT: OSCAR WRIGHT

Beneath Oscar Wright's "carloony" art and wild, junkie chic fashion, I discovered there was quite a story. After the horror he had been through as a child, I was surprised what a positive person he was. A millennial hippie without the weed. And a million-dollar free surfing salary to make it all work. —Mg.

Warriewood Headland, Sydney Northern Beaches, Australia
August 18, 2002 — 6:02 p.m.

What is it about the edge of a cliff that makes you want to stand so close to it? He looks down into the cold sea, wondering. He stands there, surfboard in hand, wondering what it would be like to jump and just keep falling forever. Below him, powerful waves slam into the cliff, sending rainbows forty feet up into the evening sun. He can taste them on his tongue. They are living things to him. He stares into the ocean. It isn't the surf that scares him; it's the falling. There is only one blue hole, eight feet square, twenty-five feet below his toes, swept by the impact of the surf. He must hit that spot perfectly. He wonders what it would be like to not make it. To just jump and find the other side. To fall forever. His childhood friend, Adam, all grown up now, stands next to him on the cliff, all nerves and laughter, waiting for his signal. But Oscar Billy Pippin Wright cannot hear him. Oscar is waiting. Not out of fear—out of curiosity. He is waiting for the wonder. Waiting not for the moment when he has to jump, but for the moment when he wants to jump. And it is this, this moment, that eve of falling, that frightens him more than anything on the face of the earth.

CRASH HOUSE

The first thing you feel when you pull up to Oscar Wright's house is that you have been here before. Or at least you have heard about a place like this so often, that it's vivid in your mind. A place that scares a quiet neighborhood. Unlike any other house in beachside Narrabeen, Sydney, Australia, Oscar's house rises like a Chinese lantern. Even in the middle of the day, it glows. Built by an eccentric some time ago who had since bailed for the warmer climes to the north. As you park out front, you feel as if the neighbors are crossing their fingers, hoping the arrival of a stranger does not mean another ear-shattering party, or worse, a ceremonial drum circle.

Before you walk around to the gate, it comes to you: this is an urban commune. And you immediately sense that this house is very important to the scheme of things in Oscar Wright's life. You will listen to him call it his first spaceship. And as he explains this to you, he will tell you the story of how he got it. He had signed the Holy Grail, his American deal with the Volcom brand, and that very day, he pulled up, looked at the house from the street, saw the for-sale sign, and bought it the next day without ever having opened the door. He could just feel it. This was home. He could make a stand here.

Now, inside the gate, half-buried female mannequins rise from the lawn like zombies, cast-off cartoon sculptures of yellow and gray lie like ancient ruins in the mud of the hedge and surfboards, lots of surfboards—scrawled-on, painted, angst-graffitied boards—are cast around the yard like fish dumped from a bait bucket. You pick your way through all of this to the front door. There is no doorknob. The door is held closed by a Bob Marley beanie wedged in the door jamb. It seems incredible to you that Oscar has only owned the place for four days and has already transformed it into the inside of his mind. You step inside and you witness the graffiti-sprayed foyer, the open living spaces, the walls piked through, all doors removed. Then the Polaroids strung together on the walls like bunting. London, art shows, Bali surfing, Swedish snow. You see the papers with scrawled notes, scribbled poems, unfinished short stories scattered on the floor and on the futons and on the couches with broken pencils and crushed crayons, and yellow paintbrushes underfoot.

You come to the main room and the "family" is there. Dashanka is first. Dashanka the muse, "Bunny Girl." She is in the kitchen making macrobiotic tacos and porridge. She drops everything she is doing, she throws her arms around you, welcomes you to the inner sanctum. Here in your arms, you hold the inspiration to almost all of Oscar Wright's art. His paintings, his sculptures, his comic books that reflect their sexy, wild counter-culture life together. Like Andy Warhol's tomato soup can, for Oscar, it's his cartoon images of Bunny Girl. And the genesis for Oscar's play on pop culture is here in the flesh. His icon, the model for the sublime cartoon images of a topless girl with playboy bunny ears, but this time around with chopped hair, cigarette butt in hand, and a middle finger thrust in the face of convention. She chirps a welcome in her native Czechoslovakian slang and gracefully guides you over to the rest of the family.

You leave her charm and embrace Adam Blakey, tall, rangy, a permanent smile curled on his lips. He hugs you so close you hear your ribs creak. Then Tim nods your way. Tim, the musician, all dark eyebrows and three-chord genius, eyes closed, guitar in hand, strumming a dark rhythm while Ryan, the skate ramp builder, sings lead. No need for a mic stand, he has wrapped strapping tape around his head that holds the microphone to his mouth. And Ryan's woman, Mylle, voice like an angel, harmonizing over the harsh chords, lost in a Rickie Lee Jones vibe. It is winter in Australia, and cold. The dress code is ragged. Hippie clothes, macramé belts, woolen caps, and hair, hair, hair, unkempt, sawed off, a study in disregard. And the men's pants, all impossibly torn up, hanging impossibly low, their waistbands defying gravity, their sweaters as moth-eaten as unearthed burial shrouds.

And then there is Oscar. The alpha male. Square-jawed, deep-voiced, filled out since you've last seen him. Taller. More confident. All ratty long hair and piano key teeth. He sits on the overstuffed couch, next to the beer carton, nodding to the music, chin raised, hearing it, smiling at you, smiling at what is all around him, at what he has made possible. What he has provided for his extended family.

In one corner, the musical instruments. Lots of them. Electric, acoustic, amps, wires, drums. Dashanka moves from the kitchen, serves Oscar his porridge, then she picks up an Irish hand drum, sits cross-legged on the floor, and joins the tribal music. For all the Woodstock overtones, not one bong can be seen. Or smelled, for that matter. And there is something strangely artful in that.

The walls are festooned with Oscar's art. Playfully sexy cartoon nudes. A lit-up, life-sized plastic statue of the Virgin Mary transformed into Bunny Girl. An entire wall a blown-up image of what looks like a South

American folk-rock band, four of the men in nothing but underwear, one of them with nothing on at all, his penis and balls gnarled as a root system. The family poses for a photo against the wall poster of the South Americans. Oscar eats his porridge. Points his spoon at the poster man's penis just behind his right shoulder, and howls.

Later, you move upstairs, another open space, airy, white, a double king-sized mattress on the floor, the bed clothes rumpled, just made love in. Surrounding all, propped up against the walls, are works in progress. More sexy images, more angst, and something else. Dashanka's art. Folk art, bent, images of bold colors and fanatic creatures in fantastic Chagall-like floating postures. Purples and indigos and pinks. Dominating the room, a twelve-by-twelve-foot projection screen. Propped up above the bed, a full-sized projector. This is for movie night. Every night. Rented or homegrown movies. All comers, all artists, are welcome. A space converted for the entire family to ritually crash where they lie, surrounding the bed, surrounding Oscar and his muse, all of them curled up like dozing chipmunks in their clothes, shoes, and sweaters. Most every night, they will fall sleep to the images and the soundtrack blasting away on the screen to the unwitnessed last credits.

You pick your way over the sleeping family and down the staircase through the kitchen for a drink of water and head out onto the back deck. You close the French doors behind you and sit at the pink, paint-splashed picnic bench and stare up into the heavens. Down at the end of the street, the Ocean crashes and sifts the sands of Narrabeen and hisses on the easterly breeze. The swell is building. The sound competes with the last of the surf movie blaring out of an open upstairs window.

You look over the fence and directly into the neighbor's picture window. It is 11:00 p.m. An older couple, kids long gone, looks back at you and then pull their curtains taut. They must pray tonight will be mercifully short. Four days now and they've already called the cops twice. Twenty-something, shiftless surfers are not supposed to be able to establish million-dollar communes next door. Not within Sydney's beachside mini-mansion compounds. Shiftless surfers are supposed to rent shabby apartments back behind the mall. Shiftless surfers are not supposed to make homes for themselves. Shiftless surfers are supposed to be lazy and ride broken bicycles with surfboards under their arms and live on welfare checks.

The neighbors' drapes are drawn tighter. Once. Twice. The surf movie upstairs stops, re-loops and starts over. There goes the neighborhood.

Again.

ITEM: On August fifteenth of 2002, *FHM Australia* noted that the new hippie chic fashion was "in with the kids." They traced it to its source and voted Oscar Wright the fifth best-dressed man in the country, behind Media Magnate Rupert Murdoch. On accepting the award, Oscar Wright says, "I love surfing so much, I would love to not know my age."

ITEM: (The following is excerpted from a letter to *Tracks* surfing magazine, blown up to a four-foot poster and glued to the wall of Oscar's late father's writing studio).

Dear Tracks,

Make sure Oscar Wright reads this.

What kind of image are you trying to portray here, Ozzie? You look like some fucking inner-city junkie. And yah, you're surfing like a flappy fucking kook at the moment, too. Do you think you can do art on boards, too? Your art skills are less than that of a two-year old; your sponsors must freak when they see the crap you put on your board. Is it what kids need to see? Surfing is about clean living, clear thinking, and matching yourself against mother nature. What do your parents think when they have to see you in your junkie outfits?

Come back to Earth, space cadet.

(Name withheld)

Below this, Oscar has roughly painted a devil character with a thought bubble that reads:

ONYA, MATEY!

OSCAR: I'm just living by example, being human, being three-dimensional. Why aspire to be mainstream when surfers are born into a slipstream?

RICK and CATHY

You stand in the work shed in the back of Oscar's childhood house up on the hill behind Narrabeen. The house where Oscar's mother, Cathy, and little sister, Annie, still live. Oscar bought that one, too. You stand with Oscar in the uneasy silence of the shed out back and feel what Oscar calls the "un-living room." His father is close here. Amongst the debris of paint and poems and smashed furniture and broken black-bottomed kneeboards and un-obtained dreams. Oscar's father is still here in this house that was once home to the coolest parents in the neighborhood. The kind of parents who would let your friends crash for weeks. The house with no schedules and no rules and late teen nights and midnight stories and scribbles on the walls and *Tintin* comics and imagination and hellfire music. The house with the funky-colored doors and the Buddha shrines and the Hindu shrines and the Jesus shrines and the kids' artwork all over and the big, simple meals that you didn't have to wash your hands for with plenty for everybody, anybody. And the front porch blocked by boxes and boxes of books, that had all been read but not forgotten, standing swollen and growing with some tired promise to drop them off at the Goodwill store so other kids could love them.

This house is where there was so much love. And the father is still here. The late Rick Wright, Oscar's father. A mad genius with a private, acute perception of a world that had disappointed him. Living with a self-inflicted gunshot of the world on his mind and a rage inside him that would explode one Christmas morning and shatter not only a family but a community. Probably manic depressive, certainly bi-polar, Rick was a friend to all, yet an enemy to himself. A gifted kneeboarder when such things were cool, a frustrated writer when such things weren't. A horticulturist who wanted more out of this world than the workaday life of a hippie dad who found out very quickly that he had mouths to feed. Who spiraled into a perception that he would never have the time or the intellectual keys that it took to be the published writer. Conradian in his pain, like Kurtz, "his mind was sane, but his soul was mad." And one early Christmas morning, Rick Wright found the exit. Excusing himself from the traditional family pancake breakfast, he quietly walked into his bedroom, shut the door, and hung himself on the doorknob by strapping his leather belt around his neck and sitting down to die. The police would later comment on the incredible willpower that this technique of suicide would demand.

The lead cop who wrote up the report was a friend of Rick's. He would report that Rick Wright "had not lost his life, he'd left it behind." And it was Oscar Billy Pippen Wright, sensing something was wrong in the house, who went looking for his father that Christmas morning. And he found him.

Oscar had just turned eighteen.

So you stand in the shed in the backyard today with Oscar Wright. In the shed that Oscar describes as his father's "important space," and you listen closely to a twenty-six-year-old Oscar talk quietly of what it all means.

He was just a crazy man. Real bad temper toward himself. Smoked a lot of weed. That seemed to help.

He hung on for while, on the edge . . . as long as I can remember, I never depended on him to lead a long life.

I guess he just couldn't break through to his other side.

Strange how I felt. As soon as I found him, I knew he was dead. And I wondered what it would be like, you know? Death. Then I ran screaming.

I never really got any counseling, just heaps of good mates . . . Counseling, maybe I need some, but it's that whole talking-to-a-stranger thing.

He was full of encouragement for me and my art. Always told me to go for it. Always told everyone to follow their dreams. My friends dug him. The most valuable thing he ever taught me was to never conspire against your heart. To never spend your days doing something you weren't born to do.

I'd love to be my father at fifteen, see if I could make it work.

Twenty days after my father died, I signed with Volcom for the first time. He would have cheered.

The new house, it's like a dream. I want to grow it like a plant. Plenty of sunshine. It's all I've ever wanted. To get a house so that I could have people come together and share, have parties, play music, make movies, whatever. I'm never alone now. I hate being alone. I love being around people.

And then Oscar stops and a silence falls in the shed. And in this space, you are with them both. His father's space that Oscar was using as his own art studio. And you realize that right here, right now, Oscar is leaving this space behind for the first and last time in his life. Oscar's new studio is down the hill in the new house. His house. And Oscar Wright ages right in front of you. He becomes a man. And so you listen to the silence, and you think of the long hours Oscar has spent in this space, making his art, listening to his dad's advice, never conforming, being what he was born to do, being with him. And it is then that you realize that you, too, love being around people and that you too hate being alone. And so you say it out loud.

And Oscar nods. And then nods again.

"Let's go back," Oscar says.

And you and Oscar leave together, arms around each other's shoulders all the way down the hill.

Word association with Oscar Wright on the way down the hill:

Love: "Finding it."

Light: "Impossible to stay out of it."

Favorite moment in life: "Taking off."

Favorite moment in art: "Finishing it."

Love: "Lots of it."

Favorite color: "Dirty."

Pro tour surfers: "Different strength."

Money: "Love it or lose it."

Fame: "A two-way radio."

THE IMPORTANCE OF BEING OSCAR WRIGHT

So you drive away from the house that Oscar built. And you think. You think on the significance of a surfer like Oscar. And you realize that, like any good human artist, with all the scars that life can heap upon them, Oscar has no business with big business. And like all good human artists, he is being recognized for it. Not only financially by the very corporations that he chooses to ignore, but by a larger group of surfers out there who are no longer feeling the need to succumb to the marketing of the pro tour as Valhalla. By surfers who need not lead or follow, but by surfers who just want to be. A scruffy-haired multitude, the new bohemians, a new wave that is choosing to listen to the voices in their own heads, to listen to their own artists within and act on that. Whether with paintbrush or surfboard, despite all that Oscar has and all that will happen to him, he will always draw outside the lines. And that is a hope for many. In Oscar, doing so lies a kind of desired prophecy. A new movement. A new belief. Drawing those who care to explore into their own third dimensions.

Warriewood Headland, Sydney Northern Beaches, Australia
August 18, 2002 — 6:03 p.m.

The time is now. Oscar Billy Pippin Wright is overwhelmed by it. He wants to jump. A giant set of waves washes over the rocks below. It is not well-timed, but his legs push off into the abyss and he is falling. And the wonder is over. The wonder is here. And it is here, falling through space, that he feels as close to his father as he can get. He is filled with the fear of falling, no way back, falling toward the other side, falling toward the eternal question, falling forever toward a cold, unknown, enveloping blackness. Then it, too, arrives, and Oscar Billy Pippin Wright plunges into the sea and is swallowed into an airless place, a dizzying place, a dark and lonely place. And for a moment, as his momentum downward stills in a swirl of hissing bubbles, he opens his eyes and looks into his fear. It is there, stretching off as endlessly as the cosmos toward the four corners of the globe. And he is not afraid of falling anymore. He knows he will never be afraid again. Oscar hesitates, cheeks bulging with air, with his father's final solution washing across his mind. And then, exhaling, with a great sweep of his arms, Oscar Billy Pippin Wright chooses to swim up to the surface again. He swims up. Up toward life. Toward love.

Toward forgiveness.

CRITICAL MASS

SUNBURNT MUSINGS ON THE 1996
NSSA NATIONAL CHAMPIONSHIPS

SURFING MAGAZINE, USA, 1996

A relentless northwest wind pressed in over the crumbling four-foot south swell. It was late afternoon and I lie on my belly in the warm sand of southern California. I was at Trestles, the famed California surf break, site of the 1996 National Scholastic Surfing Association Amateur Championships. There were a million twenty-minute heats to get through in a week. They were as relentless as the wind. After all, this was a contest that was grinding its way toward a Saturday that would feature twenty-four separate finals.

A big set of waves rolled through, and little Melanie Bartel took off late and charged down the line. Surfing desperately, as if she knew that the exclusive rights to this break were costing the NSSA eleven hundred bucks a day. I'd heard a lot of talk about money at this contest. All different kinds of money from all kinds of different people. Hell, I'd heard lots of things, but as I lie there, watching, on the beach, I knew the real truths of this contest wouldn't be found in a money trail.

I knew this from looking into the eyes of Malibu's Jordan Tappis. He'd been scraping by in his heats so far and had finally asked coach Mike Lamm's opinion on what it took to win this thing. Mike rolled this thought around a bit, considering all the things he could say, all the countless things he had already said. He finally settled for, "Go surf like Melanie." Jordan, inspired, paddled out and surfed wildly, throwing his weight around, carving, not waiting for some hopeful floater at the end of the wave. He wiped out a lot. And he didn't win. But I saw Mike Lamm tousle his hair and pat him on the back of the neck when he came in. Jordan's shy smile said that this meant more than a trophy to him.

I'd looked into the eyes of Skip Bleckley. At seven years old, he was the youngest of the brave 600 who had shown up for this thing. Skip weighed about as much as a bag of rice. He told me the whole reason he goes to school is because of Kelly Slater. He said he was "gonna be pro and make a couple three million dollars someday." Then he ran off and took on a kid twice his size in a sand fight. That's when I knew he just might make it.

I looked into the eyes of Bobby Martinez. A fourteen-year-old who already had the same Hollywood agent as Kelly Slater, Rob Machado, and Kalani Robb. Like many of the surfers here, he was already fully cash-sponsored by a number of companies. You could see that, aside from the normal concerns of a fourteen-year-old, things like acne and spin-the-bottle-games, this kid knew about the sixteen grand. That's the limit now. Amateurs are allowed to make up to sixteen grand a year, receive free travel slush funds, can appear in all the ads and videos they want, and still remain amateur. Bobby smiled like a fourteen-year-old. A really, really talented fourteen-year-old. As Bobby walked away, fellow open junior competitor Aaron Wonders, who was sitting next to me, watched him go. Then the unsponsored and sullen Aaron threw a broken seashell into the sand and said, "If you're not gettin' paid by twelve these days, forget it."

I looked into the eyes of T.J. Barron from Hawaii. All teeth and brown skin. If anyone in the contest surfed like a man, it was this nine-year-old. His semi-final heat had the biggest waves of the day. Considering that they were all still bundles of sinew, these little guys made the surf look huge. One particular set rolled through, and while most his competitors were washing around in the rinse cycle, T.J. calmly paddled up the face of a close-out and picked the perfect gap to punch through. For one moment, he made Trestles look like stormy, gnarly Haleiwa on the North Shore of Oahu. He let the next wave, an even bigger one, suck him up the face sideways before he did a no-paddle takeoff and tore like hell for the shoulder. Louie Feirrera, Hawaii's team coach, was beaming. Trestles is a walk in the park for a third grader who surfs Pipeline.

I looked into the eyes of NSSA Executive Director Janice Aragon. She was proud of the fact that the reason most of these kids go to school at all is so that they can be in these contests. She told me that these kids are looking at careers here and "a lot of money." And that plenty of the parents had changed from soccer moms and dads to surfing moms and dads "now that the cat was out of the bag." That they knew that their kid, if he played his cards right, could be a star, could bring home the bacon. I asked her what school had to do with all that bacon. After all, of the fifteen kids I asked to spell the word dictionary for me, not one got it right. One NSSA scholarship recipient had given me "dikshonary." Another kid just a blank stare.

"Well, don't blame us, blame the public school system," Janice had said. "We require report cards from these kids, and they at least have to have passing grades."

"Do you mean," I asked, "that as long as a kid got all Ds, he could still be a National Scholastic Surfing Association Champion?"

"Sure," Janice said.

At that moment, I felt the ghosts of Ted Robinson and Kelly Gibson crawl up my spine. The guys who had been the pride of the NSSA. Grade school champions, then junior college straight-A scholars. Until it was discovered that they had been falsifying their school records and playing hooky, never having spent a single second in any J.C. classroom. The NSSA went into damage control. Robinson and Gibson copped a plea and walked after signing non-disclosure agreements, surfing's version of the witness protection program. It became the biggest cover-up in surfing's history. Robinson and Gibson went on to pro careers.

I mentioned this precedent to a parent. She asked not to be identified. Parents of the amateur ranks had been asking not to be identified for years. I never got it. Until I saw some graffiti contorting the two middle letters of the NSSA logo into that of the Nazi SS forces.

Anyway, with this unidentified parent, I had fallen into a conversation about the battle of youth and drugs. This parent said she would like to see drug testing in the NSSA. And that she knew drugs were out there but that most of the kids just cover for each other. It seemed to really concern her. But not open women's competitor Jaime Lagardere, age seventeen. She had been listening to our conversation while watching a wrestling match between a girl and a boy who, after a full week of flirting, still couldn't think of a better way to get close to each other. The girl had the guy in a hammerlock. It was beautiful, in a way. Jaime just watched, amused, and then said, "Drugs? Boys are drugs."

But it was looking into the eyes of Bill Delask that put this whole event into perspective. I met Bill while he was waving his arms, in semaphore fashion, at his daughter Janey, thirteen, who was out in a heat. He explained to me that it was a signal system between the two of them, influenced by his stint in the Navy. Right arm spun in a circle means you are running out of time. Two hands in the air, set approaching. Drop the left hand means paddle south for best position, and so on. It was a strange ballet, but it was working. No wonder. Bill was also little league coach back home in Beach Haven, New Jersey.

"Mind if I smoke?" he asked.

"Fill yer boots," I said. Bill said that was the first time he'd heard that response out here in California. It was a close heat out in the water. Bill's hands shook as he lit up his Lucky Strike. He offered me one.

"Not right now," I said. Far be it from me to chastise. I wanted him to feel less criminal out here in the land of the lotus eaters.

"Boy, do I need this cigarette," he said. "Any parent that tells you they ain't shakin' when their little girl is out in a heat is lyin', by God."

I looked around at the other parents down here at the water's edge. Two of them were chewing their nails. Another was chewing tobacco. As the heat ticked away, Bill told me he was a tow-truck driver. He and his little girl had saved up every penny they had to come out and surf in this thing. Bill had been surfing all his life and this was his first visit to California.

"My youth slipped away into hard work," he said. "I'll be goddamned if I'da let Janey get as old as me before surfing out here. I figger that this whole trip already been worth from the first day. We landed at John Wayne Airport there, rented surfboards from some surf shop at a hundred bucks a pop, and found our way down to Trestles by ourselves. Next mornin' were out afor' the sun. The surf was perfect, and me an' Janey had the surf session of our lives together." Satisfied he'd told it right, Bill took the time to light another cig with his Harley Davidson zippo. He blew on the tip of the cigarette to really get it going and then he inhaled the smoke to the very tip of his toes and exhaled it in a cloud. Satisfied, he spit out a fleck of tobacco and looked around at the contest, the scaffolding, the team tents, and the people. He turned to me and said, "I don't know where all this is heading for Janey and me, I really don't. But we're here, ain't we? Ain't that the damndest thing?"

Then he hung that cigarette between his lips, held his hands over his head, and signaled for his little girl to paddle to the north a little bit.

And little Janey did.

BEYOND
THE GREAT WALL

THE FIRST SURFERS IN CHINA
SURFING MAGAZINE, USA, 1987

PHOTO CREDIT: WARREN BOLSTER

This was an early work. We were the first surfers to ever be invited to the People's Republic. The Chinese were hosting us in hopes that we could train their athletes to be gold medalists as soon as surfing made the Olympics. I had to explain to them that it would take more than just two weeks to do that. As it turned out, surfing wouldn't be in the Olympics for another thirty-three years. —Mg.

On the front sidewalk of Beijing International, a Chinese man dressed in a western-cut blue suit paces for warmth. Next to him, rising above of a scurrying crowd, a large rattling tour bus waits patiently, like an ox awaiting a new burden. The man is tall, well over six feet, and his stride is long and unhurried. He is China's former Badminton Champion. Now a specialized handler and fixer for the government, fluent in English, he was assigned these duties quite often. Greeting foreign athletic delegations, showing them the sights, getting them to their appointed rounds, keeping the rabble away from them. He stops and glances at his American-made waterproof digital watch that the government had outfitted him with. As they outfitted him with all his other watches that he wore, depending on who was showing up. They were manufactured in many different countries. Knowing foreigners' obsession with time, they were meant to put visiting international delegations at ease, seeing their schedule kept on track by a timepiece from their own country. His American guests would be arriving within the hour. He wondered if these guests would be like so many others who had flooded in when his country had finally opened her gates. Shallow and deaf to the whispered secrets of China. A practitioner of Transcendental Meditation, he recalled a passage from the first poem of the Tao Te Ching:

"The secret waits for the insight of eyes unclouded by desire. Those who are bound by desire see only the outward container . . ."

Yes, the man thought, the outward container is all that most see. Because the desire to see only that which one wants to see seems to be at the center of all Western thinking. This was the kind of thought he had been trained to swerve away from and one that made him turn quickly and continue his pacing, hoping that maybe this time things would be different.

December 19, 1987 — Somewhere Over the Hubei Province, China

A thump of turbulence awoke me. A shudder that shook me from the misery of upright airline sleep and into the consciousness of China. We were descending. It had been a rough flight, titanic thunderstorms rising into the heavens like smoke from monstrous explosions, becoming massive lanterns flashing pink bruises. Our surfing delegation had all met up in Hong Kong a few hours earlier and had just made the last CAAC flight bound for Beijing—myself, my fellow Californian Willy Morris, Hawaiians Jon Damm, Rell Sunn, and Warren Bolster, who was our photographer. I unbuckled my seatbelt and made my way to the front of the cabin where I knew I could find them in the galley. We were the only Caucasians on the plane. I found them glued to the port windows, taking in their first look at China from 30,000 feet. Over their shoulders, through a streaked window, a conveyor-belt view of the country revolved. The Yangtze River was weaving a khaki ribbon through an immense patchwork quilt of cultivated brown and drab-olive squares, as uniform as a chess board. Ruler-straight roads spider-webbed out from small settlements and stretched towards larger townships. The whole plain was butted up against a star-peaked mountain range to the east, shrouded in a ghostly mist. It started to sink in for all of us, what we were doing. A pack of surfers, upon the invitation of the Chinese Yachting Association, on our way to introduce the sport of surfing to the People's Republic of China.

The aircraft continued its choppy descent. We returned to our seats. It had taken us about two years to get this far. Months of planning, countless negotiations, setbacks, reams of telexes, faxes, and letters of marque. The entire project was shelved a few months earlier, but luckily, an eleventh-hour reprieve came in the form of Bob Roos and his Delta Institute, a San Francisco-based non-profit organization that has experience in Chinese/American delegation coordination. By lucky coincidence, Roos was due to visit Beijing and offered to talk to high-level officials on our behalf. With his help, the *SURFER* Magazine China

Exchange was kicked into high gear. I remember smiling at the thought of Marco Polo as a surfer.

November 01, 1987 — The Great Wall, 110 km Outside Beijing, China

A raw wind tugged at our hair and swung our surfboards as we continued to hump up the longest man-made structure in the world. Once here, witnessing the enormity of it, you damn near believed the myth, that the path that the wall follows was formed 2,700 years ago by a giant dragon dragging its tail. This section of The Great Wall was very steep. Willy Morris and I had shaken our two ever-present handlers and bolted up an endless stone rise. In what we all felt was an appropriate historic gesture, we had brought one surfboard each. The first surfboards to make it to the Great wall. At one point, a timeworn Chinese woman asked me what I was doing on the Great Wall with an airplane wing under my arm.

Willy and I had decided to climb to the north. But to explain our desire to clamber up and out of the tourist throng behind us is to describe our experience with China so far. We had been met at the airport as if we were Led Zeppelin, hustled into a huge tour bus, and put up in the finest hotel in Beijing. For four days, we had received five-star treatment, six-course meals, and a major tour of every great sight and temple and Holy Ground that Beijing had to offer. Our hosts had been unendingly kind, and these sights had been impressive. Beijing was a massive cement city centered around the vast square of Tienanmen. Rivers of humanity, loose-suited in quilted Mao Blue jackets, flowed about on identical black bicycles busily yet efficiently. Side alleys teemed with markets and even more people, crowds of people everywhere you looked. Heavily lidded people, red cheeked against the cold of the approaching winter. Occasional bands of soldiers in loose-fitting uniforms of green and yellow could be seen amid colossal temples and palatial grounds, spring loaded for action, oozing iron discipline. Bright banners and standards flew from everywhere they could find purchase, along with massive fifty-foot-high portraits of buttoned up, swollen-looking leaders both past and present. It was a pulsating city, crammed with a torrent of human life that swirled around its ancient temples and new hotels with the inexorable force of the tides. Facing the massif of the Forbidden Temple, we were served an elegant outdoor banquet under a pollution-burnished sky in the center of Tienanmen square. No one seemed to find anything strange about a group of surfers enjoying a six-course dinner service, complete with white tablecloths and white-gloved attendants, dining in the shadow of the Temple of Heaven. Either that or this was the most well-behaved populace on earth. Or the most well warned.

But despite all this good cheer on our behalf, I still felt an undercurrent of emptiness about the experience. It was a feeling that dogged me wherever we went. We weren't breaking any new ground here or witnessing an ancient culture, we were being ushered through pre-approved, well-trod vista points. Just as visitors to America would see the Statue of Liberty, the Grand Canyon, Mount Rushmore, Disneyland, and the Golden Gate Bridge all in one week. Take this day: as we pulled up to The Great Wall, the symbol of all that is the mystique of China, we were captured by t-shirt hawkers, Great Wall ashtray sellers, and god only knows where the world supply for those stuffed frogs playing guitars come from. As we formed an offensive, surfboards as shields, and pushed on to the wall, megaphones ordered us, in six languages, to use the handrails once we made the ramparts. The new stainless-steel handrails that had been sunk into the ancient Great Wall of China.

Still, the wind on top of the final rise was fresh as a wild stream compared to Bejing. Willy and I plopped ourselves down against the protection of a crumbled battlement. A muffled silence fell over us. There was nobody in sight up here beyond the handrails. Grass tufted between the cracks in the stones, the parapets stalwart in their original form. Before us, off to the east, stretched The Great Wall. Lunging like a Greyhound over the landscape. A graceful serpentine organism that ran itself up and over in concert with the contours of the range. Like most structures in China, its architecture was not designed to the scale of the human body. It was designed to the scale of the human spirit. After a few minutes, I stood up and let the wind tear at me. I wondered if this meant there was an offshore wind grooming surf somewhere in the South China Sea. As I stood alone, I thought of the ten million visitors the Great Wall hosts every year as one of the most popular tourist attractions on earth. Ten million people pattering about on this timeless structure with its violent, cruel history. I had fallen into a conversation days earlier at the Ming Tombs with an English-speaking Chinese tourist. Closely watched by our handlers, she had said that many Chinese felt that their country had reached its peak long ago, during the feudal ages.

"Our past was a time of great things and of a great people," she managed to say before the handlers bundled her away. "All was certain. Now it is not this way, you see." But I wasn't so sure I did. All I felt now, as I gazed out over the landscape of The Great Wall, was a sense of a million souls, a million stories, a million meanings lost to time. And my surroundings seemed a terribly lonely place, alone and forgotten in their monumental grandeur.

November 10, 1987 – Spring Bay, Hainan Island, in the South China Sea

At the top of one of the gargantuan sand dunes that flanked Spring Bay on Hainan Island in the South China sea, Jon, Willy, and I were basking in the sun like California lifeguards. Shortly, "The Thunderdome Kids" would be showing up again and our surf school for the day would begin. I could see Rell Sunn down below, surfing in the three-to-four-foot windy surf. It was astonishing entertainment for the gallery of local titanium miners that lined the beach. They mine the stuff by hand around here. They had wandered down out of their sand dune shanty town to check out all the commotion that had been going on for six days now. Our handlers and two reporters from a Beijing newspaper were with them, trying to explain things. The miners were amazed that a woman could "easy handle violence of sea." As Hawaiian royalty and a famed big wave surfer, Rell got a real kick out of that.

The colossal bay was embraced by two rocky headlands and faced the brunt of the wind swell that we had been surfing for the last week. These headlands bore the scars of gargantuan surf. The foliage had been flattened or torn away as high as forty feet in some spots. With fear in their voices, the miners that burrowed into these dunes for titanium spoke of the untamed storm surf of the typhoon season. At the moment, it was hard to believe that this place was anything but idyllic. We had long since fallen into its languorous rhythms. We were hell and gone from the official receptions and banquets of Beijing now. We were just surfers on a beach. And the local walks of life had become our friends.

It had been just six days previous that we had been bumping and chortling along in a caravan of tiny minivans. We were following a narrow dirt track that led to this coast. Trailing in our dust was a green canvas-draped military transport truck that carried our boards and gear and a handful of Chinese soldiers. We were getting very close to the sea; Rell could smell it. We had been in China for ten days and we'd finally worked our way within striking distance of some waves. Our feelings were about the only things familiar to us at this point. The anticipation, the sweaty impatience of a surfari in position to score. Yet our hunt was taking place in an otherworldly way. Our handlers, having thrown off the shackles of convention now that we were all free from Beijing scrutiny, were up front, blasting Willy's Springsteen tape turned up to ten. Any pop music tapes with intelligible lyrics were a real prize to our hosts. Many Chinese secretly learn English this way. Jon and Rell were pouring over the coastal charts, cross-referencing opinions, making decisions. Warren was in the back, all business, quietly checking his camera gear, loading some film, cleaning a lens. And me, I was staring out at the same kind of Asia I used to see every night on the six o'clock news during the Vietnam War.

We were jostling along one of the countless levees that laced out over the surrounding rice paddies. Great round holes, as precise as crop circles, about thirty feet across and about twelve feet deep, could be seen in strange rows, edges softened by lush green and yellow overgrowth. These were carpet bombing tracks. If the American A-6 Intruder pilots of the Vietnam conflict had any ordnance left under their wings after crossing back over the Gulf of Tonkin, they unloaded it here on southern Hainan Island. Damn the politics. There were suspected Chinese sympathizers in these parts, secret ground-to-air missile silos, training camps, the works. Or so it was accepted as truth.

Along this dusty track, we would pass through the occasional settlement, farmer's wood-and-mortar compounds with monstrous sway pack sows, running herds of a thousand ducks, naked street children, and market stalls with hanging flyblown meat and trays of drying rice. Out among the paddies, at what, from a distance, looked like delicate flowers, were the round bobbing, white silk sunhats, as big as wagon wheels, that the female workers wore as they bent at the waist, knee-deep in their labor. Before them, men in breech clouts drove grooves into the loamy earth behind copper-colored black-nosed oxen strapped to straining wooden plows. Now and then, a few of the people raised their brown and wizened faces in consternation, judging if our motorized procession meant any more trouble in their lives. It was a lush and swollen atmosphere that rolled by outside my window in survival mode. A harsh contrast to the electric, pulsing, air-conditioned confines of the van.

Our exotic motorcade had eventually led us to Spring Bay and its playful shore break surf. Having actually found any waves at all felt great and touched off a couple days of optimistic exploration. But after finding similar conditions wherever we went and the reefs far offshore beneath thirty feet of water, we concentrated on carving out a comfortable little niche for ourselves in the most protected corner of Spring Bay. With a prevailing cross-shore wind sweeping off the mainland of China, this geographic protection was essential for any surfable conditions.

Our days passed pleasantly from there. We would breakfast at our hilltop cinder block dormitory, usually pork testicles or goat meat, boiled carp, and fried rice with warm Pepsi from worn glass bottles. A single cantaloupe or a grapefruit would be a divine luxury that we would all share in turn. We would then caravan to the bay, two miles across the rice flats to the coastal range, a short hike in, then set up camp and "demonstrate" all day. We would return for dinner, usually something that Willy aptly named "Chainsaw Duck," some more carp, some vegetables boiled in what must have been thirty weight, washed down with more vintage warm Pepsi. Out of necessity, we developed a taste for this cuisine, especially the curried duck feet. We would then adjourn to the tearoom with our hosts and talk long into the night about surfing. They seemed most fascinated by the freedom of expression it allowed. They viewed it with the same respect as a martial art and would make nightly reports to the All-China Sports Federation about the progress of our "sporting exchange." Whether or not the Chinese were to pursue this sport on an international level was up for grabs. We were just research subjects at this point.

Third day, we had just come in from our first surf, when up at the top of the path that led onto the sand, came a marching file of nine village children. They were in varied stages of swim dress and led by a local schoolteacher. We were told that they were springboard divers in training. But since they could swim, the federation figured that was close enough. The days that followed were joyful and fulfilling as we sharpened the kids' ocean swimming and surfing skills. Their powers of concentration and emulation were astonishing, their commitment frightening. Before long, the oldest of them were making regular forays to the outside break. They began bringing these two Chinese flags to the beach with them every day, planting them in the sand in our honor. The flags also served as something to line up with on this broad expanse of beach and lent a martial order to things. At the end of the day, they would march off in single file, stoked, having reached out of their isolated world of survival for just a few gleeful hours, and head back to their villages.

The sun baked us on our last day in the surf of China. We would be leaving that night and left behind would be this completely isolated microcosm of surf spirit. One that has never existed so remotely in all the world. I could only hope that the spirit of surfing would somehow survive at this outpost.

Our handlers were perplexed after their experience with us in our natural environment. We got one of them to try surfing and he looked hooked. But what to say back in Bejing? What to report to the sporting authorities about the gold medal potential of Chinese surfers in an Olympic sport that has yet to exist in the Olympics? How were they to explain that this emotional sport was, as they told us, "less about winning and more about living"? I could only shake their hands and say thank you for everything and wish them good luck. That was about all I had.

Well, not all. I gave the kids all my surfboards, and you could see that these boards were far more valuable to these kids than gold. But privately, all I could think about, worry about, really, was what these kids would do when those surfboards wore out. There wouldn't be another within a million miles.

EPILOGUE

Off on a small muddy rise, at a fork in the trail that led to his land, a farmer and his son stood side by side. Their shadows were long, cast by an imposing sun that hung just above the horizon. A mean mosquito dusk was falling. The farmer was a man in his prime whose life of toil had twisted him into a bundle of hard, ropy muscle. His son was a twelve-year-old version of the same. They were both watching the trucks make their way off to the north for the last time, each one pulling a cloud of dust behind. The Americans that were in those trucks had been taking this farmer's son into the sea for the last few days and teaching him sport. So many changes had been coming to this land, the farmer thought. So many temptations for the young to explore. Tomorrow didn't exist anymore, only today. It made him wonder about the future for his son, so he took comfort in some words from the Tao Te Ching. "*Chasing the beasts of the field will drive a man mad. The goods that are hard to procure are hobbles that slow walking feet. But the wise man will do what his belly dictates, and never the sight of his eyes. Thus, he will choose this hardship and not that.*"

The man let his boy watch the trucks until they were beyond sight. The man then turned and started their walk home with his hand on the back of his son's neck. And all the man could think of as they made their way across the muddy levee was that it was going to take days to get his son's mind back on the tending of the fields.

THE RELENTLESS SOUL OF MADE WINADA ADI PUTRA

SURFTIME MAGAZINE, BALI, 2015

As exotic as his name, Made (pronounced Mahh-day) is as beautiful a surfer as Indonesia has ever produced. But it is that mystery around him, that rapier, cynical wit and harsh judgement of others that makes up his toughness. Fortified by all the mistrusts and confusions that arise when one is born to a tropical paradise and, by thirty years old, having witnessed part of it become a trashed-out tourist trap. —Mg.

June 01, 2015 — Kuta Beach, Bali, Indonesia

To understand the iceberg that is Made Winada Adi Putra is to reverse your thinking. Do not engage what is below the surface; beware what is above it. Particularly when he is surfing on the face of a wave, in that way of his. That matador way. His way. To watch him surf at the famed Padang Padang surf break is to witness an outright mastery of the most stunning surfing environment in the world. He even paddles around the place perfectly. Smooth, powerful, perfectly positioned at all times. Never in trouble. Never panicked. Never rag-dolled over the reef like so many others. No broken boards. Like a black cobra: elegant, smooth, and deadly. And then that way of his. When he takes off, you already know what is going to happen. He will drop and turn, and then the elegance kicks in. Not so much the jazz riffs of his cousin Garut Widiarta, or the journeyman strength moves of his cousin Raditya Rondi. No, Adi Putra has swagger. And not a cocky swagger either, but a strangely respectful one. Functional, sexy, and mystifying all at once. That swagger, in Adi Putra's case, belongs to the wave as much as it belongs to Adi Putra. And that tube technique Adi Putra employs. When the wave goes cylindrical and he stands up tall, front leg stiff, taking the weight and the momentum. Back leg deceptively active, on the gimbal of his ankle, controlling the torque and the drive. You know he is going to come out of it cool. Not like some surfers where you hold your breath, hoping against hope that they are going to reappear. No, with Adi Putra, it looks like fate and feels like magic from a magician that you look forward to fooling you. And you are so happy about it that you don't even want to know how he does it. That's the main thing. When you watch Adi Putra surf, whether at Halfway in Kuta, or Desert Point on Lombok, or Padang

Padang on Bali, or Scar Reef on Sumbawa—anywhere really—the thing is that you just cannot help yourself from believing in the way he rides. Like watching your favorite actor. Except that Adi Putra is not acting. He is very, very real.

And here is where we get to what is below the iceberg. The unseen. You might see Adi Putra around, probably down at the end of his street on the beach in Bali. Anywhere he sits, even on a plastic stool, he is always on the edge of it, spring-loaded. Surveying his domain. Suspicious. It's his territory, but it seems, to him, constantly under threat. Like a black cobra, tongue flicking, but alert, up for the hunt. And you can forget about talking to him. Not unless you are on the inside. Family. He is coiled, guarded against onslaught. His fangs are not out, but they are there. And they can drip poison. His aura expands and contracts like a concertina. At times drawing you in and at others shoving you away. You find yourself always aware of his strike zone because his words can crush you. Make you feel small. His smile at once big but dismissive. It can be downright disturbing to try and talk to him. Perhaps that's what makes his surfing so considerable. That no-talk zone. That and those eyes so busy with his relentless thoughts that have less to do with your questions and more to do with the deeply buried concerns he carries as a daily burden.

THE QUESTION OF
KELLY SLATER

TRACKS MAGAZINE, AUSTRALIA, 2009

I guess Kelly answered the question he proposed here when he won the Pipeline Masters thirteen years later, just two days shy of his fiftieth birthday. —Mg.

Those moss green eyes were looking into mine again, and I must say, it was damned good to see how bright they still burned after all these years. I had never seen Kelly Slater so fit. At thirty-seven, he looked in better shape than the eighteen-year-old kids in the room. He and I sat together, chatting in the wet heat of another Bali night. We were at Rizal Tandjung's balcony restaurant, waiting for the lights to go down. Seemed the whole world was there. All the heroes. The Rip Curl Pro contest had ended earlier that day and we had all gathered for a first look at Taylor Steele's new surfing movie, *Stranger than Fiction*. Kelly had his pretty girlfriend in hand and he gingerly sipped his red wine as we caught up on life's great events. The party swirled around us, but I could tell Kelly was in a thoughtful mood. I'd seen him like this before. He had something to say but wasn't quite sure when or how to say it.

When the lights came down and the movie started, Kelly leaned forward in the darkness, his elbows on his knees, hands clasped, and he began to watch the movie very closely. His face at my shoulder, he began whispering all sorts of questions to me about the surfing that was taking place up on the screen. I whispered my answers back. He was very quiet about it, didn't want to broadcast anything. He would comment from time to time as the best surfing the planet had to offer sailed across the screen above the packed, boozy bar. He had a wrap up on just about everyone who was surfing in the movie.

No power.

Not enough rocker.

Can't read waves.

Needs a better shaper.

Doesn't know where the power is.

No bottom turn.

Too much time looking for air.

Should look down the line more.

Too much time in beach breaks.

Board's way too small.

Hawaii will kill him.

Doesn't understand accelerating in the tube.

There was no ego in what Kelly was saying. No bitterness or sour grapes. Just pinpoint observations. I figured after all those world titles of his, he'd earned the right. It also looked like he was dead on.

Eventually, the lights came up and the party really began to howl. Dean Morrison and the beer-swilling Aussies already had lampshades on their heads. But Kelly remained quiet amid the madness. Most could feel his calm and were giving him plenty of room. He hesitated a moment, looked around the room, then leveled his eyes on me and finally said what was on his mind:

"Whose gonna take my place?" he said. *"I can't do this forever."*

We looked around together. Bruce Irons had just won the contest, but we all knew he was going to quit the tour any second now. Brother Andy was over in the corner, surrounded by fans, looking fragile, trying real hard not to drink or accept any of the more dangerous things on offer, looking like there was nothing to worry about other than everything in the whole goddamned world. The rest of the young guns in the room were incoherent with the free booze and the free weight of their own early fame and good fortune.

I looked back at Kelly and he just smiled that lonely smile of his. Then he squeezed my shoulder and stood and made his way out of the place with his girlfriend and silent dignity. I watched him go. I looked around the room again.

And I was damned if I knew the answer to his question.

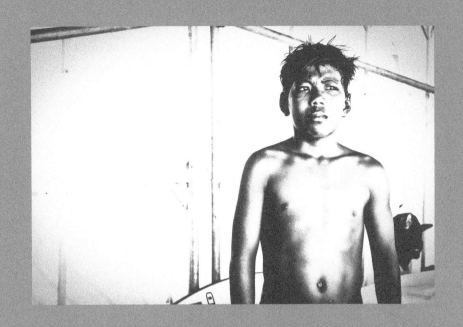

WHERE CHILDREN REIGN

THE LOST BOYS OF LAKEY PEAK
THE SURFER'S JOURNAL, USA, 2012

Where most surf breaks are dominated by grown alpha males, on a small diamond-shaped reef on Sumbawa, it is a tribe of children who hold court over one of the most perfect waves in the world. Youngsters, totally unsupervised; a herd of them, who quite literally live to surf until they are captured by puberty. A world of wonder and fragile chance, left in the wake of the first broken surfboard that washed ashore so long ago. —Mg.

The Cycle of Life

There exists a place on the edge of children's dreams, a fractured yet sweet world where there are no parents, nor rules, nor clocks, nor schedules, nor schoolteachers, nor uncomfortable clothing, nor shoes, nor Sunday School, nor anything at all to get in the way of the imaginations and wonders of a childhood spent surfing in an equatorial sea. Close your eyes and imagine a group of child Tarzans on the edge of a phantasmal jungle, all of them looking out at perfect tropical waves with mini surfboards under their arms. Do this and you just might understand the place known as Lakey Peak on the island of Sumbawa, Indonesia. But unlike the fantasy world of Peter Pan's Neverland, Lakey Peak and her child surfing tribe are as real as it gets in our surfing universe. A place where the wild things really do exist. Where the laws of the jungle still rule the days and the nights. And where the badass ten-year-old Lost Boys of Lakey Peak would eat Peter Pan alive.

Lakey Peak. Even the namesake itself suggests the ways of children. Over thirty years ago, a group of stoned English backpackers were the first westerners to see the perfect wave breaking directly offshore of the dusty Sumbawan fishing village known as Hu'u. And they named this wave "The Lucky Peak." They called it this because of the remarkable A-frame-shaped waves that crashed with metronomic precision over the outer reef of the lagoon. Waves whose shape resembled the hallucinogenic mushrooms that these backpackers were digging out of all the wild Sumbawan pony shit on the beach.

The precise nature of this wave is due to a rare bathymetric phenomenon where the rushing tidal waters of its brackish lagoon create two symmetrical outlets to the sea exactly 150 yards apart. Both outlets possess the same tidal forces, and therefore pneumatically erode the reef into the shape of an exquisitely cut diamond, oriented, as luck would have it, in perfect position for any swell that cares to come its way. From the air, this pristine reef shimmers like a green-and-brown gem in a rajah's turban.

And so the wave was discovered and the rumors spread and the western surfers arrived like Christopher Columbus himself, ready to claim it in the name of surfing and plunder all its natural riches. But unlike Columbus' victims, it was the local children of Hu'u, jungle-honed, who soon held the high ground. Lording over the waves on the broken, cast-off surfboards left behind by the invaders. Having in front of them the ultimate surfing playground, these children, who spoke only the forgotten Bima language, misunderstood the pronunciation of the giant visiting westerners and, as children do, misspelled it in their school workbooks. And so, their parents, most of whom could not read at all, painted new roadside signs to attract the foreign surfers exactly as their children had misspelled it. And so, "The Lucky Peak" became the hamlet of "Lakey Peak." And, as such, Hu'u was erased and re-plotted on the ancient charts of Sumbawa to forever bear her English name. All because of a wave that had been breaking off its shores for a million years.

On any day, a simple walk through this dusty, rooster-scrambled village will reveal the most fascinating microcosm in the surfing world, steeped in the daily hopefulness and catastrophes of a childhood life without parents. Though hard to imagine, it is easy to see how it happened. In an Islamic culture where the entire village raises the children, once this wonder called surfing was discovered, the exodus of children from all the surrounding villages and hillside jungle clearings began. This brave little tribe, answering this strange new call of the sea, gathered at the beach and stayed there. Sleeping where they could, surviving, sharing, fighting, and scratching out a surfing existence under the watchful eyes of the serene elder women. The men having long given up on the little savages because of their sons' incomprehensible lack of interest in fishing. So to this day, it is the "Ibus," the village mothers, who know the look in a little boy's eyes when not one goddamn thing an adult says is going to make a scrap of difference. These kids want to surf. All day long. So the Ibu's feed them all the rice and boiled chicken they can scrape from the half-eaten meals the westerners leave behind at their small cafes. And the Ibu's hope for the best, remaining forever hopeful that puberty will come early to these youngsters and that the dependable confusions and rages of that time will force the changes needed to survive a life at Lakey Peak. For pregnancies and marriages, in that order, are the great equalizers here, as strong and life-changing as the seismic upheavals that plague the region itself. So the Ibu's hope that the Lost Boys will become teen fathers as soon as possible, expected to provide for their elders and their new teen families. Again, in that order. So these Lost Boys will drift away from the childish frivolities of the beach and into the river of a life with much more pressing concerns. Their backs bending from all the hard work in the scorching fields and in the dengue-riddled bedrooms that create perpetual families here. Hoping the Lost Boys will become men and that they will sweat out a new existence, filled with cigarettes, hardship, diapers, anger, jealousies, lust, sins, broken bodies, and broken souls. And the Lost Boys of Lakey Peak, though tortured by the clarity of their surfing memories, will be forced to dust off these memories only in private moments of nostalgia. And the Ibu's, the mothers, will be satisfied that life in Lakey Peak is once again whirling in an orbit as dependable as the moon.

The Lovely Rose

With the poise of Cleopatra, the looks of a supermodel, and the heart of Mother Theresa, Mawar Yulia Trisnasari glides through the crowded confines of her ratty beachside cafe, serving food and issuing stern orders to the legion of brown children who gambol about the ankles of the surfing tourists like a covey of quail. She flashes knowing glances at the regulars of the Annual Rip Curl GromSearch Surf Contest, the highlight of the year here in Lakey Peak. A shrewd marketing harvest of the best little boy surfers in the world. It is Mawar who has inherited the cafe from her mother as a teen, and, alone, turned the typically shabby surfer *warung* into a kind of orphanage for the Lost Boys of Lakey Peak.

She does her best to feed them, has a standing order that she will pay for any of them who might actually show any interest in school. But most valuable to these little kids is that Mawar, a surfer herself, possessing a command of English, has rare access into the phenomena of modern Indonesian professional surfing. The visiting western surfers all want to bed and marry her immediately and Mawar leverages this into numerous unrequited relationships that benefit the kids, showering them with the western gifts from her suitors.

However, not all saint, it is rumored that Mawar has a secret love. A tall, shadowy character that might be a man of considerable influence in the halls of pro surfing. The rumor is that the Rip Curl GromSearch contest would not exist here without him. Nor would the rare sponsorship contracts that are being offered to local surfers like Oney and Andre Anwar, and, of course, the great Dedi Gun, the original Lost Boy. These contracts are the prize that makes all the young kids dream of a life as a celebrity. But few understand that it is the tedium of education that is the key. Self-educated, Dedi Gun is a kind of genius. Rip Curl has sent Oney Anwar to Australia to study and will not let him out to compete until he graduates from high school. And little twelve-year-old Andre Anwar, Oney's cousin, will soon be enrolled in the international school in Bali, compliments of Mawar, her rumored secret lover, and the Rip Curl corporation itself. But these surfing contracts, as rare as getting hit by lighting, contain the most astonishing legal clause in sports history. A contract clause that Rip Curl, learning the hard way, was forced to include for its own survival. The homesickness clause.

These kids, having grown up on the beach, having slept together for warmth since they were five, having slept on the beach curled up in damp blankets with the goats and the wild Sumbawan pony herd, who have grazed for hermit crabs together, who have slept on pool tables and in bushes and in large kitchen sinks, having faced horrific surf together, perfect surf together, having been cared for in a way they could never have imagined by Mawar, having formed a child cadre as strong as the United States Marines and a bond with the very earth they sleep on as strong as a tree root, many of them cannot break free from the gravitational forces of their flawed paradise home.

More than one has broken their lucrative western surfing contract to return from the tawdry hurly-burly of the outside world to once again sleep on the beach with their friends and the goats and the ponies. To Rip Curl, this was a deal-breaker. And many a Lost Boy has chosen it.

But the loving Mawar remains philosophical. In constant motion through the center of her universe at Fatmah's Cafe, she goes about her business of serving customers and raising the Lost Boys of Lakey Peak with an angelic grace. And Mawar Yulia Trisnasari, twenty-five years old, smiles an inner smile of fate. Knowing that the waves out on the reef, those perfect waves, the pulse of these little kids lives, will continue ticking away like dreams or time bombs. And that she will be there to help the Lost Boys of Lakey Peak navigate both.

The Second Chance

In a place where young girls walk around with the family chickens under their arms, Australian expat, Mark "Boonga" Clift, handsome, fiery blue eyes, skin from a tannery at forty-five, is timing his surf session perfectly. Standing before the well-worn, surf-sticker plastered, wall-mounted television in the corner of Fatmah's Cafe, Boonga is banging on the side of the thing with his fist. Banging away, but with certain finesse.

Apparently, it takes a special touch.

"COME ON, YOU BASTARD!"

An everyday ritual, he is trying his best to get the reception for the big game. Australian Rules Football, the mighty Perth Eagles vs. The Geelong Cats. *Bang! Bang!* goes his fist.

The TV fuzzes to life. Boonga roars with pleasure when the blurry black-and-white images of the big game appear. "YOU BEAUTY!"

He has certain affection for this television. After all, he does pay the cable. It keeps him sane here in Lakey Peak between swells. But today's challenge is that the surf is pumping. Six-to-eight-foot. Just the way this Western Australian likes it. Unmarried, a gypsy professional surf contest director, he is a lifer. He figures it like this: watch the game to get the feel of it, then paddle out, get some waves, and make it back in time for the closing minutes. It is an unwritten law that no Lost Boy may change the channel when the game is on. Boonga is also, after all, Fatmah's Cafe's best beer customer. Although the instant Boonga tears himself away from the game and runs down to the beach to paddle out onto the reef, the braver of the Lost Boys will approach the TV and switch the channel to INDO-SATELLITE TV where exhibitions like Lady Gaga's latest efforts produce a stunned, reverent silence from the Lost Boys. Even the chef comes out from the kitchen to marvel at what they all believe is a reality going on without them beyond the shores of their island.

And thus, with such Promethean abilities to capture fire from the sky, Boonga lives here between contest gigs, still with half his life to live, in the firm belief that this place is giving him his second chance at life.

So, Boonga paddles out and joins a fellow expat. A rangy, balding Colin McDonald, fifty-five. Boonga gives Colin the latest football score. Colin nods and smiles vaguely and looks back out to sea. Colin has never been happier in his life. Also an Aussie, arrived here some years ago. He forgets how many. He was restless in Australia, retired from carpentry, divorced, and lonely. His kids had grown up and all but disappeared. He was still fit from his daily surfing. Felt fit of mind too. Figured he would come to this place he heard about called Lakey Peak and just surf his blues away for a while.

Upon arrival, he met Rahma. A jovial Sumbawan woman of thirty-three, two kids, husband long gone. For Colin, it was love at first sight. The something that Colin had been looking for. A new adventure of the heart. And against his estranged family's wishes, Colin married Rahma, adopted her kids, and had one of his own with her. Nikita, the pride of his life, five months old now. So Colin now runs a small homestay for surfers behind Fatmah's Cafe with Rahma and the kids. His Nikita growing like a weed. He helps the village whenever he can, building things and fixing things. He is even training two of the Lost Boys the art of carpentry. They are doing pretty well, too. Colin doesn't even remember Australia anymore. Or football scores. Or even the names of the teams. Sitting in the lineup and waiting for a great wave, Colin looks out past Boonga at the volcanic peaks across the great bay and feels in his heart that he still has half his life to live. And that this place is giving him his second chance too.

The Ballad of Dedi Gun

"Dedi doesn't go to people," says surf photographer Mick Curley, "people go to Dedi." True words to describe the ultimate surfing icon from Lakey Peak. Dedi, a runaway from an unruly mountain town called Dompu, was the original Lost Boy. His youth in the hills unimaginable to most. A village where six-year-olds carry machetes to defend themselves against each other. A place where any gathering of more than ten people could end up in a slaughter. Weddings, birthdays, these were what Dedi recalls as "knife-sharpening" events. Dedi was a popular fat kid known as Gobo then, but he still had to sleep with a machete under his pillow, and another one by the bedroom door. Plus a rusty blade in his pocket. He provided for his family with his superior intellect. He ran a brisk business at the local dirt-floor school selling answers to all the test questions and writing everyone's papers. And the teachers knew it. And the teachers didn't care. Because he was also writing the teachers' progress reports to the local government.

After his ritual circumcision, where raw bird's eggs are placed in the mouth of the boy to keep him from screaming, Dedi escaped the village of Dompu at age nine. One day, inspired, he just began his great walk to the sea. Setting out on foot with his machete and an old plastic Coke bottle full of water. He walked for days, eating fruit from the trees, navigating by the landscape, and sleeping under the stars. After an encounter with a six-foot spitting cobra, Dedi tired of walking over land and managed to drop out of a tree onto the luggage that was strapped to the top of a passing tourist bus. When he awoke, the bus was empty and parked at Lakey Peak. One look at the Ocean was all it took. Dedi Gun swore never to leave.

A stranger, knowing no one, he collected empty bottles on the beach for a penny a pop. He lived on fruit and hand-caught crabs and tidepool fish. He ate them raw. He lived in the reeds and taught himself how to swim with the help of a toy float he found on the bank of the stream one morning. Envious of the other surfers, but too proud to beg, he made his first surfboard out of a piece of old plywood shaped with his trusty machete. This is when Mawar stepped in, deciding it was time to take this strange boy under her wing. She offered him a job at the cafe, where he slept on the pool table at night and swept during the day. It wasn't long before Mawar and the visiting guests discovered how smart Dedi was. He had already taught himself English by studying the subtitles to the *Rambo* movies that played at night on Boonga's TV. No one knew where Dedi's affinity for the sea came from. He became a good surfer overnight. Graduating from his piece of wood to a broken half of a surfboard. Jungle-powerful, Dedi soon became the most respected surfer in Lakey Peak with the worst board on earth. Not a board at all, really. On a cement wall, he had ground down and shaped a shard of a broken windowpane to serve as its fin.

A chance meeting at Lakey Peak with visiting Californian surf filmmaker Timmy Turner turned into a lifelong friendship. Timmy gave Dedi a brand-new thruster surfboard and it was as if Dedi had stepped on the third rail. His surfing became electrifying and stylish. It wasn't long before Rip Curl came knocking and the first Lost Boy contract was signed. Never forgetting his Lakey Peak roots and possessing a humble approach to life, Dedi soon graduated to the highest ranks of the Indonesian pro surfing scene and garnered the prized lifetime Rip Curl contract.

Now twenty-three, considered a demigod by everyone in Lakey Peak, Dedi, with enough hair to stuff a sofa and a personal style that includes surfing in long-sleeved Pendleton shirts, possesses a soft-spoken manner that attracts genuine affection wherever he goes. He has brought back fantastic tales of surfing in Alaska and Hawaii and even more fantastic tales of blondes and brunettes as the new generation of Lost Boys gathered at his feet, hanging on every word like a reading of *'Twas the Night Before Christmas*. His legend has grown to mythical proportion back in Dompu. His rare visits there are treated like a national holiday with droves of children just wanting to touch him for good luck. His legendary romantic exploits precede him by miles. Women of all creeds, quite literally, fall at his feet. And to accommodate his old village of Dompu, where he signs hundreds of autographs, has had to reduce his signature to a single letter.

"O"...for Ocean.

But throughout, Dedi maintains that lonely humbleness. A strange, compassionate aloneness. He remains, despite the adoration of anyone he comes in contact with, a solitary figure. He goes to the cinema by himself. And sometimes will spend the day on a Bali street corner, just watching the world end. He's up to three foreign languages now.

At Lakey Peak, the village elders often come to him in private for advice. He is considered a bit of an oracle, what with the exotic Scandinavian women he shows up with from time to time. And he is filled with the dreams of a survivor, forever faithful to Lakey Peak and what it has given him. Dedi now dreams of getting the Sumbawan government to protect Lakey Peak as a national surfing reserve. Then he, Dedi Gun, will build a traditional Sumbawan longhouse for the Lost Boys of Lakey Peak. A dormitory of sorts, and he the spirit guide, who will lead generations of the Lost Boys of Lakey Peak into their uncertain futures.

You will hear and see all of this from Dedi Gun on a star-sprung night at Lakey Peak. He will be sitting on a log on the beach, staring up at the stars as he quietly speaks of these things in perfect English. His wise, black eyes will be full of wonder at what hangs above. He will talk about the "view" of life; that if you can see things, important things, natural things, then you will be part of the "view" and that you will be happy. He will have built a small fire for the Lost Boys who will be sleeping on the beach this night, and the glow of the coals will light up his heavy, dark features. You will hear Dedi Gun and you will see him like this and you will not be able to imagine a more connected surfer on earth. A more connected human on earth. Connected to something so vast and so special and so real and so brave. And with that thought in your mind, the great Dedi Gun will shake out a sandy, moldering blanket, curl up next to his fire, and fall asleep on the beach as he first did here so long ago. And he will find sleep as he listens to the foaming waves, to the soft padding of hooves from the nearby grazing ponies, and to the singsong laughter of the Lost Boys coming from around the pool table at Fatmah's Cafe.

STATE OF GRACE

A MEXICAN SOJOURN
WATER MAGAZINE, USA, 2006

You can see a lot of things in Mexico.
You don't even have to look that hard. —Mg.

THE HOOKER
Costa Azul, Jalisco, Mexico

The night is more than slow. It is inert. She dips the middle and index finger of her right hand into the glass jar. She makes to brush a strand of hair from her eyes, instead brushes her fingers against her lips. The tequila bites. A darting tongue moves the sting from her lips to the back of her teeth. She keeps her eyes on the man behind the bar. Two beads of perspiration find their way from the nape of her neck down to where her ass meets her spine. She sits at her corner table and feels a sort of pleasure as the droplets find their way down the ropy muscles of her back. She is the kind of woman who does not scratch or itch. Every sensation reminding her that she is alive. Her small glass jar is cradled out of sight, held between her thighs on the sagging, split cane chair, snugged in her worn floral skirt. Like a rock in her hand, she can feel the power that the jar holds. Feel its power through her skirt and her rose-scented underwear, that any-man's land between her and her next performance.

A dark beer bottle, half-filled with ice, stands before her as one does every night.

This cantina does not have a proper name, so she assigns it a new one every morning. Something from a book she has finished. Summerville Manor, Sunnybrook Farm, La Buena Vista. This helps her roll the stories around in her head. The stories she makes up to amuse herself as she takes her place in the corner every evening. She prefers romances to tragedies. Happy endings. But mostly, she just thinks of the horses.

Another song ends. Behind the bar, Guillermo flips the cassette tape, nods at her, then flicks his eyes over toward the American surfers. The American surfers sit huddled, looking at each other, grinning, embarrassed. One of the surfers is sweaty with fear. She looses off an incendiary glance at the surfer she has chosen. The only one who looks like he might go through with it. The surfer feels her eyes, looks over, smiles back as if he is chewing on a marble. For the second time that night, she makes sure to turn her eyes away first. Her eyes then see Guillermo duck behind the bar to open a third crate of beer. She takes this chance to bring her jar to her mouth. She can hear the gulp. The tequila roars down her throat and pools in her belly, a wild animal going to ground.

Dear God, even tequila tastes cool on a night like this.

Her eyes are still moist from her siesta dreams. Despite the clocks that have rusted to a stop in her life, despite the timetables that have been abandoned and the maps of things to come that are misplaced forever, she still dreams. And from time to time, during the mosquito dusks of her life in this place, she sells herself to the stablemaster over at the American resort in exchange for some time with one of the tattered horses that are kept alive for the American tourists. She takes a horse—it doesn't really matter which—and she leads it along the beach. She never rides this horse. She only walks beside it, its hooves punching fetlock-deep holes on the sand berm down near the surf, throwing fans of sand behind with each step. And she talks to this horse as if it were herself. She walks, listening to herself, feeling the weight of her words drown in the weight of the hissing sea and its spilling waves. And she always takes a deep breath at the sun's last moment and holds it deep in her lungs. She holds this breath, holding the sun's glow in her chest. She can do this. Then, freeing the horse, letting the reins drag wet and sandy, she follows the horse to its stall and she returns to hers.

Across the cantina, she regards the American surfers again. American surfers had been coming to this place for some time now. She has watched them over the years, riding the waves on their surfboards not far from the cantina. It is said that the light and the waves were perfect here in this region of Mexico for the photographs that would eventually end up in the sports magazines. The magazines whose few, glossy, torn-out pages festooned the split cane walls of the cantina around her. Their faded edges curled around the tin tacks that hold them in place against the wet and the heat. It was said that these surfers before her were paid money for surfing here in front of a photographer. She understood this. She had been paid to pose for a photographer. Twice. But that was long ago, and it caused her more trouble than she cared to remember.

She tastes her fingers again and regards the angular shoulders of the American surfers. Children, all of them. Despite their age, always children. Well-fed and strong. Hurrying, sheepish, and not proud in the bed. She listens to them, looking for sign. Though young, tonight's group of surfers are surely wealthy. They are staying at the American tourist resort where the horses are kept. And although a full week has passed since their arrival, these boys are still clean. Every stitch of their clothing is brand new. On one of their shirts, she can even see the plastic nib that recently held a price tag.

She feels her surfer's eyes on her again. She looks back at him. She watches and sees it. The goading from his friends, the fifth beer. It would not be long now. Her surfer signals for a beer to be sent over to her. Guillermo shows his teeth. Then Guillermo walks over to her and replaces her beer bottle with another one half-filled with ice. As Guillermo turns, her fingers find her tequila and then her mouth. The tang of the tequila, tinted blue, makes her smile. Finally, having got enough of it in her, a soft humming has begun in the base of her spine. At times like this, her resolve to leave this life does not give in—it gives out. And she is thankful for that moment.

The surfer steps over to the bar and has a word with Guillermo. From where she sits, it looks like enough. And not in pesos either. Green, unwrinkled. Clean. She leads him by the hand back across the dirt of the courtyard and into the small room, the window curtain a worn-out dress, a cot by the window. She lights two candle stubs. She sits on the cot. The surfer stands by the door, swaying slightly. He holds his beer bottle over his balls with both hands, trying his best to look like he has been here before. But there is no stirring beyond his zipper. She tests him, speaks out loud.

The soul that sinneth shall die.

She sees that the surfer has no Spanish. She lets it begin. She has long since learned to let her soul escape when it needs to. It always came back eventually, just as the horses would return to their stalls. She stands, closes her eyes, and hears herself undress. A single move, one soft rustle, and the thing is done. She opens her eyes and suddenly she is all rust-colored skin. A taut, restless drum. She smells his fear fill the room at this, feels his heart hammer like an over-wound clock.

Children. All surfers, children. Well-fed and strong.

She lifts her eyes to his and the world becomes a jungle.

THE BEGGAR
Punta De Mita, Jalisco

He woke up hungry. But then, he was always hungry. He looked up at the sky and saw the pink of the clouds. The sun was leaving, its blazing heat already tapering off. He'd timed it perfectly. He always timed it perfectly. A little scrounging in the village in the morning, a few hours of dozing in the shade of his favorite tree during the heat of the day, and then back to the bustle of the village as it came to life in the cool of the evening. He yawned silently. Shook his head and let the shiver of it travel to his toes. He got to his feet, urinated, stretched, sneezed once, and then began his walk into town. He could hear the church bells ringing. Another festival tonight. He would work the village square, his favorite corner, by the ice cream stand. The people on that corner were a softer touch than the others, always with something to toss his way. And if the beggar waited him out, the man at the ice cream stand would always give him the stuff that had melted by the end of the night.

The path across the field led him to the road, and he began to cross it, his mouth was watering at the thought of the cool, creamy, rose-colored ice cream. He never even saw the large van full of American surfers who were racing to the beach for the last light. The front left bumper caught the beggar square, just in front of his hind legs. His long, tapered tail whipped and thumped against the fender as he was thrown under the chassis. And for an instant he even heard the crunching of his own skull under the back rear tire before a lightning bolt cracked, ending his life in a spray of stars.

Another village beggar, a small one with a liver-colored nose, happened upon the scene with the smell of fresh blood inside her dry, cracked nostrils. Her hair stood on end. Careful, she trotted out into the road to investigate. She stopped, looked toward the large van that was fast disappearing. Three human faces, with fear in their eyes, stared back out at her through the rear window. The van grew smaller. She watched it until she could no longer hear it. Then it vanished around a corner in the jungle. She watched it go, listening, making sure it was gone forever.

She tested the air once to see if other beggars were about. It wouldn't be long. Her fellow village dogs were ever vigilant. She hung her head and licked at the hot remains.

THE NOVITIATE
Santa Cruz, Nayarit

He wasn't used to seeing two perfectly sober men fight with their fists in the light of day. He had wandered down near the beach to torture himself with the thoughts of his sins. Of his weakness of flesh. And he had stopped to watch the excitement of the visiting American surfers as they rode the waves that crashed in off the river mouth of this small town. But he'd never expected this. After the initial exchange of blows the two American surfers were now rolling around in the hot black sand in each other's arms. The novitiate saw that it would soon be over. He saw the big man who was standing behind the big camera wait for a bit and then move over and patiently separate the two. It didn't take much. The surfers exchanged insults for a while until they tired of this, too. One of them picked up his surfboard, walked to the water's edge and paddled back out to sea. The other one, the tattooed one, sat down next to the big man at the camera. The novitiate stepped into the shade where some of village boys had been watching the phenomenon, grinning at the incomprehensible foolishness of fighting sober during the noonday heat.

What is this anger about?
The tattooed one stole the other's wave.
Is such a thing possible?
They seem to think so.
Why would he do something like that?
So the big man with the camera would make him famous.

The novitiate thought on this and watched as the tattooed surfer dropped his head between his knees and let the shame fall over him. It took a while. The tattooed surfer then stood up, picked up his surfboard, and walked up the beach toward the large van from the American resort.

Across the bottom of the tattooed surfer's surfboard was written boldly in English:

JESUS IS LORD

The novitiate, curious now, looked for faith in the eyes of the tattooed surfer, but saw only confusion. And something else. A weakness. He remembers his teachings.

Discontent follows ambition like a shadow, and gods suppressed become demons.

The novitiate smiled. He felt a surge of faith, close to a fire of belonging and righteousness. He felt fateful. He knew then an epiphany. He was not weak. He believed. He did not suppress his God. He was not creating demons. Yes, he sinned in a tranquil glade with a beautiful creature of God whose hair smelled faintly and magnificently of horses and tequila. But that could be forgiven, surely.

THE MARINE
Costa Azul, Jalisco

He surfaced with a gasp. Then he crawled up onto his surfboard and caught his breath. Then he paddled back outside the breaking waves and sat up on his board. He scanned the horizon for approaching waves. None. His fingers grasped the rails of his surfboard until his thumbs found the foam through the fiberglass. He breathed deeply twice, controlling red fever of rage, letting it move through him, letting it wash over him. Trying to let it go.

Anger will get you killed; control will get you home.

He closed his eyes and whispered this three times. More than once, doing so had saved his life. He found himself scanning the tree line on the beach. He picked the palm tree just to the left of the cantina. Good angle, plenty of foliage, wide, stable platform, no coconuts to shake loose and reveal his location, maybe 150 yards from the lineup, tops.

Fuck, that's point-blank.

Light wind from the east—he would have to allow for that. Sun at eleven o'clock. Evacuation route clean. Plenty of jungle behind, maybe two klicks to the far ridge, a river beyond that, float down into Puerto Vallarta, buy a guayabera, and blend in. Fly out a week later. Let the Mexicans figure it out from there.

It would be so easy. His favorite rifle, the one that kicked to the right, good cover, the targets off alert. He counted the targets. Five in the water, one on the beach. He figured it. He'd wait for a set of waves, wait for the five in the water to start paddling for these waves. He'd drop the cameraman up on the berm first. Headshot. Go after the ones in the water who had pulled back, mop up the rest in the confusion. It would take six, maybe eight pulls of the trigger.

Going for numbers, he always allowed for error. The whole operation would take maybe eighteen seconds. These calculations had taken him only five.

The marine had just arrived at Costa Azul with seven hundred bucks hazardous duty back-pay and a couple of drinkin' buddies. The divorce seemed miles away. The whole fuckin' mess seemed miles away. Until the young asswipe with the tattoos dropped down the face of a wave in front of him and forced him to straighten out toward shore. The lip of the wave had landed square on the marine's shoulders, knocking the breath out of him before driving him into the sandbar. He'd bounced hard, saw stars, and clawed his way to the surface. It all came rushing back there: what he was really good at. Pain had never made him angry. It was the fear. He'd killed for far less.

The marine watched the pack of young surfers paddle back out. He had always had a hard time finding that particular patriotic connection. Especially when he was collecting a paycheck for sitting in some tree for five days, picking off an entire village of rice farmers one by one. The marine could still see feel his first confirmed kill. An old soldier. Corded, dry muscles. A ripcord of a man. The guy was carrying mortar shells and landmine ordnance to a small launch. The marine had drawn his bead, crosshaired the enemy, squeezed the trigger. The sound of death a dampened puff. The bundle of rags on the other end of his scope had crumpled to the ground in silence.

The surfers were almost outside the break with him now. The marine looked at them closely. He looked at the surfers' lives. He knew he still had what it took to take those lives away. Easy.

Is that what I did all that for? So snot-nosed cherries like this could grow up into these cheeseburg'-eatin' assholes?

The surfer with the tattoos paddled up to the marine. The marine listened to the young surfer's voice. The surfer with the tattoos said he was sorry for dropping in on the wave in front of him. Said he was surfing for the cameraman up there on the beach. Said he was sorry again. Said he was just trying to make a living. The marine just looked at him. Thinking silently.

What in the hell would you know about making a living?

The marine formed his right hand into a pistol, thumb up with a two-fingered barrel. He raised this pistol and rested the barrel right between the eyes of the surfer with the tattoos. Then, with a *cluck* of his tongue, the marine dropped his thumb and smiled his secret smile.

THE INDIAN
Punta De Mita, Jalisco

The skin of God, the Indian whispered to himself as he watched the surf and waited in the small clearing by their tree. He finished threading the fishing line through the red clay rosary he had made and hid it in the knothole. It was one of his best and it pleased him to think that he made it with his own hands.

And of clay we are all created.

He rolled and lit a cigarette. The evening land breeze had begun and he could smell the rain in the mountains. A thundercloud thumped deeply somewhere miles away behind him. The Ocean was turning silver with the evening light and the sun blazed a blood-red path all the way to the sand. It looked thick enough to walk on.

The Indian knit his brow; there was once a hillside village of his youth. And his mother. His tiny mother. The two of them standing together on a summit, gathering firewood a long time ago. He was only six summers old and it was his first look at the Ocean. It stretched off in the distance like a gigantic, polished knife, glinting on the edge of the jungle plains, a world of green away. He had asked his mother what kind of land it was, this Ocean. She had replied that it was no kind of land at all. That it was the skin of God.

He was holding his mother's elbow when she died. She had a smile on her face. He was ten summers old by then. He had left his Huicholi village that day of her death. He went to see this skin of God. Standing on the edge of the continent, he listened to the surf and felt like he had punched a hole into a new world. He understood then what his mother was talking about. He'd never left the Ocean's side in the eight years since.

Another long roll of thunder pealed a deep bass. The Indian put out his cigarette. He waited, watching the neat lines of hissing waves wander in. He waited with the patience of history on his side. This evening was everything to him. Everything.

She will soon be here.

And she had promised.

The Indian heard the van from the tourist resort pull up into the dirt lot to his right. He heard doors opening and slamming shut and the American voices. He looked over and could see the American surfers examining a bloody smear on the front of the van, a tattered shred of dog hide. A nervous laugh came from one of them. *Gnarly,* the American said. The Indian watched them unstrap their surfboards, cradle them under their arms, and pick their way down to the surf. One of them was wearing a clay necklace that the Indian had sold him the day before. It would melt in the water.

A big man set up a tripod and camera on the beach. The Indian watched the surfers. Like most visitors to this place to whom he sold his clay pottery and jewelry, they too were blind. Blind and dissatisfied. Looking for heaven far, far from home. Some of his people had done the same and he had learned. Some of his people went to America to work and dream of an easy life. They returned with a few gold teeth and violent souls. America is free, but it is not for free. He had heard that one must pay money for everything in America. Even the smallest of things, like a place to park a car. And certainly the biggest of things, like respect.

The Indian watched the surfers move around in the surf. He had watched American surfers come here for eight years. They arrived with hope, trying to find something that was missing inside them. They always ended up discontent. They always ended up sick. Too hot. Too many mosquitoes, warm beer, no one speaking English. He had heard this so many times he assumed it was a sort of truth for them. He had seen their dissatisfaction with their lives surface time and time again. Surfers reminded him of that dog they had run over. Crazed by the sun, chasing their own tails until they made a mistake or dropped dead.

He knew that the surfers before him and the big man with the camera would all be in jail by midnight. They had given his friend a lot of money for a handful of marijuana bundled in a piece of waxed paper and tin foil. It was the same, stale bundle that his friend always sold certain visitors. The police were already waiting up the road. Depending on how much money the surfers' mothers and fathers had, they might be allowed to leave within a week. Either way, his friend with the marijuana no longer wore his clay rosaries. They were heavy and gold now.

A crunch of leaves. The Indian woman had stepped into the clearing. His throat went dry at her beauty. He could see in her eyes that she was going to keep her promise. She walked over and sat next to him. His mouth began to water. They sat silently in a hush that had fallen between waves and they thought in Huicholi together. He took the rosary from the knothole and gave it to her and kissed her cheek. He caught the faint scent of the horses still in her hair. She smiled then, kissed the rosary, and looped it around her wrist and perfect fingers. She looked out onto the surfers and saw exactly the same things in them that he did. She closed her eyes, wrinkled her small nose, drew a deep breath, and allowed the sun to see her. She exhaled. And he caught the scent of her expensive tequila. Then she lay back, pulled up her dress, and summoned him with a nod of her chin.

The Indian's heart soared. He would marry this girl. Their life together stretched out before him. It left him dizzy. The both of them, here, right here, next to the skin of God. He would ply his trade and sell to the visitors as long as they kept searching for the secret he possessed.

That which his mother had whispered last of all. A doorway to a life that would allow him to die with a smile on his lips too, allow him his state of grace. He looked around once, out at the hills of his youth in the thundering distance. Out onto the surfers floating on the skin of God. Back into the eyes of her as she lay waiting. And as he leaned over her and positioned himself, it came to him as pure and basic as a heartbeat.

His mother's whispered deathbed chant.

Heaven could be anywhere . . . why not here?

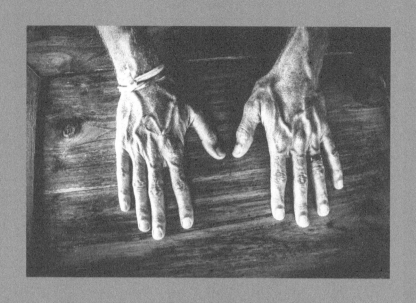

EXPAT

SOME SURFERS NEVER MAKE IT BACK
TRACKS MAGAZINE, AUSTRALIA, 2015

Expat retirees in Bali are loners or outlaws. The loners are more interesting than the outlaws. Better backstories. Less ego. In the evenings, these loner expats range around to different cafes and bars where they are sure to be recognized but not bothered too much. Heaven only knows what they do during the day. It's a very different kind of retirement. —Mg.

The fifty-nine-year-old ex-surfboard builder puts the next cigarette in his mouth. It's dry and stale. The filter sticks to his upper lip. The flame from his Zippo is big and it picks off the tips of a few eyebrows. No matter. At ten cigs a week, he doesn't smoke enough of the things to keep a pack fresh. He sits on a stool, elbows on the bench of a small cafe facing a busy backstreet shortcut for most of the scooters of Kuta, Bali. A motorcade of silky hookers, howling schoolies, pimps, hustlers, ladyboys, and families of five roar past on two wheels. A river of humanity. Mechanized. He watches it all like an adult would watch a full rollercoaster. Amused. But not in the way that makes you hop on.

Fifty-nine now, his past life in the surfboard factory back in Oz is all a blur. Retired now. If you could call it that. More like just plain tired. But not in such a bad way. Maybe the way a soldier who survived, who got out of it with his skin intact would feel at his age. And not a soldier who balanced any ledgers, earned a handful of medals or nothing, but a soldier who just did his job and didn't get clipped. Yeah, don't expect any thanks neither, ain't no gold watch waiting for nobody. That's the surfboard industry for you. Like any army, it took the simple men and women to do all the dirty work. To build a good surfboard took its toll in toxic factories of resin, fiberglass, and cruel chemicals. A job that left grooves in your face from the years of wearing industrial respirators. Stoop labor. Sweat toil. Shit like that. But what the fuck, surfboards don't make themselves and everybody needs their toys.

This thought makes him scratch a drop of sweat off the groove on the bridge of his nose.

Christ, the monsoon's hot this year.

His cigarette has burned halfway down without him taking a puff. He ashes it. He had jumped into the surfing world at around nine years old.

Jazzed on the whole lack-of-responsibility thing. He had been a stylish surfer, had even taken second place at the Queensland state titles as a nineteen-year-old. But the pro career gig had never materialized. Mainly because he was never a competitive animal. Surfing had always been so easy for him, such a natural act, that the anxiety and accolades of competition never put the hook in him. He had fiber-glassed surfboards all his life instead, just to stay in the water. The money was steady, good and honest. His role as an anonymous craftsman had kept him in for enough decades to win the race. He looked at his hands now. Thought about what they had done over the years. He smiled to himself. He had been good at his job. Still was, really. That craftsman. He orders another beer. His has gone warm. He didn't drink much these days, either.

The usual crowd was here in the bar. Most around his age. Some a decade younger. For an expat bar in Bali, you could always find a pretty good conversation at this place. Intelligent. Even provocative at times. A loud American, three outback Aussies, the Frogs, the Poms, the sunburnt boat captain, a chef, and that real nice blonde lady with the blue eyes that must have driven the boys crazy back in the day. Then there was the beggar and the thief and the swirling Balinese staff. Hell, even a dolphin trainer on his way to somewhere else. He liked listening to it all. He'd never talked that much.

The Balinese bar girl swept up to him with another bottle of beer, levered the cap off. He took it in his hand and looked at her and thanked her quietly in her language. He'd picked up the necessary phrases from a tourist brochure. The girls liked him for that. That was another reason he came here every evening. The bar girls were all caramel-colored skin and flashing brown eyes, graceful as a herd of deer. Though more than one offer had been implied for the right amount, he hadn't taken any of them home. And he wouldn't. That would spoil it. He didn't screw much either these days.

He'd first come to Bali in 1975. Just after that second place finish in the titles. Bali blew his brains out. He'd raced back to Mooloolaba and grabbed his girlfriend and his best friends and brought them back to the island show them the miracle. His girl lasted a week. A record for those times. After watching the look in the boys' eyes as they scampered down cliffs, chattered with the locals, pinballed around the Uluwatu cave at high tide, and laughed at their reef cuts and good fortune, she knew she could never change him.

You're like a heroin addict in a poppy field!

He'd never forgotten that one. About the only one he'd never forget. He'd loved her. Still did, he supposed. All that dirty blonde hair. Jesus Christ, yes.

A funny story is told next to him and the whole bench is howling. He turns his head toward the sound and grins dutifully. The bar girl catches him at it and smiles. He nods back, his beer getting warm again.

He had spent his life coming back to Bali. Then age set in and the island became something else altogether. An escape route. He returned, time and again and again. He'd had a few kids back in Oz, coupla wives, but none of it stuck. And that was all right with him. He never meant to bother nobody. That was another reason the bar girls here dug him. His surfing had slowed way down. Back injury. And that was okay, too. He knew who he was. He'd sold up back in Oz, put his dough in a safe place, and moved in with a pal in the middle of Kuta. Where else would he go?

Just then, someone lit up a clove cigarette. The smell of it gave him a memory of making love to that girlfriend in the Uluwatu cave back in '75. So vivid a memory it made his groin stir for the first time in months.

He lifts his pack of cigarettes, shakes it once, and selects one with his lips. The bar girl comes forward and lights it for him with a wooden match from a small cardboard box. She cups her hands to protect the flame, looking not at the tip of the cigarette, but into his eyes. He thanks her. In her language.

Home.

JUNGLE BOY

THE MEANING OF DYLAN WILCOXEN IN A MODERN WORLD
SURFTIME MAGAZINE, USA, 2022

More Robinson Crusoe than Peter Pan, the discovery of Dylan Wilcoxen is the stuff of myth in the surfing world. Here was this kid, raised on a remote island on the edge of the Indian Ocean, weened on the finest waves in the world since birth, whose surfing skill, by the time he was ten, was a revelation. Born to an American expat father who had no interest in the outside world and an islander mother who adhered to the custom of letting the entire village raise a child, Dylan is a being entirely of the sea. Often going weeks without uttering a single word, Dylan's lifestyle is amphibian. So focused and tuned into the rhythms of the sea, that he seems a different species, raised not on modern tech, but on the laws of the jungle. —Mg.

Kandui Resort, Mentawai Islands, West Sumatra, 2022

On an island set in the sea like a green sapphire one hundred nautical miles off West Sumatra and one and one-half degrees south of the equator, a boy pads through its jungle. It is 6:08 in the morning and he is as much a part of this remote island as the birds that are announcing the dawn. He hasn't slept much, having spent most of the night under his mosquito netting, listening to the march of the building swell coming through the pane-less window of his palm-roofed uma. Now his steps sift the white sand of a worn path to the sea, no more than a game trail marked by the split coconut husks from the small surf resort village where he lives. He holds a brand-new surfboard under his right arm, the easy weight of it feeling like a promise. Its deck freshly waxed, the scent of it, warmed by his armpit, fuses with the heavy, wet smell of the leaves that have fallen in the night. He arrives at a clearing on the edge of the jungle. His jungle. On his island. He finds the morning sky the same marbled pink as the inside of a seashell. He looks to the sea where the new swell has arrived in earnest and is hammering the offshore reefs, the hiss of its tumbling waves prevailing over all creation. Puffing his chest, he inhales the salty tang of the swell's mist deep into his lungs. He sits on his haunches, his board across his knees, and takes the measure of the day. With eyes that have seen a thousand dawns like this, he watches the cascading waves like a panther and his focus tightens and goes to ground deep within his stomach. There is only one thing now.

To ride these waves as he has done all his life. To ride them because they are his life. This boy's name is Dylan Wilcoxen. He is twelve years old.

He was born to a rare life. Brought into the world in Padang, West Sumatra. He was swept straight from the hospital out to this offshore island where his expat father, himself on the run from civilization, had carved a type of surfing resort out of the jungle. It had done a humble business since its opening, there had always been enough. His father, name of Ray Wilcoxen, had taken Dylan into the perfect surf of their island just days after the boy was born. For the first three years of his life, Dylan had rarely been clothed. From the start, his father wanted this. A very natural life for his son, a natural life on a tiny speck on the edge of the Indian Ocean. A life far from what Ray knew as the disturbed civilization that was out there beyond the island's undulating horizon. A world swollen with all the pressures to conform to whoever and whatever. A world to spend your life in being told what to do. A life full of wrong roads to take, of frustrations and regrets and missing pieces. An unnatural life. No. This was not what Ray wanted for his boy. Here on this island, with what he had built with his bare hands, Ray would watch his boy grow as an innate being. Connected to something deeper than just the sinister momentum of the mainlands of the earth. No. Here on this island, his boy would be connected to the sun on his back and the surf on his mind and the island beneath his feet. A barefoot kid, skilled in a different brand of knowledge. Ocean knowledge. Ancient knowledge. Fishing, diving, surfing, water knowledge. No police cars, no death toll news, no corruption, no principal's office, no rulers across knuckles or dunce caps in the corner. All the crap that Ray had to deal with on the streets of Los Angeles so long ago and far away. For Ray, his boy was going to get the better choice, and if the day came where his boy wanted to join the world out there, than at least it would be with an instinctive mind. But in the meantime, his boy would have this island and its waves in the palm of his hands forever, if that's what he wanted. *And isn't that what everybody out there is striving for?* thought Ray. *A place to belong? A place to thrive in ones own mind and not in the minds of others? No wars and hate and death and pollution and corruption and the rat races that erode the body and soul, bending a man to their destructive will, leaving him wrung out and regretful? Better a life healthy, natural, and wilderness strong.* To Ray, this vision was un-blurred. No one could do better than that in this batty world. The proof of it found in bearing witness to the extraordinary abilities of his son, knowing that it had something to do with living a life without the distractions of modern youth. Ray had watched his pride and joy thrive into this place. His son was imagination unbound, passion unleashed, the uncrushable powers of youth at play. And no matter what befell, Ray knew his boy would always have this island and its waves. And if that wasn't enough for the world out there, then they could all go to hell.

From where he crouches on the edge of the jungle, the boy surveys the waves as the sun breaks the horizon, dispatching the pink sky and replacing it with gold beams, one of them warming the skin of his left shoulder and cheek. Behind him, through the trees, he can hear the sounds of the resort coming to life. The ivory tinkling of dishes coming from the kitchen, the scrabbling roosters, the distant generator being fired up, and the morning voices of the guests, still sleep heavy, asking about the surf as they tottered in for breakfast.

The boy stands. Down the beach, he can see his island friends readying the jet ski for the guests. Dylan looks out at one more set of waves, props his board into the sand, and then turns and trots back toward the resort restaurant to find his father. Together, they would get the dinghy ready and decide where everyone was going to surf. He spots his father on the porch sipping his big blue mug of scalding black coffee. His father is quiet and calm, reassuring the excited guests, telling them it was a good idea to get some breakfast into their bellies, that it was going to be a helluva day.

The boy catches his father's eyes and his father raises his eyebrows. The boy raises his too and nods toward the sound of the surf and smiles broadly. His father smiles back. And in that moment the world glides into a kind of perfection.

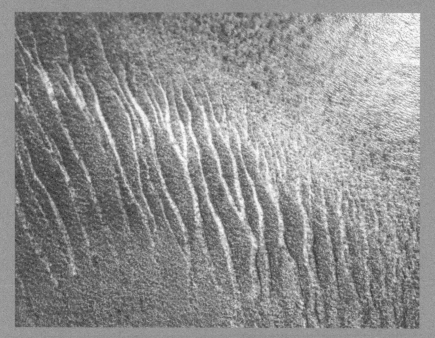

THE REEF

WALL OF SKULLS

THE BILLABONG PRO, TAHITI 2008
SURFER.COM, USA, 2008

This was the first time in my career that I was asked to report on a surf contest for a website. When I turned this in, there was much confusion. They told me that writing for the web was based on three-second attention spans. That the writing of the future was not about perspectives, it was about reactions. I didn't realize at the time how true that would become. —Mg.

DISPATCH: BILLABONG PRO TAHITI

They were called the Matahihae. Those whose "eyes are shining with anger." They lived on the Taiarapu Peninsula of O'Tahiti and would fight over territorial matters. These warriors would mark the borders of their land by building walls out of the skulls of their enemies. Their peninsula was feared throughout the realm and was spoken of in hushed whispers as Te Ahu Upo'o. The Wall of Skulls. From one of these walls, you can see the pneumatic phenomenon that is the wave that is to be surfed during this competition. Sitting on a surfboard in today's Teahupo'o channel, watching these waves myself, I wondered if those warriors of yesterday ever looked out upon their reef and drew their inspiration from this wave's ferocity, its murderous form. I cannot imagine it being overlooked.

Day One

It's the colors. The riot of them. This gets to you first. Sunrise in Teahupo'o, Tahiti. The impenetrable jungle peaks, precipitous, primordial tangles of green reaching to the heavens, flanking an unmarred cobalt sea. The silent fisherman, out on the mirror of the sky, afloat on a world of deep blue mercury. The village chickens are stirring, dogs stagger to their feet, stretch from head to tail and trot off to their daily rounds. A rooster is heard. The sun burnishes the tips of the tall, motionless palms, setting them alight in a blaze of limes and yellows. Last night's cooking fires are smoldering; sheets of smoke move like ghosts through pathways and the small yards and the rich gardens that line the single story, cement dwellings of the local people. Within one square mile of you, the best surfers in the world are waking up to a flat, peaceful Ocean and are happy for it. Most have just arrived and welcome the respite before having to paddle into the no-man's land out on the reef.

Aussie Journalist Nick Carroll is just in from his morning mile swim out to the reef. He stands at the shoreline looking back at the sea, listening to the drip of his trunks and the sound of the breathing jungle at his back. Pro surfer CJ Hobgood is sitting down to some chocolate cereal. Adrian, a local fixer that works for Billabong, is noodling around the wharf-side contest site, flipping a switch here, checking the juice on a generator there, making sure the Coke machine works. Current World Champion Mick Fanning has arrived without fanfare, unpacking his bag like he lives here, committing himself to the win. Junior Executive Holly Beck is over at the Billabong compound, sipping her coffee and checking the latest on her computer at the only internet connection for miles. A large fish jumps just offshore and in a flashing moment, is the loudest thing in the world.

You see all this on your way down to breakfast at a small beachside hut. Fresh fish and potatoes au gratin. Somehow, that makes perfect sense. Everyone is in a waiting mode. Taking their time, grooving into the place. Rumor has it that Donovan Frankenrieter and his band have arrived. Just then you see Luke Egan, contest director. He's been up for hours. He walks out onto the point of land that faces the barrier reef break. He squints and strains to see out onto the reef. Another tiny set moves through. He nods his head knowing the contest is on hold for one more day. Luke doesn't look worried. No one does. Impossible spectacle lies ahead. Any day now, the monsters will come. And the monsters will lumber in and pour themselves remorselessly over the razor-sharp reef pass, and these monsters will warp into ungodly holes in the Ocean and the Colosseum will roar.

DAY 4

CONTEST STILL ON HOLD: due to small conditions

You slip off your board on a smaller day at the Teahupo'o reef. You float on your back. The sky is an array of towering snow white clouds, gargantuan white fortresses ascending against infinite space. You slip your goggles on and take a great breath and you roll over and dive down to check out the reef. You feel good down in the cooler silence. In control. You cruise just inches above the colors. It's a tropical fish store in front of you. The back of your hand lightly brushes the bottom and you immediately feel a burning from the fire coral. And just then, you suddenly realize that even the fish are scared. The fish have all lined up in one direction as if gathering a breath and then they begin darting out to sea one by one like a fighter squadron launching off a carrier. That is when you feel all the water around you draining off the reef to feed the power of the wave. You surface and clamber onto your board and realize that, as the wave sucks the water off the edge of the reef, you are afloat on a great dome of water and that you are going to have to paddle downhill for the first time in your life. This is the biggest wave of the day. Tom Whitaker and Luke Munro are calling their friend into it. Their friend, Jeff, a car dealer from Nowra, Australia, is windmilling himself into the giant. He is not moving, so strong is the suck. You paddle down into the pit. You are now about ten feet off the edge of the reef and you begin your climb up the concave blue of the wave. The wave releases Jeff from its hold and he begins his drop just as you puncture its thick lip. You punch through into the light, feeling the dread of the wave pulling on your waist. It lets you go. You are safe but you realize you are still holding your breath from your dive. A few quick paddles and then you turn your head toward shore to watch the evidence of Jeff from Nowra getting the ride of his life. Tom and Luke are cheering from the channel. All this and the wave was only ten feet tall. The bare minimum out here. You imagine what the detonations must be like when it gets godlike. You lick the blood off the back of your hand.

That night, you are onstage down at the Marina with Donovan Frankenreiter. Two thousand screaming fans, Tahitians, and surf glitterati alike, sway to the smoky beat. Mark Occhilupo is on the mic, yowling to a cover of Van Morrison's "Brown Eyed Girl." Dave Rastovich is on the bongos. Back-up singers, Joel Parkinson, Bruce and Andy Irons. The audience, a sweaty, heaving mass, has been brought together under the Tahitian moon. Between songs, Mark asks you if you surfed today. You answer yes. Sort of. He asks you what you think of the wave. And you smile and you answer, "Even the fish are scared." Mark howls, grabs a tambourine, and swings back out on stage at the sound of Donovan's first crunch chord. The crowd surges. The waves will come to everybody and there has never been a better time to be a pro surfer in the history of mankind.

Day 5
COMPETITION UNDERWAY: 8–10 foot

You have a strong understanding of the fighter pilot mentality of the pro surfer. You know the drill. Downplay everything. Still, you must consider the hydraulics first. Imposing, heaving black foothills of water, unencumbered and uninterested in anything but ruining themselves, swinging in from the southern points of the compass after a long, silent journey across the trackless Pacific. These Ocean foothills are then arrested by a domed reef and turn their attention to its destruction. And that's just the beginning of your ride here. As these foothills stop and scream and stand up to express their outrage, two surfers, flotsam really, hand paddle around in the maelstrom on puny little surfboards looking for some kind of opportunity to make it to the channel alive. In this case, it is His Holiness, two-time champ Mr. Kelly Slater and a Hawaiian prince named Jaime O'Brien who has eyes on his throne. Within this maelstrom, Kelly commits to the incoming set of waves, and that is when it all changes. Kelly must kill this prince. In turn, these malevolent foothills seem to take an interest in Kelly himself. Only two surfers in history have been loved by waves: Tom Curren and Kelly Slater. And Prince Jaime knows this and ends up screaming to the heavens. Kelly drops in, disappears from view, emerges from another impossible cyclone of water to the gasps of onlookers in the boats in the channel. The king is one step closer to his moonshot. Ten world titles. And no one is quite sure what to make of it.

But you forget yourself. With all this thought of kings and princes, you are struck with the thought that these waves, these hydraulic monsters, would break here and crush coral and roar shoreward and resound over the village of Teahupo'o whether or not any human drama unfolded in the lineup. Which brings you back to your point about the fighter pilot mentality of the pro surfer. Bones and hearts would be broken on this day. Blood raced through veins at top fuel speeds. Announcers would bellow and women would swoon and pro surfers would bow their heads in defeat. Yet despite this, those great giant blue walls of horror, would continue to keep their appointments with the reef as they have for eons, puny human challenges or no.

Day 6
COMPETITION UNDERWAY; 6–8 foot, dropping swell

Even within the fighter pilot culture of the pro surfing, brothers Bruce and Andy Irons are still a match above the most stalwart heroes of the reef. The difference? These two break the sound barrier every time they paddle out. Pushing themselves over the ledge time and again with a loose playfulness that can be maddening to peers, joyful to fans. This is their secret: making a playground out of the torture chambers that roar in out of the blue expanse, pull the pin, and explode onto the domed Teahupo'o reef like artillery. Like bullfighters, the brothers do not mock their adversary, but move within its space. Avoiding the horns, making it look elegant, pleasing the crowd, accomplishing the impossible. And Bruce admits another secret: they always watch each other surf this particular wave. Telepathically connected. Choosing lines for each other. Guiding each other through the thunder with their eyes and a combined will. Connected between the ether of thought and mass. Silent teamwork. We've seen it too many times to doubt. Unlike any brothers who have come before, they have made a home of the death tubes of Teahupo'o. For each action, there is an equal and opposite reaction. And then there's the Irons brothers.

Day 7
FINALS COMPETITION UNDERWAY: 4–6 foot, dropping swell

On the final day of competition, you must be willing to listen. You are underwater again. You are off the reef pass of the sleepy village of Teahupo'o, Tahiti. You are suspended underwater again, this time on the edge of the channel reef of the heaviest wave on earth. But today she is playful. The surf has dropped. It is another kind of contest altogether in what you are now convinced is the most beautiful place on earth.

Beneath you is the drop-off. You can feel the abyss through the soles of your bare feet. In front of you, the reef spreads out like the center of the universe. And you think to yourself that maybe it is. You have one great lungful of air still allowing this. You look up through the mirrored surface and see again the great South Pacific clouds, pure white citadels that sail by like clipper ships on the trades. Thirty seconds left of air now. You feel the water sway and surge and you know a wave approaches. You risk it and swim closer to the reef, just on the edge. You have twenty seconds left. You stop and relax and wait and watch. The first wave rises in a triangle, a muscular thing. It draws you up slightly, letting you feel its energy. The reef begins to wind chime, a soft song of broken shells and sand dredging and dragging on the bottom. A delicate sound, considering the violence that is to come. The wave stands and pitches toward shore. And it is in that breathless moment, that silent moment, that you hear the humming.

Here comes the shadow of a surfboard racing across the reef, and then the apparition, above and to the right of you, between the reef and the sky, is a surfer riding on the surface. He is deep inside a spinning, moving, blown-glass sphere that moves past you like a planet. And you have to remember to listen.

Listen to the humming of the fins of the surfboard, to the muffled thunder of the breaking wave, to the percussion as the arcing lip penetrates the surface. The humming continues. So, mesmerized, you hold out a hand to touch the rail of the surfer as he passes. You are not close enough, but you can still feel it. The humming of the fins fade as the surfer disappears into a heaving cloud, his contrail weaving, threading up and over and into the reef. You listen until it is gone. Then you bolt for the surface. You fill your lungs with air.

Then comes a different kind of noise. From the boats in the channel, from the loudspeaker, from your world. The cheering. The horns. The sirens. In the closing moments, on this spectacular afternoon, Brazilian Bruno Santos has just defeated Tahitian Manoa Drollet to become the eighth champion of the Billabong Pro Tahiti at Teahupo'o. Heat horns are blazing, boat sirens are sounding, beer pop-tops are cracking. A grinning friend on the media boat beckons; he is waving a cold beer for you. You begin swimming for it, bubbles streaming past your ears.

You remember asking Bruno about it the night before. He answered in his thick Brazilian accent: *You must be willing to listen to her—the Ocean. You must listen to her and she will tell you what to do. You must listen to her, or she will drown you out with her own song.* So you swim on and you breathe and you listen to the bubbles and you listen to her.

You listen.

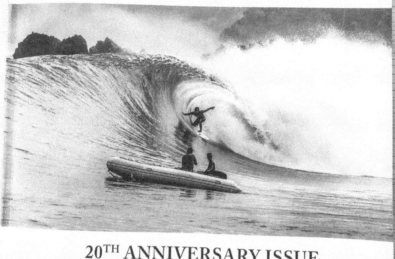

SURFTIME

passion comes in waves

20TH ANNIVERSARY ISSUE

THE HELL ZONE

IT WILL LEAVE YOU BREATHLESS
TRACKS MAGAZINE, AUSTRALIA, 2019

This story is an explanation more than anything. Why surfers find themselves on the most far-flung points of the compass. The desire. Our madness. The unquenchable thirst for the transitory thrill that comes with riding a wave. Any wave. Particularly this one on the edge of Java within the disaster shadow of Karakatau. This wave is a disaster in itself. —Mg.

THE PLACE

The Ujong Kulon National Park of northern Java is internationally rated as a category II national park—which means it could kill you. It might be neighboring Gunung Krakatau when it blows its stack. Or maybe one of the many tsunamis that scour the region out of the sight of the global news cycles. Or maybe it would be the underwater landslides that cause most of these tsunamis. Or the earthquakes that cause the rest. Or maybe it would be a saltwater crocodile. Or a leopard. Or maybe one of the last Javan tigers whose roars are rumored to still be heard here inside Ujong Kulon National Park. The good news is that you won't face any danger from the rhinoceros. A smaller, docile, Javanese species. The last wild ones on earth. There are about forty of them left in the park. Counted a while back when a crew of rhino horn poachers became extinct during an Indonesian Special Forces training sweep.

There are a few small islands in the park. The little sisters of Krakatau. One is known as Prince's Island. And if you're game and if you know how to surf on your inside right rail and if you have the balls and the right passport and right friends and plenty of money, this is where you will find the double-rectified, guaranteed, photographically certified ride of your whole goddamned life. Of course, this experience will be more transitory than you have imagined, or could imagine. Because for those seeking more than seven seconds inside the most roaring, molten-blue lava, pouring right-hand, barreling wave on the planet, the exercise is futile. Because you do not come to this specific wave to actually successfully ride the wave. In fact, you don't come here to make anything but a man of yourself.

The wave itself is a hydraulic jackhammer that pounds on an anvil of live coral. Surfing here, which is more like running into a tree trunk, offers no real exit. Once you've had enough of it, it's either a Hail Mary back into the foamball or a doggie door to oblivion. Especially since the jagged reef, with convex boils swirling around jagged towers of pronged coral heads, steepens towards shore. Like running barefoot up a hillside driveway of broken glass. You don't straighten out exactly, because there is no bellying it in. You carve out in front of the detonation and bail feet and ass first. A game of Russian Roulette, more deadly with every round you play. The human skin scraped off onto this reef on any one session is enough to feed the school of small pilot fish for hours. If ever a wave was about charging the gun nest, you're riding it. To call it suicidal is not out of the question. It takes samurai commitment (remember, they already considered themselves dead). Aptly, western surfers have named this wave *Apocalypse.*

This phenomenal, perfectly shaped wave, which attracts a select international group of half-mad barrel addicts, is watched over by rare silvery gibbons, horned banteng, Javanese lutung, crab-eating macaques, Sumatran dholes, Javanese mouse-deer, smooth-coated otters, over seventy-two species of reptiles and amphibians, all poisonous, and over 240 species of endangered birds. All who stare out unseen from the malarial jungle at man's folly upon the waves. And above all, it is those mosquito-borne malarial viruses that make photographs of the wave from land so rare. Say photographers: *Why risk it?*

Of course, any mention of this remote Prince's Island must include a conversation about Gunung Krakatau. When she detonated in 1883, the resulting tsunami, which was actually measured as far away as the English Channel, wiped out everything within its sight. Including hundreds tiny coastal villages where small groups of fishing families clung to life. On nearby Prince's Island, their forlorn coastal crops, the entire island for that matter, was buried under five feet of ash. Everybody cleared out.

Well, almost everybody.

Because when the first people decided to return to Prince's Island, they made a startling discovery. On Mount Raska, where the 330-meter-tall volcanic intrusion that thrusts up in the interior like an old goat's molar, a worn Hindu statue of Ganesh was found that dated back to the first century. Unlike any pre-Islamic statue found before. Its small size and markings gave evidence of an ancient island people, very small in size. No taller than three feet. And although the bones of these Lilliputian people were found on other islands as far southeast as Flores, none were found here; however, their etchings of tsunamis and erupting volcanoes were. Within the most hardscrabble villages of today is a belief that, since no remains have been found, these small, shy people live through the centuries. And that they still exist on Prince's Island. And to this day, they are blamed for all manner of mischief and theft and surprise teen pregnancies that occur from time to time.

"Taking the time to understand all these elements means being a long way from everything you know." For a few futile waves, being able to leave your past behind and get in touch with whatever it is that drives you to jump off the edge of the continents in the first place.

THE OTHER PLACE

This place has a heavy cement sign sunk into the dirt like a large gravestone on the outskirts of town. Painted on it are a splendid fairy wren and a red flowering gum. This sign is placed by the side of the south coast highway in a location on the planet that most people would describe as the middle of nowhere. The sign reads:

Welcome to Denmark.

That's Denmark, Western Australia. A sleepy town south of Perth. The 2,000-odd residents there like to say that while it may not be the end of the earth, you can see it from there. The place got named after a doctor, last name of Denmark, who sailed by in the Dutch fleet back in the 1800s. Apparently he was a pretty good doctor. By 1998, the town of Denmark was awarded the title of "Australia's Tidiest Town." It's that kind of place. And also the kind of place that hardworking people, those who enjoy the quiet and being able to see the end of the earth, call home.

There is also a world-class, hell-charger surfer who lives there named Cale Grigson. He considers himself the luckiest guy on earth. He is utterly un-sponsored and works for a living and works for his waves. He ships out on the big vessels that look for oil and gas in the wildest of the world's Ocean conditions. A deckhand, an all-arounder, a strong back. Cargo runs, crew transfers, evacs. He even helped look for MH370. It's hard work out there, cold, calloused hands, split knuckles work. And yet Cale sees this as a kind of freedom. He was once paid to just surf professionally. But it didn't really suit him. So the money petered out. He will tell you he was real lucky to get his freedom back after the surf sponsors let him go.

When Cale tells you the age that he began surfing, you realize that this was a very brave act for a six-year-old. The surf in this part of the world is inhumanly big and powerful. But his old man surfed, so that was that. The Aussie way. His old man was a worker, just like him. Still is. His dad was a signwriter, but the tech world sped by that honest work long ago. Now his dad paints houses. A survivor. Australian salt.

Cale is pure Aussie salt too, by default, and he uses the word "luck" every day of his life. He says everything worked out real good for him when he was moved to Denmark as that six-year-old. The place was isolated, no people. Paradise, really. A fickle bit of surfing coastline, he admits today at forty years old, but he says it has its moments. It means a lot of time behind the wheel. Cale likes to say, "If you put in the K's you get the waves." When you hear him talk like this you think about that. Where his tastes go to ground. In Denmark its either towing behind a jet ski into offshore sixty-foot bombs or paddling into muscular slabs of water over knee-deep reefs or risking the pounding, ripped-up beach breaks that would send a California lifeguard running for Escondido. And all in the roaring desert wind and the bitter, numbing cold of the southern Ocean. Cale figures surfers grow up pretty fast here. A lot faster than the pansies over on the Gold Coast in Queensland. Cale says, back in the day, a fella name of Chris Shannihan blew into town, showed up with a jet ski. And the figs to go with it. Cale says that he mind-surfed a lot before Shannihan's jet ski arrived. Just dreaming, watching heavy, cement mixer waves crush the Denmark coast. Never thinking it was really possible to ride them. But once the ski showed up, it was a big bang kind of deal. A whole new universe. And Cale puts it very carefully that it was *the* ski. Not the *skis*. There was only one back then. And it meant towing into ungodly waves at thirty knots with your nuts up in your stomach.

Cale met Hawaiian surf star Mikala Jones round about fifteen years ago when Mikala was in town sniffing around for giant waves. That's how Cale ended up at Prince's Island. He had always been interested in the wave named Apocalypse. So Mikala invited him along. When this surfer arrived at Prince's Island off Java, he immediately knew this was a "judgement wave." And by that he meant that the wave judges you. Taking off for the first time, he says, no matter what you think of yourself, it's the knowing that is so intimidating. Knowing that from the moment you take off you are going to have to bail off your board at some point. With a wave whose reef is just getting shallower with every second you ride. A wave that starts to gurgle and boil in front of you as it feels the shallow reef's pull. A train wreck of a wave. Wipe outs here were notorious for blowing ear drums out. Mikala had lost two here.

During this trip to Prince's Island, Cale thought back on all the jobs over the years, all the paychecks exchanged for all those hours of life. And he thought of the pros who get paid to just surf. Like he used to. But then he thought he wouldn't beat himself up over it. Because paying up yourself takes the pressure off. No more need to get clips and quips and selfies for the internet. Not like the other guys who need to get all the angles with their drones and harnesses and cameras clenched in their jaws. That anxiety and intensity is not on his table anymore. So for Cale, it's adventurous and personal and real again. He can focus out there and enjoy the thrill and see it. He can soak in the experience instead of trying to cover it. Now that he is paying his own way to get to these destinations, all he need hope for is getting really good waves. And he knows that the money he is spending is going to the right place for him. Spending it on something that has a true value to him. He reckons waves are a great thing to spend your money on and he really can't think of anything better to buy. The thought of being on that boat with those waves, away from everyone and everything. Isolated. It felt true. Not just a dream come true, but just, true. And he doesn't think surfing gets any better than that.

THE ONLY WAY TO GO

By boat. Run by a very earnest man named Joshua Jati Johan. *The Sirius* is a modified traditional wooden Ujong Kulon fishing boat. She has been proven strong, having recently survived the Sunda Strait tsunami that took over 500 lives. Joshua claims that on her, most surfers find the the best waves they have ever surfed. And he means waves, plural. The Prince's Island break is not the only secret out on the edge. The island is peppered with world-class empty barrels, both lefts and rights. Joshua is very proud of this and proud of his boat. After all, it has spring beds. He says his boat chef is a magician, even though he can't understand his dialect. And that his safety equipment is up to snuff, by third-world standards anyway. Fifteen years of experience in those waters makes a difference, too. He calls his journeys "surf tripping. An experience of a lifetime and the beginning of lifelong friendships forged in the fire of waves that are waiting to define you as a surfer. All you need is the desire to find out."

THE PHOTOGRAPHER

Surfing on Prince's Island is as much about a photographer as it is a surfer. Surfing here offers a lensmen a 100 percent success rate, while the surfer's is a snowball's chance in hell. Photographer Pete Frieden knows all about it. A veteran surf photographer, he has been to this hellzone more than any other photographer. But it's not the wave that worries him; it's the thought of getting badly injured here. Surfers do; this is what keeps him up in his bunk at night. It's a long five-hour boat ride back to a listing wooden dock in North Java and then an eight-hour jarring drive to the medieval surgeries of Jakarta. Where if you don't pay cash up front, they leave you in the hallway until you do.

Ask Frieden what he thinks it takes to surf this place and he'll answer: "Balls of steel, man. I mean, as a photographer, the boat angle is paradise. And the surfers are stoked because the shots are hard to believe. But it is just this giant, heaving, glorified no-hope close out. But still, that rush, those moments inside that wave, there is nothing like it in the world. Not in the entire world. It's a life-and-death wave, for sure. And it's that weird stuff that happens out there that makes you believe in the black magic they practice in the villages on land. Like the time

Mikala was here and a giant cloud of killer bees came out of nowhere and swarmed the boat. They wanted salt and if you were sweaty, you were in serious trouble. The captain had to machete the anchor line and gun it for the horizon. It's just that kind of place. And you need to be willing to hell charge this whole experience. It's a 24/7 experience of being a badass. I have seen other boats sit out there and watch all day with no takers. It's not for everybody. I mean, this wave? In the hellzone? Apocalypse? I don't know, bring a motorcycle helmet?"

THE POINT

Which brings us to an important point about surfing. Considering the immersion, the deepness of spirit and the audacious, life-and-death physical energy that remote surf travel demands, what other sports tread as close to the mysteries of nature and the ages? Perhaps there is a much more profound element of surf travel that we have yet to consider. One that helps answer the great question. That the mystery of human existence lies not in the matter of staying alive.

But in finding something to live for.

LEST WE FORGET

THAT GLORIOUS MESS BETTER KNOWN AS THE
BELLS BEACH RIP CURL PRO 2000
SURFING MAGAZINE, USA, 2000

I covered the Rip Curl Bells Beach Contest for most of my career. It really is as special a surf competition as has ever existed. Steeped in history and mayhem. Just the way we like it. The young woman featured in this story is real. —Mg.

THE LEGENDARY TORQUAY PUB, Victoria, Australia — 1:37 a.m.

It became immediately obvious to her that at Bells Beach, a day lasts twenty-four hours. She stood five foot nine inches tall, red-haired and boyish, within a sea of predominately drunken Australian surfers and holiday-makers who never seemed to sleep. And who were busy drinking gallons upon gallons of beer and slurring clever things to their patient girlfriends or to wary strangers, all of whom they hoped to screw before the sun rose again. The jukebox blasted hits long gone and a fight was brewing somewhere. She could smell it in the air. Being a musician, she was no stranger to the Australian pubdom. She had come here to be part of the ritual that her fellow Victorian countrymen simply called "Bells." That Easter holiday that coincides with a magnificent booze-up disguised as a surfing championship and music festival and everything else that is called for on such a desperate weekend for people who work for a living.

It had been a long drive from her home in the blue hills of Mt. Dandenong. She was here with her dear friend; a simple, backfire blonde whom she could always depend on to meet the right guy—the guy who would get them backstage to any venue they chose. As for herself, she was a couch sleeper, a third wheel who played the role of the quiet red-haired tag-along and in return was able to live within the epicenter of such events without committing any crimes of the heart. It suited her. This being her first Bells, she was curious about the world of the upper echelon of a sport with which she had an understanding. Her broken-down, dirty-waxed 6'8" surfboard was lying forlornly in the dew back at their campsite next to the tent that she and her blonde friend would both hopefully not have to call home for the next eight days. By the look of the proceedings between her blonde friend and the handsome Western Australian with whom she was buddy breathing, they'd have a roof over their heads before long. The red-haired girl was used to men not being interested in her until they began to lose their balance. That was cool. She was here to listen anyway, maybe get lucky enough to find some inspiration for the next song she planned to write.

Just then the jukebox caused an eruption of chants. *"You can't always get what you want . . . but if you try sometime, you just might find, you get what you need . . ."*

As the mob brayed, she wondered if they caught the irony of it. She looked around, considering the hundreds of drunken couplings that were to occur in forgettable embrace tonight. Then the fight broke out. A real beauty. It swayed in the opposite direction from her. So she took a drag off the stub of a marijuana joint that the guy next to her offered. Unique in that he was using the tip of his prosthetic arm as a roach clip. She drew deeply, not as to be half-assed, and exhaled to the sky through pursed lips to the symphony of breaking glass, splitting lips, and shattering furniture.

God, she thought, *what a glorious mess.*

THE OCCY HORROR PICTURE SHOW

With her all-access pass looped on a shoe string about her neck, she sat in the VIP bleachers among the best surfers in the world, watching the best surfing the planet had to offer. Her blonde friend was not far away, sidled up next to her Western Australian charge who, as it turned out, was no competitor at all, but actually some reporter for some website. One of those wave report operations that was busy lobbying for those internet surf cameras at every spot on the coast so that, for a buck-fifty a pop, surfers might never have to get out of bed again.

No matter—he was good-looking, and she and her blond friend had since pulled stakes, folding their sagging tent and moving into semi-residence at a rented party house full of journalists. The redhead smiled to herself; it was a bit of a coup, the house being Ground Zero for all the late-night, post-pub after-parties. A beer-soaked abattoir of romantic disasters. Fascinating material for journos and musicians alike.

Spread before her, under a mackerel blue sky, center stage in the natural cliffside amphitheater of Bells Beach, Victoria, the pro women surfers Rochelle Ballard and Megan Abubo were wildly thrashing their way through the final. The redhead was enthralled. She understood what it took as a woman to compete in a man's sport, herself the captain of the women's Victorian National Cricket team. Watching the surfing, the only other time she could think of when men witnessed women putting out efforts as brave as these was childbirth.

The beauty of the setting was intoxicating. *Surfing,* she thought, *is like riding the sky.* After all, the sea gets its color from the sky, and the rows of whitewater, so orderly and snowy-white here against the navy-blue sea and the rust-colored cliffs, were surely sisters to the equally white clouds that marched out high overhead toward the storm-swollen horizon. It felt like church, sitting there among the faithful.

At some words from the announcer, she glanced over at the current world champion, Mark Occhilupo. Mark had been taking heat all week for the most unlikely of reasons. It seems that *TRACKS magazine* had put together the official contest program and plastered its cover with a perfectly dreadful photo of Mark. She had seen it. It was impossible not to. They were everywhere, these programs. The photo, a searing cutback maneuver, was shot during the period when Marc had dropped off the tour for a couple of years and had put on 150 pounds. In an astonishing comeback, Occy was now the fittest surfer on tour. But the dumpy photo of the past was an image of a terrible time in his life. In the photo, he was well overweight and held the same expression on his face as someone who had just received a wicked left hook to the jaw. His peers had been merciless. A day didn't go by when someone didn't draw his attention to his misfortune. Mark couldn't even escape it the night before at the *TRACKS* Hall of Fame awards where he was receiving his reader's poll favorite surfer award. The redhead had sat in the audience thinking that someone who had won this award by a landslide might be spared the indignity of being roasted by the emcee once again regarding the photo. Mark wasn't. And now here at the contest, the announcer had brought it to the public's attention yet again, throwing in a clever quip that it might have had something to do with Occy losing to Mick Fanning earlier in the day. The redhead saw a shadow cross Mark's usually happy-go-lucky face. She heard him mutter to no one in particular, "That's one too many, mate. It's just not kind." Then Mark Occhilupo, world champion, stood up, walked over to a magazine rack that held hundreds of these programs and threw every one of them, handful after handful, into a nearby garbage can. Everyone tried not to watch. He then quietly returned to his seat. The redhead couldn't help it. She smiled at Mark. He felt it. Their eyes met. He silently nodded back, looked out onto the surf, and smiled himself.

HERE WALKS A MAN

The redhead had a talent for becoming invisible; she never drew attention to herself except when she was on stage and so, one enchanted late afternoon, the security being lax this the seventh day of competition, she found herself in the announcer's booth as the "Expression Session" got underway. Twenty-five of the best surfers who had already lost out of the contest, all vied for their last shot at five thousand dollars that was to be given to the surfer with the most radical, innovative, and entertaining moves. She thought they were all surfing like drunken lunatics. Cory Lopez spinning, Nathan Webster flying, young hometown hero Troy Brooks floating, and Russell Winter, from England of all places, was apparently trying to either break his board or commit suicide on the bigger sets. It was the most exuberant surfing she had ever witnessed. Made even better by the presence of Trudy Todd and Jodie Smith out there hassling the guys for waves, trading punches of their own. If only all contests were like this. She watched Richie Lovett do a reverse take-off, come unglued, and wipe out spectacularly to the cliffside audience's delight. She had overheard Richie two nights before saying that he was drawing this year's inspiration from the movie *HEAT*. That great scene where Robert De Niro tells Al Pacino that even though he has looked him in the eye over a cup of coffee, he still would not hesitate to put a bullet through him. "I will not hesitate," said Richie, right before promptly losing his first heat to Sunny Garcia. Richie, the hottest un-sponsored surfer in the world, was out there surfing for groceries at this point. The redhead silently hoped he would win; his girlfriend Amanda was the nicest person she'd met at this contest.

Just then, Sunny Garcia and his wife stepped into the booth, and the redhead knew then and there that Sunny was going to win the whole contest. The restless, animal body. The relaxed, disarming smile and the confidence that comes with having a lot of money, a beautiful wife, and, she guessed, many children. He had won yesterday's Expression Session on one move. An upside-down re-entry—an explosion more than anything else. She wondered where great surfers went at moments like that. Surfing both liberates and enslaves an individual from take-off to kick out, this much she knew. But skill on Sunny's level seemed transcendent to her. Surfers really don't go anywhere on a wave unless they go inside themselves. And that takes power. Compared to the gazelles in the water, Sunny seemed like a tawny lion, licking his lips in the shade of a tree by the watering hole. He knew they would come. And he would feed. *And power?* she thought as she stole a glance at his sea-stained eyes. *Oh, he had power.*

Outside, another set approached. She saw Sunny watch closely. Of the thirteen surfers who attempted to ride, not one stayed on their feet. Sunny didn't say a word. A ghost of a smile played across his lips. Then he gently kissed his wife on her left eyelid.

"Too easy," he said as he ran his hand through her hair.

PUSS N' BOOTS: 2:45 a.m.

On top of the kitchen counter, one of the official Rip Curl Dancers had stripped down to her thong and high-heeled boots, re-enacting her contest-winning towel dance, causing a collective heart attack that surged through the turgid standing-room-only crowd at the media party house. The music was jack-hammering and the boys clinked bottles, head-butted each other, bellowed sinfully, and slopped beer all over hell. The redhead, toward the back of the room with the rest of the girls, gently shook her head from side to side and laughed to herself. The dancer's lesbian lover was standing right next to her, egging her on with suggestive dance moves of her own. The lesbian lover had told the redhead that she and her gal play "Puss n' Boots" every chance they get.

Earlier that day, Sunny Garcia had rung the bell of the Rip Curl Pro 2000 at a place called Gibson's Steps, three hours to the south of Bells Beach in the shadow of the citadel rock formations they call "The Twelve

Apostles." After the trek back to Torquay, and the garbage fire at the pub, this party was the last blast for the tent people, holiday makers, truants, straggling surfers, and assorted cast of fringe dwellers who make Bells the Woodstock of surfing year after year. They would be going home on the morrow. The pro surfers, invisible these days except when in their heats, were long gone. The circus had pulled out of town.

Not surprisingly, the dancer on the kitchen counter lost her footing on a daub of Vegamite, sending her ass-over-teakettle into the throng, much to the delight of those who were fortunate to break her fall. The momentum of this development carried them all into the stereo player where everybody fell asunder in a tangle of electronics and speaker wires. Fast for her size, the lesbian lover stage dived off the counter and waded in affect a rescue. The redhead considered helping, but the whole thing was so damn heroic that she let things lie.

This was also looking like a break in the music so the redhead took her guitar from its case, sat on the same counter, and began to play. She was good at guitar. This settled the crowd, made it hers. Her blonde friend gazed at her with tears of envy welling in her eyes as she always did at times like this. Then the blonde dutifully retired to the treehouse in the back yard with her Western Australian. A full moon rose regally and the redhead sang of romance, inspiring the lucky ones to pair up and move into private corners, seeking the shadows. The redhead finished her last song, and with her eyes, beckoned a handsome boy into the next room. And fifteen minutes later, into the room beyond that. And finally, as they turned off the lamp, she raised her eyes to his and the world swayed and rolled. She took him places he'd never been.

DAWN'S EARLY LIGHT

At dawn, she packed up her car and drove down to Point Danger to the Anzac War Memorial. She hadn't had the chance to pay her respects at the Anzac Day parade the day before. The words on the monument inspired a song idea. She pulled her guitar out, sat on the wooden railing as the sun rose, and began to work out a bluesy tune about heartache and hope and the rage it takes to live an adventurous life. To live as a surfer and play your own song on a wave. To live as a woman and play your own song anywhere.

> This walk is so much better than the last
> Yet the old shit still hangs in the past
> Sweeter feeling, harder to walk away
> Keep it inside for a weaker day
> But there it ends but with a change
> We feel great, yet bad all the same

Her blonde friend would be rumpled and crawling out of the treehouse about now, so the redhead put her guitar back in its case and slid into her crappy little car to go fetch her friend and take them both back home to the Blue Hills. The redhead gently tapped the wheel as her song came to life in her head. She decided she would call the song "LEST WE FORGET." The same as the epitaph read on the Anzac Memorial.

She started the car, pulled out onto the road, and slipped on her sunglasses against the rising sun.

She was nineteen years old.

ANAK LAUT

THE LOMBOK CHILDREN OF THE SEA ARE RESTLESS
SURFTIME MAGAZINE, BALI, 2016

Lombok, Bali's neighbor island, has always shouldered a dark history. Civil Wars. Marauding bandits. Famines. Only a twenty-minute flight away from The Island of the Gods, it's a different world. Lombok also hosts what is considered the best shaped breaking wave on the planet. A dry, sun-blasted little corner of the island appropriately named Desert Point. The beachfront tourist area of Lombok is now being chopped up into a massive luxury resort for the Jakarta potentates, complete with an International Moto GP track that is sure to drown out the ancient sounds of the jungle. The local kids will have very little opportunity other than serving their wealthy masters. —Mg.

Up on the hill on Lombok Island, as the security gate swung open to the luxury villa, Junaidi Sayeed Alam could smell the nonbelievers. Suntan lotion, deodorant, perfume, beer...all the sour smells of white skin. He and a handful of other local surfers had competed in the surf contest earlier that day. The contest organizers from the big surf company over from Bali deemed it a charitable impulse to have them at the post-contest jubilee. It was only fair, they said. Junaidi, just sixteen, could see the pale blue glow of the pool through the gate. Shadowy figures trying not to spill their plastic cups of alcohol as they danced poolside to an angry American rap song that, played as loudly as it was, dominated all thought. In the pool, two topless girls were atop the shoulders of two large white surfers, screeching. The topless girls were trying to wrestle each other off the shoulders of their white surfers. Junaidi could see the swaying of one girl's bare breasts, shiny in the glow of the pool. His friends just kept their eyes down.

The first security guard, Junaidi's uncle, took some time looking over Juniadi and his friends. Then his uncle had to clear the whole thing with the white villa manager, who took his time looking them over, too. The manager finally nodded with a sigh, instructed Junaidi's uncle to keep a close eye, and they were allowed in. Junaidi and his friends put up as brave a front as they could, vexed at inserting themselves into a fantasy world in their own backyards. A world that could never be theirs. Their bootlegged surf brand baseball caps askew, their cleanest bootlegged surf brand t-shirts, their array of counterfeit boardshorts hanging on their slim hips, their worldly belongings, only a few crumpled packs of cheap cigarettes, stuffed in their pockets. They were all barefoot.

At the plastic, waist-high gate by the pool, the second security guard allowed Juniadi and his friends to let themselves in to the party. The second security guard did not hold open the plastic gate for Juniadi and his friends like he did for the white people. Junaidi noticed this. Juniadi's friends shambled past the bare breasts and over to the bar area. With no money, they could only make a pretense, but were able to grab a red plastic cup each. They had smuggled in enough of their backyard rice wine to see them through. They gingerly pulled small birthday balloons bursting with the stuff from out of the front of their underwear. They had already had a few slugs in the gravel parking lot, except for Junaidi, who never drank.

They all flopped down on the leather couches, trying to look like they owned the place, which in a strange way, having been born there, they did. One boy lit his cigarette from their only box of matches. The others, to conserve the matches, lit up off its burning tip. The place was packed with white surfing boys and girls. Giants all. Even the girls. The white boys were buying ten-dollar drinks for the girls. A lot of drinks. Junaidi noticed the glaze falling over the girls' eyes.

The night air was that of an oven and all Junaidi could think of was the dirt permanently ground into the pads of his feet and of the shoes he saw piled up near the front gate. A hundred pairs of sandals from two hundred different feet and all looking brand new. White or no, you still had to leave your shoes outside. Junaidi's eyes had lingered on one pair of sandals. A surf brand's best. The ones he saw in the magazine. All leather. It had filled him with resentment. Junaidi looked down at his own feet and was burdened. His splayed feet, reef-scarred like some old fisherman. For some reason, it was really riding him tonight. And he let it. Eventually bothering him so fiercely that, for the first time in his life, Junaidi emptied one of the balloons of rice wine into his mouth and took a cigarette, lit it, drew it in, and moved over to the edge of the leather couch to see where these vices would take him.

With heavy lids, he chanced a good look out over the party. The villa manager had made the girls put their tops back on. The weight of their breasts against their wet t-shirts was even more alarming. Junaidi was more aroused watching them put their tops back on than seeing their nakedness bounce to and fro. Music continued to pound. The crowd was yelling at each other to be heard above the noise and Junaidi could see inside one of the the miraculous poolside villa rooms. An oasis of unachievable sensuality. Of a kind of mating he knew nothing of. The miracle of being on top of a woman, softly lit with bedside lamps, creamy, cool sheets, white pillows. His mom and aunt were the cleaning women for this villa, so he could imagine the scent of fresh bleach and of the sun that dried those brilliant white sheets. And for a second, Junaidi was lost in a fuzzy dream. He downed another balloon. He could see himself tumbling into one of those beds with a big-breasted girl from the pool. His groin became restless and he adjusted himself. He blinked twice. Lurching away from the forbidden thought, he squared himself. His resentment flared. Junaidi lived on a dirt floor. With his mom and his three sisters and his aunt who had lost her husband. He had a tattered cot with a worn flap of cardboard for a bottom sheet and a big towel he won at a local surf contest as a blanket. He filled his t-shirt with other t-shirts for a pillow.

Junaidi had grown up surfing under a blazing sun but had always felt cast in shadow. He had competed in the local surf contests all his life, won a few trophies, a few prizes, but they always felt like handouts to him. Like the towel. Even his board was second-hand. Though he polished and re-painted and re-stickered it, it had always been someone else's first. Something they didn't want anymore. When the surf contests came over from Bali, they brought all the shiny new dreams and the shiny new Bali Hindu kid surfers and the tall white surfers, and they all tussled it out in the surf against the furnace-hot sand. It was always unsettling. As good a surfer as he was, Junaidi figured out that he was never going to be one of those white guys in the pool. None of his friends would be, either. The drugs and the cigarettes and the turpentine in the rice wine were already dicing them into mincemeat. Junaidi looked around at the party and at his friends. He'd never felt so lonely. He emptied another balloon.

His father thought his surfing was amusing and had even given him a stolen scooter with a surfboard rack on it to get to the beach. But his father also had said that surfing was no place for a grown man. Junaidi's days of hanging around the cheerless surf shop and caging a few surf lessons for the white people had become tedious. He had his mom and his aunt and his sisters to think of, too. Junaidi had tested off the charts when the local school bosses showed up. But no matter, they were really there to take all the money the government had sent from Jakarta. The village teacher, a bereaved widow who had lost her only child to Malaria, made Junaidi feel like an orphan. She had given him an email of some white Christians. They were said to give money to smart poor kids to go to a real school over on Bali. But Junaidi was no beggar. His dad had taught him that much. Even though his dad was a pirate and a thief.

Junaidi took another pull off a friend's balloon and drew in the sharp smoke of the cigarette and felt them both burn all the way in. And in that moment, he knew his path was chosen. In that moment, Junaidi left surfing and all its childish dreams behind. He stood and nodded to his friends, knowing the next time they saw him, they would fear him. He stood and took his measure in a mirror and began his rite of passage away from the party. From this life. Junaidi had never stolen a thing in his life. Even though, to his friends, if you got away with it, stealing was the coolest thing you could do. A win in a world of losing out to the wealthy who were invading their island and buying up the land like candy. But now Junaidi was headed south, far south, hours south, where he knew his father's crew was hiding, surrounded by bounty, waiting for the next opportunity. Junaidi was going to join his father and become some kind of man.

Once outside the front gate, Junaidi slipped his feet into those new leather sandals he so envied. He wiggled his toes, not ashamed anymore. They were a little big, but he figured he'd grow into them. His uncle was watching from the gate. Junaidi lifted his chin and looked straight into the eyes of his uncle. A moment. Then his uncle nodded and looked away. Junaidi walked out into the night in his sandals.

His new life was tapping its foot.

THE IMPORTANCE OF
BEING GARUT

THE WEIGHT OF THE PEACEFUL WARRIOR
SURFTIME MAGAZINE, BALI, 2013

The Balinese professional surfers are lucky princes. They have no interest in leaving these shores or proving themselves on the international pro tour, because they have nothing to prove or improve in their lives. They are family based in and of paradise. And that is where they remain. —Mg.

She was a delicate creature, but very brave. At five years old, she would look anyone straight in the eye. And she had her own style. Wore only one earring. Liked her hair in bangs, cut high on her forehead. Cute to most, but for her it was so she could see better. She wore pants, made them look right. More than loved, she was admired by adults. She was adventurous and would climb to the top of the highest trees. Higher than any of the other kids. Then, just six years old, just before joining her friends in elementary school, her grip slipped from a branch and she fell a long way to the ground. They made it to the hospital. But because her injuries were mostly internal, diagnosis was slow. By the time the doctors figured it out, she was gone. Her name was Armini Widiarta. And her little brother Garut loved her with all his heart.

Goku Restaurant, Jl. Benesari, Kuta, Bali, Indonesia.
Valentine's Day, 2016

You step into the sugar-sweet smell of BBQ smoke floating like a ghost through the small alley-side restaurant. It is a different world. A humble place, cramped, plastic chairs, but still the unofficial clubhouse of Kuta's surfing elite in Bali. One look at the walls and you know you're somewhere. A patchwork of photos torn out of surf magazines plaster the four walls. Some framed, some not, some signed, some not. Some faded and curled, some not. Some are of the people who hang out there, some are of visiting surf stars. Plenty of signatures and messages in ten different languages are scrawled on the wall in between them all, but most of the photos are of the powerful surfing family that lords over Goku's Resto like a royal court. Uncle Ganti, Made Winada Adi Putra, Made Garut Widiarta, and Raditya Rondi. The island's best surfers, spanning the generations. Cousins all. There is no place like Goku on earth.

You make your way through the place, past the kitchen girls with those enchanting Balinese smiles. You go through the kitchen and step out the back door into a typical Balinese home compound. The centerpiece is a small Hindu temple. You find yourself in the company of a mysterious savant: Hamish Humphrey. Expat photographer originally from the Seychelles. No one is quite sure how long he has been in Bali. The smart money says ten years. An astounding photographer and, because he has mastered their language, friend to the locals. An odd presence, he is lolling nearby, sixth bottle of beer in hand, naming each and every early evening constellation, and some yet to appear. Sitting next to him on the ground is the current Indonesian Surfing Champion Raditya Rondi, looking on with mild amusement to Hamish's strange accent and his abrasive comments about outer space exploration. How unnecessary it all is. Questioning why we would call life out there alien when they looked at us the same way. Hamish is holding court with the infinity and Raditya is not really listening, he just likes Hamish's sing song Seychelle accent.

And then you see Made Garut Widiarta, sitting in a doorway across the compound, scrubbing Poogie, his beloved pug, behind the ears. Garut is looking distracted, half-listening to Hamish, half in his own world. Blinking with his whole face in that way of his that curls the corners of his lips into a short burst of a smile. A tic left over from a childhood trauma. Like the way he gnaws his right thumbnail. Garut's face, with the high, classic Balinese cheekbones and wonder-filled eyes, is a welcoming sight to anyone. A bright, energetic face beneath coal-black hair. He is wearing his usually long hair short for the surf competition season.

Yet regardless of how cheerful you have always found Garut, you have always sensed a subterfuge behind that smile. A young man balancing spiritualism with driving ambition, cool peerdom with individuality. Today is no different.

You step out of the range of Hamish Humphrey's salvos against the universe and Raditya's quiet mirth and you sit on a small curb across the compound with Garut. You begin a short, restrained conversation. You find out that Garut is twenty-four years old now. That he comes from a family of thirteen brothers and sisters. That he loves his tattoos, but not the way you would think. You hear him say that the tattoo itself is not important; it's the why you wear it. You find out that his favorite moment on a wave is the bottom turn. That he feels in that moment that he can read the wave, feel its potential, and that moment gives him his greatest pleasure in the surf. You find out that he worries about getting old, that he wished he could be eighteen years old forever. You find out that he is a devout Balinese Hindu and very patriotic toward the Indonesian flag. You find out that he feels that the biggest difference he has seen in his surfing career is the equipment that the young surfers get to start out on these days. That everything is brand-new for these little kids. Boards, deck pads, boardshorts, leashes, wax. You find that he remembers the days of old, brown, broken, cast-off boards, and once even a surfboard leash partly made out of a cow's tail. You find out that his advice to the young is for them to be influenced by the visiting surf stars, but do not copy them. And above all, to honor family.

And it is in this moment, sitting in his family compound under an early evening sky, that you realize that Made Garut Widiarta is the best Indonesian surfer the world has ever seen. And that this Balinese prince before you will someday—someday soon—become a king here on Bali. All he has to do is stay alive, carry on. Legend awaits. And you realize that the importance of Made Garut Widiarta lies in his faith in his Gods, in surfing, and in his family. A role model? Garut is something more. Something genuine. Not a copy. A singular soul of Indonesian history, his pride and artistry thriving in a world around him that is not changing for the better. A world that, due to rampant tourism development, has become a construction site. And he is quite literally in the middle of it, in this compound filled with wonder and faith and trepidation for the future. But filled nonetheless. With the spirit of the island he loves. Part of its noble tradition. A brown-skinned, important talent worthy of the world's admiration.

A quiet falls over the both of you. Garut stretches and yawns and that's when you see it among the others. The tattoo under his left bicep. Ornate and graceful, it reads simply: "Armini." So you say to him, oh so quietly, looking into his eyes for longer than just a quick glance for once, you say that you heard the story about what happened to Armini. And you say that you are sorry that he lost his older sister all those years ago. And that is when Made Garut Widiarta slowly draws his knees to his chest and stares at the ground, rocking softly back and forth, blinking with his whole face in that way he does. And he says, almost a whisper now, he says, "Yeah . . . me too."

THE DELICATE DANCE

NEW DISCOVERIES AND OLD PERILS IN JAVA
SURFER MAGAZINE, USA, 2011

There might be more perfect waves in Java than anywhere else in the world. No one knows because it is one of the last explored regions of this vast Indonesian archipelago. A small fishing village whose name translates to "White Sands" is just now feeling the impact that visiting surfers will have. I watched this fisherman for days. He was questioning things, you could tell.
—Mg.

The Fisherman

Part One

He stands over his outboard motor, a worn screwdriver in his hand, remembering.

There were two of them, pearly skinned. And they had long hair growing on their faces and they came to his village and played where he had never dared. Where none of the fishermen had ever dared. The Ocean had always been a wild animal here, roaring day and night. The waves like slashing monsters that collapsed in great explosions off both sides of the walls of this small bay, leaving only a sliver of hope for the boats. A narrow, deep groove in the bottom of the sea between the two shallow, broken reefs where the water would flee in a white, racing river on its way back out to sea. This groove he used, with great care, to drive his boat out onto the rolling sea to catch fish for family and for market. This same groove took all his skill at the end of the day, fighting its great power with his outboard motor, to reach the white sands of his beach again.

And then one day they came, the two white giants. And they threw themselves into the sea and lay down on their toys and they swam into the monster waves and began playing like children. Taunting the roaring monsters, standing, riding within the monsters' mouths again and again. Getting devoured, they would surface exultant and swim their toys back into the waves to do it again and again until they too returned to shore, exhausted and burned by the sun and bloodied by the reef. It was as miraculous to the fisherman as it was silly. But that was fifteen years ago.

Part Two

He watches them eat like jungle boars. The morning's catch cooked over a fire and laid out before them on the front porch of his home within eyeshot of the great waves they have come here to play in. Nearby, three big shiny black cars, bristling with more surfboards and cameras than the entire village was worth.

He knew the tall ambitious one, Rizal Tandjung, from Bali. Had even helped him buy all the land up on the hill. They had discussed it at length over the years. How Rizal wanted to create an escape, a getaway for his family. Away from the madness of Kuta Beach, Bali. Where, because of tourism, the picked-over bones of Bali were held together with little more than memories. And in return for this help, Rizal could bring to his porch the business of the visiting surfers who were sure to come. Surfing is money. And where there is money, there is life. And hope for the fisherman's daughter. That much the fisherman believed. Because it was already happening. Over the past fifteen years, the trickle of surfers had become, if not a torrent, then at least a stream. And for the most part, they had been respectful and quiet and always in wonder of the beauty of the place. There had only been a few gross incidents and they all involved beer. Frowned upon here, any alcohol was legally forbidden. But the fisherman had his wife keep a refrigerator full of beers anyway. It was the steadiest business he had. And the backdoor payoffs to the local government were manageable for him.

Unlike the Australian madman that had set up a small bamboo structure on the berm of sand facing the waves, dreaming of starting his own beer garden in this place, he refused to pay the local bribes. As soon as the Australian opened for business, the local strongarms took it over and no one on earth was going to question the right of that. This is when the Australian drank all the beer he had at once rather than giving it to the strongarms. The Australian lost his mind and began jumping up and down on the beach with no clothes on, screeching at the full moon. He drained a full bottle of hidden gin in two minutes and then fell to the sand. The next day, his body was dragged by its feet to the fish market and covered in shaved ice. One week later, a government man in a tie arrived with the Australian's family and, without a word, they took the thing away.

The fisherman thought it very sad how a white man could possibly think that he could get away with something like that here. Paradise is never free.

Part Three

The fishing done for the day, the fisherman sits with his young daughter on the bench he built under the monkey pod tree. A bench he built so that his family could watch the surfing when all the work was done. There were six surfers in the water now. The fisherman's younger brother was holding position against the current with the outboard in the channel. The photographer in the boat stood unsteadily, swinging his camera left and right as the surfers jumped and spun and played in the waves. Three more photographers stood on the beach with wet towels on their heads against the midday heat. It seemed miraculous to him, this surfing. He still could not figure out how the surfers did not die. And he hoped they wouldn't. These surfers were going making it possible to send his daughter to school. A good school. He reached over and entwined his fingers in his daughter's hand. She smiled up at him, then moved close and dug her head into his ribs, and closed her eyes.

It wasn't as if surfing were changing everything here. It was just beginning to present new elements in unsettling ways. His daughter and wife were beginning to speak English now. He didn't speak a word of it. Listening to his wife and daughter speak it to their guests had never made him feel so simple. That was new. He had found his younger brother the other day drinking beer with the surfers. His brother had looked at him with a challenge in his eyes. And the fisherman had let it go. That had never happened before. His wife was demanding more things: a bigger cooler for the beers, a western toilet, a new generator, a new dress, things like that. And his daughter had asked for a television. He had wrinkled his nose at that. And he had heard tell of a great road that was being built along this coast and all the promised people who were to come.

He looked down at his daughter, used his little finger to move her hair out of her eyes, then gazed out over the sea and to the horizon. And he thought to himself that at least that would never change. The Ocean was something he knew very, very well. No confusion there. His had been a life of freedom, because he knew that true freedom only came to those who had a set of rules to live by. Boundaries. Belief. A noble conduct. That was freedom. And the Ocean reminded you of those things every day.

He knew that these surfers, these visitors, were bringing an even stranger influence with them. With their giant, healthy bodies and their riches and belongings and free time to play, they were bringing envy. He did not want this for his daughter. The anger. The lies.

He turned gently, not to wake his daughter, when he heard another car from the airport drive up. Four more white giants got out of the car. They had many surfboards with them. The fisherman saw his wife greet them and offer them beers and limes. And he saw them trying desperately to talk to her. They were gesturing wildly with their arms, trying to mimic a wave. He saw his wife point to the sea. And the giants began running toward the bench he sat upon. He could see in their eyes a fire. The fisherman turned back to the sea and to his daughter and held her a little closer. And for the first time in his life, the fisherman thought that not all dreams, not all desires, and not all money is good. But what does a man's dreams know of boundaries?

Then the fisherman, listening to the surfers come on, used his foot to lift the lid of the cooler at his feet, making sure the ice hadn't melted around the beer.

AUTHOR, SIKAKAP, METAWAI ISLANDS, WEST SUMATRA

AMAZING GRACE

THOUGHTS ON A SUMATRAN JOURNEY
WAVES MAGAZINE, AUSTRALIA, 2001

Surfing takes us to so many unremarkable places, too. Little forgotten corners of the world where people's lives know nothing of ours and never will. And surfing takes us to these unremarkable places and we make them remarkable by riding the waves off their shores. —Mg.

The bats were out. As they were each time twilight fell over the tattered Mentawai Island port of Sikikap off West Sumatra. These bats, with wings as supple as a goat leather jacket, swerved and flapped and swooped in a wild ballet as they plowed through the billows of mosquitoes that rose at dusk like the end of the world. The muezzin was calling the faithful over fuzzy speakers that hung from the leaning wooden light posts. The posts that ran like the ribs of a whale skeleton along the main drag. The faithful, prostrate on their woolen rugs, faced west, or thereabout, and gave thanks in this thankless place. Cerebral malaria, dengue fever, and chikungunya take half the children here before they reach three years old. This remote port is home to a small, bustling wharf-side quay that supplies petrol, water, engine parts, light bulbs, oil, grease, sweat, and the odd prostitute to the wild array of tattered sailors that ply these waters. This place is perched on the edge of the universe. If the whole place were to vanish, disappear from the face of the earth, the first people to care would be the illegal exotic fish dealers who pay the locals to scrape the reefs for the Yakuza bar aquariums back in Tokyo. The second to care would be the local pirates who rip the forests clean of old growth teak, and a long third would be the West Sumatran Government, who would simply shrug their shoulders.

The last to care would be surfers. Because sometimes the tattered boats that cart the surfers around this island chain looking for waves come in here for supplies and fuel. And if the place disappeared, if Sikikap blew up, the surfers would shrug their shoulders, too. And that would be that. Because there aren't any waves in this place. Only fuel and supplies.

Which probably explains why a group of the finest Australian junior surfers their country had to offer found themselves on shore in Sikikap.

Sweating in the surly heat, sitting in a circle of roughhewn stools on the edge of the dirt of the main drag. Sitting with some locals who regarded them as insane, hunkered down in front of the small, bare light bulb cigarette shop, drinking hot beer and smoking clove cigarettes and plunking out a rousing version of a Scottish spiritual on a handful of ten-dollar guitars. For a moment, all of Sikikap stopped what they were doing to listen to this strange sound.

Back onboard the surfers' well-appointed charter boat, the Sumatran captain was listening, too. He could hear this strange song rising over the shanty town of Sikikap, over the open sewers and the bare light bulbs and the whale bones. It carried out to the quay—to him. He asked his first mate what the song was. The first mate didn't know.

But the little girl rattling home on her bicycle past the cigarette shop did. She'd learned the song at church. That new Catholic church that was making her feel so different than her veiled Islamic friends. She knew the song she was hearing was called "Amazing Grace." And she couldn't believe that all those tall white sinners sitting in a circle in front of the cigarette shop knew the words to her favorite song.

CANGGU:
EAT, PRAY, FUCK

SOUNDBITES FROM BALIL'S FREEDOM FRONTIER
SURFTIME MAGAZINE, BALI, 2017

The changes that have come to the Canggu region of Bali over the past decade have been staggering. Once an outland of mud and back breaking toil in the rice paddies, today the new motherlode of party and rave tourism has swerved this place of ancient land right into the hands of modern rapacious developers. Canggu now rivals the reputation of Ibiza as one of the grooviest places on earth to see and be seen. —Mg.

Canggu is all on its own. Once a surfing outpost, now a colony, it's been cut off. The natural disaster known as tourism, combined with an absolute lack of civil infrastructure to handle it, has resulted in a geographical isolation due to snarled traffic. From Kuta Beach to Canggu, once mere minutes of driving, is now a bad hour of breathing near-pure carbon monoxide. This traffic is a result of a massive exodus of adventurers, scoundrels, criminals, dreamers, investors, carpetbaggers, and vegans who have forged Canggu into the most outlandish surfing community in the world. Astonishingly, usurping the Holy Grail of Uluwatu as Bali's prime surf destination. Canggu has morphed into a miasma of every surfing creed, color, and philosophy drawn to its perceived promised land of cool where any surfer on earth can reinvent themselves. Or get blown away by the cops in broad daylight. Just like a western madman did recently when he went "troppo" and attacked the police. The sun does shit to people here.

And all of this action happens minus the picture-perfect, clear blue airbrushed dream tunnels that have made Indonesia every surfer's fantasy. Canggu's best waves break within in a steaming hot beach break zone with brown, silty, rice-paddy-run-off seas up against a dark, volcanic sand beach that can burn the soles off water buffalo. A surf zone that is a bouncy castle for aerialists and a Renaissance Fair for retro riders. Canggu, the petri dish of restored western grooviness, art, fashion, food, multi-national sexual opportunity, and rampant development—complete with the subsequent environmental and cultural disaster that such prosperity exacts. But despite its long being ground zero for the surfing hipster movement, the prime destination of a diaspora that longs for the way we were in the '70s, Canggu is now reaching critical mass. Like a run-over Ibiza with rice, a place like this can only maintain its cool for so long. Today, the business of Canggu is business. And a swollen cumulonimbus of over-saturation is fast approaching from the horizon.

VOICES OF CANGGU: Dustin Humphrey, Director of *Deus Ex Machina Indonesia*, Father, Photographer, Filmmaker, Provocateur.

I talked to Dustin in his office that overlooks the Deus Ex Machina Temple of Enthusiasm. A nouveau rustic compound which accommodates a restaurant, a surf shop, a performance stage, an art gallery, a skate ramp, surfboard shaping bays, a photo studio, a barbershop, and a custom motorcycle garage. A site that, since its inception, has been more responsible for the alternative surf scene in Canggu than any other. Mostly due to Humphrey's vision of a gentler, cooler surfing world—one that belongs in the upper echelons of human achievement and art. And he's damn near achieved it. Deus truly is a temple, complete with a royal courtyard that serves as both mini music stadium and amphitheater for such guest speakers as Bob McTavish to Alex Knost. From where I sit, I can see people swanning into a retail space that looks more like a hall in the Museum of Modern Art, with elegant wine-colored alternative surfboards juxtaposed against a phalanx of enviably customized motorcycles. The scent of surf wax and chain lube go hand in hand at Deus.

"Why has Canggu become what it is? Because it looks so easy to live here. But it isn't. You gotta be somebody with something to offer or it just doesn't work. Canggu holds possibility. Like the American West back in the day. Adventurers came here to be self-made. And it happened faster than anybody could have predicted."

VOICES OF CANGGU: Gede "Ayok" Dharma, Deus Team rider, member of the Canggu Surf Community Boardriders, top local surfer, surfboard rental owner, activist, dreamer.

I sat with Ayok in the Deus restaurant. Lunch hour was booming. The grooviest people on earth surround us. And my God, the hair. Braided, beaded, ponytailed, slicked, shaven, bunned. And the jewelry, everything from love beads to tantric yoga river stones to opal medallions set in silver and all of it artfully distressed and sweat-stained. And the get-ups, bellbottoms to peggers, tight bermudas, and gossamer scarves. All thrift-store inspired but sold for top dollar. A beat-up fedora here will set you back a month's wage.

Ayok and I were sharing an organic Buddha Bowl salad, what with Canggu also now having established itself as a new culinary Eden, with hundreds of innovative restaurants popping up like the very mushrooms they sauté over liquid nitrogen. Just where everybody finds their Chia seeds in this world of rice remains a mystery, but over Ayok's shoulder I could see a pair of developers, Italian shoes, architect plans laid out on the hood of a rover, pointing to and discussing the giant cafeteria pizza joint that was going up right against the wall next to Deus. It was to be built over one of the last rice paddy lots available and would change forever the emotional landscape of what is the hottest three-way corner in Canggu. Where Deus once ruled like a lone fortress in a groomed rice paddy, now all the action on the strip was catching up and moving in right next door. Ayok speaks:

> "It's hard to talk about it. Talking about the bad things will never end, but it's good for our local people's business. Lots of money from everybody in the world. But at night, it's a bit too much now. It disturbs the spirits. It's harder and harder to hear the quiet and the spirit voices from the rice paddies and the temples that are so important to the peace of this place. The spirits used to whisper; now they have to yell to be heard. That is shame for me. I have a big hope that I was born earlier. Now there is easier work than rice, more money. But I feel sad for the young local people that wake

up in the morning and see everybody drunk trying to get home. Like that is normal life. Money life. We need their wallets, but this is what my village has become? Drunk party people that speak many different languages but never ours? We found naked people in our temple on the beach on top of each other. We had to beat them with bamboo poles to have them stop. Or people peeing on the temple walls. We bring them to the police. Would you find that in a church back in Germany or Russia or wherever they come from? Bali people are welcoming, but not to arrogant people."

As I stepped outside after our talk, I thought of that need for quiet that Ayok spoke of. Now, with all the development going on, the soundtrack to Canggu is dirt movers and jackhammers. I looked across a dusty, litter-strewn parking lot to yet another club. This one with a cowboy theme that features semi-nude local women swinging from the roof on western saddles. Next door to that, an old Dutch era building was being demolished with a wrecking ball—the rumored site of Canggu's first McDonalds.

DRAINAGE

It's an innocent-looking place. Unless you look closer. In Canggu, urban, hotel, business, private, and rice field sewer, rain, and brown-water drainage all rely on an ancient ground level runoff system about three feet wide. These broken cement and dirt ditches are open and clogged with plastic bags and God-knows-what-else and they are pungent and polluted. And they run parallel to most of the narrow roads here. There are no curbs in Canggu. These ditches run anywhere from three to six feet deep and wreak havoc with the endless flow of scooters, custom motorcycles, taxis, Ubers, and tinted-windowed SUVs that snake around what's left of the rice paddies. Get beered up and get loose as a first-time scooter renter and your vacay is over. A trip to the sketchy hospital and then home. If you're lucky.

Gerhard Engelbrecht wasn't. He was a friend of mine. A good-natured South African surf photographer and full-time philosopher. Long, sunburnt hair, unkempt goatee, startling clear blue eyes. And that strong accent. A good surfer and an even better surf photographer. He was loved here. He seemed to embody what Canggu was all about for the less wealthy, live-in expats. Fit, cool-looking, connected to the place. Good company. The kind of guy that no matter how tough you think you are, you could not help but smile when you saw him. The locals called him "friend," not "boss" like they do to the rest of the international visitors. Right down to his amulets and his bright eyes, Gerhard was part of Canggu. And like most here, he was not afraid of late, late-night beers at any of the late, late night clubs. Come to think of it, like most South Africans, I don't think he was afraid of anything.

Yet on the 12th of February 2016, like a warning shot across Canggu's bow, the dreadful news spread. In the very early hours, Gerhard Englebrecht had been found dead. Under his motorcycle in the bottom of the drainage ditch that runs smack dab through the main drag. It was easy to see how it could happen, considering the chaos of the night life here and total lack of road rules or traffic signs. You are on your own here. It's a big part of why so many people keep coming back. The thing is, nobody thought it could happen like this. Not in a place like this. Not to him. Not to them. Not to anyone they cared about. But it can. And it did.

There was a flurry of dark rumors, of a love triangle gone bad with a local married woman, of a promise unfulfilled, of money issues with the wrong people, of booze, the sun, the weather, the language, the rules, the heat, the sweat—any number of things that can get any expat into real trouble here. The things that can drain you. The things that do drain you. From mosquitoes to sunburns to neck-shattering motorcycle crashes. The things that tire you, if you choose to settle far from your blood home and come to this promised land eight degrees below the equator. One has to remember that in Bali, you don't live here, you survive here. You don't have any rights, just privileges. And any broken local trusts can send you reeling for the airport. Or worse. Paradise isn't for just anybody. Just like in any jungle, you must always maintain a circle of awareness. It's that or be eaten. Philisophically or physically there are prices to pay in paradise if you fuck up.

None of these darker rumors stuck for long on Gerhard Engelbrecht. None ever do here. Disasters are chalked up and erased quickly in a community obsessed with reinvention and expat glory. Probably just another great night for Gerhard, full of laughter, heat seeking lust and too much alcohol. And then a drainage ditch on the way home. This ditch. Waiting like fate in the blush of another drunken Bali dawn.

So here I was, a year and a half later, just outside the Deus Temple of Enthusiasm. Surrounded by the traffic and the construction and the growth of Canggu going about its mighty business of chic commerce. I was looking down into an ancient ditch that has run through this patch of land for hundreds of years. No, thousands. The place where my friend died. Things slowed way down after the incident. People went home earlier, drank a little less. But that only lasted few days. Still, Gerhard's death served as a warning all right. To everybody. Out here in Canggu it's not go big or go home. It's go big and *get* home.

At about six feet deep, I suppose that ditch did resemble a grave. The final resting place for my friend Gerhard. I dropped a single plumeria flower into it. And a handful of loamy dirt. And getting on my motorcycle and riding away, you bet I kept to the middle of the road.

Another law of the jungle.

MEN AND WOMEN

Unlike the "Hell Zone" of neighboring Kuta, overseen by the 2002 bombing memorial, you won't find many Indonesian workin' girls cruising the streets of Canggu. For the darker, danker experiences of professional sex, one must make the journey to Bali's ground zero down in Kuta. It's cheaper there, too. Out in Canggu the pickup scene is much more European. Canggu is an expensive date. And there are far more western couples out in Canggu because of it. But out in front of one of Canggu's countless thumping nightclubs, Gary "Gazza" Kilpatrick, a visitor I ran into, had this to say:

"Yeah, mate, plenty of one-nighters out here in Canggu, mate. The party circuit. Euros looking to sleep with different accents and Aussies just scrounging a root. Still cost the same though, when you look at it. To scrounge a root here, drinks, the chitchat, the hours you gotta put in. Kuta is the release valve for that bullshit. At least in Kuta you pay up front and it's all over in fifteen minutes. Still hit the surf early, mate."

I ran into an old friend, Rod Robertson, a Qantas pilot out of Brisbane. A concerned father, he was paying his adult daughter a surprise visit for her birthday. He had this to say:

"I show up and some longhaired, giant Russian surfer with Moscow mafia tattoos is plowing my daughter silly? What is this place?"

Another thing that contributes to Canggu's sensual tropical nights is the sheer number of female surf camps here. It's dizzying. On any day it seems every flag on earth is represented out in the water. Flotillas of women on soft-top surfboards, "empowering" themselves. There is a Korean women's camp, Japanese, German, Russian, and even one for gay women. This influx of women active in the surf adds to the sexual opportunity.

At a Korean BBQ joint, another element was explained to me by Mieni Khim. She was the foxy owner of the place. She answered proudly in a super-lite tee shirt, her loose breasts and their dark, hard nipples a startling challenge to anyone brave enough to take the shot.

"The women get the best of it out here in Canggu. Surfers are the best-looking crowd in the world right now. And they are single minded and totally accessible. We women just show up and look like prey. But we are not the prey. They are."

A Conversation:

As an example of the bohemian lifestyle here, consider this conversation I witnessed outside one of the popular, open-air nightclubs.

A woman who appeared to be a Russian supermodel was locked in an argument with what appeared to be a French fashion photographer. His hair was done up in a man bun. You will have to imagine the accents. They were both this side of drunk. The photographer was on a scooter with two surfboards in the rack. A seven-foot single fin snout nose and a little chocolate-colored fish design with half-moon wooden fins.

>Woman: *"I'm a creative! I need visuals to understand love! What is love? You want to sleep with me? Sleep? You go to sleep, I'm not tired! You wanna fuck? Give me a visual of it. I need the visual."*
>
>Man: *"Merde."*
>
>Woman: *"What? What? Are you stupid one?"*
>
>Man: *"Non."*

Just then, two Aussies surfers swerved up on scooters. Probably there to take advantage of the midnight three-for-one ladies' drinks special that this woman had obviously been enjoying. It's prime time for a hunter. The two Aussies, half-drunk as well, stared at the supermodel. It was impossible not to. Her macrame outfit was way sexier than being nude, her love beads hanging to her knees. She had small, shiny stars glued to her face, adding to her already celestial looks. It went quiet for few seconds. The Aussies' mouths hung open. Then the woman addressed the Aussies.

>Woman: *"You like to fuck me? Give me visual. Visual. I am a creative."*

To the Aussies, it was like buckshot into a tree full of blackbirds. The short Aussie recovered first.

>Aussie Surfer: *"Outdoors? . . . In warm mud? . . . Under tonight's full moon?"*

The woman looked at the photographer. Showed her teeth. Grabbed her fish design surfboard from the photographer's scooter and hopped on the back of the Aussie's scooter, slinging one slender arm around his waist.

>Woman: *"We go."*

And they did.

THE GROIN

We ought to be used to them by now: all these things that pop up in our lives. Or at least de-sensitized, considering how much time we spend staring at our screens. The internet doesn't have us by the balls—it has us by the eyes. Way it's going, we'll adapt to the point where we don't need vision at all. Like cave newts. But at any rate, I think the point has been made that here in Canggu, developers are busy pounding and chopping and scraping the holy hell out of the whole fucking place. So it really shouldn't have surprised anyone when a giant excavator turned up on Echo Beach in Canggu and proceeded to gouge and dig and pile up a big mess of big rocks on the sand. It popped up overnight. The rumor spread fast that a jetty construction was underway that would jut directly out onto the sandstone reef of the Canggu Rights surf break. It would destroy it, of course, the wave. The best wave in the area and the reason a lot of folks live in Canggu. Once again, they, the mysterious powers-that-be, were going to destroy the only thing that generates millions of tourist dollars through surfing. But since surfing is such an abstract thought to land-locked developers and corrupt politicians, they believe those millions are generated by people who just want to watch the sun go down.

And it was at this juncture that all those screens we stare at, for once, became useful and turned a tide for the good. Out went the words on Instagram. SAVE THE WAVE. Twenty minutes later, over a thousand people were on the beach placing themselves between excavator and the sea. Our own little Tiananmen. Locals, visitors, expats. A big Instagram party. Complete with singing. And it sorta worked. Because the cops showed up and started videoing everybody so that they would know who to kick off the island if any real trouble started, adding an international credence to the affair. The excavator was pulled back a hundred yards from the beach to give the crowd a chance to cool down. It would've been dark soon anyway.

But here's the hard news. What they were trying to build was a jetty with a platform on the end that was to extend one hundred meters "past the water's edge to provide opportunity for sunset tourist photos and selfie opportunities." That proposal has since been struck down. The compromise is that a rock wall will be constructed with a cement footpath on the berm of the beach to "save the owner's property from natural erosion." The rest of the owner's property development will be built right up to the high tide line. The new complaint is that on king tides this "rock wall" will "refract the wave action of the Ocean and turn the surfing wave into turmoil." As of September 18, 2018, the rock wall is going ahead.

But to really illustrate the separation between the church of the open sky and the state of the union in Canggu, consider this: when a certain surfer paid a visit to the Ministry of Tourism and expressed his concerns about the jetty to the highest-placed official, this official responded with, "I don't understand, what does surfing have to do with tourism in Bali?"

VOICES OF CANGGU: Damea Dorsey, Surf Photographer, Restauranteur, Impresario, Barber.

You gotta see it to believe it. Damea Dorsey has chiseled out one of the coolest places on earth. An authentic, old-time barbershop and tattoo parlor. Complete with straight razor shaves and antique sailor tattoos. The go-to place if you want to keep up with the latest tonsorial crazes that sweep through Canggu like wildfire. On the walls of the shop hang photos of famous movie stars: Marilyn, Bogey, Pacino, Elvis, but each one photoshopped with butch tattoos.

"What is the draw for all the pro surfers here?" Damea says, "The variety of waves all within the area of a football field. I can shoot here every day. And you never know who's going to paddle out. It's been an avalanche these past few years. It used to be the place to get away from it all and get a few guaranteed shots. But now it's so crowded . . . I mean, obviously when you work with great surfers, they know how to get the job done, but it's work now. But so what? You know something is going right in a community when you see hundreds of beautiful girls from all over the world cruising around with surfboards on their scooters and flowers in their hair."

The following is graffiti seen brush-painted on the new twelve-foot plywood fence blocking the beach and a giant section of Canggu waterfront in anticipation of yet another super resort. Rumors are that a twenty-five-foot sheer wall will surround the entire complex all the way to the water. White sand from Hawaii is being shipped in so that the beach won't be its usual black sand hotplate. Enormous turbine fans are rumored to be put in place to emulate a sea breeze. All this to make a more comfortable beach for the resort's strict Sharia Muslim clients. And make it impossible for the unenlightened to spy upon them and therefore soil the Sharia women who are forced to wear all-black, head-to-toe Jilbab veils at all times. The graffiti reads:

Pardon the inconvenience but Bali is under construction.

VOICES OF CANGGU: Tai Graham, 34, pro Billabong surfing ambassador, club owner, musician.

Half-Maori, half-British, all Bali, Tai is the hottest expat surfer on the island and has been for some time. Frontside, backside, fearless in big waves. Bali has figured deeply in his life since his mother moved here from New Zealand when he was seven years old. Fluent in local languages and slang, he has managed to carve out a realm like no other here. A part owner of two of the hottest clubs on the island, through his friendships he maintains his credibility by being the real deal when he hits the water. The main impression you get from Tai? This is a guy who knows exactly what he's doing here and exactly who he is.

"Things change and people change with them," Tai said. "That's the way of the world, mate. Canggu used to be jungle and people had to eat. So it was carved into rice paddies and people still had to eat. Now, it's evolved into a great place to live and surf, and people still need to eat. It's easy to sit there and complain about all that is going on here, but it's just an evolution. And in many ways the best kind. Local kids are going to better schools, better hospitals, healthier, stronger, wealthier. A better future than back-breaking work under the sun, up to your knees in the mud for pennies? You wouldn't want a better world for your kids? And their kids? Bullshit. I don't think we'll ever stop the development here. We live a great lifestyle. It will all be dealt with. Just like anywhere worth dealing with."

From an entry form for an upcoming local surfing contest:

PERERENAN SURFING CLUB PRESENTS
BOARDRIDERS CHAMPIONSHIP 2017
DATE: 01 AUGUST 2017
DIVISION: Open Men's and Women's
ENTRY FEE: Rp 250.00
BIG THANKS TO OUR MAJOR SPONSORS:
QUIKSILVER, MOONROCKS, RIP CURL, and DAVID BOWIE.

It seems David Bowie—yes *that* David Bowie—fell in love with the Balinese culture years ago. Upon his death in 2016, Bowie was cremated with full Balinese honors up in the hills that overlook Canggu. It is where he rests to this day. A fan of local surfing, it is rumored that Bowie left a certain amount of funding in his will for the local board riders' clubs.

Sunsets do take all priority in Canggu, and none more than the one that sizzles into the horizon out beyond the "Old Man's" surf spot. Once a refuge from the high-pressure lineups of neighboring Echo Beach, now Old Man's features a parking lot the size of a football field. And at thirty cents a spot, it's jammed without fail every evening. But still, this is one of the last local strongholds. The Balinese people of Canggu still hold sway with creaky bamboo warungs bursting with lurid t-shirts that blare "Up the bum, no babies!" and "I'm not gay, but twenty bucks is twenty bucks!"

These hang next to the beer openers in the shape of foot-long penises and twirling fake spinners from China. You know, everything the traveling surfer needs. Precariously perched on the small limestone berm is the local version of the giant nightclubs that dominate the beaches to the north and south. A plywood promenade where one can get everything from a gin and tonic to a fresh coconut to a ten-times repaired rental surfboard. Sitting on a small stool facing the sea, I take in the spectacle. A local reggae band on a leaning wooden stage is on the beach blasting out hit after hit. All the songs you want to hear as the sun goes down in Bali. You know, "Hotel California," "Knockin' on Heaven's Door," "Cocaine," "No Woman, No Cry," "Still Lovin' You." Which makes sense when you understand that the beach next door was re-named Echo Beach after an eighties new wave hit by Martha and the Muffins.

From where I sat with my three-dollar ice chest beer, I could count 166 people in the surf. When the sets of waves steamrolled in, it was carnage. Like a junior varsity war between Kassia Meador and Dave Rastovich, who probably have shrines of their own built for them nearby. Upright, nose-riding girl longboarders and outback-bearded guys on retro boards clunking rails all the way to their wide-legged disasters in the sandy shore break. On the beach, the entirety of the European continent was represented in a rainbow of g-strings. And that was just the men. I counted 500 hundred people on the beach, many of them women in varying stages of gestation with their long-haired, feral-chic children looking like appropriate accessories. There were eighteen different dogs running and pissing and defecating shamelessly and wildly. None of these dogs being indigenous species. Like the resort-building cranes that were swinging overhead, these dogs seemed a fitting symbol to man's need to ignore nature and warp his environment into his own image of paradise. Seems Siberian Huskies and shivering teacup Mexican chihuahuas are in high demand in Canggu.

I asked the old Balinese woman who was selling me the three-dollar beers where I should pee. She indicated the Ocean with a vague hand. Which was absolutely correct. Because vile, shattered, public toilets or no, in Canggu, it all goes there anyway. The pressure of the communal bladders here at sunset could light up a city. I asked an old-timer sitting next to me what he thought of things.

"We had Woodstock; these people have this," he said.

And I thought about the local surfers. With their club contests here and their daily battles in the lineup with both top ten pros and the hordes of famous freesurfers that come to visit. Which seems a perfect fit for Canggu. Visitors here don't want to listen to a band; they want to be in one.

The sun had set by the time I made my way back to my motorcycle past what was now the packed beer garden known as OLD MAN'S bar. Kinda like hell, where I imagine every language known to man was being shouted over the mayhem. Behind me, out there beneath a purple sky, were the waves. As they always will be. Hissing and crashing and pumping money into this place with the power of solar flares.

On my way back home to Kuta, I passed a rock club bar and skateboard park. Zoning doesn't exist in Bali. I just had to stop. Beyond its black doors was a wonderland of contradictions. Like a new beat generation joint for teens without the absinthe. The wealthy expats here have created a multitude of mixed-blood youth. They have grown up here in a culture that worships children but is not quite sure what to do with them once they hit their teens. Education here is as deplorable as the healthcare. There is a middle school here that offers macrame as a P.E. class. And like the adults, this young army has found their sophomore version of the Canggu groove. In a place where you are allowed to drive anything as soon as you can, this is a scooter-mobilized crowd. And while the grown-ups outside this place find their darkened corners of the night, so do the kids. It's expected. Cool has a Keynesian effect in Canggu. You couldn't find groovier-dressed teens in New York.

The club I was in had blacklight Jimi Hendrix posters on the wall, Sex Pistols, Blondie. The playlist while I was there included Jimi, The Who, Kiss, Led, Blind Faith, ACDC, Black Sabbath, three Doors songs, and a Johnny Cash medley. I sat at the bar, watching pro skater Greyson Thunder Fletcher and his crew fly in and out of the ten-foot skate bowl between their vodka tonics. The two junior barflies sitting next to me were sipping on tequila sunrises. Apparently a real treat for fifteen-year-olds. They and the seventeen-year-old bartender were having a real time for themselves.

I spied what had to be the owner and approached her. She looked straight out of the Haight Ashbury playbook. About the same vintage, too. I asked her what she thought of the tableau in front of us.

"Bali tells people who to be. It listens. These kids are finding the way. Listening. The future is theirs. This place is a sanctuary, where young people live on hugs, not drugs."

That much was true; I'm no narc, but I couldn't smell any weed, and magic mushrooms had recently been deemed illegal after a spate of after-hour traffic accidents that left a handful of these young drinkers to be scraped up off the asphalt, dead as doornails.

"It's a twenty-four-hour world in Canggu!" the owner went on, raising her voice above the music, sweeping her hand at the teenage crowd. "They all love each other here! They are in this together! Canggu isn't just a doggie daycare center for pro surfers, you know. These kids *live* here! They have a stake in this place. It's theirs!"

No shit there, that's for sure. These are no high schoolers bumming beers out in front of a 7-Eleven in this crowd. These guys and gals have bartenders who know exactly how they like their highballs. Heaven knows where they get all the money for it. Wait . . . sure we do. And they seem to be waiting around to inherit it all. But in the meantime, drink up!

I went into the battered black unisex toilet to pee and discovered the homemade wallpaper of Playboy and Playgirl centerfolds from the sixties. A lot of hair.

Christ. It was time for me to call it a night. I was already buzzed and the sun had just gone down. *How on earth do these kids get home at midnight?* I thought. Wait a minute . . . that's right . . . check the morgue, sometimes they don't.

I stepped outside and kickstarted my bike. "You are only old once!" that same lady proclaimed over the music as I waved goodbye: And I thought about that. Then I looked up at the light box of the club. The marquee read: CANGGU: FULL SPEED AHEAD!

And I thought *everybody* should start thinking about that.

JUNGLE LOVE

STEPHANIE GILMORE SURFS GRAJAGAN BETTER THAN YOU
SURTIME MAGAZINE, BALI, 2017

My support of female surfing is a matter of record. —Mg.

"You've come a long way, baby." So read the slogan for Virginia Slims, a "feminist" cigarette brand released in 1968. This in response to the sexual revolution and a thing called Women's Liberation. Nowadays, it's called basic human rights.

But as demeaning as that 1968 cigarette slogan may seem now, it sure worked then. Virginia Slims cigarettes carved out a dynamic market and became one of the most popular cigarette brands in history. Other brands jumped on the bandwagon. There was even a perfume called "Charlie," represented by a sassy, hair-throwing model that just slayed the men but was untouchable. So it's that marketing of the liberated woman's image, and its positive results, that is of most interest here.

Because it happened in surfing, too.

Just like the smoking of cigarettes, professional surfing was long the domain of men. Professional competitions for women were merely an afterthought. So lowly thought of that larrikin and 1998 Pipe Master Robbie Page once quipped, "Women's pro surfing...where women can act like men and look like them, too!"

But that all changed when, in 1990, a hippie photographer named Jeff Hornbaker walked into Quiksilver clothing's headquarters with a staggering new ad concept. Not only did it spike Quiksilver's dwindling profits into the black, but it also rocked the male surfing world. The subsequent campaign became the brand Roxy. And it was all about being a woman of the sea. With its imagery of beautiful women, surfing together, no men in sight, pungent flower leis about their tanned necks, straw hats plonked on their heads, and wearing "sports bikinis" against the summer sunshine of Waikiki, a new world was launched. Now a woman—any woman—could tell the men to fuck off and just go surfing on their own. And believe me, these women did. By the millions. A sexy, capable tribe was born. Surfboards replaced the spears of these Amazons and they needed approval of no man.

As for the men, two very confusing things happened in very quick succession.

One, women's professional freesurfing was born, and two, women's professional competition was entirely rebooted. Now a pro surfing woman could be a very respected, glamorous, and it has to be said, *desirable* international athlete in the mainstream media. All of the sudden, we had our own army of Maria Sharapova's.

Which brings us to our six-time surfing World Champion Stephanie Gilmore, the Charlie of our time. A woman who remains fiercely independent, who has become wealthy through athletic achievement, has a reputation as a woman for whom men are playthings, and it has to be said, performed a hyper-jump beyond such great surfing champions as Lisa Andersen and Layne Beachley. By no fault of Lisa and Layne mind you; they had to grow up surfing in men's clothes. Stephanie had designer sports bikinis. But even more than the soporific Lisa Andersen or the defensive stance Layne Beachley stood for against the misogyny of the pro tour, Stephanie Gilmore is the brassy new image of female pro surfing. Surfing gracefully but forcefully with that big smile on her face, she is counted among the greatest surfers of all time, male or female.

"With her powerful but flowing style both on land and sea," *Beach Grit Magazine* said in 2014, "she's taken a testosterone-saturated field and beautified it infinitely. Men can be beautiful on a surfboard, sure, but it always seems partially contrived. The flow Steph achieves is pure dance, the epitome of feminine beauty." Tall, wide-shouldered, and gifted, Gilmore has overcome wild odds to simply outclass most men in both personal behavior and surfing skill. Surfing's first million-dollar female pro, Stephanie Gilmore has not only overcome legions of female opponents, but the chauvinism of the male surfing scene as well. Which may be her biggest achievement. "In my eyes," Stephanie says, "the best female surfer is someone who pulls into big barrels and can take getting scraped on the reef, but can then turn around and be graceful and stylish in beautiful waves and on land in the most feminine way possible."

Stephanie recently visited the fine archipelago of Indonesia and, heading straight for the edge of the Javanese jungle, surfed Grajagan as well as it can be surfed. And in her surfing could be heard the echoes of every ambitious, talented professional female surfer who has ever come before. She wears the mantle of the newly liberated female champion, the newly liberated woman, the new Charlie, like royalty. A joy to watch, better than 99.9% of any of the men in any lineup in the world. Perhaps someday her surfing will finally serve to erode, once and for all, the misogynist hell our sport has suffered from the beginning. Forcing all us men to see the truth and to be the change. To hear the truth that has survived since that cloying, cigarette ad slogan back in 1968. "You've come a long way, baby." But this time, boys, do yourself a favor.

Drop the "baby" bit.

APOCALYPSE HERE

KRAKATAU ANAK DOESN'T CARE IF YOU SURF
SURFLINE.COM, USA, 2019

Many tsunamis come and go here in Indonesia with very little news reporting. The people get on. It's only the real monsters that you see on TV. Still, big, medium, or small, the sight of that eerie, inexorable whitewater line advancing across an entire bay and coming your way is as horrifying a sight as any human has ever faced. Believe me. —Mg.

Damn the science—this is what it was like. A group of us from Bali were on our way to help with the aftermath of Indonesia's latest Tsunami and I was lucky to be able to get a call through to my friend, Javanese surfer Diki Zulfikar, in north Java. He was there when the Tsunami slammed into his beach party and he told me the tale of that night. Diki remembers having his wife nestled under his arm as a soft breeze blew in off the Ocean at Carita Beach in far North Java. The community was listening to a band, celebrating the closing ceremonies of the Annual Carita Beach Surfing Festival.

"I had no idea that within thirty seconds we would be running for our life. When we saw the first wave coming, which was confusing at night because it was so loud, we thought it was going to stop near shore," says Diki. "But then the wave did not stop and it got bigger and bigger, five meters, more, and then we knew and all of us wished we had our surfboards, but we did not bring them to the party."

So they ran. And surfers and villagers, the women tripping over their heavy traditional head-to-toe veiled attire, got mowed down by a debris-choked, angry sea.

"Surfers were lucky; we can swim and we are strong enough to climb trees but the others...it was sad to see." Trying to flee in a shoulder-deep torrent, Diki and his wife saw the second wave coming. Frozen with fear, his wife fainted. Diki knew he had to stand his ground. "I went into surfer thought, watched it come and I was timing my move and I don't know why, but I smiled at it, the wave, like I smile at many waves when I surf, hoping this one would leave me and my wife alone. But it didn't. It wanted us both."

They took it in the teeth. Swept into the blitz, he and his wife were tumbling toward a cottage that was gutted but still standing. "I swam strong, holding my wife, and I swam into the house and I grabbed the stairs and dragged us up. That was all I could think, to go up. And that was when I saw the third wave and knew my luck was gone."

Struggling to the back of the second floor, Diki pulled his catatonic wife up into a top bunk bed and waited for the end of the world. He prayed. "Out the window, I saw many people go by, some screaming, some finished, and the wave came into the house very loudly and tried to take us too, but I would not let go of the bed and my wife. I don't know how long; maybe half hour, maybe more, the water was trying to get us. I was underwater many times, but then it got quiet and the river that goes through the village started to help drain the water back into the Ocean and we were still breathing. But I saw so many people being pulled out to sea. So many. And the surfers were helping, but could not get everybody. I stayed with my wife. Thank God my friends and me can surf. The surfers all lived, but we lost many others and my wife would not talk again for many days."

For western surfers in North Java and South Sumatra, many felt the same way as Diki, thanking their lucky stars that Saturday's Sunda Strait tsunami hit at night when they weren't surfing and that they knew how to swim. Surfers here have a distinct advantage when it comes to survival. This last point is why the death tolls of Indonesian tsunamis are so high. Swimming is not a priority of the coastal cultures throughout the archipelago due to mythology, spiritual beliefs, and female dress codes. Which is a shame, considering so many live in the crosshairs of the most active seismic roilings on the planet. And with over 17,500 islands, this country has myriad bays and crescent beaches that act as catchers' mitts for these seismic waves.

In the aftermath of this tsunami, the local media celebrated a visiting marine scientist who reported that the ability to swim would not be a factor in Tsunami survival. I called him. Of course, the guy didn't surf and had never been eaten alive by big waves or even borne witness to tsunamis like a lot of surfers and I have. Why don't scientists talk to surfers? We know all about them.

Krakatau Anak, the "child" of the main volcanic island of 1883 eruption fame, had been blowing its stack in smaller eruptions for weeks. And on

December 23, 2019, it had had enough. The devastating Tsunami was caused by a sub-Ocean landslide on the volcano's southeastern slopes. The displacement of water would have been a force unimaginable to mortals and almost impossible to detect. Hence absolutely no warning. And the fact that the volcano is a feature on the near horizon to most of the affected areas, there would also have been no time to prepare. Not to the parties on the beach or those peacefully sleeping. The first thing that came to mind to most of us in Bali was concern for our friends who might have been camped at Panaitan Island, waiting for the suicide waves of the apocalypse to happen.

"The apocalypse surf spot should be blocked by the other islands," said Indonesian Champion Dede Suryana in nearby Cimaja, Java. "But we are still waiting for my friends to call from there."

Three mornings after we arrived at Cerita Beach to help, Javanese surfer Naufel Satuwati was next to me, picking through the wreckage, when he paused, stood to stretch his back, and looked out to sea. "Krakatau called to me this morning and I looked at her. She was telling me she will do it again. That no one is strong enough to stop her. No one. Not even surfers."

MIKE PARSONS AND THE HOUNDS OF HELL

A DOMESTIC SHOWDOWN IN SAN FRANCISCO
SURFING MAGAZINE, 1991

This internal drama was unveiled for me after this American pro title contest off the frigid waters of San Francisco's Great Ocean Beach. I found myself in a small cafe across the table from Mike Parsons, and he recounted his last twenty-four hours to me as vividly as any cinematographer ever could. And this "Boy Scout Surfer" went on to ride the biggest wave in the world, landing in the Guinness Book of World Records and later that summer, into the Surfing Hall of Fame. —Mg.

THE OCEAN PARK HOTEL, SAN FRANCISCO
October 27, 1991 — 4:00 a.m.

The harder he tried, the worse it got. Mike Parsons couldn't get comfortable no matter what he did with the sheets. He'd tried to bunch up the pillow a few times but gave that up. He could move the thing with one hand like some airline pillow and it was lumpy. He'd opened up the window, but with the goddamned Muni bus roaring by every ten minutes, Jesus. He thought about getting up for a fourth drink of water, but he wasn't thirsty. He looked over at the digital clock instead. The glowing red numbers were eerie, silently counting down his life, telling him he'd been awake for twenty-two hours straight. There wasn't much left to do but lie there on his side, one arm behind his head, and stop trying. He wasn't going to sleep. Tomorrow, one way or the other, it would all be over. Mike Parsons knew he would either have it or not. The one thing he had always wanted more than anything else in his whole life. Tomorrow, Mike Parsons might be able to make the voices go away.

Six eighty-two . . . six hundred and eighty-two points . . . 6-8-2.

That's all the points lead Mike Parsons had over Shane Beschen. And Matt Archbold wasn't far behind that. For the thousandth time, Mike went through the math. *"Okay, for me to win, so-and-so has to get fifth or less and then so-and-so has to get second, and then Archie has to do something . . . yeah, yeah, and then the moon has to turn blue."*

He clenched his teeth. He took a deep breath, held it for a bit, and then did a good job of letting it go. At thirty-one years old, he'd had a better year on the American surfing tour than anybody had ever had.

The semis or better in five events. No one had ever done that. Ocean Pacific, his clothing sponsor, would have to be stoked. He'd come off the world tour months ago, walked into their offices, and told them he'd rather stay home and be the domestic champion. And that they had to give him three years to do it. They'd believed him. And here Mike Parsons was on his first run at it and it was looking good. It wasn't like he hadn't earned it. Seven years on the World Tour, seven years out there with the big boys. A million countries, surfing against the best, countless heats with the real players. During his career, he'd surfed against Tom Curren, Mark Occhilupo, Tom Carroll, Shaun Tomson, Gary Elkerton . . . the list went on. He'd won a world tour event. Won it. Took second to Tom Curren once. At Burleigh Heads, no less. He'd been in the top sixteen once back in '87. And ask anyone and they'd tell you that was a damned tough year. The best in the world and all of them in their prime. And the waves he'd faced? Ten years of the North Shore. Huge Sunset Beach finals, fifteen-foot, stormy, and gray. And that huge scary final at Margaret River. Eighteen-to-twenty-foot Indian Ocean swells slamming into some reef stuck out on a wild cape out in the middle of nowhere. He could remember people saying that they were frightened for him that day at Margaret River. Waves like that. Waves that test. It wasn't Orange County, that's for sure. Most of these American tour kids would shit their pants. Mexico? Todos Santos Island? White shark breeding grounds? Again, huge surf. Test surf. Cold and green. No one could say much against him about that, either.

Mike Parsons shifted over to his other side and cupped his face in his palm. The TV set was still glowing across the room. *Sure,* he thought as he stared into it, *I know I've done all that. Lived all that.* But still, he could hear the voices. He'd always been able to hear them. He'd never been able to shut them up. *"Mike Parsons is boring. Mike Parsons is just a contest machine. Mike Parsons doesn't do anything on a wave. Mike Parsons the buck-forty-pound weakling. Mike Parsons the robot.* The nicknames. "Parsnips" then simply "Snips," the Goody-Two Shoes, the Boy Scout . . . the Square.

Maybe, he thought. *Maybe I don't have long hair, and maybe I don't have tattoos, and maybe I don't drop acid or smoke weed or make-believe I'm a biker or try to play the guitar. Maybe I don't go out and do aerials and lip slides. Maybe I'm not cool. Maybe not . . . But I'll tell you what I am this time—I'm ahead.*

His heart was racing its own hounds of hell. The ones that had been snapping at his heels for over eight years of hard put professional surfing. He could feel them right there in his hotel room. Barking at him. And he realized that he was going to find out once and for all if the voices were right. He was going to find out whether or not he really had what it took to be a surfing champion. He closed his eyes for a few seconds, and sleep ambushed him. Then the electric clock shattered the dawn.

Ocean Beach, San Francisco
9:37 a.m.

Mike Parsons carved his board off the bottom of the wave and rocketed vertically for the lip. It was the end of his second-round heat, his fourth wave, his last chance. He wasn't going to play it safe. And for just a moment, as he swung it around off the top of the blown out, lumpy, six-foot section, he thought he was going to pull it. Then his world caved in. He caught a rail and went over the bars. It was a humiliating wipe-out.

Ten minutes later, back on shore, Mike was sure he had lost. He was sitting by himself, still in his wetsuit, his face still dripping with seawater, his eyes screwed shut, his face to the clouds. The announcement. He'd taken second place on the strength of his first three waves before the wipe-out and would be advancing into the quarterfinals. Mike Parsons dropped his head between his knees. Feeling like he had to thank someone, something, anything. He lifted his head and looked around at the freezing, windblown, six-foot surf. He looked at the small crowd lining the beach in heavy jackets against the wet Ocean breeze. He looked over at the scaffolding. He could feel a pounding behind his ears.

10:40 a.m.

He was glad for the confused surf conditions. No one could dog him, no one could ride him or starve him out of waves. This was going to be a surfing contest. Shane Beschen had advanced to the semis easily. Mike

Parsons knew he had to do the same. Simple as that. So he zipped up his wetsuit and paddled out into his quarterfinal heat. His sixth sense was telling him it was going to be a good one for him. He was right.

11:15 a.m.

Mike Parsons went and looked at the truck. The four-wheel Nissan pickup, fresh from the detailer, on display with the big surf stickers on the doors. The winner of this contest would walk away with the keys to it. The billboard standing over it read:

IT'S TIME TO SEPARATE THE MEN FROM THEIR BOARDS.

He wondered what on earth they meant by that. He made some quick calculations. If he won, all told, about a hundred grand coming his way. He promised himself that if he won, he would give the truck to his dad. His dad needed it for work. *And if anyone wanted to say that I was being some goody-two shoes for doing that, if they wanted to say I was being square, then they could just kiss my ass . . .*

1:10 p.m.

Mike Parsons stood on the seawall watching the finals. He jammed his right hand into his jacket pocket for the fifth time: he'd gnashed his index fingernail to blood. Santa Cruz's Peter Mel had knocked him out of the semifinals and now Mike Parsons was helpless. He had to watch on as Shane Beschen, Chris Billy, Chris Brown, and Peter Mel decided what the rest of his life was going to be like. The four of them were in the final.

An hour earlier, Mike had been told that if Shane Beschen won this contest then Shane would be the 1991 American Champion by six points. *Six points.* If Beschen took anything less than first then the title would be Mike Parsons by 206 points. The closest professional title race in history. The crowd was leaning into it. Mike just felt like he might throw up. He watched on in agony, in self-recrimination for losing the semifinal. The minutes ticked by. He kept no score. He just watched. And by the final horn, it looked like Shane Beschen had done enough.

2:35 p.m.

Mike Parsons stood on the scaffolding facing the crowd. His elbow was close enough to brush Shane Beschen, who stood to his right. The announcer began.

"IN FOURTH PLACE, CHRIS BILLY!" The announcer's voice had become everything. It had become all those other voices he'd heard all his life. His hounds of hell. This voice he was listening to would decide who was right. Mike Parsons or them.

"TAKING THIRD PLACE . . . PETER MEL!" The voices seemed louder than they ever had. Mike could hear them. Mike could hear them now, right now. He could just hear them saying *"We were right! We were right! Mike Parsons couldn't do it! Try as he might, he's just not a real champion!"*

Mike clenched his fists at his side. "AND IN SECOND PLACE, AND DECIDING THE 1991 CHAMPIONSHIP IN THIS, THE CLOSEST TITLE RACE IN THE HISTORY OF SURFING . . . LADIES AND GENTLEMEN . . . SHANE BESCHEN!"

A warmth flushed over Mike Parsons, threatening to bowl him over.

"MIKE PARSONS IS YOUR NEW 1991 PROFESSIONAL SURFING ASSOCIATION OF AMERICA CHAMPION!"

Mike let his hands fall behind his hips, looking for something, anything to support himself with. They found only air. Mike swayed there, blinking, fighting to make sense of things. The crowd roared. But it was strange. Because Mike Parsons couldn't hear a thing. Nothing. Nothing at all. The voices. Those voices.

They were gone.

GOING TOO FAR

SURFING AMONG THE GHOSTS OF MICRONESIA
SURFTIMEMAGAZINE, 2019

The surfing life leads to not only the most remote reaches on earth, but to those among the most world history dense. And the characters that you find there waiting for you at the end of the line are often as mad as history itself. —Mg.

Chapter One

It is impossible to partner in the mind the breathtaking beauty of Micronesia with the greatest slaughter of human bodies in history. And yet, it happened. Though the memories are fading, the Pacific theater of World War II was fought so inhumanely in Micronesia, with such horror, with such blood, with so many men, women, and children burnt and eviscerated and blown to tatters, that surfing in these graveyard waters seems near blasphemous. But history marches on, on to new historic horrors, one bloody chapter after another. And so the reeking battlefields of spilled intestines and congealing blood are forgotten by those who were never there and eventually even by time itself. We live on a planet that is not dying—but we are. And we always have been. Through our own inhumanity to our lands and seas and to each other. The earth has survived cataclysms that dwarf our pathetic human outrages. And the earth always heals itself. It's we humans who will never know how to heal anything. We will just keep taking and going to meetings about it until we die. And perhaps this is best for Micronesia.

Because the fact that men actually chose to hammer the hell out of Micronesia with ungodly atom bomb testing just so that we could blast the Japanese people of Hiroshima to kingdom come is beyond today's imaginations. A horror so complete, a memory so perfectly awful, so revengeful to the Japanese atrocities of World War II, that to this day, despite global capabilities and threats to do so from myriad countries, nuclear bombs have never been deployed anywhere by anybody since Nagasaki.

So what is the excuse to surf these waters both blasphemous and beautiful. When one considers the playful state of riding on the face of a wave here, perhaps this is a profound way to honor the dead entombed below these waters. Perhaps surfing is an exhilarating blessing, bringing an act of joy to these cleanest of the world's waters that hold such bloodstained memories. Perhaps by surfing here with no consideration at all for the horrors of war, perhaps the war of this place can be swept under the rug of the restless sea. After all, only the passions of the immediate can erase the memories of the past.

Chapter Two

Photographer Damea Dorsey recently sailed through Micronesia, bringing back with his lens not the horrors, but the sublime, pristine beauty of the last, cleanest place on earth. I sit now at his kitchen table in Umalas, Bali. It is hot in this room, like most rooms in Bali; trickle-sweat hot, and one of his semi-feral cats is licking the outside of my cold beer. Beer sweats here too. Damea's teenage children in the next room are enraptured by a *Lord of the Rings* DVD blasting at a volume set to stun. Damea lives on a small curvy road in a small curvy house on a small curvy creek with a small curvy backyard that disappears into a riot of yellow and green Bali foliage. Damea has his laptop out on the kitchen table and is scrolling through photographs of his voyage aboard mariner Martin Daly's new surveying vessel. Damea helped deliver the boat from Bali to Martin in the Solomon Islands. A check of the map makes it seem like an impossible journey. And it almost was. Damea referred to this voyage as *Searching for Martin*. Martin Daly, of *The Crossing* fame, that round-the-world surf trip on Daly's pareu-splashed Indies Trader vessel that struck such wonder into our hearts back in 1999. Lest we forget, bankrolled by Quiksilver Clothing, it was described in a press release thus:

> "The Quiksilver Crossing is vitally important because not since Charles Darwin sailed around the world on the Beagle in the 1800s has there been such an unprecedented opportunity for marine scientists to study remote reefs and evaluate their health."

Pretty heady stuff. Under the guise of these environmental studies, it was the most magnificent surf trip ever managed in the history of mankind. Martin Daly is proud to have pulled it off. He loves the unprecedented. Like his pioneering of the Mentawai Surf Charter business, his alpha maleness for all surfing maritime operations, his

Poseidon-like status in the surfing world. Martin Daly, who at his core, is really just a badass salvage diver with a sweet heart and a profound love for the sea and new challenges. And who has, as most know, all but fallen off the radar and into a mysterious self-exile in the most remote regions of the Marshall Islands of the South Pacific. Rumored to be now living as a millionaire castaway on his exclusive resort that rests on a speck of an island nearby a roaring right hand breaking reef that has the likes of Kelly Slater, Shane Dorian, and John John Florence dropping everything whenever it breaks. A resort that features a floating seaplane dock in the island's blue lagoon so that the creator of Google can drop by to get away from the pressures of all that Google dough. Though it is rumored that it was some of that Google dough that built the thing.

Looking at Damea at his kitchen table, you can see he is a very handsome man. His angular face suggests a sincerity rare in any world. He is fit, peppered with tattoos that snake out of his shirtsleeve and reach to the second knuckles of his right hand. He wears perfectly cut hair and a short, perfectly groomed beard. It's no surprise that one of his day jobs is the running of his popular vintage barbershop near Padang Padang on Bali. His eyes do not look into yours; they bore. Always interested in anything you have to say, Damea makes you feel like the only human on earth. And one cannot imagine him having any trouble with the ladies. Such is his almost childlike enthusiasm for just about everything within his grasp. Especially the adventures his photography takes him on. Even fighting an attack of the dreaded "Bali Belly," as he is on this day, does not keep him contained. He scrolls and scrolls though his photos from his recent journey from Benoa Harbor in Bali that ended on a speck of an atoll island in the Marshall Islands chain. Making his way from Bali like a modern Marlow in search of Daly's Kurtz.

Fitting of his final destination, Damea told me that Martin Daly chuckled as he mentioned that he would "find them when they got there." Damea scrolled and scrolled through his photos and spoke of his passage with the same wonder as an adventurer at the turn of the century. He spoke of dark squalls on the inside route that took him and the vessel southeast through the fabled isles. Sumbawa, then past the

Komodo of dragon fame, through the Flores Sea and past Timor, and then across the windy expanse of the Savu Sea into the Timor Sea. Then the blustery crossing to the Beagle and Van Diemen Gulfs of far north Australia. Then the long, lonely stretch transecting the Arafura Sea and into the treachery of the storied Torres Strait and onward to a lucky landfall at Port Moresby. And then setting sail again after a beer-soaked respite to sail down around the horn of Papua New Guinea, across to the Solomon Islands and to the appointed clandestine rendezvous with Martin Daly on the island of Guadacanal. That famed island salted with the bones and the relics of Operation Watchtower, the 1942 American military campaign, remembered for the sheer viciousness of the fighting. America's first major World War II offensive against the Empire of Japan.

Damea pushes his laptop aside to better tell his tale with the use of his hands. So there, Damea tells me, pulling into Guadacanal's steaming harbor of Honiara, with a halo practically above his head, was Martin Daly. All smiles, delighted with his new boat. Without the motors having even been rested, Martin took his place at the helm, fired the thing up, and set sail for a shakedown cruise through the Solomons without so much as a welcome beer on the wharfside bar.

What followed was what Damea called a "voyage within a voyage" through an island chain as remote as they come. And where there are islands in the Pacific, there are waves. Waves everywhere you look. Between raucous stories, Martin Daly helmed his boat from secret break to secret break, reveling, as he always has, in the blowing of surfers' minds. At one point pulling up to a break so remote that the chief of the small island came aboard and requested that they leave immediately. The chief felt the look of the boat was one that came to "take from the sea and to give nothing in return." Despite impassioned pleas that they were just there to surf, the chief was not buying it.

"It was incredible," said Damea. "In this modern world, here was a guy who didn't want anything more for him and his people than to just be left alone. No deals, no money, no oil exploration, no commercial fishing . . . this guy had his priorities straight."

Martin honored the chief's request, pulled anchor, and headed back for port. Not an hour later, the crew experienced what Martin would consider a lucky omen. It seems that for years, Martin has been trying to explain to certain concerned people that a pearlescent pink flying squid actually exists in Micronesian waters. Martin swore he had seen them, but had never been able to capture one. But as they left the chief's waters, one of Martin's new species came flying across the water and landed with uncertain ceremony on the aft deck of the Indies surveyor. More animated than usual, Martin's eyes were shining as he carefully placed the fragile thing in a bucket of saltwater and had Damea photograph it from every angle.

"It was like Martin's unicorn," Damea smiled. If it is a new flying species, rumor has it that scientists will name it after Martin: *Decapodiformes Dalyithicus.*

Chapter Three

The United States Navy Castle Bravo Test on Bikini Atoll, Micronesia, March 1, 1954, was the moment the atomic bomb made the jump from simply murderous to apocalyptic. The photograph of this "successful" test, a huge waterspout that blew battleships 200 feet into the air, took its place as the most iconic photograph on earth. And this nuclear test site lies about 307 nautical miles from Martin Daly's Beran Island Resort in the Marshall Islands and odds and ends of the test still wash ashore onto this island. A rusted radar buoy, a balsa wood life raft with an ecosystem of seaweed hanging from it, even a message in a bottle from a sailor who witnessed the explosion, stating it was unholy.

Damea Dorsey found the final destination of his journey on Beran Island. This after a rare invite from Martin Daly once they reached port back in Guadacanal and his flying pink squid was handed off to the proper authorities. If such a group even exists on Guadacanal. There is also surfing here on Beran Island and kitesurfing and sport fishing and a perfect anchorage and a cement pier and a floating dock all built to Martin's specs. And there is skin and scuba diving with water visibility permanently rated at infinite. The fishing and diving are so wonderful that they are known to make guests weep.

"Everything about the place feels like it's a living thing," says Damea.

"You are on this little dot in the Pacific surrounded by so much space; a place that makes you think of things you wouldn't normally think. Like never leaving the place. Like going too far to ever go back." Damea said that, from his open bedroom window while he was on the island, he could see the crescent moon illuminating clouds so beautiful that they make you talk in a whisper. Streamers of roiling nighttime steam, white against the indigo of the infinite vastness, lit by a moon racing toward its appointments to the west.

It is also said that every inch of the place reflects Martin Daly's personality. His defiance. His railing against a landlocked life and its desperate demands on mortal needs. The shaking of his fist against anything, winds or tides or storms or men, that would ever stand in the way of his unconventional path. Here on Beran, it is easy for anyone who really knows Martin to see that this is where his restless wanderings have gone to ground. His final port. A place that proves once and for all that the forces of the world, the ancient powers that have ruled earth since creation, have been defied by Martin. In comparison to the sea, he is a fragile creature, who by will, has been able to face these primitive forces and bend them into his service. And isn't it cause for wonder that a sailor like Martin has ended up in this place. This place of what will become an ancient war. This place of unspeakable bloodshed and poetic beauty. A place of thoughts filled with never going back to where one was born. A tranquil place amid all those swirling ghosts, those torn souls of war, all those other sailors who, like Martin, would never be going home again

PURPOSE BUILT

CATCHING FIRE UNDER A JAVANESE SKY
SURFTIME MAGAZINE, 2019

I once had the opportunity to see drone and satellite operations from the inside of a secret military installation. Inside one of those camouflaged shipping containers that they set up in. I could not help but think of those secret surf spots I could find on the planet with that kind of technology in front of me. That was the inspiration of this short meditation. —Mg.

Chapter One

If you were just outside of Las Vegas, Nevada, at a secret military station in the desert and you were at the controls of US spy satellite RISAT2BR1 and you happened to be a surfer, imagine what you could find. If your satellite were soaring over, say, Java, and you were curious about a surf spot you had seen in a magazine or online and you had used some simple research to get the coordinates. How you might look over your shoulder to see if anyone inside the air-conditioned shipping container you were working in was looking over your shoulder, and then, if not, to surreptitiously divert the controls to check this surf spot out real quick like. Here is what you would find with your joystick on the high-tech screen before you.

On a clear day, from outer space, you would see a large green island, a somewhat narrow island, running angled southeast on the edge of the Indian Ocean, almost kissing the island of Bali. Moving in, you would see the gray, mushrooming and then thinning, columns of smoke issuing from a few of this island's famed volcanoes. Closer in and Java would take on a relief. No longer just a green carpet, but now a personality. Still a Kelly green, but now strangely foreboding with its vast impenetrable jungles. And yet, at this point, looking soft enough for a naked human being to fall upon without injury. Closer, as this jungle became hillocks and contours and copses and rusty bare patches of earth, you would see how untrue that last thought was. Java is now a primal place. Elemental. Survival-driven. Closer, as you vector over to the coast, the first signs of a thin white border drawn like fringe between the green of land and the cobalt blue of the Indian Ocean. Wave action. Moving closer, you would see what looks like settlements near the island's bays and you would see the first signs of Ocean movement as it went about its eternal chewing away at the land. This chewing making the coastline look rough and tumble, a craggy meandering of sharp-pointed headlands and bays and coves and covelets. Still moving in, you would start to see small, tan, bowed shapes at the base of some of the coves and bays. Sand. Downturned crescents of it. A series of frowns on the edge of the island, fed by the numerous serpentine rivers and creeks and waterways that you can now see glinting like polished knives in the noon day sun. Closer still and you catch your breath when you recognize actual swell lines and swathes of sweeping whitewater. This is home territory to your mind and you scrutinize the sea for the telltale combinations of moving swell and triangles of whitewater. Or moving white bows along the inside of a headland or cove that reaches into the sea. Waves. Ridable waves. You keep moving in on your coordinates and your world begins to reveal itself. At first the size of a model train set, you spy the grid of a small burg hard against a broken-toothed bight in the coast. You can even make out a compound with a teal-colored spot that marks a swimming pool on top of the hill that faces the bay. Closer to the water, two large barrier rocks set like raw gems atop a small bay with a fingered headland to the east. Eager, you go closer and see two oblong fields of laced whitewater with a blue swirling rip cutting them in half on its way out to sea. Closer. A set of waves move through, refracting around and into the bay in a chaos that soon makes sense. Then the sign of a wake left behind one of these waves.

You stop it right there. Right. There. Surfers. You zoom in to max. You can make out bodyboarders and surfers scrambling for a set wave. And two surfers, brown as coffee, sauntering down the beach for a go-out with clean, white boards under their arms. You can imagine the sounds of the place, so you put them in your mind and the whole tableau becomes a complete experience. Live. Happening. You watch it all, drinking it in at the limits of the spy satellite's capability, until the satellite you are controlling can no longer stay on the coordinates. Until the satellite sets over the blue horizon like a tiny aluminum sun.

You take your headset off. Squeeze the bridge of your nose between your thumb and forefinger for long seconds. You breathe. Once, twice. Once more. You get back to work, distracted, envious mostly of those dissipating snake-like wakes that you saw following closely behind the moving waves. You are back to doing your duty, yet envious of those beings on the sea, wondering what drove you so far from home.

Chapter Two

Varun Tandjung and Bronson Meidy, fresh from cooling off in the swimming pool of their family villa on top of the hill, saunter down the Javan beach with their new surfboards under their arms, the hot white sand of the beach making them squint and sweat. The alpha males of the lineup, they can afford to take their time. Living atop the hill in luxury. The quivers of shiny new boards, Indonesian surfing royalty, their lives preordained. Purpose built since birth to surf. They huff to each other about how many body boarders are out, but no worry—everybody gets along. The wave off the rocky bay looks like it's handling the tide well and the rip is going to make the paddle out easy. They both make their way to water's edge, fetlock deep in the sand. And another wave rears up on the reef against the offshore winds and crashes and spits. And to them, the sky above has nothing to do with it at all.

TWO TICKETS TO PARADISE

A TOM CURREN BALI EXPERIENCE
TRACKS MAGAZINE, BALI, 2015

There is no one quite like him. Tom Curren, his three world titles and rivers and rivers of water under the bridge between us. This is the part two that took me thirty-two years to write. —Mg.

Padang Padang, Bali, Indonesia
September 01, 2015 – 6:15 p.m.

They could hear us in the lineup. Because Tom Curren and I stood facing a blazing sunset from the second story of the Pete Matthew's ultimate Padang Padang surf pad, singing out of a big picture window in full voice to the Eddie Money tune, "Two Tickets to Paradise." Tom was playing along on his guitar and we were drinking beer together. That explained the singing. That and the fact that Tom had a gig coming up at a local cafe. Part of his obligations while on a Rip Curl promo junket here in Bali. His lifetime contract and all.

I had sung and played with Tom before, a lifetime ago. Both literally and figuratively. It was odd to see my old friend. There was a full-length mirror in the room, and at my angle, I could see two Tom Currens. One a reflection and one real. But then, maybe they both were. Reflections, I mean. Looking at him, I thought, *Jesus, at fifty-one years old, everyone has the face they deserve.*

Our song ended as the sun dipped itself out and a dripping wet, reef-scraped, indestructible Chris Ward burst into the villa and ran up the stairs to tell us what a great session of waves he just had. Tom said it must have been our music. We all laughed and *click whoosh, click whoosh, click whoooosh,* opened new cans of beers and drained them, all of us braying about our great day at the same time. Then Chris Ward bounded back down the stairs and was gone.

Things settled. Tom started playing a thoughtful instrumental on his guitar.

A magenta red sky crept toward the horizon, slowly closing the eyelids of the day. Stars began to wink. I found myself listening to Tom's chord changes and nodding my head as things came to me. *Time tells,* I thought. *Hell yes, it does.* It tells everything. A real blabbermouth. How long was all this going to last? This surfing childhood? I had done this same thing with Tom Curren countless times over the last thirty years. Australia, San Francisco, Santa Barbara, our ranch days, Rincon dreams, East Australia, West Australia, Mexico, California—Christ, even Pennsylvania. Surfing forever. Never growing up. Is it possible?

Looking at Tom, it seemed possible. I mean, we surfed together as young adults, and now here we were, singing to the best waves in the world, both of us in our fifties.

But this age thing. Getting older. The haunting. Especially when it's playing the guitar right in front of you. Tricky. I looked close at the road map on Tom's face. Another parchment important to surfing's history, like a map that first showed the world that the cutback was round. Creased and torn and rolled and folded and noted upon and, finally, something regal and forever. Proof that old age is always ten years older than we are. But here in front of me was time all caught up. And let's face it, time is God.

I avoided my own reflection in the mirror.

Much later, I said goodbye to Tom and Pete and I hopped on my motorcycle for the hour-long ride home to Kuta down in the flats. It was an unattended night on the road. Tulle-fogged curves with the monsoon coming on. My single headlamp just a misty pool of light against the tangle of the jungle. Humid. Midnight. I started out easy, climbing up the big hill out of Padang Padang Valley. I couldn't help but think back again on the years in Tom's face that night. And on the life we shared together and apart. Two tickets to paradise, all right. Yeah, boy. With two very different destinations. He a family man back in Santa Barbara, me an expat writer in Bali. I hung the left at Pecatu Road on top of the Uluwatu hill and gave it a little more gas than it needed; the jungle seemed to be closer than usual on both sides.

I was close to Tom for some time in the eighties. I was there for his rise to world surfing dominance and through his first marriage. I would call his first wife Marie a good friend of mine. A visual of her and World Champion Lisa Anderson sitting on the beach together crossed my mind. I had shot the photo. Lisa was the girlfriend of another friend of mine at the time, the other odd genius, Dave Parmenter. Jesus, the characters that have walked through my life. Tom, his wife Marie, Lisa

Andersen, Dave Parmenter, me, and my brother Sam. We were quite a powerball six at the time, showing up together at the teeming contests and remote Baja islands alike. God, the conversations we used to have when we traveled together. Intellectual summit meetings. World roasts on every subject from surfing to Steinbeck. I remember once, on Isla Natividad back during the glory days, a younger pro surfer named Pat O'Connell was sitting with us, having his mind blown during our dinner conversation.

When we asked Pat his take on the subject we were discussing, he could only put both hands on either side of his head and exclaim, "I never believed anyone could even think like that!"

I was there for all three of Tom's World titles. Right there on the beach, 1985, and at the top of the stairs at Bells Beach in 1986 for his second one. There wasn't much ballyhoo. I just put my arm around him and squeezed. Ten minutes later, without one single interview, Tom disappeared down the Great Ocean Road with his wife Marie. The media ate it up. "CHAMPION SEPPO SURFER GONE MISSING!"

Those who actually knew the savant just shook their heads and smiled.

The location of that second title felt right. Tom was born in 1964. Right on the cusp of the Aussie shortboard revolution, which Tom would personally further revolutionize seventeen years later with surfboard shaper Al Merrick's refinement of the California thruster surfboard. It was the invention of Tom's famed double-pump bottom turns and sweeping roundhouse off the lips that did it. Like vertical cutbacks, those off-the-lips, they changed the game. It was all a matter of leaning back, head below the upper rail of the board, and carving the vertical with a fan of spray rather than just bashing the lip. A surfboard's wake had never gone higher into the air. And it looked like meaningful poetry. I was there for that, too. Both maneuvers quantum leaps. Both maneuvers standard operating procedure for the champions of today. Kelly, of course, the master of it, John John Florence nipping at his heels.

Tom Curren was the son of a gun maker. Surfboards designed for giant waves being called guns. Most of us know that. I had actually spent some time with Pat Curren over the years of my exposure to Tom while living in Santa Barbara, California. Looking back, their similarities were striking. Reclusive and mysterious, but with volcanic ambition. Difference was, Tom achieved his. His dad just quit and ended up in a trailer in Baja with a pack of Jack Russell Terriers for company. Details of Tom's personal life were hazy to most, but not to me. I lived with him on a daily basis. I remember watching Tom bang on his high school drums with a broken one-speaker headphone clamped to his left ear, pounding away to The Who, crashing cymbals to drown out the disharmony of his own home. *Crash! Boom! Crash!* He banged those drums in a home that was hard against the droning and swooshing of a freeway overpass. His old man left home for good when Tom was seventeen, right when Tom was coming on. Tom's mom, Janine, was a very pretty proselytizing born-again Christian who I once saw throw the family TV off the porch as she bellowed, "SATAN, GET YE BEHIND ME!" It splintered onto the scrubby front lawn of their bungalow. I always loved her for that. So did Tom, I think. By eighteen, Tom was married to a French teenager named Marie. The wedding was in Australia and in honor of it, the local radio stations kept playing Billy Idol's "White Wedding." By being his wife, Marie became damn near as famous as he was. They were global stars. Our JFK and Jackie, but just kids. And sun blond.

I watched Tom lose interest in competing in 1987 and 1988, plummeting in the ratings. Then he quit the pro tour altogether in 1989, moved to France with his young wife. Inexplicably, he returned to the tour in 1990. I watched him win seven events that year. God, what a tear. Title three. He won his final world tour event at the end of 1991, at Haleiwa on that beautiful Maurice Cole surfboard with no logos on it. Most thought it was some sublime anti-corporate statement to surf it without stickers, but I knew it was just Tom's absent-mindedness. Being chronically late for most of the heats of his career, Tom was probably just in a hurry. Like his father, Tom had exhibited savant behaviors similar to autism all his life. Genius at what he did, living in a very private world of private thoughts. A great musician, a hopeless interview subject. Not many really close friends. An introspective soul. Mischievous at times. An obtuse sense of humor. Sometimes capable of deep laughter. That was the Irish in him. Tom eventually became very fond of his drink. That was the Irish in him, too.

I made the Ungasan crossroads by the Nirmala market. No one was around, so I gunned it through the red light, feeling that freedom you get from a lonely intersection, feeling a night that was made for memories.

Tom and I drifted apart after his divorce. But he maintained a close relationship with my brother Sam. I heard tell of a few of Tom's adventures through Sam. And once, years later, I came across Tom in San Francisco. By this time, I was a starving surfer/writer living in San Francisco with a foxy flamenco dancer. I heard from a band called The Mermen that Tom's impromptu band was going to play at a local nightspot on the outskirts of town called "The Bottom of the Hill." I made my way out there with my foxy flamenco dancer. And sure enough, in front of a small crowd of Northern Californian surfers, there was Tom and his unnamed makeshift band. The front men were doing their baffled best to stay up with Tom. Because Tom had crammed himself into the back corner of the small stage, playing a borrowed, pink fur-fringed "Josie and the Pussycats" drum set. He kept his back to the crowd all night. No one was quite sure to what to think. The Mermen thought it was the greatest surf gig in history. By the end of it all, Tom was serving drinks and pulling draft beers for the crowd from behind the bar. Because of this, the crowd seemed to have forgiven the performance. I sat at the bar with the flamenco dancer until closing time and we bundled Tom into the flamenco dancer's crappy car and high tailed it back to our place in North Beach. Tom hid from the surfing world for three days there. One morning, the flamenco dancer woke me up at dawn and told me Tom, who could always be as quiet as a cat, was gone. And my girl told me she was going to miss him. Women had always been important in Tom's life. I believe he really respected them.

I never once heard Tom tell or even participate in any joke that would debase a woman. We had never once compared sensual adventures. I had never heard him interrupt when a woman was speaking. He listened. And I always had the feeling that women believed in Tom, in his quiet way, to be the only man in mortal history that understood them.

The years really stretched out after that, but I always maintained a weather eye for Tom's migrations. You never knew what a high tide would leave on the beach. Or a storm, for that matter. I know he married for a second time. A Panamanian woman, and he had two more kids. That would make four, if I was counting right. Leann, Nathan, Frank, and Pat. I met Tom's Panamanian wife once, a beautiful bronze woman with dark tectonic eyes. But, family aside, as far as I could tell from a distance, Tom remained an enigma, riding bizarre homemade surfboards without a word of explanation. About the last I'd heard of him, he was standing in front of 40,000 people at a religious rally in Anaheim Stadium.

He said to them, "The Ocean is a sign of God's power, and it's really good to live for Jesus Christ." Tom always could say surprising things. I was never sure whether he meant this one or not, but I do know he was doing it for his mother.

Al Merrick, Tom's lifetime surfboard shaper and advisor and a devout Christian as well, was always Tom's spiritual compass. Still, it was dizzying to me. Tom Curren as an evangelist? Could happen.

I was approaching the last drop down into Jimbaran, the air getting warmer and thicker as the heights of the Bukit Peninsula was left behind, and I dropped down onto the island's isthmus. My bike ticking was over smoothly, knobby tires singing. A feral dog ran across the road with a bloody chicken in its mouth. The late-night food stalls, with their steaming clouds of roasting sweetmeats and boiling rice, sped by on each side of me. Indonesian eyes watched me with a dull hope from the moment my light came into sight until the moment it was gone. Road meditating, I thought, now here we were again, Tom and I, in Bali, 2015. It had been a hell of a week. I had been roped into the emcee duties for his music gig at the Cashew Tree Cafe at Bingin earlier in the week. I had no idea what to expect. I don't think he did either. I stood onstage to introduce him. And for the life of me, I couldn't think of what to say. I eventually stammered, "PLEASE WELCOME THREE-TIME WORLD CHAMPION AND . . . AND . . . MY FRIEND, THE TOM CURREN BAND!"

Jesus.

Anyway, again, there was Tom on stage with a makeshift band. He stood in the shadows again. It was the biggest crowd the Cashew Tree Cafe had ever seen. The toilets overflowed with used beer. But people stayed anyway. Tom and what could only be called his Jam Band played for hours, with Tom off to the side, out of the lights, practically hiding behind a giant stack of Marshalls. The music was, at times, beautiful and obscure. Hard to remember, though. Forget about singing along. Very few vocals. The crowd roared when Tom stepped forward to sing. He did so once. Eyes downcast, looking like a convict, glancing at his bandmates and hoping they were catching his drift. Rick Battson, to Tom's right, former rhythm guitar for Suicidal Tendencies, said of the performance, "Great, it was great . . . except that we rehearsed all week and did not play one single song on stage that we had actually rehearsed. But that's Tom for ya."

There was this earlier in the week, too. Not many people know that Tom has a way of accidentally locking himself inside houses. I was standing at the front door of Pete Matthew's cliffside villa, talking to Tom through the door. He was locked in somehow. Couldn't figure out where he had put the keys. It was the only way out really, the front door. Because of the local marauding monkey troupes, the villas in these parts are pretty secure. The only other option was an Acapulco cliff dive into the drink sixty feet below. This was the second time I had heard of Tom accidentally locking himself inside a house. The first was in Panama, some years earlier, with my brother Sam. They were in his wife's family's apartment. And at that time, Panama apartments all had bars and security doors. Probably still do. Anyway, I remember my brother being pretty pissed off for missing a whole day of surfing, waiting for Tom's wife to come home and let them out "like puppies needing a piddle." And now, here I was, standing with Patrick Curren, Tom's eighteen-year-old son, trying to figure out how to get his dad out of the house and to the surf photo shoot at Uluwatu that Tom was an hour late for. Patrick and I were considering getting some rope to lasso Tom and sort of bungee swing him out of there when Patricks's phone rang. It was his mother. Patrick keeps his phone on speaker at all times and at full volume for some reason, so it was easy for me to hear the conversation. It went like this:

Patrick: Hi, Mom.

Mom: Hi, honey . . . how are you and your father doing?

Patrick: Dad's locked himself inside a house and we are trying to get him out.

(Long Silence)

Mom: How has the surfing been, honey?

Patrick: Good, Mom, Really fun.

Mom: That's nice.

A half hour later, after Tom risked his life by taking a monkey trail down the cliff and back up a tree, we were all standing up on top of the cliff of the Uluwatu villas, waiting for Tom to paddle it out into the surf. He had disappeared again. Patrick, me, Rip Curl execs, fans, and an impressive lineup of surf photographers were all eagerly awaiting for the drama to unfold. Tom Curren to surf the legendary left breaking waves of Uluwatu. An event of some importance. Patrick spotted Tom first. Tom had made his way into the lineup and was sitting patiently, waiting for his waves. I mean, it was a long way away and the glare was savage, but I could swear it looked like Tom was riding pretty low in the water. A big set approached, a tremor went through the watching crowd, the photographers settled behind their cameras as silent as snipers. Tom was paddling, paddling. He was in perfect position, we held our breath—the moment felt damn near historic—until Tom Curren dropped into the best wave of the day at the famed Uluwatu left and went right. Standing up on a tiny bodyboard.

That's when Pete Matthews turned to me and said, "Tom Curren's visit to Bali is not like a visit to Mars. It's a visit *from* Mars."

Spiriting through the night on my motorcycle, into the Jimbaran chicane, I could see the airport clearly. A red-eye landing. Denpasar and Kuta and Benoa Harbor winking and welcoming beyond. A pale moon had risen above the giant Mt. Agung, delicately outlined by the light of the rising moon as if by a sharpened pencil. I drove on and I wondered then when I would next see Tom Curren.

Two days previous at the big Rip Curl bash, Tom and I had come together. I was emcee at that one, too. But this time it went better for me and I was dancing in the crowd with some of the Cuervo Tequila promo girls to the heaviest Tom Curren Band jam of the night. The party was huge. On top of the Rip Curl offices no less, overlooking Kuta. The whole damn world was there. Tom had really found his band this time, and he was screaming his guitar through an extended solo that was right on the groove. I was lost in the music, hell, we all were, and the tequila didn't hurt either. Now, I am a man rarely taken by surprise, but I'll be damned. When Tommy Curren's and my eyes met, he smiled a smile at me I had not seen since we shaped our own surfboards together back in the '80s. And man, I smiled back in the same way. And I will be damned if, in that moment, he did not step down off that stage, throw his arm around me, and hand me the pick of his guitar. The music was still pounding and, by God, I took that pick and strummed away on that electric guitar as if I were Pete Townshend while Tommy played the chords with his left hand. He and I were grinning ear to ear as the crowd parted and let us do our thing. And in that moment, I was sure of some things. Sure of a lot of things, actually. Sure that Tom was still my friend. Sure that, without really knowing it, I had missed him. Sure that we had finally found each other again in each other's weathered, crow-footed eyes after all these years. Sure that I saw in his eyes that as long as he breathes, he will just be beginning. Sure that, in all of our dreams, we never have an age. And sure that our two tickets to paradise had wound up in the same place after all.

I wasn't young enough to know everything anymore, but as I turned my motorcycle left onto the bypass, home and girlfriend just minutes away, I knew this much. If anyone is going to surf forever, it's going to be Tom Curren. Because the point of all this is that in order to surf forever, you've got to become part of surfing's history. But more importantly, part of someone else's history. And it was then and there that I noticed a cool sensation on both my temples. The wind against my tears. And I knew I was right. Because someday, somewhere, somebody would grow old enough to read fairy tales again.

JUNGLE STORY

GRAJAGAN AT FORTY-EIGHT YEARS OLD
THE BLUE MAGAZINE, GERMANY, 2020

Steeped in fantasy, the waves at Grajagan, perched on the edge of a wild jungle in Java, are embedded into surfing's global conscience. As the first and longest-running surf camp on earth, "G-Land" holds us in a breathless dream. And I woke up there once with an eight-foot python digesting a rat at the foot of my mosquito net. —Mg.

THE LAST TIGER: Part One

Moving from the jungle, she padded to her place on a small rise that looks out over the Ocean. She had time yet. The late day sun was cooling and she was waiting for the scent. The scent that came when the Ocean would withdraw and the land beneath would become exposed to the sky. Then she could saunter down among the shallow green pools of water and slap fish and crabs and eels from the shallow pools with her great paws. The monkeys would follow her. And they would dart in for a steal as her pile of fish and crabs and eels grew behind her. She would roar and swipe at the monkeys and, like a flock of birds, the monkeys would scatter and reform and try again and again. When it came time to feed, she would carry her squirming pile of food in her great jaws and go back to her spot overlooking the reef. There, she would hang her head and eat slowly. And she would listen for signs of danger in the silence that came between the great waves that would roll in hissing unison across the edge of the reef in the distance. Later, the sun would set and she would return to her mate and cubs and they would hunt the wild boar together until dawn.

A noise. Her head shoots up, ears pricked, eyes searching. Men. Two men. Pale men. Approaching on foot on the beach. Always a danger, men. Though she sensed these two were weak and tired. And they carried things that did not look like danger. Unlike the steel poles the poachers used. And the two men on the beach were not interested in the jungle. They were always looking out to sea, shading their eyes with their hands again and again. Still, she decided, she would have to keep her distance until she knew more about them. How to avoid them. Or how to eat them. She left her scraps for the monkeys and, silent as smoke, vanished into the jungle.

THE DISCOVERY HEARD AROUND THE WORLD

It all started with a volcano. Rising about 10,000 feet, Gunung Agung lords over the island of Bali. The Hindu people of Bali believe that each Earth day begins when the first rays of the morning sun touch the volcano's summit. They call this moment "the morning of the world." In 1972, a young Australian filmmaker named Alby Falzon debuted a fledgling surf film that featured the first idyllic images of surfing in Bali. He had borrowed the name of his movie from this Hindu summit belief, naming his movie *Morning of the Earth* instead. And from the moment it flickered on screen in Australia, surfing in Indonesia would never be the same.

Surfers flocked to Bali in droves to ride her absolutely perfect waves. Bali was flaming sunsets over golden beaches, postcards of bare-breasted native women, and swirling, impossibly colorful dance troupes in terrifying masks. Fully booked airlines landing on runway 090 afforded a dream view out the starboard windows of the five best waves on the planet marching down the Bukit Peninsula. Surfers would deliberately book their seats on the right side of the aircraft just for the chance to glimpse this otherworldly sight. Bali was exotic, friendly, and cheap. Everything from beach huts to beer was always near at hand for the budget surfer. Why, oh why, look any further for a surfing Shangri-la? Yet it was inevitable that all these global surfing pilgrimages would eventually interrupt the idyll. And as the crowds grew and grew, a few minds turned to the possibility of new discoveries. After all, Indonesia was a country of 17,500 islands.

THE FAMILY KID

In 1972, from Kuta Beach on Bali, on a clear day, you could just see the southeast tip of Java. Shrouded in mystery like her name itself, at this time, Java was talked about in hushed tones. A land of third-world poverty, government coup attempts, student riots, bloody communist purges, ruled over by a stone-faced dictator in cop shades and military dress. Enter Bob Laverty, a surfer from Southern California who was searching for himself in the far reaches of the orient. On a local flight from Jakarta to Bali, the weather diverted his flight and Laverty found himself flying over that very same tip of Java that he had wondered about when looking on from Kuta Beach. He now was directly over the Plengkung jungle, a lonely, expansive, dried-out national nature reserve. Made only so because it was uninhabitable. But with a surfer's eye, Laverty was looking down upon row after row of crescent-swept whitewater lines that formed a perfect phalanx as they moved down from the top of the point into an enormous azure bay. Perfect surf.

The fire was lit.

Back in Bali, Laverty got to work. He got his hands on a British Admiralty chart of Java and located the bay. Next, he needed partners in crime. Brothers Bill and Mike Boyum, both Bali expats, were the best candidates, so Bob Laverty pitched them his vision. Laverty unrolled the map where his X marked the spot. A mere sixty-seven miles from where they stood in their Kuta Beach bungalow. Hire a boat? Too risky and unpredictable, especially with no knowledge of anchorages or where to hide if the Ocean turned vicious. It would have to be overland. Even though that prospect was horrendously dangerous. Mike Boyum passed on the whole adventure. But brother Bill was bitten by Laverty's bug. A loose partnership between Bill Boyum and Bob Laverty was formed.

Laverty and Bill Boyum left at dawn on rented scooters, packed with supplies and surfboards slung on straps over their shoulders. Then it was a sketchy voyage across the Bali strait into the open Indian Ocean, then to a small Javanese fishing village. The chart named this port Grajagan and it hugged the very opposite end from where they wanted to be in the great bay. Arriving at Grajagan, they entered a very different world. A world away from Hindu Bali, filled with all the puzzlements of the Muslim culture. Just as the mid-afternoon muezzin call to prayer was crying out from the mosque, Laverty and Boyum pushed their scooters onto a dugout fishing boat and pointed to the far end of the bay. The captain of the dugout took them as far as he dared. The jungle of the Alas Purwo National Reserve was a place of great superstitions. A no-man's land filled with tales of black magic, spirits, snakes, and bloodthirsty tigers. The captain dumped them a good ten miles from the top of the bay and got the hell out of there, leaving them and their scooters on a jungle-edged beachfront. The hard-packed low tide sand was okay for the scooters and they pressed on, their lust for surf making them ignore high tide and all the other warning signs. At one point, a large flock of flamingos was startled by their bikes, a species that was not even known to be in Java. Then with the tide, the sand and their luck ran out.

It was now late afternoon. They abandoned the bikes to the jungle and were now afoot. They could see the offshore spray coming off the waves five miles distant. It was slow going as the tide crept in and pushed them closer and closer to the dry, scrubby jungle. As the sun went down, they hadn't even covered half the distance. With no choice but to press on by a sliver of moonlight, they groped along until they could hear the regular sound of the surf. They then fell exhausted on the beach and slept. At one point in the night, they were awakened by the roar of a Javan tiger. Neither of them had ever heard such a spine-chilling sound in their lives. They were forced to attempt sleeping in shifts with sharpened spears fashioned from driftwood.

Boyum and Laverty woke to a blistering sunrise, sandy and sore, and looked out to sea. As the first set of waves marched in off the distant point, they stood astounded, knowing that they had found what every surfer could only dream of. Absolutely perfect, empty eight-foot waves, more dramatic and evenly formed than even the great Uluwatu, and without a hint or even a possibility of another surfer for a million miles in every direction. It was all theirs. There were no Uluwatu cliffs here, no sea snake caves to negotiate, no difficult entry or exit from the surf. Just an inviting crescent-shaped white sand beach that gave way to an easy paddle out into an empty lineup. It was, by all descriptions, an ideal fantasy setup. Laverty and Boyum, re-energized, prepared to hike the last couple of miles. And this was when they noticed the fresh paw prints of a large Javan tiger within ten feet of their small beach camp. Boyum would later say that this sobering sight was where the original idea for the treehouses came in. But more on that later.

Bill and Laverty then paddled out into the dream surf and rode undisturbed until they ran out of their rationed water. It took them three days to do it. In the tradition of the first surfers to ride a new spot being allowed to name it, they dubbed their discovery "G-Land." Even though the break was actually a long way from the town of Grajagan on a point of land known on the charts as Plengkung.

Back in Bali, the two received a heroes' welcome from a very exclusive group of surfers. Yes, it was a mad adventure. Under constant threat of malaria, reef cuts, staph infections, road accidents, heatstroke, boat disasters, storms, and apparently even tigers. But undeterred, Laverty and Boyum were already drawing up new plans for a return visit. Tragically, it never happened for Bob Laverty. On the eve of their new departure, Laverty suffered an epileptic seizure while surfing Uluwatu and was found drowned in the large surf. It was an inauspicious portent to what would become the original attempt of western colonization at Grajagan. And one that, in the minds of the Javanese, confirmed their beliefs about the malevolent spirits of Plengkung. A predictable outcome for anyone who would "pull on a tiger's tail."

Yet despite Bill Laverty's untimely passing, the lure of Grajagan proved unquenchable. Her siren's call was too strong to heed the risks. In many ways, the second journey was even crazier than the first. Because by now, Bill Boyum had talked brother Mike back into believing in the place. Together, the forward-thinking Boyum brothers were determined to own and monetize the surf break all for themselves before the inevitable mobs would descend upon it. So the concept of the surf camp was born. At first, they wanted it to be a floating camp. So the Boyum brothers gathered enough money to buy a used twenty-four-foot Radon fishing boat, which could get them from Kuta Beach to G-Land in just over four hours on a good day. On a bad day? They would probably die. They thought of this little boat as the concept for a floating surf camp, but the lack of room and the outrageous dangers this presented sank those ambitions. This was when Bill Boyum reworked his treehouse idea, relegating the Radon to a supply and guest-delivery vessel.

Mike Boyum, a drifting gypsy of a surfer with the cleverness for opportunity honed from this lifestyle, took over operations. A fitness guru, he could play the hippie and fast for days and do yoga for hours, but he could also become a formidable deal maker in a country notorious for its corruption. As stated, the Plengkung jungle was an all-but-abandoned national forest reserve. But it still meant the Boyum's camp had to be fully permitted. Naturally, and some may say fairly, considering that this was not the Boyums' birth country, bribes were essential and very tricky. Mike Boyum, having long become a master at these processes, at one point even removed a family gift gold Rolex from his own wrist and placed it on a certain politico in the name of commerce. With such savvy, during the year, Mike Boyum had obtained the necessary authorizations. In June of 1974, the finishing touches were put on a fifteen-by-fifteen-foot thatched-roof, bamboo-sided treehouse. Just one. Huge tiger prints were still occasionally seen on the beach, even though the fabled Javan tiger was supposedly extinct. Black cobras were also a big concern. Searching for firewood could end your life. To say nothing of the wild ivory-tusked pigs that could reach the height of a man's hip and rip his stomach open. Raising the treehouse twenty feet off the ground meant everybody slept a little easier.

Underneath the treehouse was a kitchen of sorts. Three single-burner stoves, four ice chests, and a fifty-pound sack of brown rice. Everything had to be duct taped shut every night, but the wild animals would just gnaw through the tape and turn the kitchen to shambles.

The surfers got used to the ruckus and could sleep through almost everything, except when the tigers came around. They would know when the tigers were there because the jungle would become completely silent.

For the next three years, G-Land was the domain of a very exclusive group of surfers. Aside from the Boyums, there was the great Gerry Lopez, who practically made it his second home, writing gushing features for SURFER from his treehouse perch that even included his personal haiku poems. Australian Peter "Grubby" McCabe was welcomed. He and Lopez would while away the hours in the surf, weaving and crisscrossing their way down the reef on the same waves. Lopez called it their "Blue Angels act."

In 1977, the camp was government registered as the Blambangan Surfing Club and began taking week-long reservations of ten surfers at a time, $200 a person, with a transportation fee on the beat-up boat from Kuta Beach in Bali. From there, the price went up quickly. By 1982, a ten-day package cost a grand.

The famed G-Land had evolved from the world's finest secret spot to the world's first surf resort. Though it still wasn't any more posh than your average Boy Scout outpost. Yet, due to the dreamscape waves, G-Land could do no wrong. And it still held on to its mystique. It was a remote fantasy adventure wave that called to that adventurous surfer within all surfers. But like all money-driven enterprises, the pristine nature of the dream was not to last. Once the Boyums' camp proved itself as a solid money-maker, other surfer-entrepreneurs bribed the right officials, other camps opened, daily boat shuttle services bloomed like mushrooms, and soon, there were up to a hundred surfers at a time in the lineup.

Gerry Lopez finally conceded to every surfer's lament. "It was the perfect setup there for a few years," he wrote twenty years after his first visit. "It was a surfing monastery. If we could have somehow kept it as such it would have stayed surfing's Holy Ground . . . I guess we just shouldn't have told anybody."

Despite Lopez's morose prayer, G-Land remains a place of mystery and adventure. It is easy to forget that it still lies on the edge of that same abandoned dry jungle, the spectacular waves coursing down that same wild point from the top of the bay. A place that will always remind you that you are on the knife's edge of an exotic, wild piece of the world. Just like the surfers who, at 1:17 a.m. on June 3, 1994, were swept from their G-Land resort beds by the full force maelstrom of a tsunami. The product of a 7.2 earthquake that rattled teeth loose a full one hundred miles away, hitting G-Land at 250 miles an hour. Australian pro-surfers Rob Bain, Simon Law, Richard Marsh, Shane Herring, and Richie Lovett were lucky to get away with their lives. It is said that their swimming skills were the only thing between them and death. With communications non-existent, they were found days later, deeply wounded and badly infected. They all lived.

The very next year, in perhaps G-Land's most glamorous period in her long history, was when the Association of Surfing Professionals included G-Land as one of their stops on the global "Dream Tour." With the pro surfers exhausted from a grueling tour in substandard waves the previous year, the G-Land concept was welcomed with open arms by all. All, that is, except the organizers. The extremely remote location of G-Land made it an organizer's nightmare. But Quiksilver, the most prestigious surf brand in the world at the time, was determined to overcome the challenges. After numerous setbacks, both logistically and legally, which included safety clauses for the surfers against wild animal attack, Quiksilver triumphed. The 1995 Inaugural Quiksilver Contest was greeted with a week of perfect six-to-eight-foot "dream surf" and was won by their sponsored world champion surfer Kelly Slater. Elated, Quiksilver followed up in 1996, with Californian Shane Beschen taking the title, and then again in 1997, with Australian powerhouse Luke Egan hoisting the winner's trophy. Each year had absolutely perfect surf. By 1998, Quiksilver, due to global economic issues and the enormous efforts needed to run these events, quit while they were ahead. The successful Quiksilver events opened the gates to a handful of regional events in the years to come, with none being more unique than *Surftime Magazine* and Coca-Cola's 2012 "Put Up or Shut Up" Competition. A winner-take-all contest format where ten surfers threw in US $1,000 each as the prize money. In perfect eight-foot surf, Bali local Tai Graham took home the US $10,000 when he was able to just nip Californian Chris Ward to take the pot. Yet despite the evolution of G-Land as a modernized, must-surf destination for thousands of surfers, that Javan mystery still presides over the camps. The local Javanese still regard this surfing outpost as a very powerful center of jungle black magic. Local villagers still believe that it was never meant for man, but only for the spirits. And they believed from the start that those who first tread upon this piece of land would eventually find a terrible end. Bob Laverty drowned soon after his G-Land discovery. While Bill Boyum abandoned the project and moved to Hawaii to raise a family, his brother Mike stayed on to run the G-Land operation. It did not end well for Mike. Not satisfied with being a surf camp owner with a $250,000 annual profit, Mike Boyum turned to drug smuggling. He was arrested in New Caledonia with Peter McCabe, where they served four years in a penal colony. Mostly on the run from that point on, Mike Boyum ended up in the Philippines. There, on the remote island of Siargao, he camped, overlooking another perfect wave.

From there, his behavior became erratic. Villagers reported that he had taken to lying out in the brutal midday Philippine sun each day to induce delirious hunger fantasies about food. After a long series of daily marathon runs and at the end of a forty-three-day fast, Mike Boyum succumbed to starvation and was buried by the local villagers in an unmarked grave.

After exorcising the demons of G-Land through elaborate ceremonies held by the Javanese, the Boyum camp was acquired by local interests in 1978. Renamed "Bobby's G-Land Jungle Surf Camp," the local belief was that the jungle spirits had been appeased. Today, more than one villager believes this was due to the human sacrifice of Laverty and Boyum. Regardless, superstitions and mysteries or no, Bobby's G-Land Jungle Surf Camp has been booked solid for over forty-two years and remains the longest-running successful surf camp in our sport's history and still maintains a household name in the sport, firmly holding a place at the top of most surfers' bucket lists.

THE LAST TIGER: Part Two

She limped on three of her four powerful legs. The three bullets had entered her right hip and two of them had split her intestines in two. She limped on, ahead of the poachers, her bottom jaw slack, her breathing rattling with the blood in her throat. Her cubs were gone, having eaten the poisoned garbage left out for the wild pigs by the humans. Her mate had died a while back, trapped in a net by poachers so as not to harm the precious fur for the taxidermist. Now it was she that was their prey, being driven toward the sea. She would have to turn and fight soon. But she limped on, weakening.

She tried to stay concealed, but reaching the edge of the jungle, she crossed a clearing, palm-sized blood drops marking her trail. She made the rise and could go no further. She lay to rest but kept her head up, waiting for the end. The familiar scent of the low-tide sea overwhelmed her. She watched the waves march down the reef and heard their familiar hissing. She roared in outrage once. It took all her strength. The monkeys, smelling the blood and fearing the roar, gazed with their blinking, thieving eyes from the canopy above. She could see the lights of the surf camps. So bright these days. So many humans. She could also see the flashlights of the approaching poachers and hear their clumsy snapping of twigs as they crept closer through the trees. A monkey screeched warning and the canopy hissed and moved and rained leaves. She could not keep her head up any longer and she rested her bottom jaw on her great paws. The moonlight cast a silvery stripe on the face of each wave that broke on the reef. Like a flashing fish making good an escape from the following whitewater.

The flashlights had found her. A poacher drew a bead on her left eye with his rifle in order to protect her valuable fur. And in one last great effort, she lifted her head and roared at the sea. The report of the rifle cut off her roar and, like smoke, both sounds echoed out over the reef and dissipated into the moonlit sky.

WARM WHISKEY FOR
ALL GHOSTS

A PORTRAIT OF BELLS BEACH, TORQUAY, VICTORIA,
AUSTRALIA
SURFING MAGAZINE, USA, 1996

The Bells Beach surf contest. Half competition, half riot. No world champion feels complete without its firehouse bell trophy. —Mg.

It Was Daytime...

And the pilot banked the old Tiger Moth biplane into a bone-shuddering turn. From 1,200 feet, in the open passenger's cockpit with the wind tugging at my hair, I looked down over my right shoulder upon the 1996 Rip Curl Pro Surf festival on Bells Beach, Victoria, Australia. Giant tents had blossomed on the bluff atop Bells Beach's amphitheater cliffs. Flags were unfurled, bleachers erected, and nothing less than a mile of bunting, merrily snapping in the wind, neatly contained the site like a dinosaur dig. As the pilot continued his arc, I looked at all the people moving about in droves down there; ant-like, purposeful. Hundreds of surfboards were strapped to the tops of cars and lying about on the ground. Their symmetrical shapes perfect from this height and shining white, like fresh fish scattered from a fisherman's net. Outside on the bowling surf, two surfers were riding back-to-back waves, their serpentine wakes leaving lacy patterns between the swells. The Woodstock of surfing was here once again.

It made me wonder what the Koories of the Wathaurong clan would have thought of all this, those Aboriginal people who used to live here in the green rolling hills that abut the break. The Wathaurong believed in Bunjil, an eagle hawk who flew in the sky and kept them safe from the bedeviling Mindi Snake, a child-stealing spirit of earth. Below me was a connection to this history: a single didgeridoo, a traditional Aboriginal wind instrument being made on-site. It was to be presented to the winner of the contest. Somewhere down there in the madness, a young local Aboriginal musician, Glen Romanis, was sitting quietly by himself meticulously dabbing an ancient, local dreamtime story onto the barrel of the instrument. Using clay ochres gathered from the nearby bluffs, he was applying these muddy paints with his fingers, tongue, and mouth. Earlier I'd told him I would be going up in this airplane in order to see a Bunjil-eye-view of Bells Beach. I'd asked him if he wanted to come along. He'd smiled. Then he closed his eyes, put his didgeridoo to his mouth, and played a lowing, growling, hypnotic piece. He finished with a strong bass note and came back to earth. Then he looked at me and looked at his didgeridoo and said, "This is my airplane, mate."

For thirty-six years, surfers have been coming to this Johanna farmland to compete at Bells Beach. And the experienced ones all know one thing: you don't happen to Bells—it happens to you.

It Was a Long Time Ago...

"After that wave of Paul Neilsen's, it's good to see that cigarettes, whiskey, and wild women haven't taken the edge off his surfing."

—Peter Drouyn, announcer, during the finals, 1976.

It Was Daytime...

And it was quite evident that no matter who won, the best surfers in this contest would be Mark Occhilupo, Gary Elkerton, and Tom Curren. And it all happened in three back-to-back heats. The event was moved to Winkipop one magic afternoon. Sunbaked, offshore, six-foot glorious Winkipop, a three-iron shot away from Bells. These three kings had been here before, had been together before. This wave was like a phone call from an old friend.

The Victorian surfing throng, two thousand strong, sat in the bushes or perched themselves on the hillside in the sun. The bricklayers and the plumbers and the carpenters and the girlfriends, freshly arrived by old Volkswagen buses, utility trucks, and kombis, munching on fish and chips served in the morning paper, and rolling the odd joint. Sitting in knit caps, paint-stained boots, ragged leather jackets, and colorful, moth-eaten homegrown sweaters. Bells has always been about festival seating.

One small tent full of judges and myself on the microphone were all we needed at this point. The top forty-four surfers, the Association of Surfing Professionals, the surfing tribe, all of us. It was the magic hour when the afternoon sun of Australia leans down toward the western horizon and reflects the colors of the land into the sea. Aqua-tinted clouds, an azure, wild Ocean dimpled by an offshore wind, the shadows of the surfers on the waves as clear as the surfers themselves. And strangely, the angle of the coast combined with the overlook angle of the cliff and the angle of the breaking wave gave us all the impression that we were viewing surfing as an optical illusion. Of course, the sponsor's rum being passed around in a wineskin might have helped that perspective.

I deliberately would not announce the surfing of these three heats blow by blow. Once a surfer would take off, I would turn off the mic. I just let the surfers ride and let the people feel whatever they wanted to feel, see whatever they wanted to see. The crowd oohed and aaahed and cheered when they felt like it and applauded without prompting.

The heat had already started while World Champion Tom Curren was still walking around the beach looking for a board to ride. It wasn't quite clear how this came to be, but that's just Tom. He saw one he liked, approached the local surfer, and asked if he could borrow the guy's board.

The starstruck local stammered, "I . . . I dunno . . . the is me wife's board."

Tom looked at the board again, considered it a while, and then asked, "How much does she weigh?"

Five minutes later, Tom Curren proved that he was still the master of the vertical connection. He proceeded to surf the borrowed board in a series of subtle, radical, complex songs. None of this new school, wing-and-a-prayer floater, hope-for-the-best recovery surfing. Go put your hands and cheek against a wall and close your eyes and think of yourself at speed, feet compressed into your surfboard wax, just about to carve down into your cutback. That's the Curren connection.

Marco Luciano Occhilupo, Italian-Kiwi kid from Cronulla, back in shape and buzzing with childish energy, surfed like a fighter pilot, banking four g, fin-bending turns. I saw Rob Machado watching the heat, absently rubbing his own legs, as if he were measuring their own power against Mark's. Gary Elkerton, the Aussie King Kong turned French expat, was forgiven by the flag-waving crowd this day. He was back after a long layoff due to a busted arm in a bicycling accident. More than understanding the wave, Gary understood himself. And he showed it with every off-the-lip that threw spray twenty feet into the air. His was a mature, merciless performance. These three old warriors dispatched Jeff Booth, Kaipo Jaquias, and Rob Machado consecutively, and it didn't surprise a soul.

This afternoon, though it would only be round three, would be the high-water mark of performance for the event. I saw Kalani Robb, Shane Dorian, and Conan Hayes huddled together in the crowd, watching closely. They might not have been taking notes, but it sure looked like they were taking note. More than seeing, you could just tell they could hear it. That beautiful noise. The sound of those people on the cliff. It was in the timbre, the tone of the applause, and the cheers. This wasn't a busload of tourists standing at the Banzai Pipeline cheering every bad wipe-out in concert with a thousand whirring motor-drives. This was the Aussie tribe, providing a soundtrack. I looked over at the three Hawaiians. I couldn't help but wonder if they got it. Maybe. All it takes is one thing: a love for Bells Beach.

It Was a Long Time Ago...

And Keith Paull was running naked through the party madness of the Torquay Pub. He would have made it, too, if Terry Fitzgerald hadn't hooked his ankle and sent him crashing into Claw Warbrick's craps game going on in the corner. With a lynch mob of gamblers in hot pursuit, Keith made it all the way to the back door. He found it locked. The fight was eventually broken up by a large female bartender.

The year was 1975.

It Was Nighttime...

And the room was haunted. It was the evening of the Australian Hall of Fame induction ceremony, held at the most impressive surfing museum in the world, a place called Surfworld, out behind the Rip Curl factory in Torquay. To walk through this place is to be proud to call yourself a surfer. This isn't just some exhibition hall with a bunch of old boards on the wall. This is the kind of place where, among other things, they have mounted on the wall an old worn tire off the first car to have ever made it out the mud track to Bells Beach. These aren't just exhibits; they're fossils.

The 1978 World Champ Rabbit Bartholomew was emcee, in fine form at that. As with all good Australian shindigs, there wasn't much food, but there sure was a hell of a lot of beer. Journalist Tim Baker summed it up nicely: "What do you mean? Beer is food!" Kelly Slater was over in the corner, laughing with Dick Garrard, a surfer who once surfed with Duke Kahanamoku. They were rapping about the tire on the wall. It was Dick's. He was telling Kelly the story of how he rolled his old Ford twice trying to get out to the surf that day so long ago.

The inductions began. We all crammed ourselves into a small back room, standing room only. By the smell of the place it was obvious more than one bottle of whisky was being passed around. By the end of it, when the magic moment came down, I found myself standing at the door, half high on the fumes alone, with Simon Anderson and Tommy Peterson. It was Bob McTavish who was being honored and inducted this night. He stood before us all with his eyes twinkling and he held his trophy as he talked to the room. We were all swaying with beer at this point as we strained to hear what he was saying. Bob abandoned his speech halfway through and asked for the lights to be brought down a bit so that he could see everyone in the room. Then he just looked at everyone, nodding time to time at some of the good, gray-haired friends who were seated in places of honor. Then he raised his voice and said, "Look, mates . . . I'm just a toymaker. An old toymaker. And it has been my pleasure to make toys for you people all my life. People who take these toys and feel the power and the beauty and the soul of the Ocean through the soles of their feet. To all the futurologists out there, to all the shapers in this room, to all surfers everywhere . . . surf until you drop, because I know I will. And I will build toys for you until I drop . . . thank you . . ."

The room was quiet for a moment. Then Simon Anderson put down his pint and started clapping. Tommy Peterson hooted. And then the whole room erupted into applause. John Elliss, editor of *Deep Magazine*, tapped me on the shoulder. He'd been rolling a cigarette. On the open flap were some words of wisdom—a fortune comes with every tobacco pouch. It read: *Happy is he who dares to defend passionately that which he loves. —Ovidius.*

It Was a Long Time Ago...

"All Bells activities seem designed to bend the body . . . then the mind."

—Claw Warbrick, 1970.

It Was Nighttime...

And Neil Ridgway, editor of *Tracks Magazine,* was huddled naked in the bushes. It was another fine end to another wild night at the Torquay Pub, the ground zero of all festivities over the Easter holidays here in Australia. But on this night, two quiet, unsuspecting citizens of Torquay were about to have a close encounter with just one of the thousands of surfers who descend upon this small hamlet each year.

It happened like this.

Neil was working his way back to the media house a full mile away, inebriated, with a small entourage following his efforts through the streets. There had been bets laid to see if he was going to make it all the way, nude, without being arrested. Just then, a cop car came rolling down the street. Neil, always a crowd pleaser, timed it just right. After all, this is a man who has run in the same condition with the bulls at Pamplona. Anyway, Neil ran across the road just behind the cop car and bailed over a small fence into someone's front yard. The cop kept rolling.

Neil stood up, hands on hips. Then he broke into "Scotland the Brave" and began to dance a jig. Just then, an older woman, standing in her picture window and regarding the nude specter dancing in the moonlight in her front yard, could be heard calling out to her husband: "John? John? There seems to be one of those surfers in our front yard . . . and he isn't wearing any clothes . . . and I think he's been drinking beer."

It Was a Long Time Ago...

"What if the surf is flat for the contest? Well, I guess as a last resort, we could just grab some dynamite and blow the whole thing up . . . "

—Claw Warbrick, responding to a question put to him by the Sydney Morning Herald, 1971.

It Was Daytime...

And I stood in an old shed that made me long for the old trials contest. You remember the trials. Those glorious do-or-die pre-contests that used to set the tone for the whole Bells affair. A qualifier that gave any soul on earth a shot at the title. They're gone now, replaced by today's contest structure that is less like war and more like surgery. There was something about the trials. It was like open season on the gods. All the hopeful, the hungry, the best young surfers in the world would show up, and try to freeze everyone in their headlights. And they often did. Unknown wildcards would fight through the four-man, twenty-minute heats and make it into the big time. In 1977, it was Simon Anderson; in 1983, it was a guy named Joe Engel. And in between were all the others who had the spirit to take a shot at it. Like in 1985, when youngsters Gary Elkerton and Nick Carroll teamed up in a second-round heat and brutally assassinated the great Shaun Tomson. Derek Hynd was always good for a dramatic effort. It was here, on one of his bizarre, gunny twin-fins, that he introduced his sliding 360, a move he'd been saving up for a year, working on it in secret, like Oppenheimer's bomb. With the skills he learned in the trials, he ended up seventh in the world. A guy named Gabe Callahan from the central coast of New South Wales made his reputation on one wave, the biggest wave ridden in the twenty-foot surf of 1981. That was the year Richard Cram was seen writing a note to his mother before his heat. Equipped only with a 6'1" single fin, he didn't expect to make it out of his heat alive. He paddled out and surfed like he was trying to kill himself. He won the heat. And I remember sitting on the bluff that day with Terry Richardson, watching the miracle of Simon Anderson's Thruster debut, and Terry turning to me after one ride and saying: "Yeah, well I reckon I could win this too if I had that board . . ."

The storage shed I was standing in was behind the Torquay Pub. Beside the paint and the sagging brooms and the cardboard boxes and two broken jukeboxes was what all those trialists had been going for. If you got in the finals, your name was painted up on these plywood panels that covered a whole wall in the pub. I looked down at these panels now, due to be painted over and used to build a new storage shed, and I read every single name. Every single goddamned one. I wasn't sure who had gathered more dust over the years. The panels themselves . . . or me.

It Was a Long Time Ago...

And the cops were rifling the American team's hotel rooms. The trouble started when Corky Carroll was suspended from the Bells World Contest for yelling obscenities at the pub owner's wife for not having enough cold beer. The rest of the team, including Rolf Arness, Brad McCaul, and David Nuuhiwa, refused to compete unless Corky was back in. So, at the big Olympic-style opening day march down in Lorne, unaware of the boycott, Dale Dobson marched alone carrying Old Glory. The cops, suspicious of such subversive ideologies and behaviors, searched the Americans' rooms and found some weed. The whole team was threatened with deportation, but it was David who decided to take the rap alone so the others could surf. Compliments of the Australian authorities, David flew back to Huntington, Corky made it to the semis, and Rolf became the world champion.

The year was 1970.

It Was Daytime...

And the announcer's booth was packed. In an 8x12 trailer, Neil Ridgway and John Elliss were hard at work trying to get little Peter Hughes' surfboard returned. Peter, Victoria's top junior surfer, was in tears, having just had his board stolen from the parking lot. Jodi Holmes, ASP media boss, was doing her best to console. Kelly Slater was in the corner, watching Lisa Andersen's final against Pauline Menczer, chewing his nails and muttering under his breath for her to "Take the next one, take the next one . . ." Kelly had lost out earlier and Lisa was Florida's last hope.

Doug "Claw" Warbrick, co-owner of Rip Curl, was telling the tale of the old, broken-down taxi that his father had given him as a thirteen-year-old kid. His dad had told him that if he could fix it, he could drive it. Claw and his friends discovered it still had reverse. And that's how they drove it to Bells for years—in reverse the whole way, five miles from town. Brad Farmer, president of the Australian Surfrider Foundation, was asking Mark Occhilupo his opinion on government graft. Mark, thinking hard, was replying that he agreed. Two female French journalists were trying to figure out a heat sheet, and three Rip Curl bikini girls were huddled in the corner, nearly naked, hiding out from the crowd and the stiff wind coming off the farmlands. The sound engineer was fighting with all his sound levels. Mark Warren was doing a live radio report. Mark handed me an article that had appeared in the Sydney Morning Herald that day. It read:

AT CHURCH? NO, WE'D RATHER BE BY THE SEA by Elissa Blake
"More Australians find a sense of peace and well-being from sitting by the Ocean watching the waves than going to church or praying, a study has shown . . ."

Just then, Jeff Darby and Glen Romanis started playing their didgeridoos. Everyone just raised their voices. I looked over at John Ellis, who was not quite sure what to say about the heat in the water at this point. So I just handed him the newspaper article. He read it once and laughed back at me through the crowd. Then he took his microphone and held it in front of the didgeridoo.

The sound engineer cranked it up.

It Was a Long Time Ago...

Here was the rumor: Michael Peterson and Owl Chapman, who'd lost out of a contest in Queensland and were subsequently broke, needed to get to Bells down south in Victoria. With no resources available, they stole a car, drove the twenty hours, and burned the car to the ground in a field behind the contest site. Peterson went on to win the event. His entire acceptance speech was only three words long: "I earnt it."

The year was 1975.

It Was Nighttime...

And it had been a long day for Kelly Slater. Earlier that afternoon, two hours and a world away from Bells down the coast at Johanna, Kelly had lost for the second time to Narrabeen's Chris Davidson. And no one hates losing more than Kelly Slater. Kelly had shown up out of nowhere at my place that night. I could tell he needed company. You could see it in his eyes—the loneliness of being the best the world had ever seen, but having still lost. The days of professional surfers traveling as a band of devil-may-care gypsies are gone as sure as yesterday. These guys live their lives on the tour like it's some witness protection program. They show up, barricade themselves in their safe houses, surf their heats, pick up their checks, and then get the hell out of there and head for home, half-dreading the next event. It's an exhausting lifestyle. Among other things, it's the goddamned money. Glamour be damned; with all the prize money and the sponsorships flying around, it's all become so serious. The judges don't fraternize with the surfers, the surfers consider the judges the enemy, the surfers themselves find it hard to be good friends with each other and form small, segregated cliques. Considering the stakes at hand, they sometimes have trouble looking each other in the eye, and thanks to arm bands and colored wrist bands and security and roped off areas, they stay even farther away from the fans. They are carted around and placed in front of video cameras and the like. It seems an odd, sterile vibe. The way I see it, anyone involved with the Association of Surfing Professionals lives with each other as they circumnavigate the globe. Like McLuhan's global village. And the greatness of any calling is the unity it creates among its participants. There is only one true form of wealth, and that is human contact. When we move toward disassociated material gain and personal isolationism, we take something beautiful and build cages for it. In the end, our coins turn to brass and will have bought nothing worth living for.

This was my food for thought as I, Kelly, and the entire crew from the media house, which had swelled to about fifteen by this time, headed down to the Torquay Pub to listen to the band. A half hour and three beers later, Kelly was sitting on a chair, guitar under arm, singing lead. Word got out fast. Another half hour and the whole place was gloriously out of control. The band had just given up their instruments to the internationals. Photographer Steve Sherman on congas and cowbell, Andrew Kidman on lead guitar, some guy from Melbourne on drums, Jesse Faen, editor of *Waves Magazine,* on bass. Jesus, that music was a mess. But, as Simon Anderson told me at the bar, at least it was loud.

Everyone was dancing, the pool tables were doing brisk business, and a whole crew of bearded punters were still betting on the dog races on TV.

At one point, I found myself behind the bar with Brian Doherty, the pub manager, who was sketching out his new fin design on the employee chalkboard for me. It involved a turbine engine. I told Tommy Peterson about it once I was back in the fray. He just looked at me and said, "Mate, on a night like this, just about anything would make sense."

It Was a Long Time Ago...

"A lot of people got drunk and nostalgia flowed from open taps and open arms and open beds were shared . . ."

—John Witzig, *Tracks*.

The year was 1971.

It Was Daytime...

And the PA died at noon. Thank God. When I thought about it, it really couldn't have come down any other way. Here I was, sitting on the berm far south of the main contest site at Johanna with Claw Warbrick, surveying the scene. The power and the glory of pro surfing had somehow miraculously reincarnated itself. Just a simple club contest at this point. A card table on an empty beach, a handful of judges, offshore four-to-five-foot surf. How could you possibly lose with a contest that you had to take your shoes off and cross a stream to get to? The whole pro tour was dependent on the power of one car battery in the sand. The ghosts of Bells were smiling.

From where I sat, I could see Sunny Garcia sitting quietly with his wife, crunching on an apple, waiting for his final against Todd Prestage. Over to my left, Barton Lynch was laughing and playing in the sand with his daughter, and Mark Occhilupo was waxing up for his fifth free surf of the day down at the water's edge. Behind me, Sean Davey was trying his hand at the didgeridoo trophy. A small local crowd had gathered, maybe twenty people, mostly curious farmers and fox hunters from the surrounding hills. It was enough.

The surfing so far had been much like the contest: loose and free. The final was a groovy affair. Todd Prestage, jumping out of his skin to be in his first final, and Sunny Garcia a little nervous at having to defend his title in the only Bells final to ever be held in left-breaking waves. As it turned out, they were both up to it. Much must be said for Todd though. Cool and aggressive, he peppered his rides with big sky off the lips and it paid off. It rattled Sunny a bit, who finally got angry enough halfway through the heat to start throwing his weight around. So, with the boys in the lifeguard boat yelling out the scores to the surfers in the water, the lead changed hands four times in ten minutes. And even though he was defeated in the end, Todd Prestage became a man that day. All alone in the final against the powerful Hawaiian, Todd injected a renewed belief in the Aussie battler directly into the bloodstream of the professional surfing world.

On the beach, the winner's podium was a couple cardboard boxes full of Aussie meat pies. The famed Bells trophies sat atop them. Claw took one look at the trophies and said: "They've never looked better, mate . . ."

The crowd was so small by now that the acceptance speeches were as quiet as a conversation in an afternoon pub. Sunny got the Bell, the didge, and the first back-to-back wins since Mark Richards did fifteen years previous.

And the rest of us? As we made our way back to the car park a mile down the beach, I thought of all the contests these days; Bells just might be our most sacred. A contest that is more a state of mind than anything else. A contest where, professional or not, one can be a part of the future and still celebrate surfing's past. A place where you can find all you are looking for. And where you can still hear the warm whiskey voices of surfing's ghosts in the wind.

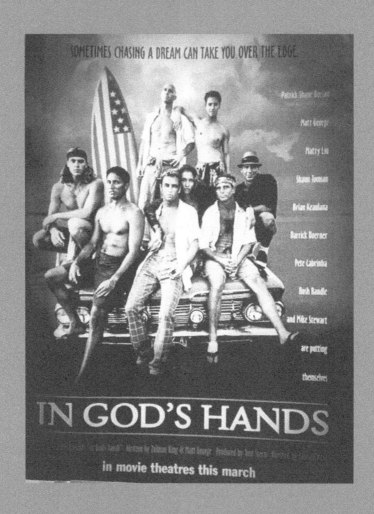

IN GOD'S HANDS

THE MOVIE, PART ONE
BEACHGRIT.COM, 2021

IMAGE COURTESY OF COLUMBIA TRI-STAR PRODUCTIONS

How it came to be that I wrote, co-produced, and was a leading man in a Columbia Tri-Star international feature film release is a book for another time. But In God's Hands *was a surfing drama that took me around two worlds: our planet and the topsy turvy world of Hollywood. This published essay was just a soundbite of the madness that ensued. —Mg.*

Think of it as a disaster movie. I have. For lo' these many years. To be invited to Hollywood to write a movie about surfing and then to have them actually want to make it and then to talk them into hiring all your friends to do it with you and then to have to stand by and watch the Hollywood machine turn the story into a compost heap was absolutely heartbreaking. But at least my friends and I had a ball making it. Surfers like Matty Liu (who surfed the giant waves of *Jaws* in the climax of the movie, but did not make the final cut), Shane Dorian (who I believe was at a surf contest in Brazil when I called him. He was ranked fifth in the world at the time but he jumped on board just to get out of the crappy surf in Brazil), Shaun Tomson, 1978 world champion (who, when I called him, asked, "Will they clear the lineups for us so we can surf alone?"), Brian Keaulana (who no surf movie maker in their right mind would *not* call, considering how many lives he has saved as a Hawaiian lifeguard), Derrick Doerner (big wave legend who provided the name for the movie after describing a terrifying wipeout at Waimea Bay), Dave Kalama (who was convinced we were all gonna die doing our own stunts without any jet-ski experience and came damned close to being right), Pete Cabrinha (genius who had just invented kite surfing, which did not make the final cut either), Rush Randle (sailboard champion who was the strongest man in the world and who, when he hugged me in thanks, bruised two of my ribs), and yes, even Bret Michaels, the lead singer of the hair band *Poison*. So for those brave enough to sit through *In God's Hands* once again, here is a series of behind-the-scene capers to keep you occupied.

EXT. PADANG PADANG, BALI — NIGHT

I had never heard anyone laugh at ten million dollars before. But the other producers did. Still, there it was, our budget. So yeah, as big as ten million dollars sounds, we were still broke the whole time and it often fell on me to make things happen time and again. Me, who had zero experience making a big Hollywood movie.

Anyway, we were in Bali and I wrote this huge party scene that was to take place on the famed beach of Padang Padang. I needed at least fifty people as extras, but the other producers came to me and said that they couldn't pay for any. So I grabbed my co-stars Shane Dorian and Matty Liu and we walked down Jalan Legian, the main tourist drag, handing out my homemade flyers that announced a huge blow-out full moon party the very next night at Padang Padang (even though the full moon was ten days away). "Wanna be in a Hollywood movie?" the flyer read. "Show up and get down! No one refused! All the free beer you can swill!" I also spread the underground rumor that it was going to be a shroomfest. Remember, this was 1996, and you could still get magic mushrooms on your Caesar salad in Bali. The thing was, we didn't have any shrooms and between the three of us, we could afford about a six pack of Bud, which we were drinking while we handed out the flyers. So I guess you could say it was all left "In God's Hands."

But wait. We needed a band. Another thing the flyer promised. And that's when we heard a noise that sounded a lot like an electronic cat fight in a slaughterhouse. It was coming from one of the more notorious welcome bars on the Legian Kuta strip. A few of the ladies, and, well, a few of the men, in skirts and makeup were hanging out front and looking for early customers. Matty realized we had found exactly what we needed. Dragging us into the place, Matty introduced us to the source of the catfight. It was a Russian industrial metal band called KAOS who had rented the place for practice with a jug of black-market vodka. All the band demanded from us for the gig was a tip jar, a stage, and ice cubes for their last jug of vodka (which was, honest to god, black vodka, by the way. Christ, I've never figured that out). I said sure, easy. I grabbed a sharpie, wrote their band name on the flyers, and the deal was set.

Have you ever accidentally thrown a baseball through a window? We should have known better. This is a tourist town smack dab in the middle of the global Dharma bum trail. So, when we pulled up to the White Monkey surf shop at Padang Padang, our staging area for the night of production, the police had already dispatched a squad of bruisers to handle all the traffic. And honestly, I was considering paddling out to sea and never coming back. Because how the hell was I gonna throw a full moon party with no moon, no booze, and no party favors for over a thousand people?

Do you believe in Karma? Well, mine must have been teed up, because it soon became apparent that the experienced international party jet-set never believes what's on a fucking flyer anyway. Just let them know the location, and a river of firewater will flow and stash bags of exotic pharmaceuticals from all points of the compass will be emptied into lungs and throats. So if you pause on the big party scene of the movie that we shot in the rain all night, you can see most of this famous cast of surfers, along with the pink elephant multitude and the film crew, had all gone nuts.

So, under the deluge of the skies the river broke through, generators blew out, the stage collapsed, someone's hair was set on fire by the sparklers, the tide came in, the body painting contest turned the beach into a nudist colony, and there was even a spaced-out impromptu marriage between the female camera operator and the mohawked drummer of KAOS. Which was officiated by Bret Michaels, cast member and executive producer, complete with his famous male mascara. (And for you romantics, rumor has it that the happy couple are still together in 2021.)

Fast forward. By dawn, the beach looked like the morning after the D-Day invasion. That or a human version of turtle breeding season. Dozing couples of all genders lying in sandy humps in each other's arms, some of them even copulating on their last reserves. And the walking wounded were making their way up through the famous cave stairs with hangovers that I swear to god you could actually hear.

Meanwhile, Shane, Matty, Shaun Tomson, Bret Michaels, and I were up on the shaded remnants of the listing bamboo stage. (KAOS had fled at dawn, fearing Indonesian immigration reprisals for starting a riot, but they made sure we knew where to find them if we did this sort of thing again.) And being very South African, Shaun had somehow found some Earl Grey tea that wasn't spiked with psilocybin and we all sat with our pinkies up, considering the impressive wreckage before us.

Shaun broke the silence. "So, Shane . . . if you didn't body shave, you'd be quite a hairy bastard, yeah?" Even a female survivor of the night who was sitting on Bret Michaels' lap busted up. (She was the Ibizian fire dancer and hula hoop instructor who had thoughtfully provided all the sparklers that lit a number of heads of hair on fire.) And that was when Bret grabbed a beat-up beach guitar and serenaded in the new day of what was one of the many mad moments in the remarkable surfing production that was *In God's Hands*. Bret, in a very amused frame of mind with the Ibizian beauty breathing in his ear, chose to sing the acoustic version of his number-one hit from 1988. And it could not have been more fitting.

Every rose has its thorn
Just like every night has it's dawn
Just like every cowboy sings his sad, sad song
Every rose has its thorn
Yeah it does . . .

THE BALI YOU REMEMBER

WHERE DREAMS BECOME REALTY
TRACKS MAGAZINE, AUSTRALIA, 2012

That is no misspelling in the subtitle. The land-grabbing and development here is dizzying. This was written as a sequel to my "FLESH AND BLOOD" feature. A confession. I wrote this for myself, then sent it out freelance. I was surprised when it got published. —Mg.

June 10, 2012 — Uluwatu, Bali, Indonesia

It is your birthday. You are fifty-three years old. You are a surfer. Today, you find yourself eight degrees below the equator, standing on a cliff's edge in the backyard of a luxury villa of Uluwatu, Bali, overlooking the famed surf break. Considering a fall over the vertical 300-foot limestone cliff makes your knees go wobbly. You have your surfboard under your arm and a waterproof pack on your back. You are going to climb down the cliff's southern path and you are going to walk, surf, and paddle the entire Bukit Peninsula over the next three days. You will be dusting off memories. Your first visit here was twenty-eight years ago. When things were much different.

With your peripatetic lifestyle, you and Bali have crossed paths innumerable times in the past. But you live in in Bali now. With a full-time job here, the proper green card, and a local woman you are planning to marry, you are no expat. You are an immigrant. Drawn to this far-off place, far from the USA because of the different brand of freedom it offers. An adventurous kind. A romantic kind. And because you have never been able to shake her call. A courtesan, Bali makes you feel special, makes you feel like you are the only one on earth who loves her in the right way. Even though millions of others can have her, too. And they do. Anytime they like. You are drawn to Bali and the Bukit Peninsula because of the daredevil rules here. Watch your back, make the right friends, no sudden moves. Like any jungle, that's what gets you noticed—sudden moves. And then you get eaten. And you find there is a strange beauty in knowing that. Here, it's every man, woman, and child for themselves. Survival, but with perfect waves and the freedom of taking care of oneself without anyone sticking their nose in your business. Unless, of course, you fuck up. Then it's all over. As sure as a popped balloon. If not the horrors of the Kerobokan jail, then surely an escort to the airport and an economy flight back to wherever the hell you came from. But you love the risk. Bali is Dodge City with palm trees. And you, the gambler, but you are not drawn to the dark side. The illegal. Because knowing you can be anyone you want to be here is enough. You can reinvent yourself. Or just be who you always were with no trouble from nobody. No government, no cops, no hassles. Just keep your paperwork in order and don't pop any flares. Then it's all smiles. As long as you are aware that here, the smiles are like icebergs, where unimaginable dangers lurk below. Romantically, philosophically, physically. Good luck. As long as you keep your nose clean, don't misstep, and thank the spirits everyday—whether you believe in them or not—you just might make it. Remember, you have no rights here. Only privileges. Only savvy will see you through. From the booze-addled, sex-brutalized carnival of the construction site formerly known as Kuta Beach, to the eat, pray, love of the creaking bamboo forests of Ubud. And you know this. Learned this. All the while, Bali intertwined herself with your fate. Your station in life. You are here now. You are fifty-three years old.

You reach the bottom of the cliff, just. The frayed rope section was a little hairy. You walk the beach along the secret cove, past the topless sunbathing Germans, crunching along in the seashell sand, your feet covered in mittens of the stuff. That has never changed. You can smell the cliffside Uluwatu village up ahead. The cliff sagging under the weight of the astonishingly irresponsible real estate development. The luxury villas, the beer-soaked warungs—bars and resorts—the sewage, the litter, and the paper money that drives it all into the sea. Scads of paper money. You can remember a time when there were only three warungs up there. So it goes.

The surf's not half bad and there's only sixty-five guys out. It is off-season, after all. You'll put in at the cave, grab a wave, and make your way to Padang Padang for the night.

You can see the Bukit white kids are out in the surf, their porcelain skin standing out amongst the brown. There is always brown skin in the lineup now; that is one thing that has changed for the better. The locals have taken this place back from the invaders. Not the empires of the

Dutch, the English, nor the Japanese could take this island forever. Why should it be any different for the Western surfers? We could only hold the place so long. Too much treasure. The twelve-year-old Balinese girl, who once carried your surfboards in on the footpath to Uluwatu for one dollar, is now a millionaire. Her family was able to lease their cliffside land to one of the Korean Resort Developments for twenty years and six million in cash. The Koreans brought the money in suitcases that night. It took the young lady's family all night to count it. And another day to wrap it in foil and plastic and bury it in various secret locations near the temple. The young lady, now a rich woman of forty, still sells her homemade bracelets to the tourists for a dollar a pop. As she always has. All her life. This woman has no idea what she is going to do with her share of the millions. Despite the fact she has never been more than four miles from the Uluwatu Temple, she is thinking of buying a car. Though she's not sure she wants to go anywhere.

You see the great Australian surfer Jim Banks and his son Harley take off on the same wave. You'd put Harley at about thirteen. Just like the other kids out there. Luca Carlisle, Luan Huberman, Dyou Worawong, Max Desantis, and the others. Their names tell the story. They live here too, growing up with their expat parents. Or fathers who have married locally. Bali is not a place you go to live as a white person—it's a place you end up. The kids are growing up in the shadow of the temples. Their lives are a mélange of languages, mixed blood, exotic scents, monsoons, bigotry, jealousy, and fantasy surfscapes. Their playgrounds are the best waves in the world. They breathe in the belonging to a place that will never belong to them. Paddling out day after day into international lineups of every creed and color on earth. Rubbing shoulders with their heroes, the Indonesian greats, and international surf stars alike. They have backstage passes to every party, every contest, every happening. Thirteen years old and already familiar with the taste of the gin and tonics. The Kuta township to the north sees to that, like a hooker with a heart of a gold. Which Kuta is, actually.

The white kids are growing up here as a man-child cadre. They stick together, stay close, relate, compete now and then. They all want to be surf champions. That's the ticket here. Then you don't have to be a real estate hustler. Surfing champions. An impossible dream on an island where the local surf brands don't sponsor little white kids. Viewing most of them like white pegs trying to fit into brown holes. Still, they live in a dream that takes guts. Carving out their place while delicately balanced on the tightropes of mixed culture.

Your hands on each rail, you lay your board in the water at the Uluwatu cave. You look back inside its cavernous walls. It breathes a great breath back at you. It always has. No matter what, no matter what anyone says, it's still the most exotic entry point into any surfing lineup in the world. This mysterious cave, a surf star itself, held in your imagination for twenty-eight years now. You've paddled out through her when she was a maelstrom of tangling sea snakes with your heart in your throat. And you have swum in her crystal-clear pools with exotic beauties at midnight. And your heart was in your throat then, too. You have honored this cave. Approached her like a church. The hush of the place is something you always remember. Everyone talks in whispers in the Uluwatu cave. Japanese, Indonesian, Korean, Russian, Aussie, and American. Hushed. You have never heard so much as a shriek from a child inside her dripping limestone overhangs. From her old wooden ladder days to her modern Dr. Seuss cement stairs, you have loved her.

Just the other day, you paddled from within her to the crowded lineup with thirty other surfers. You all paddled out and sat just beyond the waves and held hands in a big circle. Here, you were going to promise the local environmental, non-profit white guy that you would keep the place clean. To honor the water. Then another set of waves came through and everyone just tore over each other to catch one. The mad, hungry Uluwatu lineup. After all, everyone had just spent ten precious minutes away from the waves, holding hands in a big circle and promising to keep things clean around the place. A guy sure could use another wave after spending so much time holding hands. The thought makes you huff a laugh to yourself as you jump off the edge of the green-and-black reef and stroke as hard as you can to miss the oncoming set over the racetrack reef section. You feel the weight of your backpack for the first time. The trouble it's going to cause you.

You make it outside and sit up and watch Jim Banks swoop by you, front hand cupped like it's protecting a lit match, eyes as intense as when he was a boy. And you knew him as a boy. You look at the young kids in the lineup and hope they realize some shit. Knowing that if they realize some shit, then maybe the Bukit stands an even chance. And you think, if only everybody realized that it was all about water. Life-giving water, evaporated from the sea, kidnapped up into the pregnant clouds, sailing inland to the hills and mountains, disgorging the bounty of distilled fresh water, falling upon the riches of the earth, and then moving, racing, running, following her secret paths of least resistance, roiling, running, flowing, always headed home. A raindrop becomes a rivulet, a creek, a stream, a river, and then, finally, the sea and home.

And us. Waiting for her. Floating on the edge of water's home, playing in her sea waters. When just below our feet, it is her returning fresh water that carves our reefs into magnificent crescent sculptures, refracting the sea's power, allowing us to ride within the sea's hollows. Providing to the end.

You hope at least these kids out at Uluwatu realize this. Realize that they ask everything from water. Everything. And that it asks nothing of them. And you hope these kids realize how all the grown-ups on earth, with all their great advice and rules and truths and stinking lies, have treated the Ocean like a global garbage can. And you hope these white kids figure out how to change things. Make it worth money to someone to clean up the water. Because the only way things ever change anywhere in this fucked-up world is to make it worth money to someone. Anyone. Because there is only one real problem in this world.

We think we have time.

You catch a wave, kick out, and, with a wave to Jim Banks, paddle on.

At dusk, you make it into the small cove of Padang Padang a half mile to the north. You paddle past its famed reef, hollow waves as usual, but very small, about chest high. The tattooed Russian bodyboarders are just lording over the place, spending more time in the tube than any conventional surfer could ever imagine. You give a thumbs up to one of the Russians after his outrageous ride and across the cultures, he salutes. This place was anyone's game these days.

You make shore and walk up to your favorite warung. The one with the ninety-year-old Ibu who has served *nasi goreng*—fried rice—to the greatest surfers in the world since 1967. You negotiate a small price and pitch your two man tent on the rattan-covered massage table next to the dripping cliff wall. You buy three warm beers and then fill your thermos with the water seeping from the limestone cliffs an arm's reach away. Ibu doesn't bat an eye. She's familiar with your colorful behaviors. You and her her thirty-five-year-old granddaughter were once a couple. So this night, you drink deeply of the warm beer and of the cliff water. Both taste as earthy and fresh as your own blood.

At 9:00 p.m., the hissing lanterns are turned down and the beach workers all begin the long walk up the steep temple stairs for home. Darkness falls and it is muted and complete. Walking waist-deep into the Ocean, you urinate underneath an indigo dome of stars. Returning your water to the endless cycle. You rinse off the sand on your feet with the ice water long melted in the battered cooler full of clinking warm beers. You slip into your tent to sleep.

The thirty-five-year-old granddaughter slips into your tent as well. As she had done so many times before in 1996, when you were making a Hollywood film here at Padang Padang. You had pitched your tent then too, eschewing the movie crew villa rooms for a more trustworthy belonging. This was all before your split with her and the heartache and before her two kids and the deadbeat Norwegian husband and all troubles that had dogged you both since. This was before she escaped Norway and returned from the land of ice and snow to sell sarongs to the tourists again here on her birthright beach, her sandy haired boys scrabbling it out in the sands with the rest of the urchins. A cycle as endless as water itself in this place. You had asked her why, after all this time, she had returned to you this night. And she had whispered onto your face, onto your lips, that there were no mosquitoes in your tent. And both your laughter echoed against the cliff wall for the first time in a very long time. And that seemed enough. As natural as a heartbeat, you held each other close and dozed through a night of soft rains without making love. You smelling of the Ocean and she of the temple's incense.

Dawn. The eleventh. She is gone, her bouquet a floating apparition. Old Ibu has descended the worn stone stairs after the morning offerings of flowers and holy water in the temple perched on the cliff above you. She has *nasi goreng* waiting for you in her spitting, battered iron skillet. You crawl out of your tent and sit on her wooden bench and you nod a good morning. Old Ibu just rests her hand on the back of your neck for a long moment, looking out to sea. Perhaps remembering the giant electric generator you had managed to steal from that movie production. It was all in the paperwork, a simple omission, a strike of a pen. It was easily overlooked within the madness of trying to make a the first Hollywood movie ever allowed in Bali. You had stolen the thing because of your love for the granddaughter and given the generator to her and her family when the Hollywood movie cleared out. The generator that had become her family fortune and they had managed it as a business. And though cranky, it still brought electricity to the fairy lights strung between the warungs every night. Ibu's hand is warm and dry and file rough on your nape and after a few gentle pats, Ibu turns back to her day's work.

You pack up and shoulder your waterproof backpack and take to the water. The surf has dropped. Still absolutely perfect at two foot. You paddle out through the calm channel, remembering how different it was last year. And about that six o'clock set of waves that had become Bukit lore. You remember. At first it was thought to be a cloud. But then it was moving too fast. It was October 17, 2011. And the Bukit was about to be slammed by the biggest set of waves in living memory. All that day, the Bukit was as big and as good as it gets. And no place on the planet was better than Padang Padang. Not everyone wanted a piece of it, but the luminaries were all there. Made Winada Adi Putra, standing tall, Mustofa Jeksen at play in his Spiderman mask, Rizal Tandjung, Jason

Childs tear-assing around on his jet ski with his faithful Man-Friday, snapping photos like mad. The Balawista lifeguards at the ready, oiled down tourists gawking, and set after perfect set pouring over the reef under a blistering hot sky. By noon, most surfers had howled themselves hoarse.

By five o'clock, most had gone in, not able to lift their arms for one more. But by six o'clock, those who remained witnessed the unforgettable. Made Lana, at outside corner Uluwatu, was the first to deal with the great waves. He dropped into history and oblivion on one. At Padang Padang, two minutes later, no one was prepared. The only guys who stood a chance were Jason Childs and his man on the jet ski. They had just cleared the top of the first giant when it roared and shut down the entire bay behind them, bypassing the Padang Padang reef and roiling into one long, serpentine, hydraulic monster to the break called Impossibles. Bingin became no more than a shore break. Dreamland was nonexistent, Balangan dismissed. Jimbaran Bay awash. And Jason Childs and the Balawistas were out until dark, effecting rescues. And it was said that even an airplane taking off at the airport had its wings soaked with the offshore spume of the great waves that washed ashore and expired at the end of runway 270.

So you paddle out, remembering, through the Padang Padang channel, past the reef, out into deep water. You sit up on your board. Looking back at the white sands of Padang Padang, the beauty of the cove, the perfection of it, and you wish it well. Knowing that, for the rest of your life, for all your life, it will remain indelible. As it always has. And you wonder if you need to thank Hollywood for that. Then you belly down, adjust your backpack, and start making your way north, up through the Impossibles lineup. North.

Toward a place you were personally responsible for destroying.

June 11, 2012 — Bingin Beach

You pitch your tent on the beach in exactly the same spot that you photographed from twenty-six years ago. You had to hike in back then. The waves only a rumor. It was an hour and fifteen minutes of streaming sweat down a limestone path through a dry jungle back then. You had followed a little boy who carried you and your friend's four surfboards on his head. An impossible load. You couldn't have done it. You had come out onto the beach at what would become Dreamland. Not a thing there. Not a soul. A sparkling creek, inviting, singing, emptying itself into a turquoise sea. In the distance, the prize. The most perfectly shaped left-hand wave possible.

You were working for *SURFER Magazine* and you had time to shoot three photos of the sight before you and your friend started running for it, the little boy keeping pace with all your boards. The two of you built a small shelter on the beach and, for the next eight days, surfed the spot called "Bingin" with no more than four other white guys at a time. When you filed your story two weeks later with *SURFER Magazine,* the bonanza began. The best-shaped, most friendly wave on the Bukit. Uncrowded perfection. The dream. But you'd have to find it yourself.

Later that year, you had found yourself at the Action Sports retailer show in Long Beach, California. You had sold one of the photos to the Pro-lite Surfboard luggage company. It was the first of the three photos you took that day that depicted the little boy, surfboard Pro-lite bags piled on his head, perfect empty surf peeling in the distance against an impossibly exotic background. Pro-lite had turned it into a billboard on the front of the Long Beach Convention Center. Inside the great Convention Hall another giant light box, as tall as a canoe, shone through the masses. Crowds were gathered before the photo. Dreaming. Planning. You remember being proud at the time.

You are tired now from the day. You slip into your tent below the rocks at Bingin where you had once built a hut out of rice bags and driftwood. Above you, a hundred luxury villas pepper the cliffs. Twice that in warungs, backpacker hotels, and ding repair shops. By the lights of these structures, you can just see the measured white hissing of the waves. Waves that are so crowded by day that it is difficult to see the wave itself. Almost settled in, a local cliffside hotel owner and an armed security guard roust you like a roadside bindlestiff. They tell you that you either have to stay at their cliffside hotel and spa for two hundred bucks a night, or you have to clear out. You pack up and paddle out into the night.

Karma.

Dreamland had just been too hard to look at as you paddled past it in the dark. The thumping music from a dozen different cliffside clubs hammering away. And then the giant, gray, shoddy cement edifice gouged clumsily into the north cliff. A real honest-to-god hatchet job of a big ugly hotel and bar complex. Chinese money. Crassly renamed "The New Kuta Beach: The Bali You Remember." It was hard to remember the days of yore at Dreamland. The cool little warungs of Dreamland beach, cleaner than anywhere else on the island. All gossamer, swaying mosquito nets over cool, crisp, bleach scented sheets. The open warungs, the cool green surf, the icy Coca-Colas and cold beers. The talcum-white sand. The photographers from around the world who came to shoot for fashion magazines. The light reflecting off the limestone cliffs unique in all the world. Nothing like it. Life on a beach through a filtered light. All forever young. Now beaten and bruised under tons of cement, varicose veined, spitting diseased blood into the sea. Ten-dollar margaritas. Rattling, giant tour buses waiting like a sad herd of pachyderms in the parking lot, chugging exhaust into the atmosphere hour after hour. Machines and drivers both hopeless beasts of burden. And you. Bastard. You helped start it all with your photographs.

June 12, 2012 — Balangan

You spend the next night at Balangan beach, the last undeveloped beachfront on the Bukit. Though it wouldn't be for long. You'd pitched your tent above the creek mouth, up against the south hill of Balangan. You had left an offering upon arrival at Balangan's powerful temple, Dalan Pura. Literally a bat cave. Dug into the cliff. With her swooping bats and a single, eternal light bulb illuminating the Hanuman Monkey God deity back in the recesses. There wasn't a soul around and you let the wonder of it fill you.

Now in your tent. Early evening. You didn't bring a camera this time. You have deliberately chosen the most exposed bivouac you could, facing the twinkling lights of Kuta and the roaring airport runway a mile and a half away. The great modern terminus of the Bukit Peninsula. One hundred and six flights a day. You stick your head out of the tent. You watch for a while, a soft rain dripping through your eyelashes and onto your lips, thinking of how peaceful Kuta looked from a distance. And how a crash of rhinos would appear the same.

You had to peg your tent down. Not a smart camp. Exposed to the sky, rain, tradewinds, and the spirits. Another penance. You tried to drift off to sleep on the hard, volcanic ground. The farmer of this land gave you a wide berth. So did the cows. As they would any spirit they thought mad.

Tomorrow, you plan to paddle around the corner to Jimbaran Bay. Toward your final destination. You will paddle past Honeymooners Cove. A cliffside surf spot, a holy site that is being ground up by the new Five Seasons resort. Then you will paddle past the last remaining beach warungs. Then you plan to make shore and stand upon the exact spot in the sand where the main blast of the 2005 Bali bombings erupted within the field of white tablecloths of the beach-side sunset dining. Where twenty human beings became bloody rags, even though twenty-two had died.

No one wanted to count the Jihadist bombers.

And this will be the fitting end of your sojourn. Fitting because you plan to pray for forgiveness when you get there. Forgiveness for being a part of the bombings. You, a western visitor who helped turn this island into a target. Who helped inspire the exodus of western influence. You who contributed to the western crowding and avarice and development and environmental and spiritual erosion of the island. You who contributed to that which drew the hordes and the hounds of hell.

Listening to the rain, you calm down. There is still hope for this place called the Bukit Peninsula. And Bali. Because the outside world may be able to blow out her candles, but not her flames. Which is why here in Bali, you must care for this place as the precious gem it is. You have no choice. You've crossed the line. And you cannot go back to the west. Even though you are a western surfer. Because you helped create this place. And what you see now is what you get for it. So you plan to ask forgiveness and take the Bali dream differently in your hands. You've crossed the line. You cannot go back. You are in love with an island that is not yours. And never will be. And there is nothing to be done about that. But you must endure this love. Spread a different message. One of repair. Like an adopted child trying to return the new parent's love. And you hoping the gods of this place will someday cremate your sins. Even the ones that would never, could ever be your fault.

FAREWELL TO THE
KING...FOR NOW

SURFTIME MAGAZINE, INDONESIA, 2023

I believe that this will be the last story I ever write about Kelly. After thirty-five years of a relationship that has always had a patina of wariness on both our parts, due to the fact that I am a surf journalist, it's time to stop writing about him and just enjoy his company as a friend. —Mg

---

On February 5, 2022, when Kelly Slater won his eighth Pipeline Masters title only six days before his fiftieth birthday, a full thirty years after his first Pipeline Masters title, I wasn't surprised at all. At this, our sport's most prestigious tournament, I had already seen him do it seven times. But it did make me think about the last time I spent some time with him. It was during his summer sojourn to Bali in 2020.

A miraculous visit, considering the labyrinth of red tape one had to go through to travel anywhere during the Covid-19 global lockdown. Rumor was he got in on an essential business visa, and that made a lot of sense to me; Bali had the best waves on the planet at the time. And though an immigration agent might have a hard time buying it, waves are his business. And he has monetized them on land as well as sea. Let us not forget that this man manufactured his own Ocean in the middle of California's central valley, which features the most extraordinarily perfect artificial surfing wave in history. The Surf Ranch, now a spectacular playground, literally, for the rich and famous. Yes, Kelly Slater is a businessman.

Thinking back now on his visit to Bali, the fallout from that incendiary visit is still descending on the streets of Kuta. After all, it was akin to a royal mission of reassurance during a murderous global pandemic. And, man, did he make the most of it. It would be hard to find someone who loves to go surfing outside the contest arena more than him. Though rumors flew that he was in Bali to seek a healing from a barrage of personal subterfuge in his life—his career, finances, his girl, the vagaries of his anti-vax stance that had enraged fans. Yet I say "incendiary visit" because his surfing here in Bali was electrifying. And it is so hard not to say "as usual." Every day, absolutely every day, for long, sunburned hours, he would light up lineups from Java to Sumbawa. Ripping Keramas, Desert Point, G-Land, Scar Reef, Padang

Padang, Uluwatu, Kuta Beach, and more. Kelly, with the help of local wave whisperer Nick Chong, seemed to be wherever the surf was best during what had been the most excellent surf season in Bali for the last quarter century. As an island known for its healing properties, perhaps he instinctively chose this environment for introspection, as well as to recharge his extroverted approach to every wave he catches. Observers here witnessed his explosive sessions with a sense of wonder.

Kelly quietly went about his days, attending the odd evening gathering and working closely with local shaper Mike Woo on top-secret surfboard designs said to be based on the ergonomics of a white shark. That really lit up the rumor mill. Yet just short of his 49th birthday, Kelly Slater was still making his statement in the water as the best surfer the world has ever seen. And nowhere was this more evident than in the simple beach breaks that front Kuta Beach.

"In a way," said top photographer Pete Frieden, a fellow Floridian who has photographed Kelly since he was a child, "Kelly's beach break surfing in Bali was like a return to Florida. Like Sebastian Inlet on the best day of the century." Again, rumors flew as to where Kelly would be surfing every day, as they would around any surf celebrity who was tearing around a small island on a scooter with a surfboard in its side rack. But Kelly spent his last days at Kuta, concentrating on the perfect sandbars that have formed just off the downtown beaches. Sandbars, phenomena in themselves, the likes of which have not been seen for years. The product of the pandemic, actually. With no tourist industry to use and abuse them, all the waterways, both above and below ground in Bali, had been flowing full and trash-free onto the sea. Distributing their sands to their rightful homes, forming a series of humping peaks from the Airport jetties to Canggu. A mid-to-high tide summer wonderland of playful surf. Not the famed Indonesian barrels, but more like quarter pipes where Kelly could jam his rail work and pop his aerials. And that was one of the more startling revelations. Kelly Slater as a master aerialist. Setting up his airs on his all-black, secretive twin fin designs, made of entirely new composite compounds, at twice the speed of anyone. Kelly was hitting his airs on these superboards with commitment and an 80 percent success rate. To say nothing of his other skills. Carving 360s, massive roundhouse cutbacks, fin humming bottom turns. Though everyone else wanted to be surfing near him, the lineup cleared the runway once he took off.

"Do you think he is doing this as practice for the title final at Trestles?" said Arya Subiyakto, one of the most respected surfing figures in Indonesia. "Because if he is, Toledo and Medina are in a shitload of trouble."

Regardless of the answer, Kelly maintained a gentle presence on land. Sitting alone under his favorite shade tree, semi-concealed from small knots of tourists on the beach, Kelly looked meditative between surf sessions. And it was a quiet goodbye to the island as Kelly left the water for the last time of the summer season in Bali. Walking up the beach a little girl, who had no idea who he was, asked him what was on the deck of his surfboard. Kelly took the time to explain the function of surfboard wax and had her scrape her fingernails across the deck of a surfboard that he wouldn't have let any other soul on earth touch. I met him on the promenade to say goodbye and good luck out there on the pro tour. We chatted a bit and compared notes about the trouble we were having with our women—my wife and his long-time girlfriend. Like most men, we left it with laughter at how women can just be colossal pains in the ass and there isn't a goddamn thing we can do about it. Another little kid approached with his beaming Australian family, and Kelly took the time to shake his hand. The little kid was catatonic to be standing next to his hero, couldn't say a word. Kelly asked his parents his name and then crouched down to the kid's level and just looked him in the eyes.

"You're gonna make it, Alex," was all Kelly said, with a light squeeze of the shoulder. The kid staggered away with his proud family. Then, sure that our paths would cross again, Kelly and I shook hands and said a simple goodbye, then I grabbed my board and paddled out into the surf.

Out beyond the breaking waves, I sat on my board and took in a sky that the sunset had set ablaze. And I couldn't help but think about Kelly. Especially about our ages and how he has refined his to the point that at fifty, he still strikes fear into competitors who weren't even born by the time he won his first world title. How he now had a whole world behind him and a whole world ahead. Of how surfing is the whole world to him and how that whole world is his. Considering his competitive fervor over his astonishing career, I wondered if there was ever an end of the day for Kelly, or if there was only tomorrow. And I thought of how he is too old to die young, a living legend already an heirloom of surfing's history. He stands atop Olympus. The master of the only sport on earth that takes place on a dynamic moving surface. And I wondered if it would ever be enough for him. If you can't ever get enough of what you want, you will always be poor. And I hoped that someday, he would be rich in that aspect, finally have enough of winning, I really did. Like a moth that can no longer blame the flame, with a body that must, like an aging fighter jet still in service, be showing signs of metal fatigue, just how much further can this man go? How much further would he *need* to go? A tiger can only last as long as its teeth. If it wasn't winning the Pipeline Masters against the best twenty-year-old surfers in the world at fifty years old, what possible crowning achievement would become his chorale finale of his concluding symphony? What would it take to distill the torments of a life of ferocious competition into a message in a bottle that he could finally toss into the sea? What would it be that could contain all the creativity and rage and redemption and poetic fury of his life and lay it in clover as a thing of wonder and beauty and vitality laid to rest? What could take all this suffering and this desire and all this winning and set it in a halcyon chalice to be regarded forever as something incandescent, something superhuman?

I surfed a wave to shore then. And as I strolled up the sand, I thought of those infamous words that I had written about Kelly over thirty years previous. And it stopped me in my tracks. Devil knows they still rang true. The world was still whirling around Kelly like a maelstrom as he lay in the eye of the storm. And it still hadn't got a hold of him just yet. At fifty, he was still going. And going. No, all the madness that the waning fame and fortunes of retirement could bring would have to wait for Kelly Slater just a little while longer. And right then, right there, I could only pray that he still sleeps like an angel.

THEY ARE WHO
YOU ARE

A FINAL NOTE

PHOTO CREDIT: JAMES METYKO

The brand of stories in this book lives inside surfers. Inside their dreams. Indelible. And surfing needs its storytelling in order to exist and inspire further quests. Surfing lends itself to such mythological comparisons because of where it takes place. The Ocean. Because it is there, like Everest. Like the great mountains, the Ocean too is imbued with an awesome power and presence. A mysterious reality that we have no business challenging, a place not meant for humans. And yet surfers still go, still seek it out. A place of extraordinary violence. The only place on earth where you can still be attacked and eaten by a dinosaur. At the very beginning of this book, there is a quote from Euripides' play *Medea*, whose underlying message examines the power of emotion and how it drives people to do things they would normally not do, to be places they would normally not be. The enterprise of finding purpose in what one's heart is capable of facing.

And so, when it comes to writing about surfing and its people in this frame of mind, taking its measure, the art of getting inside the heads of surfers lies in the ability to not just hear what the subject is saying, but to listen to what they are not saying. To not just scratch the surface, but to actually get to know these heroes of ours and their stories and the places where they take place. This is essential to understanding the very mysticism that we assign to our own inner surfing identity. These heroes and these stories hold keys. Keys that open passages to the performances of our daily lives. Like it or not, these famous surfers and these stories influence the way we dress, the way we think, the way we see ourselves, the way we see others, what we ride, what we value, what we believe, what we do, the way we surf, the way we speak, the very way we live and love. And man, if that's not just about the most important truth for any surfer to accept, I don't know what is. This has always been the essence of surfing tales. Seeking a story's humanness. Seeking the hero's humanness. Reveal theirs and we reveal our own.

It is a basic human instinct to seek the depth of our passions, to plumb the well of our souls. Whether you ride in one-foot surf or twenty. Whether you are a pro or a beginner. It is life, liberty, and the pursuit of happiness. And it is imperative for the individual to ensure this right for themselves. To capture the inspirations of our sport's pantheon of greats and our compelling stories is important, so that they might not only inspire us to tackle our dreams but so our dreams might live forever. And so they should. If you are a surfer, they are who you are. And even if you are not, if you are passionate enough in your own pursuits and if you read closely enough and if you take a wild shot at revealing your own soul to yourself, *really* take the shot, well, you will live forever in these pages too.

ACKNOWLEDGEMENTS

This book never would have happened without the involvement and support of an extraordinary group of people from all corners of the globe. First, I must thank all the surfers who chose to be so honest with me. I remain a proud member of that tribe. Secondly, I feel it is remarkable that the editorial team at Di Angelo Publications invested such time and expertise in a collection of my life's work so far. What they have taught me about writing and publishing eclipses anything that I have been taught about writing before. I thank Sequoia Schmidt for her patience and leadership, Alma Felix for her kindness and whip cracking, Editor Cody Wooten for helping keep this book badass, Ashley Crantas for exemplifying the truths within it and keeping it on point, Thai Little for a cover design that perfectly reflects the adventure of it all, and Kimberly James for designing into a state that to me is as beautiful as a perfectly shaped wave. And lastly, though it seems an impossibility, I would like to offer my respect to the great oceans themselves, all of whose waves I have proudly experienced in my attempt to mine their mysteries.

"There is, one knows not what sweet mystery about this sea, whose gently awful stirrings seem to speak of some hidden soul beneath..."

-Herman Melville-

MATT GEORGE

ABOUT THE AUTHOR

For over thirty-five years, Matt George's feature articles and photographs have stood among the most influential works in surfing journalism. Accepting a post as Senior Contributing Editor for SURFER Magazine in 1985, George traveled the world as he covered all aspects of the sport, garnering a sterling list of awards and achievements along the way. George is also known for the writing and co-production of the Columbia Tri-Star Feature film In Gods Hands, a big wave surfing drama, and the creation of the NBC drama series, Wind on Water. He remains a senior contributor for all the major surf magazines and websites and is an in-demand public speaker. He resides in Bali, Indonesia, and is currently the Editor-in-Chief of South East Asia's Surftime Magazine. He still surfs every day.

CATHARSIS

ABOUT THE PUBLISHER

Di Angelo Publications was founded in 2008 by Sequoia Schmidt—at the age of seventeen. The modernized publishing firm's creative headquarters is in Houston, Texas, with its distribution center located in Twin Falls, Idaho. The subsidiary rights department is based in Los Angeles, and Di Angelo Publications has recently grown to include branches in England, Australia, and Sequoia's home country of New Zealand. In 2020, Di Angelo Publications made a conscious decision to move all printing and production for domestic distribution of its books to the United States. The firm is comprised of ten imprints, and the featured imprint, Catharsis, was inspired by Schmidt's love of extreme sports, travel, and adventure stories.

DI ANGELO PUBLICATIONS
A Modernized Publishing Firm